Optimizing Oracle Performance

Other Oracle resources from O'Reilly

Related titles

Oracle in a Nutshell

Oracle PL/SQL Programming

Oracle PL/SQL Language
  Pocket Reference

Oracle Essentials: Oracle 9i,
  Oracle9 & Oracle8i

Mastering Oracle SQL

Oracle SQL*Plus Pocket
  Reference

Learning Oracle PL/SQL

TOAD Pocket Reference
  for Oracle

Oracle Books Resource Center

oracle.oreilly.com is a complete catalog of O'Reilly's books on Oracle and related technologies, including sample chapters and code examples.

oreillynet.com is the essential portal for developers interested in open and emerging technologies, including new platforms, programming languages, and operating systems.

Conferences

O'Reilly & Associates brings diverse innovators together to nurture the ideas that spark revolutionary industries. We specialize in documenting the latest tools and systems, translating the innovator's knowledge into useful skills for those in the trenches. Visit *conferences.oreilly.com* for our upcoming events.

Safari Bookshelf (*safari.oreilly.com*) is the premier online reference library for programmers and IT professionals. Conduct searches across more than 1,000 books. Subscribers can zero in on answers to time-critical questions in a matter of seconds. Read the books on your Bookshelf from cover to cover or simply flip to the page you need. Try it today with a free trial.

Optimizing Oracle Performance

Cary Millsap
with Jeff Holt

O'REILLY®

Beijing · Cambridge · Farnham · Köln · Paris · Sebastopol · Taipei · Tokyo

Optimizing Oracle Performance
by Cary Millsap with Jeff Holt

Published by O'Reilly & Associates, Inc., 1005 Gravenstein Highway North, Sebastopol, CA 95472.

O'Reilly & Associates books may be purchased for educational, business, or sales promotional use. Online editions are also available for most titles (*safari.oreilly.com*). For more information, contact our corporate/institutional sales department: (800) 998-9938 or *corporate@oreilly.com*.

Editor:	Jonathan Gennick
Production Editor:	Jane Ellin
Cover Designer:	Ellie Volckhausen
Interior Designer:	David Futato

Printing History:

September 2003:   First Edition.

ISBN: 0-596-00527-X

[M]

*I dedicate this book with love to Mindy,
Alexander, and Nikolas.*

—Cary Millsap

*I dedicate this book to every manager with a bent
ear and a soft couch.*

—Jeff Holt

Table of Contents

Part II.   Reference

Part III.   Deployment

Part IV.   Appendixes

Foreword

Seldom does an editor have the privilege of editing a book such as this one. From the moment I first saw Cary Millsap's and Jeff Holt's proposal for a book called *Optimizing Oracle Response Time* (that was the original working title) I knew I'd struck gold. This book has everything an editor dreams of: talented authors, rigorous research, groundbreaking material.

I remember well my first foray into Oracle performance tuning. It was back in the Oracle7 days when I was becoming grounded in Oracle. I'd just been handed DBA responsibility for all the databases used by my development group, and what better way to begin my career as an Oracle DBA, I thought, than to make an impact via some serious tuning? So I bought a book. And I read the Oracle manual. I learned about the buffer cache, the shared pool, and hit-ratios.

It all seemed so simple. The previous DBA had never done any tuning, so all I needed to do was tweak a few parameter settings, use hit-ratios to find the optimum memory allocations for the buffer cache and shared pool, and then I could kick back, bask in the glory of a job well done, and drink in the praises from my fellow developers who would no doubt be awed at how fast I could make their programs run.

Only it didn't work the way I'd envisioned. I doubled the size of my buffer cache, but nothing seemed to run any faster. I cut my buffer cache in half from its original size, but nothing seemed to run any slower. I increased the shared pool. I decreased the shared pool. I tinkered with this parameter and that parameter, and always the database stubbornly seemed to run on at the same speed as ever. Obviously this tuning business was more difficult than I'd envisioned, and I just wasn't smart enough to "get it." Humbled, I set aside my dreams of becoming a crackerjack performance tuner.

Fortunately, for my ego and probably for my career as well, I eventually discovered SQL trace, and learned how to generate trace files and use *tkprof* to report on their contents. I was no good at tuning the database as a whole, I decided, but I did become reasonably good at using SQL trace to identify and fix badly performing SQL statements.

Eventually, I came to the conclusion that what really mattered was what users were complaining about. Users don't care about hit-ratios, nor about disk-throughput; they don't care whether latch contention exists, nor do they care about any other arcane statistic that you or a system administrator might think to worry about. Users only care about one statistic: *how fast their jobs run.* For the most part, I gave up worrying about anything other than what my clients were worrying about. When a client complained about slow performance, I measured my success not by any arcane ratio or statistic, but by how much time I could save them. Still, I was often haunted by thoughts that I was missing something about this tuning business, that there was some level to which I just wasn't capable of ascending. Real DBAs, I felt, monitored statistics such as hit-ratios to keep up with the overall performance of their databases. Why couldn't I make that work?

Cary's and Jeff's proposal, my conversations with them, their class which I attended, and this book freed me from the vestiges of guilt and shame over my lack of success tuning databases at the instance level using hit-ratios and other instance-wide statistics. I'd learned to focus on user response time; Cary and Jeff validate that. I'd become frustrated, indeed I felt belittled, at my inability to manage performance by monitoring hit-ratios and other instance-wide statistics; Cary and Jeff throw hit-ratios out the window. My greatest tuning successes came from using trace file statistics (SQL trace and *tkprof*) from a specific job to determine what SQL statements were consuming the greatest time; Cary and Jeff take the use of trace file statistics to a whole new level.

By now you can see why I was, and am, so excited by this book. Everything about Cary's and Jeff's method resonates with my own experience. As I talked with them, every time they brought up a new point I found myself nodding my head thinking: "yes! yes! of course!" When they first talked to me about their vision for this book, they were "preaching to the choir," though they probably didn't know it at the time. What's so exciting is that Cary and Jeff saw clearly where I saw only dimly. There is indeed a level above where I was at, but it's one that I *am* capable of ascending to, and it's one you too can reach with Cary and Jeff's help.

After talking with Cary and Jeff about their plans for a book, I knew I had to have it as an O'Reilly publication. I thoroughly enjoyed editing their work. I learned a lot from reading the chapters over and over again, and I know you will too. I can't recommend this book strongly enough. I'm glad you bought it; you won't regret the investment. And if you're reading this Foreword in a bookstore aisle, please, don't put the book back on the shelf. Invest the price of this book in your own development. You'll reap returns many times over. I'm sure of it.

—*Jonathan Gennick*

Preface

Optimizing Oracle response time is, for the most part, a solved problem. I hope that I have written effectively enough that, after reading this book, this idea will come to fruition in your own experience.

However, if you're like most people, you probably don't feel that way yet. For most people, Oracle performance improvement projects are long, frustrating battles against some invisible enemy that evades detection no matter how much time or extra computer hardware you throw at the situation. The root cause of the problem is that most education about tuning is broken. My aims in this book are to show you why, and to reveal to you what you should do instead.

Bad tuning methods have prospered among the Oracle community for a long time. For well over a decade, the Oracle community has been afflicted with lots of performance problems but a virtual absence of competent training programs for performance analysts. The result has been a lucrative seller's market for the Oracle performance analyst. Throughout the 1990s in many parts of the world, a consultant could name his own price and bill by the hour for time spent attempting to improve performance. The tuning methods that evolved in this environment were geared more toward maximizing a consultant's revenue intake than maximizing the success of your system.

Why I Wrote This Book

I began my Oracle career in 1989 as a new employee of Oracle Corporation itself. By 1992, I felt reasonably competent as a performance specialist. My performance optimization method was one that many people still teach today: fix the ten things I knew how to fix, and then pray that the cause of the performance problems had been some combination of those ten things. In late 1992, I was charged with leading a national group. Beginning promptly with that promotion to manager, my hands-on technical skills (such as they were) began their decay. By the end of 1993, I felt like I had logged more career hours in Excel and PowerPoint than in Oracle products.

In 1995, I proposed the construction of a new group in Oracle Corporation that would be called the System Performance Group (SPG). SPG became one of the largest and best collections of Oracle performance experts in the world. By 1996, it had become abundantly clear to me that my feelings of reasonable competence in 1992 had been false. Specifically, I was receiving engagement summaries from a few of my staff that depicted an absolutely stunning leap forward in project efficiency.

These analysts were wasting virtually *no* time whatsoever in their performance improvement projects. They were predicting the exact impact upon application response times that would result from the implementations of specific performance improvement recommendations. By the end of one of these analysts' first day on site, he would have solved more performance problems more conclusively than I would have solved in a whole week back in 1992. It was as if these people were doing system performance surgery with CAT scans and laser scalpels in an environment where I had formerly known only of leeches and bone saws.

The informal name of the technology these analysts were using was the "Oracle wait interface." This "wait interface" was, to the extent of my knowledge back then, a collection of V$ tables and some new trace data that could tell an analyst how the Oracle kernel was spending the user's response time. Anjo Kolk's internal Oracle paper, "Description of Oracle7 Wait Events and Enqueues," released in the mid-1990s, first made Oracle insiders aware of the potential of this new instrumentation. As with any emerging technology, however, remarkable successes were restricted mostly to the few practitioners who possessed extraordinary talent to begin with.

Repeatability was the problem. In the work of my most talented colleagues, I could smell the potential of a repeatable performance optimization method, but never more than about 10% of my 85 performance specialists could repeat the spectacular results of my few top consultants. The methods simply required more intuition and experience than we could count on people to summon.

In October 1999, I resigned from my position as vice president at Oracle Corporation. After taking the weekend off, I began work with Gary Goodman and Jeff Holt to build a company known now to several thousand performance analysts as *hotsos. com.* Since 1999, I have been able to dedicate my professional life to one goal:

> To create a performance optimization method that *works* and that *can be taught effectively* to the typical Oracle database administrator.

In the more than three years since beginning this project, we have devoted over six man-years of full-time research to derive and test the results that you will see in this book. In the process, we have instructed students at the rate of about 250 per year in our Hotsos Clinic events. Our goal in the course is the same as the goal of this book, to transfer understanding of a reliable new method that will revolutionize your effectiveness as a performance optimizer. Using the same techniques presented in this book, students have returned home from class to improve the response time of critical business actions from hours to seconds on their first day back at work.

The "Oracle wait interface" is, by the time of this writing, prominently in the public attention among database administrators. Although it took nearly ten years since its introduction in Oracle release 7.0.12, messages about the "wait interface" are today being carried forward by hundreds of performance practitioners who are delivering wait-based tuning presentations at conferences and posting wait-based tuning information on public forums like *Oracle-L* (*http://www.cybon.com/~jkstill/util/util_master.html*).

However, at the time of this writing, Oracle's extended SQL trace facility is still sorely underutilized in the general market, for several reasons:

- Although the pseudo-error debugging event 10046 feature has been around for a long time, Oracle Corporation did not formally support its customers' use of *extended* (i.e., LEVEL > 1) SQL trace data until the release of the DBMS_SUPPORT.START_TRACE_IN_SESSION procedure.

- Oracle Corporation's own documentation and most of the books you buy have dedicated only minimal attention to the extended SQL trace facility.

- There have been many misconceptions about extended SQL trace data that unfairly limit analysts' perception of its trustworthiness. Even at the time of this writing, most analysts don't realize that trace files do convey information about time that an Oracle session has spent paging, swapping, or waiting for CPU.

- There have been no tools available that assist you in collecting properly time-scoped and program-scoped diagnostic data.

- There have been few tools to help you interpret properly scoped trace data in a useful way. Oracle's *tkprof* tool has performed adequately in unit testing environments since its release in Version 6. However, after retrofitting in Version 9, *tkprof* does a lackluster job of accounting for a session's total response time. It does a poor job of helping you diagnose the events that occur *between* database calls. And it doesn't help at all in determining the recursive relationships among cursor actions.

Oracle's extended SQL trace facility has become the principal performance diagnostic feature of the Oracle kernel for our staff at *hotsos.com*. We have acquired this capability because since 1999 we've been able to do extensive research of the behavior of over a thousand real SQL trace files collected from real application systems running on a variety of platforms all over the world.

We have attacked both the education problem and the tools problem. In our Hotsos Clinic events, we have subjected our method to the rigorous scrutiny of several hundred students of performance analysis. With our free tool called *Sparky*, we have introduced the first tool in the world that helps you collect properly scoped SQL trace data. Because of our *Hotsos Profiler* software tool, we have helped solve hundreds of difficult real-life performance problems for our customers in hundreds of analyses that have averaged less than one hour each in duration. (You can obtain more information about Hotsos Clinic events and Hotsos software tools at *http://www.hotsos.com*.)

This book is the fruit of all three investments. Its intent is to eliminate the obstacles that have prevented the world from exploiting Oracle's extraordinary "new" performance instrumentation to its fullest capacity.

Audience for This Book

Responding to an Oracle performance problem can be a complicated task involving people from several departments within your business (users, system managers, database managers, network managers, application developers, and so on) and possibly even from several of your hardware and software vendors as well. I have written this book for the person called the *performance analyst*. The performance analyst is one person, or perhaps a small team of people, who are responsible for the following activities in a performance improvement project:

Targeting
> The performance analyst is responsible for properly designing a performance improvement project to fix the right problem.

Analysis
> The performance analyst is responsible for ensuring that a performance improvement project will achieve the desired target with the least economic investment.

Implementation
> The performance analyst is responsible for ensuring that the performance improvement project results in real progress in the actual live system.

Because this is a book about a new performance improvement method that is more radical than you're probably accustomed to, I have included text to help motivate the necessary changes in fundamental approach among project sponsors and project managers. Part I of this book is especially important reading for sponsors and managers who don't understand the need for change in Oracle performance improvement methods.

Structure of This Book

This book is divided into four parts, with twelve chapters and five appendixes in total.

Part I, *Method*, is about *targeting*. It is written in an informal, narrative style that sponsors and managers of performance improvement projects can read from front to back without getting distracted by a lot of technical details. It includes the following chapters:

- Chapter 1, *A Better Way to Optimize*, explains why Oracle performance improvement is so difficult using conventional methods. It explains three important advances from other industries that Oracle performance analysts have ignored for decades. Finally, it describes the new performance improvement method to which the remainder of the book is dedicated.

- Chapter 2, *Targeting the Right User Actions*, describes why many performance improvement projects are doomed from the beginning by poor project specifications. It explains how to construct a foolproof specification for your performance improvement project.

- Chapter 3, *Targeting the Right Diagnostic Data*, describes how errors in diagnostic data collection are the root cause of many failed performance improvement projects. It describes why many projects cannot ever succeed without properly scoped diagnostic data, and it introduces three distinct sources of such information on Oracle systems.

- Chapter 4, *Targeting the Right Improvement Activity*, explains how performance improvement projects can be held to the same standard of *informed consent* that other scientific endeavors require. It describes how to forecast performance improvement project costs and benefits and how to find the economically optimal performance improvement activity from the universe of things you *could* do about system performance.

Part II, *Reference*, is about *detail*. It is written in a deeply technical style in which I try to provide what a performance analyst needs to implement the method. It contains the following chapters:

- Chapter 5, *Interpreting Extended SQL Trace Data*, describes the content of an Oracle extended SQL trace file. It describes the meaning of fields in a trace file, and it explains the relationships of time statistics throughout a trace file.

- Chapter 6, *Collecting Extended SQL Trace Data*, explains how to collect the properly scoped extended SQL trace data that you'll need to analyze a performance problem.

- Chapter 7, *Oracle Kernel Timings*, explains how software like the Oracle kernel measures itself and how you can verify the self-diagnostic behavior of your own system. It goes on to explain several sources of unaccounted-for time in Oracle trace files and why these lapses in timing data often contain performance diagnostic data in and of themselves.

- Chapter 8, *Oracle Fixed View Data*, explains some of the many deficiencies of Oracle's dynamic performance views. It presents descriptions of several popular V$ fixed views and examples of their use. You might be surprised to find out that some of the things you thought you knew about Oracle's dynamic performance views are untrue.

- Chapter 9, *Queueing Theory for the Oracle Practitioner*, is one of my favorites. It explains the physical phenomenon of queueing and how to use the body of mathematical knowledge called *queueing theory* to understand and even predict the performance of systems including Oracle database applications.

Part III, *Deployment*, returns to the informal, narrative style that I hope will encourage project sponsors and managers to follow along. It covers the issues of how to complete the job for maximal positive impact in the following chapters:

- Chapter 10, *Working the Resource Profile*, describes a step-by-step method for analyzing Oracle response time data that leads to maximized performance improvement at minimized cost. It describes the tremendous economic benefits of waste removal and explains how to think "outside the box" to achieve performance improvements you might never otherwise have considered. Finally, it explains how to tell when your performance optimization work is complete, a task that is astonishingly difficult in conventional performance improvement methods.

- Chapter 11, *Responding to the Diagnosis*, describes how to improve application performance in response to various patterns you'll find in your performance diagnostic data. It places particular emphasis upon *how* to eliminate wasteful work from your system, and it covers important response time components that are documented either poorly or not at all in other works.

- Chapter 12, *Case Studies*, is the capstone chapter of the book. It documents four complete cases from problem identification, through the targeting, analysis, and deployment processes, to show you exactly how the method works in real life.

Part IV, *Appendixes*, contains the following:

- Appendix A, *Glossary*, contains definitions of technical terms used throughout the book.

- Appendix B, *Greek Alphabet*, is a table of Greek letters and their English equivalents, intended to simplify your reading of Chapter 9.

- Appendix C, *Optimizing Your Database Buffer Cache Hit Ratio*, inspired by Connor McDonald's *http://www.oracledba.co.uk*, is the best proof I know that having a great database buffer cache hit ratio does not mean that you have a great system. The Perl program shown in this chapter can make your cache hit ratio anything you want it to be!

- Appendix D, *M/M/m Queueing Theory Formulas*, is a summary of formulas used in Chapter 9.

- Appendix E, *References*, contains bibliographic information about the several dozen references used in the book.

Which Platform and Version?

This book contains examples from Oracle kernel releases 8 and 9 on operating systems including Linux, Sun Solaris, IBM AIX, HP-UX, OSF-1, VMS, MVS, and Microsoft Windows. Most of the features described within this book are virtually independent of operating system, and most work equally well in Oracle releases from 7.0.12 through 9.2.0.

As I write this book, Oracle Corporation has not yet unleashed Oracle release 10. I'm not officially endowed with any foreknowledge of the release 10 kernel, but I have my suspicions about what they're doing with it. Where possible, I've identified areas in which the upcoming changes in release 10 will likely alter your world beyond what I've described in this book.

Some chapters are immune. The entirety of Part I and most of Part III will remain unchanged after Oracle release 10 comes onto the market. Most of Part II, you might be surprised to learn, is Oracle version independent. The core messages of Chapters 5, 7, 8, and 9 will remain unchanged by release 10. For example, though Chapter 7 gives examples of how Oracle Release 7, 8, and 9 kernels do their work, it also shows you how to find out whether release 10 behaves any differently. Though Chapter 8 shows details of Oracle9i V$ views, which will change in release 10, the basic problems of polling and summarization will remain relevant in release 10.

Some features mentioned in this book are not available on every version of Oracle from 7 through 9 (TRACEFILE_IDENTIFIER is one example). I've made no effort to list the Oracle kernel version in which new features appear. However, for features that may not be available in the release of Oracle that you're using, I generally provide two or more ways to accomplish a task. Therefore, if the elegant way to accomplish a task isn't available in your environment, then I have probably described an alternate way to get the job done.

What This Book Is and Is Not

This book is different from any other book about Oracle performance on the market. It is not a book of tips and techniques. It is a book dedicated to helping you remove performance pain faster and more completely than you've ever thought possible. I believe that doing this, however, requires a book that will change your whole mindset about performance.

This book describes a method for optimizing the performance of an Oracle system, but it goes an important step further. The method prescribed in this book optimizes the performance of the whole *performance improvement project*. The goal of this book is not to make one system faster; it is to make *you* faster and more efficient at optimizing *any* system.

This book focuses more completely upon performance problem *diagnosis* than upon *repair* tasks. In my experience, diagnosis is where people usually mess up. There are lots of experts out there responding sensibly to poorly collected diagnostic data in poorly specified projects. It is usually easy to solve a problem when it is presented to you correctly. It can be impossible to solve the right problem when you're focused on the wrong problem. This book contains many examples of working on the wrong problem, and it explains how never to make that mistake again.

This is not a book about system management or capacity planning, although almost all the information in this book is relevant to the system manager's and capacity planner's job. It is not a compendium of all the Oracle "wait events." I cover the events that we have encountered most frequently in the hundreds of trace files we've analyzed, but I leave detailed treatment of each event to other sources, such as you might find on the Internet. I use *google.com* as my primary source of information about wait event definitions. Authors are continually adding to the Internet repertory of detailed information about the wait events.

Finally, this is a book for the performance optimization *practitioner*. It's not a book of theories. Every piece of information in this book is included because my students, my colleagues, and I need to have the information available to do our jobs of improving Oracle performance.

About the Tools, Examples, and Exercises

I've chosen Perl as the primary demonstration programming language for this book. It may seem odd that a book about Oracle doesn't use SQL or PL/SQL as a demonstration language, but once you begin reading you'll begin to understand. A lot of this book isn't about Oracle, it's about *performance*, and the issues of performance are much broader than the SQL and PL/SQL languages are capable of handling elegantly. Perl allows me to illustrate realistic experiments using a free, portable tool that is simple to install. I hope that this choice will maximize the probability that you will actually try some of the experiments that I describe.

I've chosen Microsoft Visual Basic as the demonstration programming language for some of the queueing theory material because Microsoft Excel is the de facto workbook software today. Again, I hope that this choice will maximize the probability that you will actually use the material I'm offering here.

You can download all the listings in this book at the following URL:

> *http://www.oreilly.com/catalog/optoraclep/*

This book contains exercises. This is unusual both for an O'Reilly book, and for a book about Oracle. I use exercises for the following reasons:

1. To encourage you to try exactly what you've just read.

2. To stimulate you to apply things that you've just read, but with different input values.

3. To stimulate you to apply things that you've just read, but on your own system.

4. To admit that I don't know the answer to every interesting question out there, but at least I have made it as far as defining the problem. This way, others can

better understand that a problem exists, and they can work on solving it only if the economics of their particular situation warrant the effort.

5. To encourage the use of this book as a textbook in formal education courses. I have been using draft versions of this book very successfully as the text material for my company's Hotsos Clinic 101 (*http://www.hotsos.com*) since 2002.

Most of the exercises don't have a single correct answer. For the ones that do, check *http://www.oreilly.com/catalog/optoraclep* for updated solutions.

Citations

This book cites several outside resources. For these citations, I use a standard academic format that is easy to decode. When you see the citation, "[Bach (1986) 148]," it is a reference to page 148 in the document identified in Appendix E as "[Bach (1986)]." The document in this case is a book written by Maurice Bach, published in 1986.

Conventions Used in This Book

The following typographical conventions are used in this book:

Italic
> Used for filenames, directory names, and URLs. It is also used for emphasis and for the first use of a technical term.

`Constant width`
> Used for examples and event names and to show the contents of files and the output of commands.

`Constant width bold`
> Indicates user input in examples showing an interaction. It is also used to emphasize parts of `constant width` text, such as output listings.

> Indicates a tip, suggestion, or general note.

> Indicates a warning or caution. For example, I'll tell you if a certain setting has some kind of negative impact on the system.

Comments and Questions

We have tested and verified the information in this book to the best of our ability, but you may find that features have changed or that we have made mistakes. If so, please notify us by writing to:

O'Reilly & Associates, Inc.
1005 Gravenstein Highway North
Sebastopol, CA 95472
(800) 998-9938 (in the United States or Canada)
(707) 829-0515 (international/local)
(707) 829-0104 (fax)

There is a web page for this book, which lists errata, examples, or any additional information. You can access this page at:

http://www.oreilly.com/catalog/optoraclep/

To comment or ask technical questions about this book, send email to:

bookquestions@oreilly.com

For more information about books, conferences, Resource Centers, and the O'Reilly Network, see the O'Reilly web site at:

http://www.oreilly.com

You can also visit the authors' web site at:

http://hotsos.com

Acknowledgments

Mindy, Alexander, and Nikolas Millsap
> My wife and my boys are an inspiration to me each day, and I want to acknowledge the sacrifice they've made to make this project possible. I wrote this book on their time, and I hope that the results of this project in some way pay them back for all the time they have let me invest into it. Thank you, Mindy, Alex, and Nik.

Van and Shirle Millsap
> At the beginning of every school year, my parents would take me into school and introduce themselves to my teachers. On the way to school, they would always tell me the same thing:
>
> > There are two answers to every question your teachers will ask you while you're in school. There's the correct answer, and there's the answer that the teacher wants. I expect you to know them both.
>
> Thank you, Mom and Dad. You have no idea how much you've helped me in this lifetime.

Jeff Holt

Of the many blessings bestowed upon *hotsos.com* in its three years, none is more important than to have secured the participation of one Mr. Jeffrey L. Holt. Jeff was one of the top performance analysts in that 85-person group that I left at Oracle. He is now our Chief Scientist at *hotsos.com*. In the past three years, Jeff's principal job has been to teach *me* how to optimize an Oracle system. My job has been largely to deactivate the intuitive part of Jeff's brain.

Jeff is one of those talented people who understands how to solve a problem long before he can explain how he did it. I'm an obsessive-compulsive pedant who spends more time trying to figure out *why* an answer is correct than he does trying to figure out the answer. I believe that if a method relies on its user's intuition and experience, then the method is neither repeatable nor teachable. I believe that without rigorous elimination of experience, intuition, and luck from the performance improvement process, it is impossible to create an acceptably high-quality Oracle performance optimization method.

You can see, then, what Jeff has been dealing with. Jeff has been limitlessly intelligent and patient throughout the entire process of having the insides of his head taken out and put back in again lots of times. Thank you, Jeff.

Gary Goodman

Gary Goodman is my friend and co-founder of *hotsos.com*. Without the long walk that occurred back in the summer of 1999, there's no telling what I'd be doing today. Actually, without the long walk that occurred back in the summer of 1989, I might have never worked for Oracle Corporation. Without the job that Gary does every day, there would be no *hotsos.com* and no book that you're now holding in your hands. Thank you, Gary.

Mogens Nørgaard

Mogens Nørgaard is my award-winning friend from Denmark who first introduced me to the then-mysterious "Oracle wait interface." Mogens is the first human on the planet to require his entire technical staff at Oracle Corporation to use the wait interface and only the wait interface in diagnosing Oracle performance problems. Mogens is also the founder of the world-famous Oak Table Network (*http://www.oaktable.net*), a collection of people who I consider to be the dominant minds in the Oracle performance space. Without Mogens' friendship, support, and social arrangement-making, this book would probably have never happened. Thank you, Mogens.

Anjo Kolk

Anjo Kolk is the father of Oracle response time optimization methods. Since I first met Anjo sometime in the early 1990s, he has never balked at investing time from his busy schedule to teach my groups and me how things really work. Thank you, Anjo.

Virag Saksena

Virag Saksena is the first consultant in my System Performance Group at Oracle Corporation who showed me a glimpse of what the world of performance improvement projects *could* be like. Virag's talent is in a sense the spark that lit the fire that became this book. Thank you, Virag.

Jonathan Lewis, Connor McDonald, and Frank Hansen

For a multitude of reasons including their provision of feedback that improved the quality of this book. Thank you, gentlemen.

Jonathan Gennick and the staff at O'Reilly & Associates

Rick Greenwald told me that there are three types of book publishers in the world: those who publish a book that's worse than the author's original manuscript, those who publish a book that's as good as the manuscript, and those who publish a book that's better. Jonathan's leadership has made this book better than the one I would have written without O'Reilly.

I would like to express my sincerest gratitude to the customers of *hotsos.com*, who have provided sustenance to my family and stimulation to my mind. Your support is the reason that the material in this book can exist. Finally, thank you to the many people who have taught me many things, including:

Steve Adams	Nancy Dushkin	Jonathan Intner
Micah Adler	Julian Dyke	Lynn Isabella
Philip Almes	Morten Egan	Ken Jacobs
Andy Bailey	Jean Emerson	Neil Jensen
Karla Baisey	Bjørn Engsig	Phil Joel
Vladimir Barriere	Dave Ensor	Guðmundur Jósepsson
Ken Baumgardner	Barry Epstein	Derry Kabcenell
Curtis Bennett	Henry Fahey	George Kadifa
Darren Bock	Mark Farnham	Mike Kaul
Kenneth Brady	Robert Feighner	Brian Kush
Phillip Briggs	Peter Gram	Armand Sadat Kyaee
Michael Brown	Donald Gross	Tom Kyte
Tim Bunce	Kyle Hailey	Ray Lane
Dr. Burt Burns	Stephan Haisley	Sang Chul Lee
Lasse Christensen	Theresa Haisley	Jonathan Lewis
Carol Colrain	Ray Hamlett	Margaret Lewis
Rudy Corsi	Ahmer Hasan	Jim Littlefield
Carol Dacko	Jim Herndon	Juan Loaiza
Dominic Delmolino	Dave Herrington	Andrea Lopez
David Dempsey	Carol Hipp	Scott Lovingfoss
Kirti Deshpande	Dr. Myron Hlynka	Roderick Mañalac
Johannes Djernæs	Torben Holm	Laura Mazzarella
Greg Doherty	Mark Horstman	Connor McDonald
Ellen Dudar	Mamdouh Ibrahim	Daniel Menascé

Rick Minutella
Michael Möller
James Morle
Craig Newburger
Mark Pavkovic
Charles Peterson
Nagesh Pillarisetti
Nick Popovic
Lyn Pratt
Darryl Presley
Dr. Ray Quiett
Willis Ranney
Matt Raue
Andy Rivenes
Hasan Rizvi
Jesse Ruder
Bob Rudzki
Sandy Sanderson
Matt Seaton
Craig Shallahamer
Pete Sharman
Robert Shaw
Roger Siemens
Dr. John Slocum
Jerry Snow
Bill Stangel
Jared Still

Marcela Studnicka
Torfi Ólafur Sverrisson
Irfan Syed
Tony Taylor
Lawrence To
Dan Tow
Joakim Treugut
Hank Tullis
Peter Utzig
Gaja Krishna Vaidyanatha
Thierry Vergult
Michel Vetsuypens
Dr. Anita Walker
Dr. Bill Walker
Mike Wielonski
Gerald Williamson
Liz Wiseman
Brian Wolff
Graham Wood
Jimmy Harkey, for introducing me to the
    axiomatic approach to problem-solving
Rachel Rutti, for introducing me to Eli Goldratt's
    The Goal
The members of the Oak Table Network
The many contributing members of *Oracle-L*
And Gram... I miss you more than I ever imagined.

## PART I

Method

## CHAPTER 1

A Better Way to Optimize

For many people, Oracle performance is a very difficult problem. Since 1990, I've worked with thousands of professionals engaged in performance improvement projects for their Oracle systems. Oracle performance improvement projects appear to progress through standard stages over time. I think the names of those stages are stored in a vault somewhere beneath Geneva. If I remember correctly, the stages are:

Unrestrained optimism
Informed pessimism
Panic
Denial
Despair
Utter despair
Misery and famine

For some reason, my colleagues and I are rarely invited to participate in a project until the "misery and famine" stage. Here is what performance improvement projects often look like by the time we arrive. Do they sound like situations you've seen before?

Technical experts disagree over root causes

The severity of a performance problem is proportional to the number of people who show up at meetings to talk about it. It's a particularly bad sign when several different companies' "best experts" show up in the same meeting. In dozens of meetings throughout my career, I've seen the "best experts" from various consulting companies, computer and storage subsystem manufacturers, software vendors, and network providers convene to dismantle a performance problem. In exactly 100% of these meetings I've attended, these groups have argued incessantly over the identity of a performance problem's root cause. For *weeks*. How can dedicated, smart, well-trained, and well-intentioned professionals all look at the same system and render different opinions—often even *contradictory* opinions—on what's causing a performance problem? Apparently, Oracle system performance is a very difficult problem.

Experts claim excellent progress, while users see no improvement

Many of my students grin with memories when I tell stories of consultants who announce proudly that they have increased some statistic markedly—maybe they increased some hit ratio or reduced some extent count or some such—only to be confronted with the indignity that the users can't tell that anything is any better at all. The usual result of such an experience is a long report from the consultant explaining as politely as possible that, although the users aren't clever enough to tell, the system is eminently better off as a result of the attached invoice.

The story is funny unless, of course, you're either the owner of a company who's paying for all this wasted time, or the consultant who won't get paid because he didn't actually accomplish anything meaningful. Maybe this story seems funny because most of us at some time or another have *been* that consultant. How is it possible to so obviously improve such important system metrics as hit ratios, average latencies, and wait times, yet have users who can't even perceive the beneficial results of our effort? Apparently, Oracle system performance is a very difficult problem.

Hardware upgrades either don't help, or they slow the system further

Since first picking up Neil Gunther's *The Practical Performance Analyst* in 1998 [Gunther (1998)], I have presented to various audiences the possibility of one particularly counterintuitive phenomenon. "Do you realize that a hardware upgrade can actually *degrade* the performance of an important application?" Every audience to which I've ever presented this question and the facts pertaining to it have had virtually identical reactions. Most of the audience smiles in disbelief while I describe how this can happen, and one or two audience members come to the podium afterward to rejoice in finally figuring out what had happened several months after their horrible "upgrade gone wrong."

Hardware upgrades may not often cause noticeable new performance problems, but they can. Very often, hardware upgrades result in no noticeable difference, except of course for the quite noticeable amount of cash that flows out the door in return for no perceptible benefit. That a hardware upgrade can result in no improvement is somewhat disturbing. The idea that a hardware upgrade can actually result in a performance *degradation*, on its face, is utterly incomprehensible. How is it possible that a hardware upgrade might not only not improve performance, but that it might actually *harm* it? Apparently, Oracle system performance is a very difficult problem.

The number one system resource consumer is waste

Almost without exception, my colleagues and I find that 50% or more of every system's workload is *waste*. We define "waste" very carefully as any system workload that could have been avoided with no loss of function to the business. How can completely unnecessary workload be the number one resource consumer on so many professionally managed systems? Apparently, Oracle system performance is a very difficult problem.

These are smart people. How could their projects be so messed up? Apparently, Oracle system optimization is very difficult. How else can you explain why so many projects at so many companies that don't talk to each other end up in horrible predicaments that are so similar?

"You're Doing It Wrong"

One of my hobbies involves building rather largish things out of wood. This hobby involves the use of heavy machines that, given the choice, would prefer to eat my fingers instead of a piece of five-quarters American Black Walnut. One of the most fun things about the hobby for me is to read about a new technique that improves accuracy and saves time, while dramatically reducing my personal risk of accidental death and dismemberment. For me, getting the "D'oh, I'm doing it wrong!" sensation is a pleasurable thing, because it means that I'm on the brink of learning something that will make my life noticeably better. The net effect of such events on my emotional well-being is overwhelmingly positive. Although I'm of course a little disappointed every time I acquire more proof that I'm not omniscient, I'm overjoyed at the notion that soon I'll be better.

It is in the spirit of this story that I submit for your consideration the following hypothesis:

> If you find that Oracle performance tuning is really difficult, then chances are excellent that you're doing it wrong.

Now, here's the scary part:

> You're doing it wrong because you've been *taught* to do it that way.

This is my gauntlet. I believe that most of the Oracle tuning methods either implied or taught since the 1980s are fundamentally flawed. My motivation for writing this book is to share with you the research that has convinced me that there's a vastly better way.

Let's begin with a synopsis of the "method" that you're probably using today. A method is supposed to be a deterministic sequence of steps. One of the first things you might notice in the literature available today is the striking *absence* of actual method. Most authors focus far more attention on tips and techniques than on methods. The result is a massive battery of "things you might want to do" with virtually no structure present to tell you *whether* or *when* it's appropriate to do each. If you browse *google.com* hits on the string "Oracle performance method," you'll see what I mean.

Most of the Oracle performance improvement methods prescribed today can be summarized as the sequence of steps described in Method C (the *conventional* trial-and-error approach). If you have a difficult time with Oracle performance optimization, the reason may dawn on you as you review Method C. One of the few things that this method actually optimizes is the flow of revenue to performance specialists who take a long time to solve performance problems.

Method C: The Trial-and-Error Method That Dominates the Oracle Performance Tuning Culture Today

1. Hypothesize that some performance metric x has an unacceptable value.
2. Try things with the intent of improving x. Undo any attempt that makes performance noticeably worse.
3. If users do *not* perceive a satisfactory response time improvement, then go to step 1.
4. If the performance improvement *is* satisfactory, then go to step 1 anyway, because it may be possible to produce other performance improvements if you just keep searching.

This trial-and-error approach is, of course, not the only performance improvement method in town. The *YAPP Method* first described by Anjo Kolk and Shari Yamaguchi in the 1990s [Kolk et al. (1999)] was probably the first to rise above the inauspicious domain of tips and techniques to result in a truly usable deterministic sequence of steps. YAPP truly revolutionized the process of performance problem diagnosis, and it serves as one of the principal inspirations for this text.

Requirements of a Good Method

What distinguishes a good method from a bad one? When we started *hotsos.com* in 1999, I began spending a lot of time identifying the inefficiencies of existing Oracle performance improvement methods. It was a fun exercise. After much study, my colleagues and I were able to construct a list of objectively measurable criteria that would assist in distinguishing *good* from *bad* in a method. We hoped that such a list would serve as a yardstick that would allow us to measure the effectiveness of any method refinements we would create. Here is the list of attributes that I believe distinguish good methods from bad ones:

Impact
> If it is possible to improve performance, a method must deliver that improvement. It is unacceptable for a performance remedy to require significant investment input but produce imperceptible or negative end-user impact.

Efficiency

A method must always deliver performance improvement results with the least possible economic sacrifice. A performance improvement method is not *optimal* if another method could have achieved a suitable result less expensively in equal or less time.

Measurability

A method must produce performance improvement results that can be measured in units that make sense to the *business*. Performance improvement measurements are inadequate if they can be expressed only in technical units that do not correspond directly to improvement in cash flow, net profit, and return on investment.

Predictive capacity

A method must enable the analyst to predict the impact of a proposed remedy action. The unit of measure for the prediction must be the same as that which the business will use to measure performance improvement.

Reliability

A method must identify the correct root cause of the problem, no matter what that root cause may be.

Determinism

A method must guide the analyst through an unambiguous sequence of steps that always rely upon documented axioms, not experience or intuition. It is unacceptable for two analysts using the same method to draw different conclusions about the root cause of a performance problem.

Finiteness

A method must have a well-defined terminating condition, such as a proof of optimality.

Practicality

A method must be usable in any reasonable operating condition. For example, it is unacceptable for a performance improvement method to rely upon tools that exist in some operating environments but not others.

Method C suffers brutally on every single dimension of this eight-point definition of "goodness." I won't belabor the point here, but I do encourage you to consider, right now, how your existing performance improvement methods score on each of the attributes listed here. You might find the analysis quite motivating. When you've finished reading Part I of this book, I hope you will revisit this list and see whether you think your scores have improved as a result of what you have read.

Three Important Advances

In the Preface, I began with the statement:

> Optimizing Oracle response time is, for the most part, a solved problem.

This statement stands in stark contrast to the gloomy picture I painted at the beginning of this chapter—that, "For many people, Oracle system performance is a very difficult problem." The contrast, of course, has a logical explanation. It is this:

> Several technological advances have added impact, efficiency, measurability, predictive capacity, reliability, determinism, finiteness, and practicality to the science of Oracle performance optimization.

In particular, I believe that three important advances are primarily responsible for the improvements we have today. Curiously, while these advances are new to most professionals who work with Oracle products, none of these advances is really "new." Each is used extensively by optimization analysts in non-Oracle fields; some have been in use for over a century.

User Action Focus

The first important advance in Oracle optimization technology follows from a simple mathematical observation:

> You can't extrapolate detail from an aggregate.

Here's a puzzle to demonstrate my point. Imagine that I told you that a collection of 1,000 rocks contains 999 grey rocks and one special rock that's been painted bright red. The collection weighs 1,000 pounds. Now, answer the following question: "How much does the red rock weigh?" If your answer is, "I know that the red rock weighs one pound," then, whether you realize it or not, you've told a lie. You don't know that the red rock weighs one pound. With the information you've been given, you *can't* know. If your answer is, "I *assume* that the red rock weighs one pound," then you're too generous in what you're willing to assume. Such an assumption puts you at risk of forming conclusions that are incorrect—perhaps even stunningly incorrect.

The correct answer is that the red rock can weigh virtually any amount between zero and 1,000 pounds. The only thing limiting the low end of the weight is the definition of how many atoms must be present in order for a thing to be called a *rock*. Once we define how small a rock can be, then we've defined the high end of our answer. It is 1,000 pounds minus the weight of 999 of the smallest possible rocks. The red rock can weigh virtually anything between zero and a thousand pounds. Answering with any more precision is *wrong* unless you happen to be very lucky. But being very lucky at games like this is a skill that can be neither learned nor taught, nor repeated with acceptable reliability.

This is one reason why Oracle analysts find it so frustrating to diagnose performance problems armed only with system-wide statistics such as those produced by *Statspack* (or any of its cousins derived from the old SQL scripts called *bstat* and *estat*). Two analysts looking at exactly the same *Statspack* output can "see" two completely different things, neither of which is completely provable or completely disprovable by the *Statspack* output. It's not *Statspack*'s fault. It's a problem that is inherent in any performance analysis that uses *system*-wide data as its starting point (V$SYSSTAT, V$SYSTEM_EVENT, and so on). You can in fact instruct *Statspack* to collect sufficiently granular data for you, but no *Statspack* documentation of which I'm aware makes any effort to tell you why you might ever want to.

A fine illustration is the case of an Oracle system whose red rock was a payroll processing problem. The officers of the company described a performance problem with Oracle Payroll that was hurting their business. The database administrators of the company described a performance problem with latches: *cache buffers chains* latches, to be specific. Both arguments were compelling. The business truly was suffering from a problem with payroll being too slow. You could see it, because checks weren't coming out of the system fast enough. The "system" truly was suffering from latch contention problems. You could see it, because queries of V$SYSTEM_EVENT clearly showed that the system was spending a lot of time waiting for the event called latch free.

The company's database and system administration staff had invested three frustrating months trying to fix the "latch free problem," but the company had found no relief for the payroll performance problem. The reason was simple: payroll wasn't spending time waiting for latches. How did we find out? We acquired operational timing data for one execution of the slow payroll program. What we found was amazing. Yes, lots of other application programs in fact spent time waiting to acquire cache buffers chains latches. But of the slow payroll program's total 1,985.40-second execution time, only 23.69 seconds were consumed waiting on latches. That's 1.2% of the program's total response time. Had the company completely *eradicated* waits for latch free from the face of their system, they would have made only a 1.2% performance improvement in the response time of their payroll program.

How could system-wide statistics have been so misleading? Yes, lots of non-payroll workload was prominently afflicted by latch free problems. But it was a grave error to assume that the payroll program's problem was the same as the system-wide average problem. The error in assuming a cause-effect relationship between latch free waiting and payroll performance cost the company three months of wasted time and frustration and thousands of dollars in labor and equipment upgrade costs. By contrast, diagnosing the real payroll performance problem consumed only about ten minutes of diagnosis time once the company saw the correct diagnostic data.

My colleagues and I encounter this type of problem repeatedly. The solution is for you (the performance analyst) to focus entirely upon the *user actions* that need optimizing. The business can tell you what the most important user actions are. The system cannot. Once you have identified a user action that requires optimization, then your first job is to collect operational data *exactly* for that user action—no more, and no less.

Response Time Focus

For a couple of decades now, Oracle performance analysts have labored under the assumption that there's really no objective way to measure Oracle response time [Ault and Brinson (2000), 27]. In the perceived absence of objective ways to measure response time, analysts have settled for the next-best thing: *event counts*. And of course from event counts come ratios. And from ratios come all sorts of arguments about which "tuning" actions are important, and which ones are not.

However, users don't care about event counts and ratios and arguments; they care about *response time*: the duration that begins when they request something and ends when they get their answer. No matter how much complexity you build atop any timing-free event-count data, you are fundamentally doomed by the following inescapable truth, the subject of the second important advance:

> You can't tell how long something took by counting how many times it happened.

Users care only about response times. If you're measuring only event counts, then you're not measuring what the users care about. If you liked the red rock quiz, here's another one for you: What's causing the performance problem in the program that produced the data in Example 1-1?

Example 1-1. Components of response time listed in descending order of call volume

Response Time Component	# Calls
CPU service	18,750
SQL*Net message to client	6,094
SQL*Net message from client	6,094
db file sequential read	1,740
log file sync	681
SQL*Net more data to client	108
SQL*Net more data from client	71
db file scattered read	34
direct path read	5
free buffer waits	4
log buffer space	2
direct path write	2
log file switch completion	1
latch free	1

Example 1-2 shows the same data from the same program execution, this time augmented with timing data (reported in seconds) and sorted by descending response time impact. Does it change your answer?

Example 1-2. Components of response time listed in descending order of contribution to response time

Response Time Component	Duration		# Calls	Dur/Call
SQL*Net message from client	**166.6s**	**91.7%**	**6,094**	**0.027338s**
CPU service	9.7s	5.3%	18,750	0.000515s
unaccounted-for	2.2s	1.2%		
db file sequential read	1.6s	0.9%	1,740	0.000914s
log file sync	1.1s	0.6%	681	0.001645s
SQL*Net more data from client	0.3s	0.1%	71	0.003521s
SQL*Net more data to client	0.1s	0.1%	108	0.001019s
free buffer waits	0.1s	0.0%	4	0.022500s
SQL*Net message to client	0.0s	0.0%	6,094	0.000007s
db file scattered read	0.0s	0.0%	34	0.001176s
log file switch completion	0.0s	0.0%	1	0.030000s
log buffer space	0.0s	0.0%	2	0.005000s
latch free	0.0s	0.0%	1	0.010000s
direct path read	0.0s	0.0%	5	0.000000s
direct path write	0.0s	0.0%	2	0.000000s
Total	181.8s	100.0%		

Of course it changes your answer, because response time is dominatingly important, and event counts are inconsequential by comparison. The problem with the program that generated this data is what's going on with SQL*Net message from client, not what's going on with CPU service.

If you are an experienced Oracle performance analyst, you may have heard that SQL*Net message from client is an *idle event* that can be ignored. You must *not* ignore the so-called idle events if you collect your diagnostic data in the manner I describe in Chapter 3.

If the year were 1991, we'd be in big trouble right now, because in 1991 the data that I've shown in this second table wasn't available from the Oracle kernel. But if you've upgraded by now to at least Oracle7, then you don't need to settle for event counts as the "next-best thing" to response time data. The basic assumption that you can't tell how long the Oracle kernel takes to do things is simply incorrect, and it has been since Oracle release 7.0.12.

Amdahl's Law

The final "great advance" in Oracle performance optimization that I'll mention is an observation published in 1967 by Gene Amdahl, which has become known as *Amdahl's Law* [Amdahl (1967)]:

> The performance enhancement possible with a given improvement is limited by the fraction of the execution time that the improved feature is used.

In other words, performance improvement is proportional to how much a program uses the thing you improved. Amdahl's Law is why you should view response time components in *descending* response time order. In Example 1-2, it's why you don't work on the CPU service "problem" before figuring out the SQL*Net message from client problem. If you were to reduce total CPU consumption by 50%, you'd improve response time by only about 2%. But if you could reduce the response time attributable to SQL*Net message from client by the same 50%, you'll reduce total response time by 46%. In Example 1-2, each percentage point of reduction in SQL*Net message from client duration produces nearly twenty times the impact of a percentage point of CPU service reduction.

Amdahl's Law is a formalization of optimization common sense. It tells you how to get the biggest "bang for the buck" from your performance improvement efforts.

All Together Now

Combining the three advances in Oracle optimization technology into one statement results in the following simple performance method:

> Work first to reduce the biggest response time component of a business' most important user action.

It sounds easy, right? Yet I can be almost certain that this is *not* how you optimize your Oracle system back home. It's not what your consultants do or what your tools do. This way of "tuning" is nothing like what your books or virtually any of the other papers presented at Oracle seminars and conferences since 1980 tell you to do. So what is the missing link?

The missing link is that unless you know how to extract and interpret response time measurements from your Oracle system, you can't implement this simple optimization method. Explaining how to extract and interpret response time measurements from your Oracle system is a main point of this book.

 I hope that by the time you read this book, my claims that "this is *not* how you do it today" don't make sense anymore. As I write this chapter, many factors are converging to make the type of optimization I'm describing in this book much more common among Oracle practitioners. If the book you're holding has played an influencing role in that evolution, then so much the better.

Tools for Analyzing Response Time

The definition of *response time* set forth by the International Organization for Standardization is plain but useful:

> *Response time* is the elapsed time between the end of an inquiry or demand on a computer system and the beginning of a response; for example, the length of the time between an indication of the end of an inquiry and the display of the first character of the response at a user terminal (source: *http://searchnetworking.techtarget.com/sDefinition/0,,sid7_gci212896,00.html*).

Response time is an *objective* measure of the interaction between a consumer and a provider. Consumers of computer service want the right answer with the best response time for the lowest cost. Your goal as an Oracle performance analyst is to minimize response time within the confines of the system owner's economic constraints. The ways to do that become more evident when you consider the components of response time.

Sequence Diagram

A *sequence diagram* is a convenient way to depict the response time components of a user action. A sequence diagram shows the flow of control as a user action consumes time in different layers of a technology stack. The *technology stack* is a model that considers system components such as the business users, the network, the application software, the database kernel, and the hardware in a stratified architecture. The component at each layer in the stack demands service from the layer beneath it and supplies service to the layer above it. Figure 1-1 shows a sequence diagram for a multi-tier Oracle system.

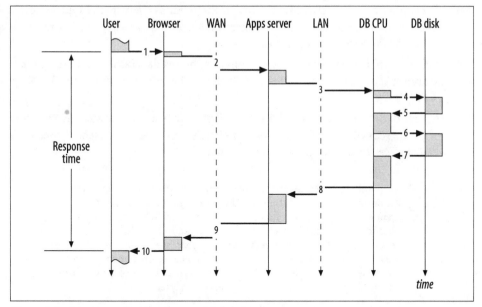

Figure 1-1. A sequence diagram for a multi-tier Oracle system

Figure 1-1 denotes the following sequence of actions, allowing us to literally *see* how each layer in the technology stack contributes to the consumption of response time:

1. After considering what she wants from the system, a user initiates a request for data from a browser by pressing the OK button. Almost instantaneously, the request arrives at the browser. The user's perception of response time begins with the click of the OK button.

2. After devoting a short bit of time to rendering the pixels on the screen to make the OK button look like it has been depressed, the browser sends an HTTP packet to the wide-area network (WAN). The request spends some time on the WAN before arriving at the application server.

3. After executing some application code on the middle tier, the application server issues a database call via SQL*Net across the local-area network (LAN). The request spends some time on the LAN (less than a request across a WAN) before arriving at the database server.

4. After consuming some CPU time on the database server, the Oracle kernel process issues an operating system function call to perform a read from disk.

5. After consuming some time in the disk subsystem, the read call returns control of the request back to the database CPU.

6. After consuming more CPU time on the database server, the Oracle kernel process issues another read request.

7. After consuming some more time in the disk subsystem, the read call returns control of the request again to the database CPU.

8. After a final bit of CPU consumption on the database server, the Oracle kernel process passes the results of the application server's database call. The return is issued via SQL*Net across the LAN.

9. After the application server process converts the results of the database call into the appropriate HTML, it passes the results to the browser across the WAN via HTTP.

10. After rendering the result on the user's display device, the browser returns control of the request back to the user. The user's perception of *response time* ends when she sees the information she requested.

A good sequence diagram reveals only the amount of detail that is appropriate for the analysis at hand. For example, to simplify the content of Figure 1-1, I have made no effort to show the tiny latencies that occur within the Browser, Apps Server, and DB CPU tiers as their operating systems' schedulers transition processes among *running* and *ready to run* states. In some performance improvement projects, understanding this level of detail will be vital. I describe the performance impact of such state transitions in Chapter 7.

In my opinion, the ideal Oracle performance optimization tool does not exist yet. The graphical user interface of the ideal performance optimization tool would be a sequence diagram that could show how every microsecond of response time had been consumed for any specified user action. Such an application would have so much information to manage that it would have to make clever use of summary and drill-down features to show you exactly what you wanted when you wanted it.

Such an application will probably be built soon. As you shall see throughout this book, much of the information that is needed to build such an application is already available from the Oracle kernel. The biggest problems today are:

- Most of the non-database tiers in a multi-tier system aren't instrumented to provide the type of response time data that the Oracle kernel provides. Chapter 7 details the response time data that I'm talking about.

- Depending upon your application architecture, it can be very difficult to collect properly scoped performance diagnostic data for a specific user action. Chapter 3 explains what constitutes proper scoping for diagnostic data, and Chapter 6 explains how to work around the data collection difficulties presented by various application architectures.

However, much of what we need already exists. Beginning with Oracle release 7.0.12, and improving ever since, the Oracle kernel is well instrumented for response time measurement. This book will help you understand exactly how to take advantage of those measurements to optimize your approach to the performance improvement of Oracle systems.

Resource Profile

A complete sequence diagram for anything but a very simple user action would show so much data that it would be difficult to use all of it. Therefore, you need a way to summarize the details of response time in a useful way. In Example 1-2, I showed a sample of such a summary, called a *resource profile*. A resource profile is simply a table that reveals a useful decomposition of response time. Typically, a resource profile reveals at least the following attributes:

- Response time category
- Total duration consumed by actions in that category
- Number of calls to actions in that category

A resource profile is most useful when it lists its categories in descending order of elapsed time consumption per category. The resource profile is an especially handy format for performance analysts because it focuses your attention on exactly the problem you should solve first. The resource profile is the most important tool in my performance diagnostic repertory.

The idea of the resource profile is nothing new, actually. The idea for using the resource profile as our company's focus was inspired by an article on profilers published in the 1980s [Bentley (1988) 3-13], which itself was based on work that Donald Knuth published in the early 1970s [Knuth (1971)]. The idea of decomposing response time into components is so sensible that you probably do it often without realizing it. Consider how you optimize your driving route to your favorite destination. Think of a "happy place" where you go when you want to feel better.

For me it's my local Woodcraft Supply store (*http://www.woodcraft.com*), which sells all sorts of tools that can cut fingers or crush rib cages, and all sorts of books and magazines that explain how not to.

If you live in a busy city and schedule the activity during rush-hour traffic, the resource profile for such a trip might resemble the following (expressed in minutes):

```
Response Time Component            Duration        # Calls     Dur/Call
-----------------------------   ----------------  -----------  ------------
rush-hour expressway driving     90m   90%             2           45m
neighborhood driving             10m   10%             2            5m
-----------------------------   ----------------  -----------  ------------
Total                           100m  100%
```

If the store were, say, only fifteen miles away, you might find the prospect of sitting for an hour and a half in rush-hour traffic to be disappointing. Whether or not you believe that your brain works in the format of a resource profile, you probably would consider the same optimization that I'm thinking of right now: perhaps you could go to the store during an off-peak driving period.

```
Response Time Component            Duration        # Calls     Dur/Call
-----------------------------   ----------------  -----------  ------------
off-peak expressway driving      30m   75%             2           15m
neighborhood driving             10m   25%             2            5m
-----------------------------   ----------------  -----------  ------------
Total                            40m  100%
```

The driving example is simple enough, and the stakes are low enough, that a formal analysis is almost definitely unnecessary. However, for more complex performance problems, the resource profile provides a convenient format for proving a point, especially when decisions about whether or not to invest lots of time and money are involved.

Resource profiles add unequivocal relevance to Oracle performance improvement projects. Example 1-3 shows a resource profile for the Oracle Payroll program described earlier in "User Action Focus." Before the database administrators saw this resource profile, they had worked for three months fighting a perceived problem with latch contention. In desperation, they had spent several thousand dollars on a CPU upgrade, which had actually degraded the response time of the payroll action whose performance they were trying to improve. Within ten minutes of creating this resource profile, the database administrator knew exactly how to cut this program's response time by roughly 50%. The problem and its solution are detailed in Part III of this book.

Example 1-3. The resource profile for a network configuration problem that had previously been misdiagnosed as both a latch contention problem and a CPU capacity problem

```
Response Time Component            Duration        # Calls     Dur/Call
-----------------------------   ----------------  -----------  ------------
SQL*Net message from client     984.0s  49.6%       95,161     0.010340s
SQL*Net more data from client   418.8s  21.1%        3,345     0.125208s
```

Example 1-3. The resource profile for a network configuration problem that had previously been misdiagnosed as both a latch contention problem and a CPU capacity problem (continued)

db file sequential read	279.3s	14.1%	45,084	0.006196s
CPU service	248.7s	12.5%	222,760	0.001116s
unaccounted-for	27.9s	1.4%		
latch free	23.7s	1.2%	34,695	0.000683s
log file sync	1.1s	0.1%	506	0.002154s
SQL*Net more data to client	0.8s	0.0%	15,982	0.000052s
log file switch completion	0.3s	0.0%	3	0.093333s
enqueue	0.3s	0.0%	106	0.002358s
SQL*Net message to client	0.2s	0.0%	95,161	0.000003s
buffer busy waits	0.2s	0.0%	67	0.003284s
db file scattered read	0.0s	0.0%	2	0.005000s
SQL*Net break/reset to client	0.0s	0.0%	2	0.000000s
Total	1,985.4s	100.0%		

Example 1-4 shows another resource profile that saved a project from a frustrating and expensive ride down a rat hole. Before seeing the resource profile shown here, the proposed solution to this report's performance problem was to upgrade either memory or the I/O subsystem. The resource profile proved unequivocally that upgrading either could result in no more than a 2% response time improvement. Almost all of this program's response time was attributable to a single SQL statement that motivated nearly a billion visits to blocks stored in the database buffer cache.

 You can't tell by looking at the resource profile in Example 1-4 that the CPU capacity was consumed by nearly a billion memory reads. Each of the 192,072 "calls" to the CPU service resource represents one Oracle database call (for example, a parse, an execute, or a fetch). From the detailed SQL trace information collected for each of these calls, I could determine that the 192,072 database calls had issued nearly a billion memory reads. How you can do this is detailed in Chapter 5.

Problems like this are commonly caused by operational errors like the accidental deletion of schema statistics used by the Oracle cost-based query optimizer (CBO).

Example 1-4. The resource profile for an inefficient SQL problem that had previously been diagnosed as an I/O subsystem problem

Response Time Component	Duration		# Calls	Dur/Call
CPU service	48,946.7s	98.0%	192,072	0.254835s
db file sequential read	940.1s	2.0%	507,385	0.001853s
SQL*Net message from client	60.9s	0.0%	191,609	0.000318s
latch free	2.2s	0.0%	171	0.012690s
other	1.4s	0.0%		
Total	49,951.3s	100.0%		

Example 1-4 is a beautiful example of how a resource profile can free you from victimization to myth. In this case, the myth that had confused the analyst about this slow session was the proposition that a high *database buffer cache hit ratio* is an indication of SQL statement efficiency. The statement causing this slow session had an exceptionally high buffer cache hit ratio. It is easy to understand why, by looking at the computation of the cache hit ratio (CHR) metric for this case:

$$CHR = \frac{LIO - PIO}{LIO}$$
$$\approx \frac{10^9 - 507385}{10^9}$$
$$\approx 0.9995$$

In this formula, LIO (*logical I/O*) represents the number of Oracle blocks obtained from Oracle memory (the database buffer cache), and PIO (*physical I/O*) represents the number of Oracle blocks obtained from operating system read calls.[*] The expression LIO – PIO thus represents the number of blocks obtained from Oracle memory that did not motivate an operating system read call.

Although most analysts would probably consider a ratio value of 0.9995 to be "good," it is of course not "perfect." In the absence of the data shown in Example 1-4, many analysts I've met would have assumed that it was the imperfection in the cache hit ratio that was causing the performance problem. But the resource profile shows clearly that even if the 507,385 physical read operations could have been serviced from the database buffer cache, the best possible total time savings would have been only 940.1 seconds. The maximum possible impact of fixing this "problem" would have been to shave a 14-*hour* execution by a mere 16 minutes.

Considering the performance of user actions using the resource profile format has revolutionized the effectiveness of many performance analysts. For starters, it is the perfect tool for determining what to work on first, in accordance with our stated objective:

> Work first to reduce the biggest response time component of a business' most important user action.

Another huge payoff of using the resource profile format is that it is virtually impossible for a performance problem to hide from it. The informal proof of this conjecture requires only two steps:

> *Proof*: If something is a response time problem, then it shows up in the resource profile. If it's not a response time problem, then it's not a performance problem. *QED*

Part II of this book describes how to create resource profiles from which performance problems cannot hide.

---

[*] This formula has many problems other than the one illustrated in this example. Many authors—including Adams, Lewis, Kyte, and myself—have identified dozens of critical flaws in the definition of the database buffer cache hit ratio statistic. See especially [Lewis (2003)] for more information.

Method R

The real goal of this book is *not* just to help you make an Oracle system go faster. The real goal of this book is to optimize the *project* that makes an Oracle system go faster. I don't just want to help you make one system faster. I want to help you make *any* system faster, and I want you to be able to accomplish that task in the most economically efficient way possible for your business. Method R is the method I will describe by which you can achieve this goal. Method R is in fact the basis for the remainder of this book.

Method R is conceptually very simple. As you should expect, it is merely a formalization of the simple "Work first to reduce the biggest response time component of a business' most important user action" objective that you've seen many times by now.

Who Uses the Method

An immediately noticeable distinction of Method R is the type of person who will be required to execute it. Method R specifically can *not* be performed in isolation by a technician who has no interest in your business. As I have said, the goal of Method R is to improve the overall value of the system to the *business*. This goal cannot be achieved in isolation from the business. But how does a person who leads the execution of Method R fit into an information technology department?

The abominable smokestack

Most large companies organize their technical infrastructure support staff in a manner that I call the "abominable smokestacks," like the departmental segmentation shown in Figure 1-2. Organizational structures like this increase the difficulty of optimizing the performance of a system, for one fundamental reason:

> Compartmentalized organizational units tend to optimize in isolation from other organizational units, resulting in locally optimized components. Even if they succeed in doing this, it's not necessarily good enough. A system consisting of locally optimized components is not necessarily itself an optimized system.

One of Goldratt's many contributions to the body of system optimization knowledge is a compelling illustration of how local optimization does not necessarily lead to global optimization [Goldratt (1992)].

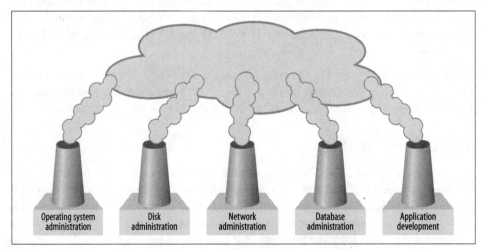

Figure 1-2. Typical organizational structure for a technical infrastructure department

The smokestack mentality is pervasive. Even the abstract submission forms we use to participate in Oracle conferences require that we choose a smokestack for each of our presentations (conference organizers tend to call them *tracks* instead of smokestacks). There is, for example, one track for papers pertaining to database tuning, and a completely distinct track for papers pertaining to operating system tuning. What if a performance optimization solution requires that attention be paid iteratively to both components of the technology stack? I believe the mere attempt at categorization discourages analysts from considering such solutions. At least analysts who do implement solutions that span stack layers are ensured of having a difficult time choosing the perfect track for their paper proposals.

 One classic aspect of segmentation is particularly troublesome for almost every Oracle system owner I've ever talked with: the distinction between application developers and database administrators. Which group is responsible for system performance? The answer is *both*. There are performance problems that application developers will not detect without assistance from database administrators. Likewise, there are performance problems that database administrators will not be able to repair without assistance from application developers.

The Goal

One inspiration behind Method R is the story told in Eli Goldratt's *The Goal* [Goldratt (1992)]. *The Goal* describes the victory of a revolutionary new performance optimization method over a method that is culturally ingrained but produces inferior results. Goldratt's method applies to factory optimization, but his story is eerily reminiscent of what the Oracle community is going through today: the overthrow of an optimization method based upon a faulty measurement system.

The Goal dismantles a lot of false ideas that a lot of analysts think they "know" about optimization. Two of the most illuminating lessons that I learned from the book were:

- *Cost accounting* practices often promote bad optimization decisions. Oracle practitioners use cost accounting practices when they target a system's hit ratios for optimization.

- A collection of optimized components *is itself not necessarily optimized*. This explains why systems with 100% "best in class" componentry can have performance problems. It explains why so many slow Oracle systems have dozens of component administrators standing behind them who each swears that his component "can't possibly be the cause of a performance problem."

If you haven't read *The Goal*, then I think you're in for a real treat. If you have read it already, then consider reading it again with the intent to apply what you read by analogy to the world of Oracle performance. The cover says that "*Goal* readers are now doing the best work of their lives." This statement is a completely accurate portrayal of my personal relationship with the book.

The optimal performance analyst

A company's best defense against performance problems begins with a good performance analyst who can diagnose and discourse intelligently in all the layers of the technology stack. In the context of Figure 1-2, this person is able to engage successfully "in the smoke." The performance analyst can navigate above the smokestacks long enough to diagnose which pipes to dive into. And the best analyst has the knowledge, intelligence, charisma, and motivation to drive change in the interactions among smokestacks once he's proven where the best leverage is.

Of the dozens of great Oracle performance analysts I've had the honor of meeting, most share a common set of behavioral qualities that I believe form the basis for their success. The best means I know for describing the capabilities of these talented analysts is a structure described by Jim Kennedy and Anna Everest [Kennedy and Everest (1994)], which decomposes personal behavioral qualities into four groups:

Education/experience/knowledge factors
In the education/experience/knowledge category, the capabilities required of the optimal analyst are knowledge of the *business goals*, *processes*, and *user actions* that comprise the life of the business. The optimal analyst knows enough about *finance* to understand the types of input information that will be required for a financially-minded project sponsor to make informed investment decisions during a performance improvement project. And the optimal analyst of course understands the technical components of his application system, including the *hardware*, the *operating system*, the *database server*, the *application programs*, and any other computing tiers that join clients to servers. I describe many important technical factors in Part II of this book.

Intellectual factors
The optimal performance analyst exhibits several intellectual factors as well. Foremost, I believe, is the strong sense of *relevance*—the ability to understand what's important and what's not. Sense of relevance is a broad category. It combines the attributes of *perceptiveness*, *common sense*, and good *judgment*. General *problem solving* skills are indispensable, as is the ability to *acquire and assimilate new information quickly*.

Interpersonal factors
The optimal performance analyst exhibits several interpersonal factors. *Empathy* is key to acquiring accurate information from users, business owners, and component administration staff. *Poise* is critical for maintaining order during a performance crisis, especially during the regularly scheduled panic phase of a project. *Self-confidence* is necessary to inspire adequate morale among the various project victims and perpetrators to ensure that the project is allowed to complete. The optimal analyst is *tactful* and successful in creating *collaborative* effort to implement a solution plan.

Motivational factors

Finally, the optimal performance analyst exhibits several important motivational factors. She is *customer oriented* and *interested in the business*. She *enjoys a difficult challenge*, and she is *resourceful*. I have found the best performance analysts to be always mindful that technical, intellectual, interpersonal, and motivational challenges are all surmountable, but that different problem types often require drastically different solution approaches. The best performance analysts seem not only to understand this, but to actually *thrive on the variety*.

Your role

As a result of buying this book, I want you to become so confident in your performance problem diagnosis skills that a scenario like the following doesn't scare you one bit:

Scene: Big meeting. Participants include several infrastructure department managers, you, and a special guest: the CEO, whose concerns about online order form performance are critical enough that he has descended upon your meeting to find out what you're going to do about it....

Senior manager of the system administration department ("System manager"): In two weeks, we're going to upgrade our CPU capacity, at a cost to the business of US$65,000 in hardware and upgraded software license fees. However, we expect that because we're doubling our CPU speeds, this upgrade will improve performance significantly for our users.

CEO: (Nods.) We *must* improve the performance of our online order form, or we'll lose one of our biggest retail customers.

You: But our online order form consumes CPU service for only about 1.2 seconds of the order form's 45-second commit time. Even if we could totally *eliminate* the response time consumed by CPU service, we would make only about a one-second improvement in the form's response time.

System manager: I disagree. I think there are so many unexplained discrepancies in the response time data you're looking at that there's no way you can prove what you're saying.

You: Let's cover this offline. I'll show you how I know.

(Later, after reconvening the meeting.)

System manager: Okay, I get it. He's right. Upgrading our CPU capacity won't help order form performance in the way that we'd hoped.

You: But by modifying our workload in a way that I can describe, we can achieve at least a 95% improvement in the form's commit response time, without having to spend the money on upgrading our CPUs. As you can see in this profile of the order form's response time, upgrading CPU capacity wouldn't have helped us here anyway.

I've witnessed the results of a lot of conversations that began this way but never veered back on-course when it was the *You* character's first turn to speak. The result is often horrifying. A company works its way through the alphabet in search of something that might help performance. Sometimes it stops only when the company runs out of time or money, or both.

Perhaps even more painful to watch is the conversation in which the *You* character *does* speak up on cue but then is essentially shouted down by a group of people who don't believe the data. Unless you can defend your diagnostic data set all the way to its origin—*and* how it fits in with the data your debaters are collecting—you stand a frighteningly large chance of losing important debates, even when you're right.

Overcoming Common Objections

I hope that I've written this book effectively enough that you will want to try Method R on your own system. If you can work alone, then most of the obstacles along your way will be purely technical, and you'll probably do a great job of figuring those out. I've tried hard to help you overcome those with the information in this book.

However, it's more likely that improving the performance of your system will be a collaborative effort. You'll probably have to engage your colleagues in order to implement your recommendations. The activities you recommend as a result of using Method R will fall into one of two categories:

- Your colleagues have heard the ideas before and rejected them
- They've never heard the ideas before

Otherwise, your system would have been fixed by now. Either way, you will probably find yourself in an environment that is ready to challenge your ideas. To make any progress, you will have to justify your recommendations in language that makes sense to the people who doubt you.

 Justifying your recommendations this way is healthy for you to do anyway, even in the friendliest of environments where your words become other people's deeds almost instantaneously.

The most effective ways I've found to justify such recommendations are:

Proof-of-concept tests
> There's no better way to prove a result than to actually demonstrate it. Dave Ensor describes this as the *Jeweler's Method*. Any good jeweler will place interesting merchandise into a prospective customer's hands as *early* in the sales process as possible. *Holding* the piece activates all the buyer's senses in appreciating the beauty and goodness of the thing being sold. The buyer's full imagination goes to work for the seller as the buyer locks in on the vision of how much better life will become if only the thing being held can be obtained. The method works wonderfully for big-ticket items, including jewelry, cars, houses, boats, and system performance. There's probably no surer way to build enthusiasm for your proposal than to let your users actually *feel* how much better their lives will become as a result of your work.

Direct statistics that make sense to end users

If proof-of-concept tests are too complicated to provide, the next best thing is to speak in direct statistics that make sense to end users. There are *only three* acceptable units of measure for such statistics:

- Your local currency
- The duration by which you'll improve someone's response time
- The number of *business* actions per unit of time by which you'll improve someone's throughput

Any other measure will cause one of two problems. Either your argument will be too weak to convince the people you're trying to persuade, or, worse yet, you'll succeed in your persuasions, but because you were thinking in the wrong units of measure you'll risk producing end results with inadequate "real" benefit. Real benefit is *always* measured in units of either money or time. Succeeding in your proposal but failing in your end result of course causes an erosion of your credibility for future recommendations.

Track record of actualized predictions

If you have the luxury of a strong reputation to enhance your persuasive power, then merely making your wishes known may be enough to inspire action. However, if this is the case, *beware*. Every prediction you make runs the risk of eroding your credibility. Even if you have the power to convert your instructions into other people's tasks, I strongly encourage you to assess your recommendations privately using proof-of-concept tests or direct statistics that make sense to end users. Don't borrow from the account of your own credibility until you're certain of your recommendations.

"But my whole system is slow"

At *hotsos.com*, we use Method R for our living. After using the method many times, I can state categorically that the most difficult step of Method R is one that's not even listed: it is the step of convincing people to use it. The first objection my colleagues and I encounter to our focus on user actions is as predictable as the sunrise:

"But my *whole system* is slow."

"I need to tune my *whole system*, not just one user."

"When are you going to come out with a method that helps me tune my *whole system?*"

We hear it everywhere we go.

What if the whole system is slow? Practitioners often react nervously to a performance improvement method that restricts analysis to just one user action at a time. Especially if users perceive that the "whole system" is slow, there is often an overwhelming compulsion to begin an analysis with the collection of system-wide statistics. The fear is that if you restrict the scope of analysis to anything less than the entire system, you might miss something important. Well, in fact, a focus on prioritized user actions *does* cause you to miss some things:

> A focus on high-priority user actions causes you to overlook irrelevant performance data. By "irrelevant," I mean any data that would abate your progress in identifying and repairing your system's *most important* performance problem.

Here's why Method R works regardless of whether a system's problem is an individual user action or a whole mess of different user actions. Figure 1-3 shows the first information that analysts get when they learn of system performance problems. Legitimate information about performance problems usually comes first from the business in the form of user complaints.

 It *is* possible for information providers to be the first to know about performance problems. In Chapter 9 I describe one way in which you can acquire such *a priori* knowledge. But it is rare for information providers to know about performance problems before their information consumers tell them.

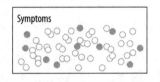

Figure 1-3. What performance analysts first see when there's a performance problem. Shaded circles represent user actions that are experiencing performance problems

Upon receipt of such information, the first impulse of most analysts is to establish a cause-effect relationship between the *symptoms* being observed and one or more *root causes* that might be motivating the symptoms. I wholeheartedly agree that this step is the right step. However, many projects fail because analysts fail to establish the *correct* cause-effect relationships. A core strength of Method R is that it allows you to determine cause-effect relationships more quickly and accurately than with any other method.

Figure 1-4 shows why. It depicts three possible sets of cause-effect relationships between problem root causes and performance problem symptoms. Understanding the effectiveness of Method R for each of these scenarios compared to conventional tuning methods will help you decide for yourself whether Method R is an effective system-wide optimization or not. The three possible scenarios depicted in Figure 1-4 are:

- At one extreme, case (a) depicts that every user-discernible symptom on the system is caused by a single "universal" root cause.
- In case (b), there is a many-to-many relationship between symptoms and root causes. Some symptoms have two or more contributory root causes, and some root causes contribute to more than one symptom.

- At the other extreme, case (c) depicts a situation in which every symptom is linked to its own distinct root cause. No single root cause creates negative performance impact for more than one user action.

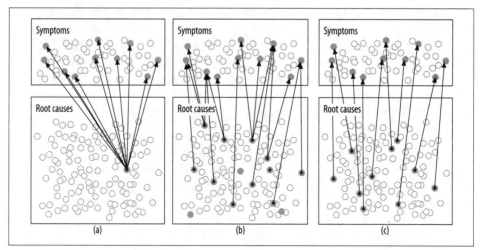

Figure 1-4. *Three possible sets of cause-effect relationships (depicted by arrows) between root causes and performance problem symptoms*

Of course it is easy to draw pictures of cause-effect relationships between root causes and performance problem symptoms. It's another matter entirely to determine such cause-effect relationships in reality. The ability to do this is, I believe, the most distinguishing strength of Method R. Let me explain.

For problems resembling Figure 1-4(a), Method R works quite well. Even if you were to completely botch the business prioritization task inherent in the method's step 1, you'd still stumble upon the root cause in the first diagnostic data you examined. The reason is simple. If all symptoms have the same root cause, then no matter which symptom you investigate, you'll find the single, universal root cause in that symptom's response time profile.

Method R also works well for problems resembling Figure 1-4(b) and (c). In these cases, the only way to provide system-wide relief is to respond to each of the root causes that contributes to a symptom. Constraints on analyst labor (your time) probably make it impossible to respond to all the symptoms simultaneously, so it will probably be important to prioritize which activities you'll conduct first. This requirement is precisely the motive for the work prioritization inherent in Method R. Remembering that the true *goal* of any performance improvement project is *economic*, the proper way to prioritize the project activities is to respond to the most important *symptoms* first. Method R is distinctive in that it encourages alignment of project priorities with *business* priorities.

By contrast, let's examine the effectiveness of Method C for each of the same three scenarios. Remember, the first step of Method C is:

> Hypothesize that some performance metric x has an unacceptable value.

In the context of Figure 1-4, this step is analogous to searching for the shaded circles in the portion of the diagram labeled *root causes*. After identifying probable root causes of performance problems, Method C next requires the analyst to establish a cause-effect relationship between root causes and symptoms. One problem with Method C is that it forces you to compute this cause-effect relationship rather more by accident than by plan. The conventional method for determining this cause-effect relationship is literally to "fix" something and then see what impact you created. It's a trial-and-error approach.

The challenge to succeeding with Method C is how quickly you can identify the right "unacceptable" system metric value. The longer it takes you to find it, the longer your project will drag on. Certainly, your chances of finding the right problem to solve are greatest when there's only one problem in the whole system. However, it's not certain that finding the root cause will be easy, even in an "easy" case like Figure 1-4(a). Just because there's only one root cause for a bunch of problems doesn't mean that there will be only one system-wide performance statistic that looks "unacceptable."

The real problem with Method C becomes apparent when you consider its effectiveness in response to the cases shown in Figure 1-4(b) and (c). In both of these cases, when we look "from the bottom up," there are several potential root causes to choose from. How will you determine which root cause to work on first? The best prioritization scheme would be to "follow the arrows" backward from the most important business symptoms to their root causes. The root causes you'd like to address first are the ones causing the most important symptoms.

However, Method C creates a big problem for you at this point:

> System-wide performance metrics provide insufficient information to enable you to draw the cause-effect arrows.

You *cannot* reliably compute the cause-effect relationships shown in Figure 1-4 unless you measure response time consumption for each user action—"from the top down" in the context of the drawing. Understanding what information is required to draw the cause-effect arrows reveals both the crippling flaw of Method C and the distinctive strength of Method R. It is impossible to draw the cause-effect arrows reliably from root causes to symptoms (from the bottom to the top). However, it is very easy to draw the arrows from symptoms to root causes (from the top down), because the resource profile format for targeted user actions tells you exactly where the arrows belong.

Without the cause-effect arrows, a project is rudderless. Any legitimate prioritization of performance improvement activities *must* be driven top-down by the economic priorities of the business. Without the arrows, you can't prioritize your responses to the internal performance metrics you might find in your *Statspack* reports. Without the arrows, about the only place you can turn is to "cost accounting" metrics like hit ratios, but unfortunately, these metrics don't reliably correspond to the economic motives of the business. The Oracle Payroll situation that I described earlier in this chapter was rudderless for three months. The project concluded on the day that the team acquired the data shown in Example 1-3.

 Ironically, then, the popular objection to Method R actually showcases the method's greatest advantage. We in fact designed Method R specifically to respond efficiently to systems afflicted with several performance root causes at once.

The reason Method R works so well in system-wide performance crises is that your "whole system" is not a single entity; it's a collection of user actions, some more important than others. Your slow user actions may not all be slow for the same reason. If they're not, then how will you decide which root cause to attack first? The smart way is by prioritizing your user actions in descending order of value to your business. What if all your slow user actions actually *are* caused by the same root cause? Then it's your lucky day, because the first diagnostic data you collect for a single process is going to show you the root cause of your single system-wide performance problem. When you fix it for one session, you'll have fixed it for every session. Table 1-1 summarizes the merits of conventional methods versus the new method.

Table 1-1. The merits of Method C and Method R. Method R yields its greatest comparative advantage when "the whole system is slow"

Figure 1-4 case	Method C effectiveness	Method R effectiveness
(a)	Effective in some cases. Existence of only one problem root cause increases the likelihood that this root cause will be prominent in the analysis of system-wide statistics.	Effective. Even if business prioritization is performed incorrectly, the method will successfully identify the sole root cause on the first attempt.
(b)	Unacceptable. Inability to link cause with effect means that problems are attacked "from the bottom up" in an order that may not suit business priorities.	Effective. Business prioritization of user actions ensures that the most important root cause will be found and addressed first.
(c)	Unacceptable. Same reasons as for (b).	Effective. Same reasons as above.

"The method only works if the problem is the database"

Another common objection to Method R is the perception that it is incapable of finding and responding to performance problems whose root causes originate outside the database tier. In a world whose new applications are almost all complicated multitier affairs, this perception causes a feeling that Method R is severely limited in its effective scope.

Method R itself is actually not restricted at all in this manner. Notice that nowhere in the four-step method is there any directive to collect response time data *just for the database*. The perception of database focus arises in the *implementation* of step 2, which is the step in which you will collect detailed response time diagnostic data. This book, as you shall see, provides coverage only of the response time metrics produced specifically by the Oracle kernel. There are several reasons for my writing the book this way:

- When performance problems occur, people tend to point the finger of blame first at the least well-understood component of a system. Thus, the Oracle database is often the first component blamed for performance problems. The Oracle kernel indeed emits sufficient diagnostic data to enable you to prove conclusively whether or not a performance problem's root cause lies within the database kernel.

- At the time of this writing, the Oracle kernel is in fact the most robustly instrumented layer in the technology stack; however, many analysts fail to exploit the diagnostic power inherent in the data this instrumentation emits. Oracle's diagnostic instrumentation model is very robust in spite of its simplicity and efficiency (Chapter 7). Vendors of other layers in the application technology stack have already begun to catch onto this notion. I believe that the response time diagnostic instrumentation built into the Oracle kernel will become the standard model for instrumenting other application tiers.

Even without further instrumentation of non-database tiers, if your performance problem *is* in the database, Method R helps you solve it quickly and efficiently. If your problem is *not* caused by something going on in your database, then Method R helps you *prove* that fact quickly and efficiently. Regardless of where in your architecture your root cause resides, Method R prevents you from trying to fix the wrong problem.

The proof is in the experience. Method R routinely leads us to the doorstep of problems whose repair must be enacted either inside or outside of the database, including such cases as:

- Query mistakes caused by inefficiently written application SQL statements, poor data designs, ill-advised indexing strategies, data density mistakes, etc.

- Application software mistakes caused by excessive parsing, poorly designed serialization (locking) mechanisms, misuse (or disuse) of array processing features, etc.

- Operational mistakes caused by errors in collection of statistics used by the cost-based optimizer, accidental schema changes (e.g., dropped indexes), inattention to full file systems, etc.

- Network mistakes caused by software configuration mistakes, hardware faults, topology design errors, etc.

- Disk I/O mistakes caused by poorly sized caches, imbalances in I/O load to different devices, etc.
- Capacity planning mistakes resulting in capacity shortages of resources like CPU, memory, disk, network, etc.

"The method is unconventional"

Even if Method R could prove to be the best thing since the invention of rows and columns, I expect for some pockets of resistance to exist for at least a couple of years after the publication of this book. The method is new and different, and it's not what people are accustomed to seeing. As more practitioners, books, and tools adopt the techniques described in this book, I expect that resistance will fade. In the meantime, some of your colleagues are going to require careful explanations about why you're recommending a completely unconventional performance optimization method that doesn't rely on *Statspack* or any of the several popular performance monitoring tools for which your company may have paid dearly. They may cite your use of an unconventional method as one of the reasons to reject your proposals.

One of my goals for this book is certainly to arm you with enough knowledge about Oracle technology that you can exploit your data to its fullest diagnostic capacity. I hope by the end of this book I'll have given you enough ammunition that you can defend your recommendations to the limit of their validity. I hope this is enough to level the playing field for you so that any debates about your proposed performance improvement activities can be judged on their economic merits, and not on the name of the method you used to derive them.

Evaluation of Effectiveness

Earlier in this chapter, I listed eight criteria against which I believe you should judge a performance improvement method. I'll finish the chapter by describing how Method R has measured up against these criteria in contrast to conventional methods:

Impact
Method R causes you to produce the highest possible impact because you are always focused on the goal that has meaning to the business: the response time of targeted user actions.

Efficiency
Method R provides excellent project efficiency because it keeps you focused on the top priorities for the business, and because it allows you to make fully informed decisions during every step of the project. *Project* efficiency is in fact the method's key design constraint.

Measurability
Method R uses end-user response time as its measurement criterion, not internal technical metrics that may or may not translate directly to end-user benefit.

Predictive capacity

Method R gives the unprecedented ability to predict the impact of a proposed tuning activity upon a targeted user action, without having to invest in expensive experimentation.

Reliability

Method R performs reliability in virtually every performance problem situation imaginable; a distinction of the method is its ability to pinpoint the root cause of any type of performance problem without having to resort to experience, intuition, or luck.

Determinism

Method R eliminates diagnostic guesswork first by maintaining your focus on business priority, and second by providing a foolproof method for determining the true relationships between problem symptoms and their root causes.

Finiteness

Method R has a clearly stated termination condition. The method provides the distinctive capacity to prove when no further optimization effort is economically justifiable.

Practicality

Method R is a teachable method that has been used successfully by hundreds of analysts of widely varying experience levels to resolve Oracle performance problems quickly and permanently.

The next chapters show you how to use Method R.

## CHAPTER 2

Targeting the Right User Actions

One of the first steps in any project is to figure out what the project is supposed to accomplish. The formal written result of figuring out the project's goal is called the project's *specification*. An Oracle performance improvement project, like all sorts of other projects, needs a specification. Otherwise, you have nothing that you can use to measure the success or failure of your project.

Many Oracle performance improvement projects are crippled from their beginnings with poor specifications. You've probably seen the cartoon in which a programmer's manager says, "You start coding. I'll go find out what they want." A lot of people try to "tune their systems" without ever really knowing what they're out to accomplish. On the other hand, there's no need for a system to languish for months while analysts try to construct the "ultimate" project specification, charging time and materials rates while they inch forward. Constructing a good specification for an Oracle performance improvement project should usually consume no more than a couple of hours.

The aim of this chapter is to help you get your performance improvement project started on the right foot, so that your project will optimize the economic value of a system. I'll explore some bad project specifications and explain why they hurt the projects they were supposed to help. I'll describe some specifications that have worked well, resulting in projects that have quickly created great positive economic impact to their systems. Throughout the chapter, I'll list some attributes that have distinguished good specifications from bad ones.

Specification Reliability

A project specification can be called "reliable" only if any project that successfully fulfills the letter of that specification also fulfills the specification's true intent.

Unfortunately, the most commonly used specifications for performance improvement projects are unreliable. Examples of specifications include:

- Distribute disk I/O as uniformly as possible across many disk drives.
- Ensure that there is at least x% of unused CPU capacity during peak hours.
- Increase the database buffer cache hit ratio to at least x%.
- Eliminate all full-table scans from the system.

Each of these specifications is unreliable because the letter of each specification can be accomplished without actually producing a desired impact upon your system. There is a simple game that enables you to determine whether you have a reliable specification or not:

> To establish whether or not the specification for a performance improvement project is reliable, ask yourself the question: "Is it possible to achieve the stated goal (the specification) of such a project without actually improving system performance?"

One easy way to get the game going is to imagine the existence of an evil genie. Is it possible for an evil genie to adhere to the letter of your "wish" (the project specification) while producing a project result that actually contradicts your obvious underlying goal? If the evil genie can create a system on which she could meet your project specification but still produce an unsatisfactory performance result, then the project specification has been proved unreliable.

The evil genie game is a technique employed in thought experiments by René Descartes in the 1600s and, more recently, by Elizabeth Hurley's character in the film *Bedazzled*. Here's how the evil genie game can play out for the bad specifications listed earlier:

Distribute disk I/O as uniformly as possible across many disk drives

This specification is a perfectly legitimate goal for trying to prevent performance problems when you are configuring a new system, but it is an unreliable specification for performance *improvement* projects. There are many systems on which making significant improvement to disk I/O performance will cause either negligible or even negative performance impact.

For example, imagine a system in which each of the most important business processes needing performance repair consumes less than 5% of the system's total response time performing disk I/O operations. (We have hundreds of trace files that fit this description at *hotsos.com*.) On such a system, no amount of I/O "tuning" can create meaningful response time improvement of more than 5%. Since distributing disk I/O uniformly across many disk drives can result in a system without meaningfully improved performance, this specification is unreliable.

Ensure that there is at least x% of unused CPU capacity during peak hours

There are several ways that an evil genie could accomplish this goal without helping the performance of your system. One way is to introduce a horrific disk I/O bottleneck, such as by placing the entire database on one gigantic disk drive with excessively poor I/O-per-second capacity. As more and more user processes stack up in the disk I/O queue, much CPU capacity will go unused. Since increasing the amount of unused CPU can result in worse performance, this specification is unreliable.

Increase the database buffer cache hit ratio to at least x%

This one's easy: simply use Connor McDonald's innovative demonstration that I include in Appendix C. The application will show you how to increase your database buffer cache hit ratio to as many nines as you like, by adding CPU-wasting unnecessary workload. This additional wasted workload will of course degrade the performance of your system, but it will "improve" your buffer cache hit ratio. Connor's application is, of course, a trick designed to demonstrate that it is a mistake to rely on the buffer cache hit ratio as a measure of system "goodness." (I happen to know that Connor is definitely *not* evil, although I have on occasion noticed him exhibit behavior that is at least marginally genie-like.)

There are subtler ways to degrade a system's performance while "improving" its cache hit ratio. For example, SQL "tuners" often do it when they engage in projects to eradicate TABLE SCAN FULL row source operations (discussed again in the next specification I'll show). Another way an evil genie could improve your cache hit ratio in a way that harms performance is to reduce all your array fetch sizes to a single row [Millsap (2001b)]. Because it is so easy to increase the value of your buffer cache hit ratio in ways that degrade system performance, this specification is particularly unreliable.

Eliminate all full-table scans from the system

Unfortunately, many students of SQL performance optimization learn early the *untrue* rule of thumb that "all full-table scans are bad." An evil genie would have an easy time concocting hundreds of SQL statements whose performance would degrade as TABLE SCAN FULL row source operations were eliminated [Millsap (2001b); (2002)]. Because eliminating full-table scans can actually degrade performance, the action is an unreliable basis for a performance improvement project specification.

The cure for unreliable performance improvement specifications is conceptually simple. Just say what you mean. But of course, by the same logic, golf is simple: just hit the ball into the hole every time you swing. The problem in curing unreliable performance improvement specifications is to figure out how to specify what you really mean in a manner that doesn't lead to other errors. For example, a performance specification that comes closer to saying what you really mean is this one:

Make the system go faster.

However, even this specification is unreliable. I've seen dozens of projects with this specification result in ostensible success but practical failure. For example, a consultant finds, by examining V$SQL, a batch job that consumes four hours. He "tunes" it so that it runs in 30 minutes. This is a project success; the consulting engagement summary says so. However, the success was meaningless. The batch program was already as fast as it needed to be, because it ran in an otherwise vacant eight-hour batch window. The expensive input into performance improvement (the consultant's fee) produced no positive value to the business.

Worse yet, I've seen analysts make some program *A* go faster, but at the expense of making another vastly more important program *B* go slower. Many systems contain process interdependencies that can cause this situation. On these systems, "tuning" the wrong program not only consumes time and money to execute the tuning project, it results in actual *degradation* of a system's value to the business (see the section "Case 1: Misled by System-Wide Data" in Chapter 12 for an example).

This "make the system go faster" specification is just too vague to be useful. In my service line management role at Oracle Corporation, I had many discussions about how to specify projects—the whole idea of packaged services requires contract-quality specification of project goals. Most participants in those meetings understood very quickly that "make the system go faster" is too vague. What I find remarkable today is that most of these people saw the vagueness in entirely the wrong place.

Most people identify the *go faster* part of the specification as the root of the problem. People commonly suggest that "make the system go faster" is deficient because the statement doesn't say, numerically, how *much* faster. In my Oracle meetings, explorations of how to improve "make the system go faster" generally led to discussion of various ways to measure actual and perceived speeds, ways to establish "equivalency" metrics such as count-based utilization measures (like hit ratios), and so on. Of course, the search for "equivalency" measures finds a dead end quickly because—if you execute the evil genie test correctly—such presumed equivalency measures are usually unreliable.

Figuring out how much faster a system "needs to go" often leads into expensive project rat holes. (An exception is when an analyst has found the maximum allowable service time for an operation by using a model like the queueing theory one that I describe in Chapter 9.) When our students today discuss the "make the system go faster" spec, it usually takes very little leading for students to realize that the real problem is actually hidden in the word *system*. For example, consider the following commonly suggested "improvements" to the original "make the system go faster" specification:

- Make the system go 10% faster.
- Make the system complete all business functions in less than one second.

First of all, each specification expressed in this style is susceptible to the same evil genie tricks as the original spec. But by adding detail, we've actually weakened the original statement. For example:

Make the system go 10% faster
> Do you really expect that *every* business transaction on the system can go 10% faster? Even those that perform only a couple of Oracle logical I/O calls (LIOs)

---

to begin with? On the other hand, is 10% really enough of an improvement for an online query that consumes seventeen minutes of response time?

Make the system complete all business functions in less than one second
Is it really good enough for a single-row fetch via a primary key to consume 0.99 seconds of response time? On the other hand, is it really reasonable to expect that an Oracle application should be able to emit a 72-page report in less than one second?

Do these two formats actually lead to an improvement of the original "make the system go faster" specification? They do not. A bigger problem is actually the lack of definition for the word "system."

The System

What is *the system?* Most database and system administrators interpret the term much differently than anyone else in the business does. To most database and system administrators, *the system* is a complex collection of processes and shared memory and files and locks and latches, and all sorts of technical things that can be measured by looking at "V$ tables" and operating system utilities and maybe even graphical system monitoring dashboards. However, *nobody* else in the business sees a system this way. A user thinks of *the system* as the collection of the few forms and batch jobs in that user's specific job domain. A manager thinks of *the system* as a means for helping improve the efficiency of the business. To users and managers, the redness, yellowness, or greenness of your dashboard dials is completely and utterly irrelevant.

Here's a simple test to determine for yourself whether I'm telling the truth. Try to imagine yourself as a user who has just waited two hours past your reporting deadline this morning because your "fifteen-minute report" required three full hours to run. Try to imagine your reaction to a database administrator who would say the following words in front of your colleagues during a staff meeting: "There was absolutely nothing wrong with the system while your report was running, because all our dashboard dials were green during the entire three-hour period."

Please remember this when you are acting in the role of performance analyst: a *system* is a collection of end-user programs. An end-user is watching each of these programs attentively. (If no one is watching a particular program attentively, then it should be running only during off-peak time periods, or perhaps not at all.) The duration that each program requires to deliver a requested chunk of business value is that program's response time. The response time of an individual user action is practically the only performance metric that your business cares about. Hence:

Response time for an end-user action is the first metric that you should care about.

Economic Constraints

When you eliminate the ambiguity of the word "system," you take one big step closer to a foolproof goal:

> Improving the performance of program A during the weekday 2:00 p.m. to 3:00 p.m. window is critical to the business. Improve the performance of A as much as possible for this time period.

But is this specification evil genie–proof? Not yet. Imagine that the average run time of program A is two minutes. Suppose that the evil genie could reduce the response time from two minutes to 0.25 seconds. Great... But at a cost of $1,000,000,000. Oops. Maybe improving response time only to 0.5 seconds would have been good enough and would only have cost $2,000. The specification omits any mention of an economic constraint.

There *is* an optimization project specification that I believe may actually be evil genie–proof. It is the optimization goal described by Eli Goldratt in [Goldratt (1992), 49]:

> Make money by increasing net profit, while simultaneously increasing return on investment, and simultaneously increasing cash flow.

This specification gives us the ultimate acid test by which to judge any other project specification. However, it does fall prey to the same "hit the ball into the hole on every swing" lack of detail that I discussed earlier.

Making a Good Specification

Let's stop fooling around with faulty project specifications and start constructing some good ones. It shouldn't take you more than a couple of hours to create a good specification for most performance improvement projects. Here's how:

1. Identify the user actions that the *business* needs you to optimize, and identify the contexts in which those actions are important.
2. Prioritize these user actions into buckets of five.
3. For each of the actions in your top bucket, determine *whom* you can observe executing the action in its suboptimal context and *when* you can make the observation.

User Action

In this book, I try to make a careful distinction between *user actions*, *programs*, and *Oracle sessions*. A *user action* is exactly what it sounds like: an action executed by a user. Such an action might be the entry of a field in a form or the execution of one or more whole programs. A user action is defined as some unit of work whose output and whose performance have meaning to the business. The notion of *user action* is especially important during project specification because the user action is precisely the unit of work that has business meaning.

A *program* is of course a sequence of computer instructions that carries out some business function. A user action might be a program, a part of a program, or multiple programs. An *Oracle session* is a specific sequence of database calls that flow through a connection between a user process and an Oracle instance. A program can initiate zero or more Oracle sessions, and in some configurations, more than one program can share a single Oracle session. The notion of an *Oracle session* is important during data collection because the Oracle kernel keeps track of performance statistics at the Oracle session level.

Oracle does make a distinction between a *connection* (a communication pathway) and a *session*. You can be connected to Oracle and not have any sessions. On the other hand, you can be connected and have many simultaneous sessions on that single connection.

Identifying the Right User Actions and Contexts

The first step in your specification is to identify the user actions that the *business* needs you to optimize. If you mess up this step, it is likely that your performance improvement project will fail. It is vital for you to obtain a list of *specific user actions*. The ones you select should be the ones that are the most important in the business's pursuit of net profit, return on investment, and cash flow.

I emphasize "that the *business* needs you to optimize" because you are specifically *not* looking for a database administrator's opinion about performance at this point. One of the most common mistakes that Oracle performance analysts make is that they consult their V\$ views to learn where their system needs "tuning." Your V\$ views can't tell you. I'll describe in Chapter 3 some of the technical reasons why it's unreliable to consult your V\$ views for this information.

Finding out what your business needs is usually easy. It is almost never the result of a long goal-definition project. It is almost always the result of asking a business leader who speaks in commonsense language, "If we could make one program faster by the end of work today, which program would you choose?" The following examples illustrate the type of response that you're looking for:

- We manufacture disk drives. We have a warehouse full of disk drives that are ready to ship. We receive hundreds of telephone calls each morning from angry customers who placed orders with us over two weeks ago, demanding to know the status of their shipments. At any given time, there is an average of over two dozen empty FedEx trucks parked at our loading dock. If you go down to the loading dock, you can see that our packers and the truck drivers are sitting on boxes drinking coffee right now. They can't load the boxes on the trucks because the program that prints shipping labels is too slow. Our business's most important performance problem is the program that prints shipping labels.

- We're spending too much on server license and maintenance fees. We have 57 enterprise-class servers in our shop, and we need to cut that number to ten or fewer. We already house 80% of our enterprise data on one large storage area network (SAN). However, our total CPU workload that is presently distributed across 57 servers is probably too large to fit onto ten machines. Our business's most important performance problem is eliminating enough unnecessary CPU workload so that we can perform the server consolidation effort and ditch about fifty of our servers.

The hardest part is usually gaining access to the right people in the business to get the information you need. You might have to dig a little bit for your list. The following techniques can help:

Ask your boss where the performance risks are
> Steer him away from answers that refer to technical components of the database. Force the conversation into the domain of user language. Ask which user is giving him the most flak about system performance, and then book a lunch with the user. The loudest user is not necessarily the one with the business's most critical problem, but understanding that user's problems are probably a good start.

Take a user to lunch
> Buy him a sandwich, and ask down-to-earth questions like, "If I could make something you use faster today, what would you want it to be?"

Find a sales forecast for your business
> Consider which application processes are going to be the most important ones to facilitate your company's planned sales growth. Are those processes running as efficiently as they can?

If you get stuck in your conversations with people with whom you're trying to identify user actions that are important to the business, ask them which actions fit into these categories:

- Actions that are business critical
- Actions that run a long time
- Actions that are run extremely often
- Actions that consume a lot of capacity of a resource you're trying to conserve

In addition to identifying which user actions require optimization, you need to identify the *context* in which those actions are important. For example:

- Is the action always slow?
- Is it slow only at a particular time of day (week, month, or year)?
- Is it slow only when it runs at the same time as some other program(s)?
- Is it slow only when the number of connected users exceeds some threshold?

- Is it slow only after some other program runs (upload, delete, etc.)?

Without context, you run the risk that you'll collect performance diagnostic data for the "problem" action and then find after all your effort that there's apparently nothing wrong with it. You have to identify how to find the user action when it is performing at its worst. Otherwise, you're not going to be able to see the problem. This concept is so important that I'll say it again:

> You have to identify how to find the user action when it is performing at its *worst*.

In this step, it is usually important to select more than one user action, especially in situations where many users perceive many different performance problems. This is true even in situations where the number-one system performance problem has a priority that clearly exceeds everything else on the system. The reasons for this advice come from the experience of using the method many times:

- Because cost is a factor in net benefit, the business net benefit of improving, for example, user action #3 may actually exceed the business net benefit of improving user action #1.

- Producing significant improvement quickly in *any* of a system's top five most important performance problems can create a significant political advantage, including factors like project team morale and project sponsor confidence.

- You might not know how to improve performance for user action #1. But fixing, for example, user action #3 may eliminate so much unnecessary workload that #1 becomes a non-issue.

- You can't tell which performance improvement action will produce the greatest net benefit to the business until you can see a high-level cost-benefit analysis for the user actions in your top-five bucket.

Prioritizing the User Actions

Once you have constructed the list of candidate user actions, you need to rank the importance of their improvement to the business. Everything you do later will require that you have chosen the most important actions to optimize first. Business prioritization is vital for several reasons, including:

The most important actions will get fixed the soonest
> This is the most important reason. Quite simply, if you don't optimize the most important business processes first, then you're not optimizing.

Trade-off decisions will always favor more important user actions
> On occasion, you may find that an optimization for one user action inflicts a performance penalty upon another. This happens frequently when the optimization strategy you choose is to increase the capacity of some component. However, because I hope to convince you to increase capacity only when necessary (that is, *rarely*), such trade-offs should be rare.

Less important user actions enjoy collateral benefits

The term *collateral damage* has been introduced into our language by discussions of accidents that occur during wartime. The opposite of collateral damage is *collateral benefit*—a benefit yielded serendipitously by attending to something else. Collateral performance benefits occur frequently on computer systems in which we eliminate huge amounts of unnecessary work.

It's easy to over-analyze at this stage, but there's actually no need to spend much time here. All you need are rough categories. I recommend grouping your user actions into prioritized buckets of no fewer than five. This way, you won't be tempted to obsess over the precise ranking of actions that are close in importance. For example, if you have ten important problem user actions, then create no more than two groups of five. If you have more than ten problem actions (I've visited sites whose lists numbered in excess of fifty), then I suggest partitioning your list into three parts:

1. The five most important user actions (your first bucket).
2. The five next most important user actions (your second bucket).
3. The remainder of the important user actions you've listed (the union of your third and subsequent buckets)

Be especially wary of executing any prioritization task with the participation of large groups. Every user, of course, will try to convince you that his actions are the very most supremely important actions on the entire system. And of course, every action on the system cannot take top priority. Most of the time that you might spend negotiating whether a user action belongs in one group or another could be invested more wisely in other steps of the method. If you find that the whole prioritization task is consuming more than just a few minutes, then step back and just make some sensible decisions. Assure the users whose actions don't fall into the top priority class that they haven't lost anything; you'll attend to their problems too.

Determining Who Will Execute Each Action and When

The final step in the construction of a good spec for your performance improvement project is the specification of how you'll be able to find each targeted action when it next runs in its targeted context. This information will allow you to find the programs implementing those actions so that you can measure their performance.

Often, the success of a diagnostic data collection effort will be determined by your ability to establish simple human contact with a person who will execute the slow action and answer the following simple questions:

- When is the next time that this person expects for the action to exhibit the performance problem?
- How can you watch?

The answers to these questions unambiguously define the parameters you'll use for your diagnostic data collection process, which I describe in Chapter 3.

If you have a tool that constantly monitors the appropriate performance statistics for every individual user action on your system, then predicting who will run a problem program and when it will happen becomes unnecessary. The luxury of having such data for every user action on your system will allow you to respond to a complaint about an action in the recent past instead of having to predict their occurrences in the imminent future. Such tools are expensive, but they do exist.

If you do not own such a tool, then you'll have to be more selective in which diagnostic data you'll want to collect, and the step described in this section will be essential. For you, I hope that Chapters 6 and 8 will provide significant value.

Specification Over-Constraint

I've discussed the reliability problems introduced by specifications that are too vague. Equally devastating is the specification that is too precise. Many specifications that go into too much detail actually conflict with the optimization goal. A specification that requires some specific program performance improvement *and* a 10-point improvement in the database buffer cache hit ratio might actually be impossible to achieve. It is entirely possible that improving the performance of a specified program might result in a dramatically lower system-wide cache hit ratio. (See [Millsap (2001b)] for an example.)

Another fun example occurred several years ago when I was an Oracle Corporation employee. A performance specification required that, on a particular client-server application form, navigation from one field to the next must occur within 0.5 seconds. The specification further required for the client system to be in Singapore and for the server system to be in Chicago. Furthermore, the specification required that we could not modify the prepackaged application, which made an average of six synchronous database calls across the wide-area network (WAN) per field.

The objective as stated in the specification was unachievable, because the specification is *over-constrained*; it in fact conflicts with the physical laws of our universe. There is no way that six round-trip network transmissions can occur between Singapore and Chicago within the span of half a second. Even if we could eliminate all components of response time except for the theoretically smallest amount of time required for the data transmission at its fastest theoretically possible rate (that is, if we could ignore the time consumed by cable, hubs, routers, the database, and so on), executing six round-trip communications per field will require *at least* 0.6 seconds per field.

> *Proof*: Assume that all practical influences other than the speed of light have no effect upon performance of field-to-field navigation. The speed of light in a vacuum is approximately 299,792,458 meters per second. The distance along the Earth's surface

from Singapore to Chicago is approximately 15,000,000 meters. Therefore, the distance traversed by six round-trips for each field is $2 \times 6 \times 15,000,000$ meters, or approximately 180,000,000 meters per field. Obeying the relationship $d = rt$, we find that $t = d/r \approx 0.6$ seconds per field. Reintroducing all of the practical influences upon performance that we have ignored up to now will only degrade performance further. Therefore, the requirement specification cannot be met. QED.

There is *no way* to meet this specification without relaxing at least one of its constraints. The most important constraint to eliminate first was the requirement that each field must execute an average of six round-trips between the client and the database server. The most important task of the existing performance improvement project was to show the proof of why any project with the given specification was doomed to failure. Until this proof became known, people on the project had continued to waste time and money in pursuit of an unattainable goal.

Good projects don't come from bad project specifications. Whether the problem is sloppy targeting or a specification that is utterly unattainable, you cannot afford to base your performance improvement project upon a faulty specification.

## CHAPTER 3

Targeting the Right Diagnostic Data

Once you have correctly targeted the user actions for which the business most needs performance improvement, it is data collection time. Diagnostic data collection is the project phase in which the typical performance analyst really begins to feel a sense of progress. There are very few arguments in Oracle literature today about how one should go about collecting performance diagnostic data. However, there should be. The way that you collect your diagnostic data has a tremendous influence over a project's potential for success. In fact, unless you are exceptionally lucky, a performance improvement project cannot proceed beyond a botched data collection.

I hope that this chapter will surprise you. It describes a couple of very important flaws in the standard data collection procedures that are deeply institutionalized in the Oracle culture. In the hundreds of flawed Oracle performance improvement projects that my colleagues and I have helped repair, a contributing factor to failure in nearly every project was one or more errors in data collection. Unfortunately, virtually every document written about Oracle performance prior to the year 2000 leads its reader to make these errors. I believe that the commonsense examples described in this chapter will forever change your attitude toward diagnostic data collection.

Expectations About Data Collection

The whole point of data collection in a performance improvement project using Method R is to collect response time data for a *correctly targeted user action*. No more, no less. Unfortunately, many application designers have complicated the data collection job significantly by providing insufficient instrumentation in their applications.

 Many companies, especially Oracle Corporation, are improving the response time instrumentation in newer application releases.

The data collection lessons you learn in this chapter will make data collection seem more difficult than you had probably expected. The benefit of doing it right is that you will reduce your overall project costs and durations by eliminating expensive and frustrating trial-and-error analysis/response iterations.

A Method R performance improvement project proceeds much differently than a project that uses the conventional trial-and-error approach introduced as Method C in Chapter 1. Figure 3-1 illustrates the difference. A project practitioner typically begins to feel like he is making real progress when the targeting and data collection phases are complete and he enters the analysis/response phase of a performance improvement project. The Method C practitioner typically reaches this milestone (marked t_1 in Figure 3-1) before the Method R practitioner working on the same problem would (marked t_2). If you don't expect this, it can become a political sensitivity in a Method R project. The time between t_1 and t_2 is when your risk of losing commitment to the new method is at its greatest.

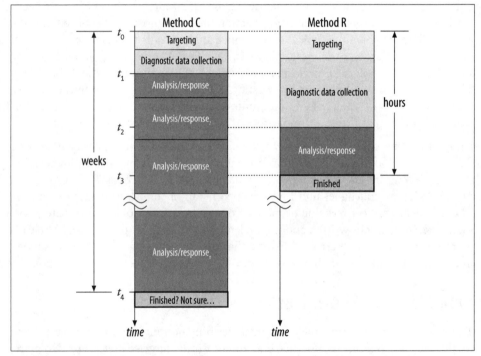

Figure 3-1. The targeting and diagnostic data collection phases of Method R consume more time than in conventional methods, but total project duration is typically much shorter

Finishing the data collection phase quickly is not the goal of a performance improvement project. The correct goal is to optimize the system with the smallest possible investment of resources. Method R is optimized for this goal. In fact, my colleagues and I created Method R specifically to help our customers fix performance improvement projects that had dragged on for weeks or even months without meaningful progress. In the overwhelming majority of Method R projects we've led, we've been able to demonstrate how to achieve the optimization goal within one hour of obtaining correctly scoped diagnostic data. Once you have collected the *right* performance diagnostic data, Method R will require only a single analysis/response phase before you'll make progress against your targeted user action.

Method C practitioners spend most of their time in trial-and-error mode trying to determine the cause-effect relationship between the hundreds of possible problem causes and the business symptom that is most in need of improvement. A huge inefficiency of Method C is the need to perform, on average, several iterations of analysis and response activities before you'll stumble upon a symptom's root cause. Each iteration of analysis and response tends to consume more time than the prior one, because analysts usually try the easiest responses they can think of first, saving the more time-consuming and expensive tuning activities for later in the project after the cheaper ideas are discarded.

The final blow to Method C is that there's really no quantitative way to determine when you're "finished tuning." In many projects, Method C users never positively identify an actual contributory cause of a performance problem. Even in "successful" projects, practitioners spend weeks, months, or even years without really knowing whether a targeted performance problem has been truly perfected (*optimized*) or merely partially improved (*tuned*). The problem of not knowing whether a user action could be further tuned leads to a condition that Gaja Vaidyanatha and Kirti Deshpande cleverly call *Compulsive Tuning Disorder*, or CTD [Vaidyanatha and Deshpande (2001) 8]. I joke that CTD is a debilitating condition caused by *hope*. More specifically, CTD is caused by an absence of complete information that would allow you to prove conclusively whether the performance of a given user action has any room for improvement. Method R fills this information gap, eliminating the possibility of CTD.

The first time you use Method R, collecting the diagnostic data will probably be the most difficult phase of your project. For some applications, diagnostic data collection is a cake walk. For other applications, proper diagnostic data collection can legitimately become quite a difficult challenge. Chapter 6 describes which kinds of applications are easy and which are hard, and it illustrates some of the techniques that my colleagues and I have used to overcome various challenges. The good news is that once you've figured out how to collect good diagnostic data for a targeted user action in your application, the process will be much easier and less time-consuming on your next performance improvement project. Method C, on the other hand, will always suffer from the problem of multiple analysis/response iterations, regardless of where you are on the experience curve.

I believe that in the future, most application software vendors will make it very easy for users and analysts alike to collect precisely the diagnostic data that Method R requires. Newer releases of Oracle's E-Business Suite are simplifying the diagnostic data collection process, and everything I hear indicates that the Oracle release 10 kernel and application server software are headed in the same direction. If the dominance of methods analogous to Method R in other industries is any indication, then success in simplifying diagnostic data collection should practically universalize the adoption of Method R for Oracle performance improvement projects.

Different Methods for Different Performance Problems?

Could it be that conventional methods are more effective for "simple" performance tuning problems, and that Method R is more effective for "complex" ones? The problem with that question is this: How do you know whether a performance tuning problem is "simple" or "complex" without engaging in some kind of diagnostic data collection?

One approach that we considered during the construction of Method R was to collect very easy-to-obtain diagnostic data to use in deciding whether the more difficult-to-obtain diagnostic data were even necessary to collect. We found this approach to be sub-optimal. The problem with it is that there's virtually no situation in which you can be *certain* about cause-effect relationships without the *correct* diagnostic data (and of course, sometimes the *correct* diagnostic data are difficult to obtain). The doubt and ambiguity that are admitted into a project by the analysis of easy-to-obtain diagnostic data rapidly deteriorate the efficiency of a performance improvement project. The thought-blocking fixations that I've seen caused by bad diagnostic data at many projects remind me of a wonderful quotation attributed to Cardinal Thomas Wolsey (1471–1530): "Be very, very careful what you put into that head, because you will never, ever get it out."

A dominant goal during the construction of Method R was that it must be *deterministic*. Determinism is a key attribute that determines how teachable (or automate-able) a method can be. We wanted to ensure that any two people executing Method R upon a given performance problem would perform the same sequence of tasks, without having to appeal to experience, intuition, or luck to determine which step to take next. Our method achieves this by creating a single point of entry, and a well-defined sequence of if-then-else instructions at every decision point thereafter.

Data Scope

Good Oracle performance data collection requires good decision-making in two dimensions. You must collect data for the right *time scope* and the right *action scope*. Let's begin by drawing a user action's response time consumption as a sequence of chunks of time spent consuming various resources. Figure 3-2 shows the result. To keep it simple, our imaginary system consists of only three types of resource, called C, D, and S. Imagine that these symbols stand for CPU, disk, and serialization (such as the one-at-a-time access that the Oracle kernel imposes for locks, latches, and certain memory buffer operations). In Figure 3-2, the time dimension extends in the horizontal direction.

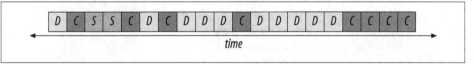

Figure 3-2. The consumption of three types of resource over the duration of a user action

We can denote a system that is executing several user actions at the same time by stacking such drawings vertically, as shown in Figure 3-3. In this drawing, the action dimension extends in the vertical direction.

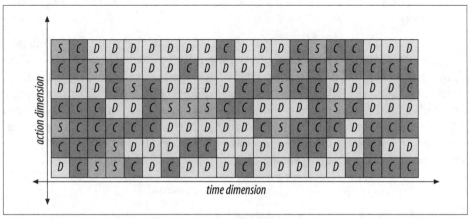

Figure 3-3. By adding a vertical dimension, this drawing depicts a system containing seven concurrent actions, each consuming three different types of resource through time

The following sections use this graphical notation to illustrate why the data collection methods that many Oracle experts have been teaching since the 1980s are actually what have been killing performance improvement projects all over the world.

Scoping Errors

In the system shown in Figure 3-3, imagine that the targeting process described in Chapter 2 has revealed the following: the most important performance problem for the business is that a user named Wallace endures an unacceptably long response time between times t_1 and t_2, as shown in Figure 3-4.

 In the following discussions, I shall use the mathematical notation for a *closed interval*. The notation $[a, b]$ represents the set of values between a and b, inclusive:

$$[a, b] = \{\text{all } x \text{ values for which } a \leq x \leq b\}$$

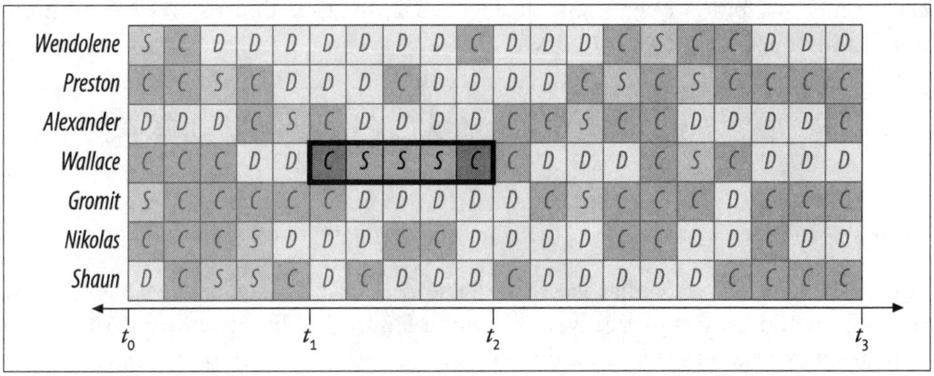

Figure 3-4. This system's most important user, Wallace, experiences unacceptable performance in the time interval [t_1, t_2]

From the picture in Figure 3-4, it is easy to see that during the problem time interval, Wallace's response time was consumed predominantly by S and secondarily by C, as shown in Table 3-1. Of course, repairing Wallace's performance problem will require a reduction in time for Wallace's action spent consuming either S, or C, or both. Amdahl's Law indicates that any percentage reduction in consumption of S will have 1.5 times the response time impact that an equivalent percentage reduction in consumption of C will have, because the response time contribution of S is 1.5 times the size of the response time contribution of C.

Table 3-1. Resource profile for Wallace's action for the time interval [t_1, t_2]

Resource	Elapsed time	Percentage of total time
S	3	60.0%
C	2	40.0%
Total	5	100.0%

Perhaps the most common data collection error is to collect data that are aggregated in both dimensions. Figure 3-5 shows what this mistake looks like. The heavy, dark line around all the blocks in the entire figure indicate that data were aggregated for all processes (not just Wallace's), and for the whole time interval [t_0, t_3] (not just [t_1, t_2]). Counting the time units attributable system-wide during the [t_0, t_3] interval produces the resource profile shown in Table 3-2. As you can see, Wallace's performance problem—which we know to have been too much time spent doing S—has been thoroughly buried by all of the irrelevant data that we collected. The result of the botched data collection will be a longer and probably less fruitful performance improvement project than we want.

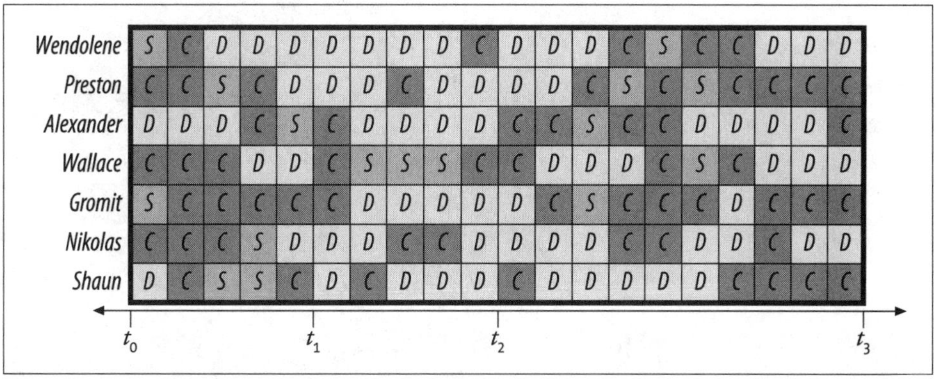

Wendolene	S	C	D	D	D	D	D	D	D	C	D	D	D	C	S	C	C	D	D	D
Preston	C	C	S	C	D	D	D	C	D	D	D	D	C	S	C	S	C	C	C	C
Alexander	D	D	D	C	S	C	D	D	D	D	C	C	S	C	C	D	D	D	D	C
Wallace	C	C	C	D	D	C	S	S	S	C	C	D	D	D	C	S	C	D	D	D
Gromit	S	C	C	C	C	C	D	D	D	D	D	C	S	C	C	C	D	C	C	C
Nikolas	C	C	C	S	D	D	D	C	C	D	D	D	D	C	C	D	D	C	D	D
Shaun	D	C	S	S	C	D	C	D	D	D	C	D	D	D	D	D	C	C	C	C

t_0 t_1 t_2 t_3

Figure 3-5. Collecting data that are improperly scoped on both the time and action dimensions will completely conceal the nature of Wallace's problem in the time interval $[t_1, t_2]$

From the data shown in Table 3-2, you simply cannot see that S is Wallace's principal problem root cause. It would actually be *irresponsible* to assume that S might be the root cause of Wallace's problem.

Table 3-2. Resource profile for the entire system for the time interval $[t_0, t_3]$

Resource	Elapsed time	Percentage of total time
D	66	47.1%
C	58	41.4%
S	16	11.4%
Total	140	100.0%

Unfortunately, the deeply flawed data collection method illustrated here is the default behavior of *Statspack*, the *utlbstat.sql* and *utlestat.sql* script pair, and virtually every other Oracle performance tool created between 1980 and 2000. Of the most deeply frustrating performance improvement projects with which I've ever assisted, this type of data collection error is far and away the most common root cause of their failure.

The remedy to the data collection problem must be executed on *both* dimensions. Repairing the collection error in only one dimension is not enough. Observe, for example, the result of collecting the data shown in Figure 3-6. Here, the time scoping is done correctly, but the action scope is still too broad. The accompanying resource profile is shown in Table 3-3. Again, remember that you *know* the root cause of Wallace's performance problem: it is a combination of S and C. But the data collected system-wide provides apparent "evidence" quite to the contrary, even though the data were collected for the correct time interval.

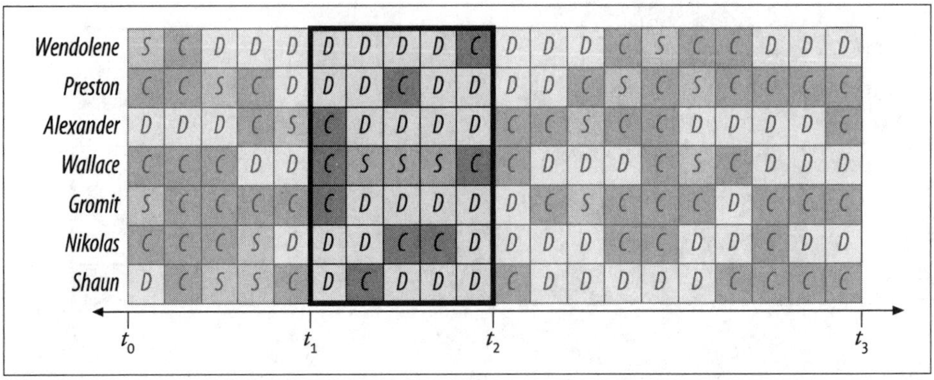

Figure 3-6. Collecting data that are scoped improperly on the action dimension also conceals the nature of Wallace's performance problem, even though the data were collected for the correct time scope

Table 3-3. Resource profile for the entire system for the time interval [t_1, t_2]

Resource	Elapsed time	Percentage of total time
D	23	65.7%
C	9	25.7%
S	3	8.6%
Total	35	100.0%

Finally, examine the result of collecting data for the correct action scope but the wrong time scope, as shown in Figure 3-7. Table 3-4 shows the resource profile. Once again, presented with these data, even a competent performance analyst will botch the problem diagnosis job. Wallace's problem is *S* and *C*, but you certainly wouldn't figure it out by looking at Table 3-4.

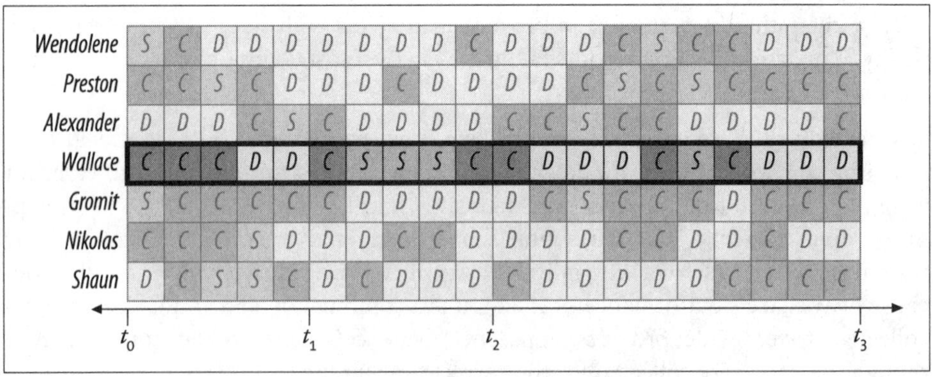

Figure 3-7. Collecting data that are scoped improperly on the time dimension also conceals the nature of Wallace's performance problem, even though the data were collected for the correct action scope

Table 3-4. Resource profile for Wallace's action for the time interval [t_0, t_3]

Resource	Elapsed time	Percentage of total time
D	8	40.0%
C	8	40.0%
S	4	20.0%
Total	20	100.0%

From this sequence of simple examples, it is easy to see why proper diagnostic data collection is so vital to a performance improvement project. The examples also clearly reveal the identity of the two dimensions along which you can assess whether or not a given diagnostic data collection can be deemed *proper*:

> Reliable problem diagnosis cannot proceed unless the data collection phase produces response time data for exactly the right *time scope* and exactly the right *action scope*.

Long-Running User Actions

When you have a really long-running user action, do you need to collect performance diagnostic data for the whole thing? Perhaps you have an action that ran in ten minutes last week, but today it has already run for over four hours, and you're wondering whether you should kill it. Do you have to restart the job in order to collect diagnostic data for it? Sometimes, I hear about batch jobs that run for several *days* before their users give up and terminate the jobs instead of letting them finish.[*] Do you really need to collect performance diagnostic data for the whole job?

The answer is no. Of course, collecting performance diagnostic data for some subset of an action's performance problem duration introduces a type of time-scoping error, but it is actually useful to collect time-subset diagnostic data in some circumstances. For example:

- If a user action is supposed to run in n minutes, then collecting data for just $n + m$ minutes will reveal at least m minutes of response time that shouldn't exist. For example, if a job is supposed to run in 10 minutes, then 25 minutes' worth of diagnostic data will reveal at least 15 minutes of workload that shouldn't exist.

- If a user action consists of a long sequence of repetitive tasks, then performance diagnostic data collected for a small number of the tasks will reveal the resources consumed by the whole action, as long as the tasks are homogeneous.

In Chapter 6, I discuss some collection errors that might occur if your data collection process begins in the midst of a database action. But in many cases, collecting time-subset diagnostic data can help you along your way.

---

[*] In some of these cases, I've been able to prove that if the job were left to run to completion, it would not be able to complete in our lifetimes.

"Too Much Data" Is Really Not Enough Data

It is tempting to say that the scoping problems in Tables 3-2 through 3-4 were the result of collecting "too much data." However, the problem with these three resource profiles was not necessarily in what data were *collected*, it is more an issue of how the data were *aggregated*. Look again at Figure 3-5. There is plenty of information here to produce a correctly scoped resource profile. The problem with Table 3-2 is in how the data from Figure 3-5 were aggregated. The same can be said for Figures 3-6 and 3-7 and their resource profiles. The problem is not that the figures contain too *much* data, it's that their corresponding resource profiles are aggregated incorrectly.

Poor aggregation is an especially big problem for projects that use SQL queries of Oracle V$ fixed views as their performance diagnostic data sources. Oracle V$ views by their nature provide data that are either aggregated for an entire instance since instance startup, or for an entire session since connection. For example, using V$SYSSTAT or V$SYSTEM_EVENT is *guaranteed* to produce the action scoping errors depicted in Tables 3-2 and 3-3. Even meticulous use of V$SESSTAT and V$SESSION_EVENT makes you prone to the type of time scoping error depicted in Table 3-4 (as you can see by experimenting with my *vprof* program described in Chapter 8).

When used with careful attention to time scope, Oracle's V$SESSTAT and V$SESSION_EVENT views provide a high-level perspective of why a user action is taking so long. However, for the next level of your diagnosis, you'll need to know details that V$SESSTAT and V$SESSION_EVENT can't provide. For example, what if your preliminary analysis indicates that your targeted user action is spending most of its time waiting for the event called latch free? Then you'll wish you had collected data from V$LATCH (and perhaps V$LATCH_CHILDREN) for the same time interval. But even if you had, you'll notice that neither fixed view contains a session ID attribute, so collecting properly action-scoped data about latches on a busy system will be impossible.

The problem of acquiring secondary detail data from V$ views is an extremely serious one. It's by no means just a problem with V$LATCH. What if the dominant consumer of response time had been CPU service? Then you need properly time- and action-scoped data at least from V$SQL. What if the dominant consumer had been waits for db file scattered read? Then you need properly time- and action-scoped data at least from V$FILESTAT. What if the problem had been waits for buffer busy waits? Then you need V$WAITSTAT. In Oracle9*i* there are roughly 300 events that beg for details from any of dozens of V$ fixed views. Even if you could query from all these V$ views at exactly the right times to produce accurately time-scoped data, you'd still be left with aggregations whose values fall short of what you could acquire through other means.

Happily, there are at least three ways to acquire the drill-down data you need. The first doesn't work very well. The second is expensive, but you might already have the capability. The third is available to you for the price of the book that you are holding. The following section explains.

Oracle Diagnostic Data Sources

There are at least three distinct ways to access Oracle's operational timing data:

- Querying Oracle fixed views using SQL (fixed views are the views whose names begin with the prefix V\$, GV\$, or X\$).

- Polling Oracle shared memory segments directly to obtain the same V\$ data (that is, accessing the same V\$ data without using SQL).

- Activating Oracle's extended SQL trace facility to emit the complete historical timing activity of an Oracle session to a trace file.

Although V\$ data and extended SQL trace data look like quite different things, it's all the same data, just presented through different user interfaces. In Chapter 7, I describe where the base information comes from.

After devoting three years full-time to studying Method R and its data collection requirements, my personal opinion on the merits of these three approaches is as follows:

Querying V\$ data through SQL

Using SQL to acquire data from V\$ fixed views is an excellent way to compile information about *resource consumption* (that is, to acquire information about how many times various resources have been visited). See Tom Kyte's excellent example at *http://asktom.oracle.com/~tkyte/runstats.html* for more information. V\$ data are especially valuable during application development. Using SQL to acquire *timing* data through the V\$ fixed views, it's easy to get started experimenting with Oracle's operational timing data. But for several reasons listed in Chapter 8, the timing data you will obtain from this data source are unreliable for several problem types. Using SQL to acquire *timing* data from V\$ fixed views provides much less capability than the other two approaches.

One fixed view called X\$TRACE does provide a means to access extended SQL trace data through SQL. However, the X\$TRACE feature is presently undocumented, unsupported, and unstable. If Oracle Corporation fortifies the X\$TRACE facility in the future, it may render obsolete my pessimistic comments about drill-down with fixed view data. But as of Oracle release 9.2, the feature is not ready for production use.

Polling V\$ data directly from Oracle shared memory

If you already own a tool that allows you to properly manipulate the time scope and action scope of your diagnostic data, then high-frequency polling directly from shared memory is probably an excellent approach for you. High-frequency polling gives you diagnostic data that reliably help you solve many types of performance problem. However, attaching to shared memory and then storing gigantic masses of data requires either a lot of study and hard work, or a financial investment in a tool to do it for you. Such tools are expensive.

Activating the extended SQL trace facility

The extended SQL trace facility also offers outstanding diagnostic reliability, but without the research or investment pain that high-frequency polling requires. The principal disadvantage of using extended SQL trace is that you'll be able to collect diagnostic data only for those user actions that you can expect beforehand to exhibit suboptimal performance behavior. This can require some patience when a performance problem occurs only intermittently. With polling, you'll be able to construct properly scoped diagnostic data for any historical user action that you might like to analyze, but *only* if you have invested into enough un-aggregated diagnostic data storage. Extended SQL trace data provides an excellent low-cost substitute for high-frequency polling.

In Table 3-5, I've tried to translate my opinion into a numerical format for your convenience.

 This technique of creating the illusion that a man's opinion can be manipulated arithmetically is something I picked up from reading *Car & Driver* magazine.

I believe that extended SQL trace data offers the best performance optimization value of the three diagnostic data sources identified in this chapter. In the past three years, my colleagues and I at *hotsos.com* have helped to diagnose and repair production performance problems in well over 1,000 cases using *only* extended SQL trace data. Our field testing has shown that, when used properly, the extended SQL trace feature is a *stunningly* reliable performance diagnostic tool.

Table 3-5. My opinion on the relative merits of the three Oracle operational timing data sources. Scores range from 1 to 10, with higher scores representing better performance in the named attribute

	Diagnostic data source		
Attribute	**V$ fixed views**	**Oracle shared memory**	**Extended SQL trace data**
Ease of getting results now	9	1	8
Ease of storing the retrieved data	7	1	10
Ease of parsing the retrieved data	8	1	7
Minimal invasiveness upon Oracle kernel	2	10	7
Minimal invasiveness upon other resources	8	4	7
Capacity for historical drill-down analysis	1	8	7
Cost to develop tools to assist in analysis	9	1	6
Diagnostic reliability	3	9	9
Total	**45**	**35**	**61**

For More Information

Chapters 5 and 6 contain the information you will need to put extended SQL trace data to use, as soon as you're ready for it. Chapter 8 provides some guidance for you in the domain of Oracle's V$ data sources. I do not discuss in this text how to obtain performance information directly from an Oracle SGA. Very few of the people who have figured out how to map the Oracle SGA are willing to talk about it publicly. Kyle Hailey is one professional who has figured it out and who has been willing to describe the process [Hailey (2002)]. As a technician, I find the subject of direct Oracle SGA memory access to be irresistible. However, as a practitioner and a student of optimization economics, I have found Oracle extended SQL trace data absolutely unbeatable.

## CHAPTER 4

Targeting the Right Improvement Activity

When you have collected properly scoped diagnostic data for some targeted user actions, it's time to figure out how to repair the problem:

> Execute the candidate optimization activity that will have the greatest net payoff to the business. If even the best net-payoff activity produces insufficient net payoff, then suspend your performance improvement activities until something changes.

Performing this task well requires thinking in two distinctly different fields. First, there's the job that everyone knows about: the technical job of figuring out which changes might cause performance improvement. The analysis that you might *not* have expected is the job of predicting the financial impact of each change. This is the job that many performance analysts don't do very well (most analysts don't do it very well because they don't try to do it at all). It is the job that is almost impossible to perform with conventional "Oracle tuning" methods. But by not predicting the financial impact of a change before you make it, you lose the ability to make well-informed performance improvement decisions that suit the priorities of your business.

A New Standard of Customer Care

In many ways, Oracle performance analysis is still in its infancy. The age of response time–based optimization methods—ushered in by the likes of Juan Loaiza, Roderick Mañalac, Anjo Kolk, and Shari Yamaguchi—is certainly a big technical leap forward. But technical advances represent only a part of our field's necessary growth path. The standard of quality with which we treat our customers (our users, our managers, our consulting clients...) is another tremendous growth opportunity for us.

The Stanford University *Human Subjects Manual* illustrates how I believe we ought to treat our customers. The following text is an excerpt from the chapter entitled "Informed Consent" [Stanford (2001)]:

> The voluntary consent of the human subject is absolutely essential. This means that the person involved should:
>
> •Have the legal capacity to give consent;

- Be so situated as to be able to exercise free power of choice, without the intervention of any element of force, fraud, deceit, duress, over-reaching, or other form of constraint or coercion; and

- Have sufficient knowledge and comprehension of the subject matter and the elements involved as to enable him or her to make an informed and enlightened decision.

This latter element requires that all of the following be made known to the subject:

i. The nature of the experiment;

ii. The duration of the experiment;

iii. The purpose of the experiment;

iv. The method and means by which the experiment is to be conducted;

v. All inconveniences and hazards reasonably to be expected;

vi. The effects upon the subject's health or person which may possibly come from his or her participation in the experiment.

I find the idea of *informed consent* extremely relevant to our profession. Thankfully, few Oracle analysts live under the kinds of literally life-and-death pressures that medical practitioners deal with every day. But, regularly, many of us are enlisted to execute very technical tasks that few non-specialists understand, in situations that involve very high stakes for the customers who need our help. The doctrine of informed consent is a sort of "bill of rights" that protects any customer who lives on the short end of the teeter-totter in a technology balance of power.

But living up to the standard of informed consent is virtually impossible for practitioners who use the conventional Method C Oracle tuning approach. The Method C technology simply doesn't provide you with the information you need to predict how a project—or even a small piece of a project—is going to turn out. You can't tell your customers something you don't know. One of the most important benefits of Method R is that it puts within reach the technical tools that enable us to enact this *informed consent* standard of customer care within our profession.

How to Find the Economically Optimal Performance Improvement Activity

By now, you've probably noticed that a central theme of Method R is careful *targeting*. How you respond to your diagnostic data fits the theme. Your response consists of three targeting steps:

1. First, the analyst *targets* the user actions for which performance improvement provides the best potential economic value to the business (Chapter 2).

2. Next, the analyst *targets* the correct time scope and action scope for diagnostic data collection (Chapter 3).

3. Finally, the analyst *targets* for implementation the performance improvement activity with the best expected net payoff (Chapter 4).

As I described in Chapter 1, the data format that best facilitates this third act of targeting is the *resource profile*. However, a resource profile is only part of the information that you'll need. After you learn from your resource profile where a user action's time went, your next step is to mine the diagnostic data to determine *why* a targeted component of response time took so long. Fortunately, if you have collected well-scoped extended SQL trace data, then everything you'll need is already in your possession. If you have *not* collected well-scoped extended SQL trace data, then you probably shouldn't have escaped the bounds of Chapter 3 just yet.

Once you have collected properly time- and action-scoped diagnostic data for each of your few (one to five) targeted user actions, the following algorithm combines the technical and financial analysis elements required to reveal the optimal action for your business:

1. For each targeted user action:

    a. Assemble your diagnostic data into a format that helps you attribute root causes to elements of the action's response time consumption.

    b. Estimate the net payoff of the best few options for performance improvement. Add the option and its expected net payoff to the list of candidate performance improvement activities.

2. From the list of candidate performance improvement activities, determine which activities will provide the best net payoff for the business.

When you've performed these steps, you've identified the performance activities that will most benefit your business. The next thing you'll do is set this book down and go convert your performance improvement plan into reality.

 Method R is a significant departure from conventional "tuning" approaches. Method R is not about chasing down a list of ratios or even wait events that look suspicious. It's about aligning the priorities of performance improvement with *business need*. Your *business* drives prioritization decisions in an optimized performance improvement project, not your technology.

Making Sense of Your Diagnostic Data

Part II contains all the information you will need to respond to properly scoped performance diagnostic data. As you'll see, the Method R pathway through your diagnostic data is deterministic. Therefore, assembly of raw Oracle trace data into something you can analyze conveniently is a task that can be automated. Some form of automation is essential if your job includes analyzing several megabytes of raw trace data. At the time of this writing, I am aware of three tools that Oracle Corporation provides to help:

tkprof

> *tkprof* is a trace file formatter that takes raw Oracle trace data as input and emits a text file that shows performance statistics aggregated by SQL statement. Different command-line options allow you to select the order in which the SQL statements are shown. *tkprof* was designed for unit-level performance testing of SQL applications, and it does an excellent job in that role. Oracle9i is the first release in which *tkprof* processes the Oracle "wait event" data required by Method R. Prior versions of *tkprof* simply ignore the wait data. (Chapter 5 explains the significance of Oracle "wait events.") For more information about *tkprof*, see the Oracle *Performance Tuning Guide and Reference* (*http://technet.oracle.com*) and *MetaLink* documents 41634.1, 29012.1, and 1012416.6.

trcsummary

> *trcsummary* is a tool that Oracle Corporation advertises as "not available for general customer use." It uses *awk* and *nawk* to parse an Oracle trace file and provide similar output to that produced by *tkprof*. It was apparently designed to overcome some of the deficiencies of early *tkprof* releases. For more information about *trcsummary*, see Oracle *MetaLink* document 62160.1.

Trace Analyzer

> Trace Analyzer is a set of SQL*Plus scripts and PL/SQL code that reads a raw SQL trace file, loads its content into a database, and then prints a detailed report. Trace Analyzer is capable of processing Oracle "wait event" data. For more information about Trace Analyzer, see Oracle *MetaLink* document 224270.1.

Of these three options, Oracle's Trace Analyzer is the newest and most comprehensive, but it is also the most cumbersome to use. It is very slow, and the prodigious quantity of un-prioritized output that it emits can require days of analysis to decipher.

The trace file analyzer I use is a commercial product in which I meddled while Jeff Holt did all the real work, called the *Hotsos Profiler*™. We built the Hotsos Profiler because no other tool on the market took us from *data collected* to *problem solved* as fast as we needed. The Hotsos Profiler takes just a few seconds to convert a multi-megabyte extended SQL trace file into an HTML document that reveals the root cause of virtually any performance problem within two mouse clicks. With Hotsos Profiler output, I expect to understand the net payoffs of all my best performance improvement options within one hour of acquiring a properly scoped trace file. You can read about the Hotsos Profiler at *http://www.hotsos.com*.

Once you have assembled your diagnostic data into a format that you can analyze, your next job is to determine how you might go about improving the performance of your targeted user action. Your work at this point becomes a brief iterative process that looks something like this:

1. Use the resource profile to identify the components of response time that appears to offer the best net payoff opportunity. Then find the diagnostic data elements that will illustrate why the components account for so much response time.

2. Assess ideas that you believe will best reduce time spent in the response time component targeted in step 1. To do this, you'll typically test a performance improvement idea on a testing system. The result of such a test provides the data you need to forecast the net payoff of a project to implement an idea. Assess enough ideas to convince yourself that you're not overlooking any high-payoff performance improvement opportunities.

I defer the technical details of how to execute these steps to Part III. The remainder of this chapter is devoted to the task of forecasting the net payoff of a project.

Forecasting Project Net Payoff

The point of a performance improvement project is *economic optimization*. When you undertake a performance improvement project, you're implementing a willingness to make a time and materials investment in exchange for an improved amount of economic value coming out of the system. Optimizing successfully requires that each of your work steps be an *informed* action. That is, you should know the costs and benefits of every step you take *before* you take it.

The rule that should guide your behavior is simple: before making any investment, you should understand the expected *net payoff* of that investment. The *net payoff* of a project is the present value (PV) of the project's *benefits* minus the present value of the project's *costs*. The concept of present value is conceptually simple: ·

> A dollar today is worth more than a dollar tomorrow, because the dollar today can be invested to start earning interest immediately. [Brealey and Myers (1988), 12]

The PV formula is the tool you need to "normalize" future cash flows into present-day dollars so that you can make an apples-to-apples comparison of investments and payoffs that are expected to occur at different times in the future. To forecast the net payoff of a proposed project, then, you'll need to execute the following steps:

1. Forecast the business benefits of the proposed activity and the timings of those benefits.

2. Forecast the business costs of the proposed activity and the timings of those costs.

3. Compute the PV of each cash flow component by using the formula:

$$PV = \frac{C}{1+r}$$

where C is the future cash flow, and r is the rate of return that you demand for accepting delayed payment. Microsoft Excel provides a built-in PV function to perform this calculation.

For example, if you expect a rate of return of $r = 0.07$ (this is the approximate average rate of return of the U.S. stock market over the past 90 years), then the present value of a dollar received one year from now is only about $0.934579. In other words, if you expect a 7% rate of return, receiving $1 in one year is of equivalent value to receiving $0.934579 today. The reason is that you can invest $0.934579 today, and if you receive 7% interest on that money, in one year it will be worth $1.

4. Compute the net payoff of the proposed activity by summing all the benefit PVs and subtracting all the cost PVs.

Once you know the PV of each proposed activity, you (or your project's decision-maker) can make simple comparisons of proposed activities based on their estimated financial values.

Forecasting Project Benefits

The resource profile vastly simplifies the task of forecasting the business benefit of a proposed performance improvement activity. I remember painfully the days before Method R, when the only ways we had to forecast business benefits were to extrapolate well beyond our mathematical rights to do so. For example, I can remember when professional analysts used to forecast results like this:

> "I have reduced the number of extents in your sales order table from 3,482 to just 8. It is expected that this improvement will increase across-the-board Order Entry performance by 30 percent."

> "Increasing the buffer hit ratio from 95 to 99 percent can yield performance gains of over 400 percent."

I have *books* that say stuff like this. Did you ever wonder where a number like "30" or "400" comes from in statements like these? Unless such a number comes from a properly scoped resource profile, then you can virtually be assured that it came from a place where unsubstantiated estimates hide when they're not being drafted into service by a consultant whose earnings capacity relies upon an ability to inspire customer hope.

 I always derive a kind of sinister enjoyment when I see benefit statements written with phrases like, "It is expected that...." The use of passive voice in situations like this is a grammatical tool that authors use when they want to make it possible later to disassociate themselves from their own guesses.

I hope this book will help you both make better performance improvement decisions and insist upon better decisions from the professionals who are supposed to be helping you.

Monetizing the benefits

There are two steps in forecasting the benefits of a proposed performance improvement action:

1. Estimate the amount of response time you can eliminate from a targeted user action. Part III describes how to do this.

2. Estimate the cash value to the business of that response time improvement. Arithmetically, this calculation is straightforward. It is the product of the following three quantities:

> The number of seconds you can remove from a user action
> > multiplied by
>
> The number of times the user action will be executed over the period during which the business benefits are being forecast
> > multiplied by
>
> The cash value of one second of response time to the business

Step 1 is simple in practice. As you'll learn in Part III, a resource profile generated on a production system provides all the *before* timing statistics you need, and a resource profile generated on a test system helps you forecast your *after* timing statistics. Step 2 is usually simple as well, until it comes time to estimate the cash value of one second of response time to the business. Many businesses simply don't know this number. Some businesses do. For example, your company may already know information like the following:

> Improving the speed of the return materials authorization process from 5 days to 2 hours will be necessary to prevent losing our largest retail customer. An annual sales impact of over $100,000,000 hangs in the balance.

> Reducing the time it takes to invoice our customers from 4 days to 1 day will reduce our working capital requirement by €325.000.

> Improving the performance of the form through which our users pay invoices will improve accounting staff morale, reduce staff turnover, and reduce overtime wages, resulting in annual cost savings of over £60.000.

> Increasing the number of orders processed on the system from the current state of 40 orders in a peak hour to 100 orders per hour will increase annual sales revenue by over ¥100,000,000.

For businesses that don't have such concrete "dollar"-per-second value specifications, it is usually good enough to express project value in terms of un-monetized response time savings over some reasonable period. A resulting net payoff statement might look like this:

> I expect Project A to be complete within two weeks at a cost of $10,000. I expect as a result, we will reduce end-user response times by over 128 hours per week.

With the "dollar"-per-second value specification in hand, though, the net payoff statement makes decision-making a little easier:

> I expect Project A to be complete within two weeks at a cost of $10,000. I expect as a result, we will reduce end-user response times by over 128 hours per week, which will save the company over $70,000 in labor expenses per year.

Monetizing the expected benefits of a project is often an unnecessary academic exercise. This is especially likely in projects in which the cost of the appropriate remedy action is low compared to the obvious business value of the repair. For example, the following requirements range widely from very vague to very specific. However, each provides a perfectly legitimate level of detail in its place:

> I don't know how long this report should run. I just know that how long it's running now can't be right. We'll appreciate anything you can do to help.

> We can't live with the application unless you can reduce the response time for this transaction from several minutes down to only a couple of seconds.

> This transaction must respond in 1.0 seconds or less in 95% of executions.

> This transaction must consume less than 13 milliseconds on an unloaded system.

I explain in Chapter 9 how and why you might formulate extremely detailed requirements like the final two shown here with only the limited information available from an application unit test. In such detailed specifications, it will usually be important for your project sponsor to assign a business value to the requirement. I've witnessed several projects that survived only because during the course of the project, the project sponsor relaxed several of his original specifications when he found out how much it was going to cost to actually meet them.

If you can't monetize the benefits

It's often not a problem if you can't reasonably approximate the "dollar"-per-second value of response time reductions. If the remedy you propose is *in*expensive to obtain, then your project sponsor will probably never require a cash benefit justification. In this case, the only person who will really miss the data is *you*—you'll miss the opportunity to quantify the financial impact of your good work. If the remedy you propose is very expensive, then an inability to affix a reasonable value to your expected response time savings will result in one of three outcomes:

- Your project sponsor will estimate the financial benefit and make a well-informed financial decision about your project direction.
- The project will be allowed to continue in spite of the lack of objective financial justification, which may or may not be a mistake—you won't know until the project is done.
- The project will simply be called off on the grounds that "it will cost too much." The best way I know to combat a project termination threat is to prove the financial benefit of the project net payoff. If the project can't stand up to the scrutiny of financial justification, then termination is almost certainly the right answer.

The financial benefit estimation task is in place solely to provide the data that you or your project sponsor will need to make financial decisions about your project. It's nothing more than that. Don't diminish your credibility by letting unnecessarily detailed forecasting of business value bog down your project.

A Warning About Thinking in Percentage Units

The resource profile format makes thinking in percentages easy. If a performance improvement activity will eliminate x percent of some duration that accounts for y percent of your total response time, then the action will eliminate $x \times y$ percent of your total response time. For example, if you can eliminate 50% of some duration that accounts for 80% of your total response time, then you'll reduce total response time by 40% ($0.5 \times 0.8 = 0.4$).

But beware any time you use percentages as decision-making tools. Percentages are always susceptible to ratio fallacies. For example, which is better: to improve response time by 20% of A, or to improve response time by 90% of B? The correct response to the question is that, without knowing the values of A and B, you can't answer the question. If you answered either A or B, then you have become the victim of a ratio fallacy.

Forecasting Project Cost

Forecasting a project's net payoff requires both a forecast of benefits and a forecast of costs. Forecasting *costs* is the easier of the two tasks, because there's so much more infrastructure in place to help you do it. Lots of people are good at estimating the level of investment required to try something. Consultants, for example, take courses in proposal development that fine-tune their skills in estimating project costs. Consultants who can't estimate project costs with reasonable accuracy go out of business (and typically then go to work for other consultants who can).

For you to produce reasonable project cost forecasts, you of course must understand the tasks that will be required to implement a proposed performance improvement. I have provided a lot of information in Part III that I hope will stimulate you to better understand many of those tasks and materials.

Forecasting Project Risk

Even the best projects usually miss their forecasts. It is virtually impossible to predict the precise benefit or cost of any complicated activity. Therefore, the best forecasters integrate the concept of risk into their assessments. Before a project has completed, its cost and benefit are random variables. A random variable is a concept that mathematicians use to describe the result of a process that cannot be predicted exactly, but that is constrained in some understandable way. Each variable has an expected value, but each has properties of variance that you need to understand going into the project. Financial analysts use the word "risk" to refer to what statisticians measure as "variation" [Kachigan (1986); Bodie, et al. (1989)].

What Is Your Project's "Cost Constraint"?

Many people, when asked "What is your project cost constraint?", are tempted to give a fixed numerical answer like "ten thousand dollars." But a good financial officer would probably answer that the real constraint depends upon the value of the improvement to the business and the rate of return on investments that the business requires.

For example, imagine that the presumed budgetary limit is $10,000. Say that the return on investment that the business requires is 35%, and imagine that you've identified a performance improvement that will bring an incremental $1,000,000 of value this year to the business. Then if the business can truly trust your $1,000,000 estimate of benefit value, it should be willing to invest up to $740,741 into your project. The analysis boils down to whether the $740,741 that the business will have to procure from un-budgeted sources can be expected to fetch a higher return in your project or elsewhere.

It is possible to measure the risk of a project that has occurred in the past, if you have data from enough projects to draw statistically valid conclusions. To consider how it is possible to measure project risk, imagine that thirty different project teams were to embark upon thirty identical performance improvement projects. It is virtually inconceivable that all thirty projects would come in at the exact same cost and deliver the exact same benefit. If we could perform such an experiment in real life, then with so many project teams participating, we would actually have enough data at the conclusion of our experiment to determine a statistical pattern in the costs and benefits. If you were to plot a histogram of, for example, project costs across all thirty executions of the project, you might end up with the one shown in Figure 4-1.

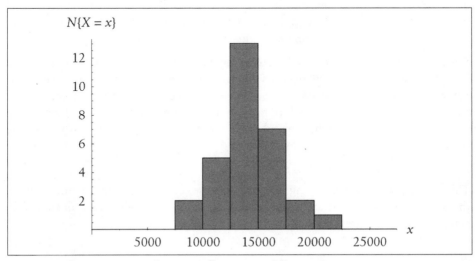

Figure 4-1. Thirty executions of a project all came in at different costs

The costs depicted in Figure 4-1 exhibit a clear tendency to cluster around the value 15,000 (imagine that this figure represents units of your local currency). If the cost numbers happened to be skewed rightward and distributed over a wider range, like the ones shown in Figure 4-2, then, quite simply, the project's risk is greater: there's a greater chance that the project will overrun its cost estimate.

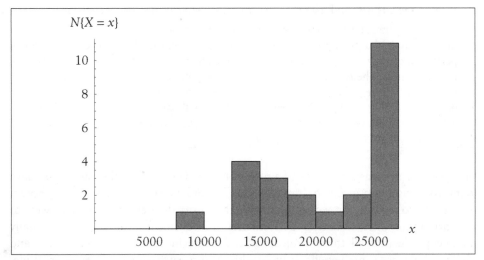

Figure 4-2. The larger cost variance for this project indicates increased project risk

If you had the luxury of having project cost and benefit data from large numbers of projects that are exactly like the one you're undertaking, then of course you'd be a lot better able to predict the true cost and benefit of your project. But you probably don't have this kind of data unless you're a company that does the same type of project over and over again. (Companies who execute the same type of project over and over again can get quite good at predicting project costs and benefits.)

Several factors influence the risk of cost overruns and benefit shortfalls in a project. The dominant factor is *experience*. Doing something that nobody has ever done before is understandably risk-intensive. But even executing a simple project with a team that has never done it before can produce unpredictable results. Experience isn't the only thing, though. One of my favorite lessons from athletics is this one [Pelz (2000)]:

> Practice makes *permanent*. Only *perfect practice* makes perfect.

This is a scientist's way of saying that just because someone has done something ten thousand times doesn't mean he does it well.* A consistent track record of success in similar projects is a tremendous risk reduction factor.

---

* A related observation is this: meeting a given quality standard ensures only *consistent* quality, not necessarily *high* quality.

You can get as fancy at forecasting variances as you want. However, don't lose sight of the goal of your adventures in risk forecasting. What you're really looking for is the ability to predict two things that your customer needs to know, and that can come directly from the "informed consent" text cited earlier in this chapter:

v. All inconveniences and hazards reasonably to be expected

vi. The effects upon the subject's health or person which may possibly come from his or her participation in the experiment

You'll never be able to predict the exact costs and benefits of every project action you recommend. But, by using the techniques described in this book, you will be able to refine your predictive abilities very rapidly.

Reference

## CHAPTER 5

Interpreting Extended SQL Trace Data

To succeed, a performance analyst must understand the language in which a system communicates information about its performance. Unfortunately, for over a decade, the domain of Oracle time statistics has been one of the most misunderstood areas of the Oracle kernel. To understand the response time instrumentation that the Oracle kernel provides, you must understand how the Oracle kernel interacts with its host operating system. It is this operating system that allocates resources to the Oracle kernel process itself, and it is the operating system that actually supplies the timing statistics that Oracle uses to describe its own performance.

Trace File Walk-Through

I believe that the best way to begin the study of Oracle operational data is with a tour of Oracle's *extended SQL trace* output. SQL trace output is unsurpassed as an educational and diagnostic aid, because it presents a linear sequential recorded history of what the Oracle kernel does in response to an application's demands upon the database.

The SQL trace feature has been a part of the Oracle kernel since Version 6, which should be older than any version of Oracle that you are currently running. In 1992, with the release of the kernel Version 7.0.12, Oracle Corporation significantly enhanced the value of SQL trace data by adding information about the durations of non–CPU-consuming instructions that the Oracle kernel executes.

Let's begin our study with the "Hello, world" of Oracle response time data. Example 5-1 shows one of the simplest SQL*Plus sessions you can run. The session activates the extended SQL trace mechanism for itself. It then queries the string "Hello, world; today is *sysdate*" from the database and exits.

*Example 5-1. Input for a SQL*Plus session that generates extended SQL trace data for a simple query*

```
alter session set max_dump_file_size=unlimited;
alter session set timed_statistics=true;
```

Example 5-1. Input for a SQL*Plus session that generates extended SQL trace data for a simple query (continued)

```
alter session set events '10046 trace name context forever, level 12';
select 'Hello, world; today is '||sysdate from dual;
exit;
```

The trace file shown in Example 5-2 reveals the sequence of actions the Oracle kernel performed on behalf of this session. If you've learned to view SQL trace data only through the lens of Oracle's *tkprof*, then you're in for a treat. By upgrading your understanding of extended SQL trace data in the raw, you'll earn the ability to diagnose more classes of performance problem than can be detected with *tkprof* alone. After becoming fluent with raw trace data, many analysts are surprised by how many deficiencies they find in *tkprof*.

Example 5-2. Raw extended SQL trace data produced by a SQL*Plus session using Example 5-1 as input

```
/u01/oradata/admin/V901/udump/ora_9178.trc
Oracle9i Enterprise Edition Release 9.0.1.0.0 - Production
With the Partitioning option
JServer Release 9.0.1.0.0 - Production
ORACLE_HOME = /u01/oradata/app/9.0.1
System name:    Linux
Node name:  research
Release:    2.4.4-4GB
Version:    #1 Fri May 18 14:11:12 GMT 2001
Machine:    i686
Instance name: V901
Redo thread mounted by this instance: 1
Oracle process number: 9
Unix process pid: 9178, image: oracle@research (TNS V1-V3)

*** SESSION ID:(7.6692) 2002-12-03 10:07:40.051
APPNAME mod='SQL*Plus' mh=3669949024 act='' ah=4029777240
=====================
PARSING IN CURSOR #1 len=69 dep=0 uid=5 oct=42 lid=5 tim=1038931660052098 hv=1509700594
ad='50d6d560'
alter session set events '10046 trace name context forever, level 12'
END OF STMT
EXEC #1:c=0,e=1,p=0,cr=0,cu=0,mis=0,r=0,dep=0,og=4,tim=1038931660051673
WAIT #1: nam='SQL*Net message to client' ela= 5 p1=1650815232 p2=1 p3=0
WAIT #1: nam='SQL*Net message from client' ela= 1262 p1=1650815232 p2=1 p3=0
=====================
PARSING IN CURSOR #1 len=51 dep=0 uid=5 oct=3 lid=5 tim=1038931660054075 hv=1716247018
ad='50c551f8'
select 'Hello, world; today is '||sysdate from dual
END OF STMT
PARSE #1:c=0,e=214,p=0,cr=0,cu=0,mis=0,r=0,dep=0,og=4,tim=1038931660054053
BINDS #1:
EXEC #1:c=0,e=124,p=0,cr=0,cu=0,mis=0,r=0,dep=0,og=4,tim=1038931660054311
WAIT #1: nam='SQL*Net message to client' ela= 5 p1=1650815232 p2=1 p3=0
FETCH #1:c=0,e=177,p=0,cr=1,cu=2,mis=0,r=1,dep=0,og=4,tim=1038931660054596
```

Example 5-2. Raw extended SQL trace data produced by a SQL*Plus session using Example 5-1 as input (continued)

```
WAIT #1: nam='SQL*Net message from client' ela= 499 p1=1650815232 p2=1 p3=0
FETCH #1:c=0,e=2,p=0,cr=0,cu=0,mis=0,r=0,dep=0,og=0,tim=1038931660055374
WAIT #1: nam='SQL*Net message to client' ela= 4 p1=1650815232 p2=1 p3=0
WAIT #1: nam='SQL*Net message from client' ela= 1261 p1=1650815232 p2=1 p3=0
STAT #1 id=1 cnt=1 pid=0 pos=0 obj=221 op='TABLE ACCESS FULL DUAL '
XCTEND rlbk=0, rd_only=1
```

It's not difficult to step through a trace file this small by hand. At the end of this chapter, I'll describe each action in overview, to give you a feel for what kind of data you'll find in the trace file. In the meantime, let's just hit the highlights.

At the beginning of a trace file is a preamble, which reveals information about the trace file: its name, the release of the Oracle kernel that generated it, and so on. Next is a line that identifies the session being traced (session 7, serial number 6692 in our case), and the time the line was emitted. Notice that the kernel identifies every SQL statement used by the session in a PARSING IN CURSOR section. This PARSING IN CURSOR section shows attributes of the SQL text being used, including the SQL text itself.

The action lines in a trace file are lines beginning with the tokens PARSE, EXEC, and FETCH (and a few others) and the WAIT lines. Each PARSE, EXEC, and FETCH line represents the execution of a single database call. The c and e statistics report on how much total CPU time and total elapsed time, respectively, were consumed by the call. Other statistics on a database call line reveal the number of Oracle blocks obtained via operating system read calls (p) or by two modes of database buffer cache retrieval (cr for consistent-mode reads and cu for current-mode reads), the number of misses on the library cache endured by the call (mis), and the number of rows returned by the call (r). The tim value at the end of each database call line lets you know approximately what time it was when the database call completed.

The WAIT lines are an exciting "new" addition to Oracle trace files, since they have been available only since about 1992. These WAIT lines are part of what distinguish *extended* SQL trace data from plain old regular SQL trace data. Each WAIT line reports on the duration of a specific sequence of instructions executed within the Oracle kernel process. The ela statistic reports the response time of such a sequence of instructions. The nam attribute identifies the call, and the p1, p2, and p3 values provide useful information about the call in a format that is unique to each different nam value.

The STAT lines don't convey direct response time information until Release 9.2. However, even prior to 9.2, they're of immense use in performance analysis, because they contain information about the execution plan that the Oracle query optimizer chose for executing the cursor's SQL. Finally, the XCTEND line is emitted whenever the application being traced issues a commit or a rollback instruction.

That's it. Everything you need to account accurately for a session's response time is in the trace file. One of the best things about the data is that you can see *exactly* what a session did during the course of its execution. You don't have to try to extrapolate details from an average, like assessing V$ data forces you to do. All the details are laid out in front of you in chronological order,* and they're stored in an easy-to-parse ASCII format.

Extended SQL Trace Data Reference

One of the reasons for Oracle Corporation's enormous success in the high-performance database market is the easy accessibility of detailed response time data. Beginning with extended SQL trace files and extending throughout several fixed views, the Oracle kernel provides you all the detail you need in order to know *why* an application has consumed exactly the response time that it did. The only thing that might be missing is whether you understand how to exploit all that detail. Filling this gap is the mission of my work in this book.

Trace File Element Definitions

Several good sources exist to describe the format of each trace file line [Oracle *MetaLink* note 39817.1; Kyte (2001) 464–475; Morle (2000) 133–142]. However, none goes far enough to enable full accounting of session response time. Full response time accounting is the goal that you will achieve with the book you are reading now. The following sections describe the meaning of each of the performance-related statistics reported in Oracle's extended SQL trace data.

Cursor numbers

Each line emitted to a trace file corresponds to one "action" executed by the Oracle kernel program. Each line uses the string #ID to identify a cursor upon which the kernel performed the action. For example, the following line shows a fetch executed upon cursor #1:

```
FETCH #1:c=0,e=177,p=0,cr=1,cu=2,mis=0,r=1,dep=0,og=4,tim=1038931660054596
```

The cursor numbers are relevant only within the scope of the trace file. Furthermore, the Oracle kernel makes a cursor number available for reuse within a trace file when a cursor is closed. Hence, trace file lines containing references to a given cursor number do not all necessarily refer to the same cursor. Fortunately, a given trace file contains a time-ordered record of every cursor creation; each PARSING IN CURSOR token indicates a cursor birth (or rebirth). For example, the following are two PARSING IN CURSOR lines from the trace file in Example 5-2:

```
=======================
PARSING IN CURSOR #1 len=69 dep=0 uid=5 oct=42 lid=5 tim=1038931660052098
hv=1509700594 ad='50d6d560'
```

---

* There are a few inconsequential exceptions to strict chronological ordering, which you shall see shortly.

```
alter session set events '10046 trace name context forever, level 12'
END OF STMT
...
=====================
PARSING IN CURSOR #1 len=51 dep=0 uid=5 oct=3 lid=5 tim=1038931660054075
hv=1716247018 ad='50c551f8'
select 'Hello, world; today is '||sysdate from dual
END OF STMT
```

The first PARSING IN CURSOR section indicates that cursor #1 was associated with the ALTER SESSION statement. Later in the same trace file, the Oracle kernel reused ID #1 for the cursor associated with the SELECT statement.

Session identification and timestamps

A line beginning with the token *** indicates the system time obtained immediately before the *** line itself was emitted to the trace file. For example:

```
*** 2002-12-02 22:25:53.716
*** SESSION ID:(8.6550) 2002-12-02 22:25:53.714
```

This information helps the performance analyst by establishing a mapping from Oracle's tim value clock to the system wall clock. The Oracle kernel helpfully emits a *** line into the trace data any time there has been a significant amount of time (tens of seconds) elapsed since the emission of the previously emitted trace line. This feature is helpful because it allows you to resynchronize your understanding of the correct wall clock time over large spans of WAIT lines, which contain approximate elapsed durations (ela), but no internal clock (tim) values. If you want to emit this line yourself to your trace data, you can do so by calling DBMS_SYSTEM.KSDDDT.

A line containing the token SESSION ID:(m.n) identifies the trace file lines that follow the SESSION ID line as being associated with the Oracle session with V$SESSION.SID=m and V$SESSION.SERIAL#=n. The session identification lines help you ensure that you are analyzing the correct trace file. In Oracle multithreaded server (MTS) configurations, the lines are especially valuable, because each Oracle kernel process can service requests on behalf of many Oracle sessions. Lines containing a session ID signal which session's work is represented in the raw trace lines that follow.

Did you notice that the timestamp and session identification lines shown here are printed out of time sequence? (The first line marks time 22:25:53.716, and the second one marks a time 0.002 seconds earlier.) This phenomenon is similar to the one described later in "Cursor identification."

Application identification

If the application has set its module name or action with the DBMS_APPLICATION_INFO package, then the Oracle kernel will emit an APPNAME line when level-1 SQL tracing is activated. For example:

```
APPNAME mod='SQL*Plus' mh=3669949024 act='' ah=4029777240
```

The individual values in this line are as follows:

mod

    The name of the module set with the SET_MODULE procedure.

mh

    A "hash value" that identifies the module.

act

    The name of the action set with either SET_MODULE or SET_ACTION.

ah

    A "hash value" that identifies the action.

Cursor identification

A PARSING IN CURSOR section contains information about a cursor. For example:

```
=====================
PARSING IN CURSOR #135 len=358 dep=0 uid=173 oct=3 lid=173 tim=3675359494 hv=72759792
ad='bb13f788'
select vendor_number, vendor_id, vendor_name, vendor_type_lookup_code, type_1099,
employee_id, num_1099, vat_registration_num, awt_group_id, allow_awt_flag, hold_all_
payments_flag, num_active_pay_sites, total_prepays, available_prepays from po_
vendors_ap_v where (VENDOR_NUMBER LIKE :1) AND ( active_flag = 'Y' and enabled_flag =
'Y' ) order by vendor_number
END OF STMT
```

The PARSING IN CURSOR line itself contains information about cursor #ID. Text between the PARSING IN CURSOR line and the corresponding END OF STMT line is the cursor's SQL text. The Oracle kernel usually emits this section at the conclusion of a parse call, just before the kernel emits a cursor's PARSE line. However, if tracing was not active when the parse call completed, the kernel will usually emit the section near the beginning of the trace data (just before the completion of the first traced database call, but potentially after one or more WAIT lines), as if the Oracle kernel were executing the following pseudocode:

```
# Upon completion of Oracle kernel activity required by a db call...
if SQL tracing level >= 1 {
    if db call is PARSE or pic[cursor_id] is unset {
        emit "PARSING IN CURSOR" section
        pic[cursor_id] = 1
    }
    emit statistics for the db call
}
```

Thus, Oracle reveals information in the trace file about a cursor even if tracing was not active at the conclusion of the cursor's parse call.

Each PARSING IN CURSOR line contains the following information about a cursor:

len

    The length of the SQL text.

dep

> The recursive depth of the cursor. A dep=*n* + 1 cursor is a child of some dep=*n* cursor (*n* = 0, 1, 2, ...). Several actions motivate recursive SQL, including database calls that require information from the Oracle database dictionary, statements that fire triggers, and PL/SQL blocks that contain SQL statements. See "Recursive SQL Double-Counting" later in this chapter for further discussion of the "recursive" SQL relationship.

uid

> The schema user ID of the user who parsed the statement.

oct

> The Oracle command type ID [Oracle OCI (1999)].

lid

> The privilege user ID. For example, if FRED calls a package owned by JOE, then a SQL statement executed within the package will have a uid that refers to FRED, and an lid that refers to JOE.

tim

> If a tim value is 0, then TIMED_STATISTICS for the session was false when the database call time would have been calculated. You can thus confirm whether TIMED_STATISTICS was true by observing tim values. In our field work, my colleagues and I have found that specific non-zero tim values associated with PARSING IN CURSOR sections are largely irrelevant.

> In Oracle9*i*, tim is a value expressed in microseconds (1 μs = 0.000 001 seconds). On some systems (such as our Linux research servers), tim field values are unadulterated gettimeofday values. On other systems (like our Microsoft Windows research machines), the origin of tim field values can be much more mysterious. In releases prior to Oracle9*i*, tim is a V$TIMER.HSECS value expressed in centiseconds (1 cs = 0.01 seconds).

hv

> The statement ID of the SQL statement. The hv may look unique, but it is not. Occasionally (albeit rarely), distinct SQL texts share the same hv value.

ad

> The library cache address of the cursor, as is shown in V$SQL.

Database calls

A *database call* is a subroutine in the Oracle kernel. If level-1 SQL tracing is active when a database call completes, then the Oracle kernel emits a database call line upon completion of that database call. PARSE, EXEC, and FETCH calls are the most common types of database call. For example:

```
PARSE #54:c=20000,e=11526,p=0,cr=2,cu=0,mis=1,r=0,dep=1,og=0,tim=1017039304725071
EXEC #1:c=10000,e=12137,p=0,cr=22,cu=0,mis=0,r=1,dep=0,og=4,tim=1017039275981174
FETCH #3:c=10000,e=306,p=0,cr=3,cu=0,mis=0,r=1,dep=2,og=4,tim=1017039275973158
```

Other database call types (for example, ERROR, UNMAP, and SORT UNMAP) are explained in Oracle *MetaLink* note 39817.1. Each database call line contains the following statistics:

c

The total CPU time consumed by the Oracle process during the call. Oracle9*i* expresses c in microseconds (1 μs = 0.000 001 seconds). Prior kernel versions express c in centiseconds (1 cs = 0.01 seconds).

e

The amount of wall time that elapsed during the call. Oracle9*i* expresses e in microseconds (1 μs = 0.000 001 seconds). Prior kernel versions express e in centiseconds (1 cs = 0.01 seconds).

p

The number of Oracle database blocks obtained by the call via operating system disk read calls. The name p is supposed to be mnemonic for the word "physical," but note that not every so-called Oracle "physical" read visits a physical disk device. Many such reads are serviced from various caches between the Oracle kernel and the physical disk.

cr

The number of Oracle database blocks obtained by the call in *consistent mode* from the Oracle database buffer cache. A read executed in consistent mode can motivate additional consistent mode reads from undo blocks, which are stored in rollback segments.

cu

The number of Oracle database blocks obtained by the call in *current mode* from the Oracle database buffer cache. A read executed in current mode is simply a read of the current content of a block.

mis

The number of library cache misses encountered during the call. Each library cache miss motivates a *hard parse* operation.

r

The number of rows returned by the call.

dep

The recursive depth of the cursor. A dep=n + 1 cursor is a child of some dep=n cursor (n = 0, 1, 2, ...). See the "Cursor identification" section earlier in this chapter for more details.

og

The optimizer goal in effect during the call. Oracle uses the values shown in Table 5-1.

tim

See the "Cursor identification" section listed previously for details.

Table 5-1. Oracle query optimizer goal by og value (source: Oracle MetaLink note 39817.1)

og value	Oracle query optimizer goal
1	ALL_ROWS
2	FIRST_ROWS
3	RULE
4	CHOOSE

Note that the Oracle kernel does not emit a database call line into the trace file until the action has *completed*. Thus, an extraordinarily long database operation might cause the Oracle kernel to work for several hours without emitting *anything* to the trace file. Poorly optimized SQL can produce EXEC calls (for updates or deletes) or FETCH calls (for selects) that consume CPU capacity for several *days* at a time.

Wait events

An Oracle *wait event* is a sequence of Oracle kernel instructions that is wrapped with special timing instrumentation. If level-8 or level-12 SQL tracing is active when a wait event completes, then the Oracle kernel emits a WAIT line upon completion of that event. For example:

```
WAIT #1: nam='SQL*Net message to client' ela= 40 p1=1650815232 p2=1 p3=0
WAIT #1: nam='SQL*Net message from client' ela= 1709 p1=1650815232 p2=1 p3=0
WAIT #34: nam='db file sequential read' ela= 14118 p1=52 p2=2755 p3=1
WAIT #44: nam='latch free' ela= 1327989 p1=-1721538020 p2=87 p3=13
```

Each WAIT line contains the following statistics about work executed during the event:

nam

> The name assigned by an Oracle kernel developer to reveal which part of the Oracle kernel code is responsible for this portion of your response time.

ela

> The elapsed duration of the named event's execution. Oracle9*i* expresses ela in microseconds (1 μs = 0.000 001 seconds). Prior kernel versions express ela in centiseconds (1 cs = 0.01 seconds).

p1, p2, p3

> The meanings of these parameters vary by nam. A complete catalog of parameter descriptions for each event type is available by running the following SQL:
>
> ```
> select name, parameter1, parameter2, parameter3
> from v$event_name order by name
> ```

Note that WAIT lines appear in the trace data *before* the database call that motivated them. This occurs because the Oracle kernel emits lines into the trace file as events complete. Thus, if a fetch call requires three OS read calls, the three waits for the read calls will appear in the trace file before Oracle emits the information about the completed fetch call.

The WAIT lines in SQL trace data are one interface to the new Oracle feature introduced in 1992 that has been so important in revolutionizing the ease with which we can diagnose and repair performance problems today.

Bind variables

If level-4 or level-12 SQL tracing is active when the Oracle kernel binds values to place-holders in an application's SQL text, the kernel emits a BINDS section. For example:

```
=====================
PARSING IN CURSOR #1 len=105 dep=0 uid=56 oct=47 lid=56 tim=1017039275982462
hv=2108922784 ad='98becef8'
declare dummy boolean;begin fnd_profile.get_specific(:name, :userid, :respid,  :
applid, :val, dummy);end;
END OF STMT
...
Several lines have been omitted for clarity
...
BINDS #1:
 bind 0: dty=1 mxl=2000(1998) mal=00 scl=00 pre=00 oacflg=01 oacfl2=0 size=2000
offset=0
    bfp=025a74a0 bln=2000 avl=19 flg=05
    value="MFG_ORGANIZATION_ID"
 bind 1: dty=2 mxl=22(22) mal=00 scl=00 pre=00 oacflg=01 oacfl2=0 size=72 offset=0
    bfp=025a744c bln=22 avl=04 flg=05
    value=118194
 bind 2: dty=2 mxl=22(22) mal=00 scl=00 pre=00 oacflg=01 oacfl2=0 size=0 offset=24
    bfp=025a7464 bln=22 avl=05 flg=01
    value=1003677
 bind 3: dty=2 mxl=22(22) mal=00 scl=00 pre=00 oacflg=01 oacfl2=0 size=0 offset=48
    bfp=025a747c bln=22 avl=03 flg=01
    value=140
 bind 4: dty=1 mxl=2000(1998) mal=00 scl=00 pre=00 oacflg=01 oacfl2=0 size=2000
offset=0
    bfp=025ba490 bln=2000 avl=00 flg=05
```

A BINDS section contains one or more bind subsections, one for each variable being bound. The number following the word bind indicates the ordinal position, beginning at 0, of the bind variable within the SQL text. Each bind section contains several statistics about the bind. The most important ones for use in performance analysis are:

dty

> The external data type of the value supplied by the application [Oracle OCI (1999)]. Oracle publishes two sets of data types: *internal* and *external*. The internal data type definitions reveal how the Oracle kernel stores its data on the host operating system. The external data type definitions reveal how the Oracle kernel interfaces with application SQL.

> The external data type of a bind value is important. Occasionally we find SQL statements for which the Oracle query optimizer flatly refuses to use an obviously helpful index. Sometimes such a case is caused by a mismatch

between the column type and the value type, which can force an implicit type coercion function to be executed upon the column, which prevents the optimizer from choosing that index.

avl

The length, in bytes, of the bind value.

value

The value that is bound into the statement execution. The Oracle kernel sometimes truncates values that it emits into the trace file. You can determine exactly when this has happened by simple inspection; truncation has occurred any time the avl value is larger than the length of the value field.

Row source operations

If level-1 SQL tracing is active when a cursor is closed, then the Oracle kernel emits one STAT line for each row source operation in the cursor's execution plan. For example:

```
STAT #1 id=1 cnt=55 pid=0 pos=1 obj=0 op='SORT UNIQUE (cr=39741 r=133 w=0
time=1643800 us)'
STAT #1 id=2 cnt=23395 pid=1 pos=1 obj=0 op='VIEW  (cr=39741 r=133 w=0 time=1614067
us)'
STAT #1 id=3 cnt=23395 pid=2 pos=1 obj=0 op='SORT UNIQUE (cr=39741 r=133 w=0
time=1600554 us)'
STAT #1 id=4 cnt=23395 pid=3 pos=1 obj=0 op='UNION-ALL  (cr=39741 r=133 w=0
time=1385984 us)'
```

If a trace file does not contain the STAT lines you were hoping to find, it is because tracing was deactivated before the cursor closed. The STAT lines will of course be absent any time you trace a well-designed persistent service that neither terminates nor closes its cursors more than once every several weeks.

Each STAT line contains the following statistics about the cursor's execution plan:

id

The unique ID of the row source operation within the STAT line set.

cnt

Number of rows returned by this row source operation.

pid

ID of this operation's parent operation.

pos

The best we can determine, an arbitrary number. It might seem that this value might define the "position" of a row source operation within a set of operations belonging to a single parent, but it appears that sibling row source operations are ordered in increasing ID order.

obj

Object ID of the row source operation, if the operation executes upon a "base object." A row source operation such as NESTED LOOPS, which itself does not access a base object, will report obj=0. (The NESTED LOOPS operation's children *do* access base objects, but the NESTED LOOPS row source operation itself does not.)

op

The name of the row source operation. Beginning with Oracle Release 9.2.0.2.0, the kernel emits additional information into the STAT lines [Rivenes (2003)]. The new information reveals several useful statistics for each row source operation, including:

cr

Number of consistent-mode reads.

r

Number of Oracle blocks read with OS read calls.

w

Number of Oracle blocks written with OS read calls.

time

The elapsed duration, expressed in microseconds (us).

The statistics for a parent row source operation include a roll-up of the statistics for its children.

 Oracle's *tkprof* utility produces erroneous results in more cases than you might have imagined, especially in STAT line processing. Oracle's *tkprof* has an exceptional reputation for reliability, but I'm convinced that one reason the tool maintains this reputation is that people simply never bother to double-check its output. To confirm or refute whether *tkprof* is giving correct output is impossible to do without studying raw trace data. Most people are reluctant to do this. I hope this book helps encourage you to make the effort.

Transaction end markers

If level-1 SQL tracing is active when a commit or rollback occurs, then the Oracle kernel emits an XCTEND line upon completion of the call. For example:

```
XCTEND rlbk=0, rd_only=0
```

Each XCTEND line contains the following statistics about work executed during the commit or rollback:

rlbk

True (1) if and only if the transaction was rolled back.

rd_only

True (1) if and only if the transaction changed no data in the database.

Notice that the XCTEND marker has no cursor ID reference. This is because there is a one-to-many relationship between a transaction and the cursors that participate in the transaction.

Reference summary

Table 5-2 summarizes the raw trace data statistics that will be most interesting to you during your performance analysis work.

Table 5-2. Descriptions of selected elements from extended SQL trace data

Field	Occurs in...			Description
	Cursor ID	Database call	Wait event	
c		✓		Total CPU time consumed by the database call. Reported in microseconds on Oracle9*i*, centiseconds on prior releases.
cr		✓		Number of Oracle blocks obtained from the database buffer cache in consistent mode.
cu		✓		Number of Oracle blocks obtained from the database buffer cache in current mode.
dep	✓	✓		The recursive depth of the cursor.
e		✓		Elapsed duration consumed by the database call. Reported in microseconds on Oracle9*i*, centiseconds on prior releases.
ela			✓	Elapsed duration consumed by the wait event. Reported in microseconds on Oracle9*i*, centiseconds on prior releases.
hv	✓			Statement ID.
mis		✓		Number of misses upon the library cache.
nam			✓	Name of the wait event.
p		✓		Number of Oracle blocks obtained via operating system read calls.
p1, p2, p3			✓	Information about the wait event; varies by value of nam.
tim	✓	✓		The internal Oracle time at which an event completed.

Oracle Time Units

Oracle9*i* kernels report SQL trace timing statistics in microseconds (1 μs = 0.000 001 seconds). Oracle release 6, 7, and 8 kernels report SQL trace timing statistics in centiseconds (1 cs = 0.01 seconds). Table 5-3 summarizes the unit of measure that the Oracle kernel uses for each type of time statistics in extended SQL trace data.

Table 5-3. Trace file time statistic units by Oracle version

Oracle version	c	e	ela	tim
9	μs	μs	μs	μs
8	cs	cs	cs	cs
7	cs	cs	cs	cs
6	cs	cs	N/A	cs

Table 5-4 explains the meaning of the time units that you will use as an Oracle performance analyst.

Table 5-4. Time units commonly used by computer performance analysts

Unit name	Abbreviation	Duration in seconds (s)		
Second	1 s	1 s	1E-0 s	1. s
Centisecond	1 cs	1/100 s	1E-2 s	0.01 s
Millisecond	1 ms	1/1,000 s	1E-3 s	0.001 s
Microsecond	1 μs	1/1,000,000 s	1E-6 s	0.000 001 s

Response Time Accounting

The Oracle kernel emits two categories of time into a trace file:

1. Time consumed *within* a database call
2. Time consumed *between* database calls

A session's total response time is the sum of all time spent within database calls, plus the sum of all time consumed between database calls. To keep from over- or under-accounting for response time in your trace file, you must know the proper category for each line of your trace file.

Time Within a Database Call

The trace file excerpt in Example 5-3 shows actions that consume time within three different database calls. The first database call to complete was a parse call that consumed 306 μs. The kernel helpfully supplied the PARSING IN CURSOR section before emitting the PARSE line so that you and I can tell what got parsed. Next, the kernel emitted an EXEC line, which means that an execute call completed upon the cursor, consuming an additional 146 μs of elapsed time. The next actions to complete are two operating system read calls denoted on the two WAIT lines. The "parent" operation responsible for issuing these read calls is the fetch call whose statistics are reported on the FETCH line.

Example 5-3. This trace file excerpt demonstrates the consumption of time within three database calls

```
=====================
PARSING IN CURSOR #4 len=132 dep=1 uid=0 oct=3 lid=0 tim=1033064137929238 hv=3111103299
ad='517ba4d8'
select /*+ index(idl_ub1$ i_idl_ub11) +*/ piece#,length,piece from idl_ub1$ where obj#=:1
and part=:2 and version=:3 order by piece#
END OF STMT
PARSE #4:c=0,e=306,p=0,cr=0,cu=0,mis=0,r=0,dep=1,og=4,tim=1033064137929139
EXEC #4:c=0,e=146,p=0,cr=0,cu=0,mis=0,r=0,dep=1,og=4,tim=1033064137931262
```

Example 5-3. This trace file excerpt demonstrates the consumption of time within three database calls (continued)

```
❶  WAIT #4: nam='db file sequential read' ela= 13060 p1=1 p2=53903 p3=1
❷  WAIT #4: nam='db file sequential read' ela= 6978 p1=1 p2=4726 p3=1
❸  FETCH #4:c=0,e=21340,p=2,cr=3,cu=0,mis=0,r=0,dep=1,og=4,tim=1033064137953092
STAT #4 id=1 cnt=0 pid=0 pos=0 obj=72 op='TABLE ACCESS BY INDEX ROWID IDL_UB1$ '
STAT #4 id=2 cnt=0 pid=1 pos=1 obj=120 op='INDEX RANGE SCAN '
```

The lines for the read calls occur in the trace data *before* the line for the fetch that motivated them because the Oracle kernel emits the statistics for an action upon that action's completion. The Oracle kernel instructions that produced these trace lines looked something like this:

```
fetch IDL_UBL$ query
        execute some of the instructions necessary for the IDL_UBL$ fetch
        perform a single-block I/O call upon file 1, block 53903
        emit ❶"WAIT #4: nam='db file sequential read' ela=13060 ..."
        execute some more fetch instructions
        perform a single-block I/O call upon file 1, block 4726
        emit ❷"WAIT #4: nam='db file sequential read' ela=6978 ..."
        execute the remainder of the fetch instructions
        emit ❸"FETCH #4:c=0,e=21340,..."
close the cursor
etc.
```

The fetch call consumed a total elapsed duration of 21,340 μs. The components of the response time for the fetch call are shown in Table 5-5.

Table 5-5. Components of the fetch call response time

Response time	Component
13,060 μs	db file sequential read
6,978 μs	db file sequential read
0 μs	Total CPU
1,302 μs	Unaccounted for
21,340 μs	Total elapsed time for the fetch

The e statistic for a database call is the elapsed duration of the entire database call. Thus, the value of e includes the duration of all CPU time consumed by the call (reported as the value of c), plus all of the elapsed time consumed by wait events executed in the context of the database call (reported as ela values). Figure 5-1 shows the relationship; formally, we write:

$$e \approx c + \sum_{db\ call} ela$$

This is the fundamental relationship of Oracle time statistics within a single database call. The relationship is only approximate because of factors including measurement intrusion effect, quantization error, time spent not executing, and un-instrumented Oracle kernel code segments, which I discuss in Chapter 7.

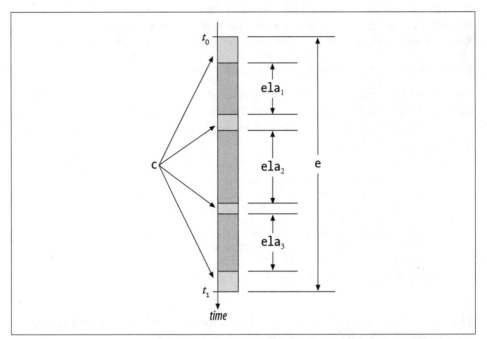

Figure 5-1. The fundamental relationship of Oracle time statistics within a single database call: the total elapsed duration (e) approximately equals the total CPU time for the call (c) plus the sum of the durations of its wait events ($\sum ela$)

Time Between Database Calls

The Oracle kernel also emits elapsed durations for wait events that occur *between* database calls. Examples of wait events that occur between database calls include:

```
SQL*Net message from client
SQL*Net message to client
single-task message
pipe get
rdbms ipc message
pmon timer
smon timer
```

The trace file excerpt in Example 5-4 shows wait events that occur between database calls. The application depicted here makes the scalability-inhibiting mistake of parsing too often. As you can see, the excerpt shows two consecutive parse calls (bold) of the exact same SQL text. The WAIT lines (bold and italic) occur *between* the parse calls both in the sense of where they are located in the trace file and also because the elapsed times of these actions are not tallied into the elapsed time of the second parse call. You can confirm this by noticing that the elapsed duration recorded for the second PARSE line (e=0) is too small to contain the elapsed duration for the SQL*Net message from client event (ela= 3).

Example 5-4. This trace file excerpt demonstrates the consumption of time between two identical parse calls on an Oracle8i system

```
=====================
PARSING IN CURSOR #9 len=360 dep=0 uid=26 oct=2 lid=26 tim=1716466757 hv=2475520707
ad='d4c55480'
INSERT INTO STAGING_AREA (TMSP_LAST_UPDT, OBJECT_RESULT, USER_LAST_UPDT, DOC_OBJ_ID,
TRADE_NAME_ID, LANGUAGE_CODE) values(TO_DATE('11/05/2001 16:39:06', 'MM/DD/YYYY HH24:MI:
SS'), 'if ( exists ( stdphrase ( "PCP_MAV_1" ) ) , langconv ( "Incompatibility With Other
Materials" ) + ":   " , log_omission ( "Materials to Avoid:   " ) )', 'sa', 222, 54213, 'NO_
LANG')
END OF STMT
PARSE #9:c=0,e=0,p=0,cr=0,cu=0,mis=1,r=0,dep=0,og=4,tim=1716466757
WAIT #9: nam='SQL*Net message to client' ela= 0 p1=1413697536 p2=1 p3=0
WAIT #9: nam='SQL*Net message from client' ela= 3 p1=1413697536 p2=1 p3=0
=====================
PARSING IN CURSOR #9 len=360 dep=0 uid=26 oct=2 lid=26 tim=1716466760 hv=2475520707
ad='d4c55480'
INSERT INTO STAGING_AREA (TMSP_LAST_UPDT, OBJECT_RESULT, USER_LAST_UPDT, DOC_OBJ_ID,
TRADE_NAME_ID, LANGUAGE_CODE) values(TO_DATE('11/05/2001 16:39:06', 'MM/DD/YYYY HH24:MI:
SS'), 'if ( exists ( stdphrase ( "PCP_MAV_1" ) ) , langconv ( "Incompatibility With Other
Materials" ) + ":   " , log_omission ( "Materials to Avoid:   " ) )', 'sa', 222, 54213, 'NO_
LANG')
END OF STMT
PARSE #9:c=0,e=0,p=0,cr=0,cu=0,mis=0,r=0,dep=0,og=4,tim=1716466760
```

With this knowledge, you can refine your understanding of the relationship among c, e, and ela statistics for an entire trace file. Given what you've seen so far, total response time for a session equals the total amount of time spent within database calls, plus the total amount of time spent between database calls. We can state this formally as:

$$R = \sum e + \sum_{\substack{between \\ calls}} ela$$

$$\approx \left[\sum c + \sum_{\substack{within \\ calls}} ela \right] + \sum_{\substack{between \\ calls}} ela$$

$$= \sum c + \sum ela$$

However, there is one final complication: the double-counting imposed by the presence of recursive SQL.

Recursive SQL Double-Counting

Recursive SQL is the SQL associated with any database call that has a dep value that is greater than zero. A dep=*n* + 1 database call (for *n* = 0, 1, 2, ...) can be regarded as a child of some dep=*n* database call. Application sessions routinely produce complicated enough trace data to produce a whole forest of relationships among SQL statements that act as each other's parents, children, siblings, and so on. Each SQL trace file contains enough information to enable you to determine the exact parent-child relationships among database calls. To account for a session's response time without double-counting some statistics, you must understand how to determine the recursive relationships among database calls.

Parent-child relationships

The term *recursive* denotes the Oracle kernel's execution of database calls within the context of other database calls. Activities that inspire recursive SQL include execution of DDL statements, execution of PL/SQL blocks with DML statements within them, database call actions with triggers on them, and all sorts of routine application DML statements that motivate data dictionary access. Any database call that can execute another database call can motivate recursive SQL.

Example 5-5 is a trace file excerpt that contains evidence of recursive SQL in action. In this excerpt, you can see information about a new cursor labeled #2, which is associated with the following SQL text:

```
select text from view$ where rowid=:1
```

This SQL text appears nowhere within the source of the application that was traced. This SQL was motivated by the parse of a query from the DBA_OBJECTS view.

Example 5-5. A trace file excerpt containing evidence of recursive SQL. The three cursor #2 actions at dep=1 are recursive children of the dep=0 parse action upon cursor #1

```
====================
❶   PARSING IN CURSOR #2 len=37 dep=1 uid=0 oct=3 lid=0 tim=1033174180230513
hv=1966425544 ad='514bb478'
select text from view$ where rowid=:1
END OF STMT
❷   PARSE #2:c=0,e=107,p=0,cr=0,cu=0,mis=0,r=0,dep=1,og=4,tim=1033174180230481
❸   BINDS #2:
 bind 0: dty=11 mxl=16(16) mal=00 scl=00 pre=00 oacflg=18 oacfl2=1 size=16 offset=0
    bfp=0a22c34c bln=16 avl=16 flg=05
    value=00000AB8.0000.0001
❹   EXEC #2:c=0,e=176,p=0,cr=0,cu=0,mis=0,r=0,dep=1,og=4,tim=1033174180230878
❺   FETCH #2:c=0,e=89,p=0,cr=2,cu=0,mis=0,r=1,dep=1,og=4,tim=1033174180231021
❻   STAT #2 id=1 cnt=1 pid=0 pos=0 obj=62 op='TABLE ACCESS BY USER ROWID VIEW$ '
====================
❼   PARSING IN CURSOR #1 len=85 dep=0 uid=5 oct=3 lid=5 tim=1033174180244680
hv=1205236555 ad='50cafbec'
```

Example 5-5. A trace file excerpt containing evidence of recursive SQL. The three cursor #2 actions at dep=1 are recursive children of the dep=0 parse action upon cursor #1 (continued)

```
select object_id, object_type, owner, object_name from dba_objects where object_id=:v
END OF STMT
❽    PARSE #1:c=10000,e=15073,p=0,cr=2,cu=0,mis=1,r=0,dep=0,og=0,tim=1033174180244662
```

The rule for determining the recursive relationships among database calls is simple:

> A database call with dep=n + 1 is the recursive child of the first subsequent dep=n database call listed in the SQL trace data stream.

Example 5-6 shows by example why this is true. The Oracle kernel can emit trace data for a database call only after the action has completed. (The kernel cannot compute, for example, the call's elapsed time until after the call has completed.) Thus we can reconstruct the sequence of instructions that generated the SQL trace data shown in Example 5-5. Specifically, in this example, all the database calls for the VIEW$ query are recursive children of the parse call for the DBA_OBJECTS query. The indentation levels for procedures in the call stack shown in Example 5-6 highlight the recursive parent-child relationship among database calls.

Example 5-6. This sequence of Oracle kernel instructions emits SQL trace data in the order shown in Example 5-5. In this listing, indentation is proportional to call stack depth

```
parse DBA_OBJECTS query
    # query VIEW$ to obtain the definition of DBA_OBJECTS
    parse VIEW$ query
        # execute the instructions necessary for the VIEW$ parse
        emit ❶"PARSING IN CURSOR #2 ..."
        emit ❷"PARSE #2: ..."
    bind to the VIEW$ cursor
        # execute the instructions necessary for the VIEW$ bind
        emit ❸"BINDS #2: ..."
    execute the VIEW$ cursor
        # execute the instructions necessary for the VIEW$ exec
        emit ❹"EXEC #2: ..."
    fetch from the VIEW$ cursor
        # execute the instructions necessary for the VIEW$ fetch
        emit ❺"FETCH #2: ..."
    close the VIEW$ cursor
        # execute the instructions necessary for the VIEW$ close
        emit ❻"STAT #2: ..."
    # execute the remaining instructions for the DBA_OBJECTS parse
    emit ❼"PARSING IN CURSOR #1 ..."
    emit ❽"PARSE #1: ..."
```

Figure 5-2 shows a graphical representation of the parent-child relationships among the database calls.

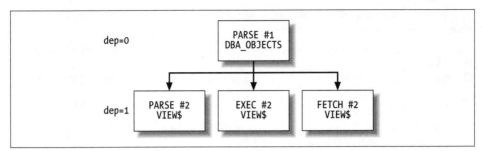

Figure 5-2. The recursive call stack for Example 5-5 expressed graphically

Recursive statistics

In Oracle releases through at least Oracle9*i* Release 2, a database call's c, e, p, cr, and cu statistics contain an aggregation of the resources consumed by the database call itself and its entire recursive progeny.

> A database call's *recursive progeny* consists of all recursive descendants of the database call, including children, grandchildren, great-grandchildren, and so on.

Figure 5-3 illustrates such a relationship for a fictional set of database calls. Each node (rectangle) in the graph represents a database call (e.g., a PARSE, EXEC, or FETCH). A directed line from some node *A* to another node *B* denotes that database call *A* is a recursive parent (that is, the *caller*) of database call *B*. The cr=*n* listed inside the node is the statistic that the Oracle kernel will emit for the database call. The value of cr_{self} is the number of consistent-mode reads executed by the database call itself, exclusive of its children's call counts.

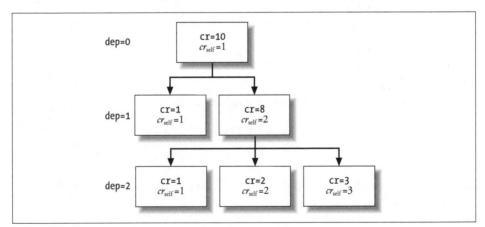

Figure 5-3. Each of a database call's c, e, p, cr, and cu statistics is an aggregation of consumption on that statistic for that database call's entire recursive family tree

The kernel emits only the progeny-inclusive statistics, but from these statistics you can derive the progeny-exclusive statistics shown inside the nodes. For example, if the numbers inside the nodes in Figure 5-3 had been omitted, it would be easy to fill them in. Each node's value is simply the statistic value for that node minus the sum of the statistic values reported for that node's direct descendants. The value of a node at dep=k is thus the cr value reported for that database call minus the sum of the cr values of its dep=k + 1 descendants. Or, to generalize, we can say that the quantity s of a resource consumed by a database call at dep=k is:

$$s = \mathsf{s}_k - \sum_{children} \mathsf{s}_{k+1},$$

where s_i is the value of a statistic in the set {c, e, p, cr, cu} reported by the Oracle kernel at recursive depth i.

You can use this technique easily enough on real trace data. Again consider the database calls described in Example 5-5. Figure 5-4 illustrates the progeny-inclusive elapsed time value for each database call (denoted e) and the progeny-exclusive elapsed time contribution for each database call (denoted e_{self}).

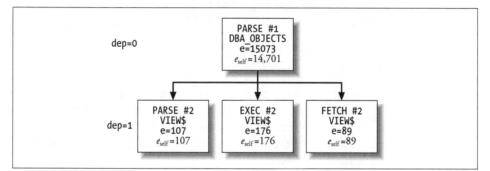

Figure 5-4. The recursive call stack for Example 5-5 expressed graphically

Table 5-6 shows all the progeny-exclusive statistics associated with each database call in Example 5-5. The progeny-exclusive contribution to elapsed time for the PARSE #1 database call, for example, is:

$$e = \mathsf{e}_0 - \sum_{children} \mathsf{e}_1$$
$$= 15,073 - (107 + 176 + 89)$$
$$= 14,701$$

Table 5-6. The c, e, p, cr, and cu statistics for a cursor include that cursor's activity by itself plus the activity of all of its recursive children. You can derive a cursor's individual activity by using subtraction

Resources consumed by…	c	e	p	cr	cu
PARSE #1, including its recursive progeny	10,000	15,073	0	2	0
PARSE #2, a child	0	107	0	0	0
EXEC #2, a child	0	176	0	0	0
FETCH #2, a child	0	89	0	2	0
PARSE #1 excluding its recursive progeny	10,000	14,701	0	0	0

Now we have enough information to complete the response time accounting formula. When we eliminate the double-counting influences of recursive SQL, we have, finally:

$$R = \sum_{dep=0} e + \sum_{\substack{between \\ calls}} ela$$

$$\approx \left[\sum_{dep=0} c + \sum_{\substack{within \\ calls}} ela \right] + \sum_{\substack{between \\ calls}} ela$$

$$= \sum_{dep=0} c + \sum ela$$

That is, the total response time for a trace file approximately equals the sum of the file's e values for database calls at recursive depth zero, plus the sum of the file's ela values for wait events that occur between database calls. A file's total response time approximately equals the sum of the file's c values for database calls at depth zero, plus the sum of all the file's ela values.

Evolution of the Response Time Model

In the 1980s, when most of today's "tuning methods" were invented, Oracle's SQL trace facility did not yet have the capability to emit wait event timing information—the WAIT lines—into the trace file. The c, e, and tim data were the only trace data elements that we had. Of course, if most of an application's response time had been spent consuming CPU, then the c and e data told us most of what we needed to know about the performance of our database calls. However, if some of a database call's response time was *not* due to CPU consumption, then our analysis became more difficult.

For example, consider the following fetch call statistics obtained from an application running on Oracle 8.1.7.2:

```
FETCH #1:c=80741,e=151841,p=9628,cr=34304348,cu=10,mis=0,r=0,dep=0,og=4,tim=87762034
```

This fetch call consumed 1,518.41 seconds of elapsed time, only 807.41 of which was spent on the CPU. Where did the other 711.00 seconds of response time go? Was it latch contention? Enqueue waits? Long disk queues? Excessive paging? We simply cannot know by looking at this FETCH line. Its statistics contain insufficient information to determine where the unaccounted-for 711 seconds of elapsed time went. Certainly, a large p value is a clue that some of the unaccounted-for e time might have been consumed by OS read calls, but there are roughly 200 different wait events that Oracle could have executed during those 711 seconds. From viewing only the fetch statistics shown here, we *cannot know* how the 711 seconds were consumed.

In 1992 with the release of kernel Version 7.0.12, Oracle Corporation published an elegant solution to this problem. The new mechanism that Oracle provided was simply to instrument several events executed by the Oracle kernel that consume elapsed time but not CPU capacity. The value of the so-called wait data is absolutely extraordinary. It helps to fill in the time gap between e and c. Anjo Kolk and Shari Yamaguchi were the first to document the use of "wait data" in the document that became the landmark *YAPP Method* [Kolk and Yamaguchi (1999)].

Let's revisit our previous example, in which we had 711 seconds of unaccounted-for time. Instructing the Oracle kernel to produce the WAIT statistics adds 9,748 more lines of data to our trace file before the fetch call. Executing the Perl program in Example 5-7 upon 9,749 lines of trace data produces the following resource profile:

```
$ prof-cid waits.1.trc
  Duration    Pct  Oracle kernel event
  --------- ------  ----------------------------------------
   807.41s  53.2%  total CPU
   426.26s  28.1%  direct path write
   197.29s  13.0%  db file sequential read
    76.23s   5.0%  unaccounted-for
     8.28s   0.5%  latch free
     2.87s   0.2%  db file scattered read
     0.05s   0.0%  file open
     0.02s   0.0%  buffer busy waits
     0.00s   0.0%  SQL*Net message to client
  --------- ------  ----------------------------------------
  1518.41s 100.0%  Total response time
```

Now we know. Over 53% of the response time for the fetch was consumed on a CPU in user mode. Over 28% was consumed *writing* (surprise!) to disk. Another 13% was consumed by reading from disk, and roughly another 6% of the response time was consumed in various other wait events.

Example 5-7. A Perl program that creates a resource profile from raw SQL trace data for a single, simple Oracle database call (with no associated recursive database calls)

```
#!/usr/bin/perl

# $Header: /home/cvs/cvm-book1/sqltrace/prof-cid.pl,v 1.4 2003/03/20 23:32:32 cvm Exp $
# Cary Millsap (cary.millsap@hotsos.com)
```

Example 5-7. A Perl program that creates a resource profile from raw SQL trace data for a single,
simple Oracle database call (with no associated recursive database calls) (continued)

```
# Copyright (c) 1999-2003 by Hotsos Enterprises, Ltd. All rights reserved.

# Create a resource profile for a single database call.
# Usage: $0 file.trc

# Requires input of Oracle extended SQL trace data (level 8 or level 12)
# that has been pre-filtered to contain only a single database call (that
# is, a single PARSE, EXEC, FETCH, UNMAP, or SORT UNMAP with no recursive
# children) and the WAIT lines associated with that db call. Example input
# file content:
#
#   WAIT #2: nam='db file sequential read' ela= 0 p1=2 p2=3240 p3=1 WAIT
#   #2: nam='db file sequential read' ela= 0 p1=2 p2=3239 p3=1 FETCH
#   #2:c=213,e=998,p=2039,cr=100550,cu=5,mis=0,r=0,dep=0,og=4,tim=85264276

use strict;
use warnings;
my $cid;            # cursor id
my %ela;            # $ela{event} contains sum of ela statistics for event
my $sum_ela = 0;    # sum of all ela times across events
my $r = 0;          # response time for database call
my $action = "(?:PARSE|EXEC|FETCH|UNMAP|SORT UNMAP)";
while (<>) {
    if (/^WAIT #(\d+): nam='([^']*)' ela=\s*(\d+)/i) {
        $ela{$2} += $3;
        $sum_ela += $3;
    }
    elsif (/^$action #(\d+):c=(\d+),e=(\d+)/i) {
        $ela{"total CPU"} += $2;
        $r = $3;
    }
    if (!defined $cid) {
        $cid = $1;
    } else {
        die "can't mix data across cursor ids $cid and $1" if $1 != $cid;
    }
}
$ela{"unaccounted-for"} = $r - ($ela{"total CPU"} + $sum_ela);
printf "%9s  %6s  %-40s\n", "Duration", "Pct", "Oracle kernel event";
printf "%8s-  %5s-  %-40s\n", "-"x8, "-"x5, "-"x40;
printf "%8.2fs  %5.1f%%  %-40s\n", $ela{$_}/100, $ela{$_}/$r*100, $_ for sort { $ela{$b}
<=> $ela{$a} } keys %ela;
printf "%8s-  %5s-  %-40s\n", "-"x8, "-"x5, "-"x40;
printf "%8.2fs  %5.1f%%  %-40s\n", $r/100, 100, "Total response time";
```

Note the row labeled "unaccounted-for" in our resource profile. Consider how it was
computed. The total elapsed time—in fact the *response time*—for the fetch call is
simply the value of e for the fetch. The raw trace data account for this response time
in two ways:

- The total CPU time component of the fetch call's response time is recorded as the c statistic on the FETCH line itself.
- The system-call time components of the response time are recorded as ela statistics on all of the WAIT lines associated with the fetch.

The "unaccounted-for" duration is thus the leftover amount Δ (delta) expressed in the following formula:

$$e = c + \sum_{db\ call} ela + \Delta$$

How Oracle response time accounting has evolved since Oracle Version 6 is an interesting story. In Version 6, Oracle's SQL trace facility printed database call response times (e) and CPU consumptions (c) to the trace file, but that was the *only* response time data that the Oracle kernel published. The first Oracle response time model was simple. It was "response time equals CPU consumption plus some unidentified other stuff," or:

$$e = c + \Delta$$

This model is effective when Δ is small, but it is not reliable for diagnosing many types of response time problems that occur when Δ is large. In the Version 6 days, most analysts were taught to assume that large values of Δ were attributable to time consumed by operating system read calls. This assumption is often incorrect (as was the case in the resource profile shown previously), but it has helped analysts solve many application performance problems. One reason for the model's success in spite of its over-simplicity is that so many Oracle application problems are caused by fetch calls that access the database buffer cache excessively. These cases create small Δ values for which the $e = c + \Delta$ model works just fine.

Oracle kernel developers were among the first to encounter the most serious inadequacies of the model. The range of potential root causes for large Δ values was so large that some important high-end response time problems simply could not be solved without more operational data. Oracle's *extended* SQL trace data, introduced to the general market in 1992 with release 7.0.12, is an elegant solution to the problem. Extended SQL trace data include those WAIT lines that tell us how much time the Oracle kernel spends "waiting" for the execution of key events. The new, significantly improved response time model made possible by the new extended SQL trace feature of Oracle release 7.0.12 is the one that we use today:

$$e = c + \sum_{db\ call} ela + \Delta$$

As it happens, extended SQL trace data provide significantly more diagnostic power than most analysts have ever believed. Of the few analysts who even realize that the gap Δ exists, some deem the existence of the gap a deficiency of extended SQL trace data that renders the data unreliable. On the contrary, as you shall see, there is good information buried in the value of Δ. There are several contributory causes of non-zero Δ values, as I explain in Chapter 7. Understanding these causes helps you exploit the full diagnostic power of Oracle's extended SQL trace data.

Walking the Clock

As you try to extract response time information from raw trace data, you'll need to be able to interpret the time sequence of events using a process we call "walking the clock." Walking the clock requires a few pieces of knowledge about how the Oracle kernel manages time data:

- The value of a line's tim field is the approximate time at which the action represented by that line *completed*.

- A database call's e field value contains the total elapsed time consumed by that action. This value includes both the CPU time consumed by the action (the value of the c field) and the time consumed by events executed during the course of the action (the sum of the appropriate ela field values).

- Recursive SQL causes double-counting. That is, the value of a database call's e field when dep=n + 1 is already included in the subsequent e value for which dep=n.

- Don't expect perfection from clock walks. Off-by-one errors are common in Oracle8i trace files. Errors of seemingly much greater magnitude are common in Oracle9i trace files; however, with the microsecond timing resolution of Oracle9i, the errors are smaller than they look.

Oracle Release 8 and Prior

Here is an example of some trace data that will demonstrate how to walk the clock through trace files emitted by Oracle8i and prior kernels:

```
EXEC #13:c=0,e=0,p=0,cr=0,cu=0,mis=0,r=0,dep=2,og=3,tim=198360834
FETCH #13:c=0,e=0,p=0,cr=3,cu=0,mis=0,r=1,dep=2,og=3,tim=198360834
EXEC #12:c=2,e=4,p=0,cr=27,cu=0,mis=0,r=0,dep=1,og=4,tim=198360837
FETCH #12:c=2,e=10,p=10,cr=19,cu=4,mis=0,r=1,dep=1,og=4,tim=198360847
```

Table 5-7 shows the associated clock-walk.

Table 5-7. Walking the tim clock for Oracle8i database calls

Line (k)	e	Predicted $tim_k = tim_{k-1} + e_k$	Actual tim_k	Error
1	0		198360834	
2	0	198360834 + 0 = 198360834	198360834	0
3	4	198360834 + 4 = 198360838	198360837	1
4	10	198360837 + 10 = 198360847	198360847	0

Occasionally, there'll be an off-by-one error such as the one that distinguishes the predicted *tim* value in line 3 from the actual *tim* value found there. Don't let a ±1-cs error disturb you. Oracle8*i* kernels round their time values to the nearest centisecond, so what appeared to be the addition of ...834 + 4 might actually have been the addition of ...833.7048 + 3.5827, which after rounding would have produced the observed value of ...837.

The following Oracle8*i* trace file excerpt contains database calls and wait events:

```
PARSE #494:c=4,e=5,p=11,cr=88,cu=0,mis=1,r=0,dep=2,og=0,tim=3864619462
WAIT #494: nam='latch free' ela= 2 p1=-2147434220 p2=95 p3=0
WAIT #494: nam='latch free' ela= 2 p1=-2147434220 p2=95 p3=1
EXEC #494:c=0,e=4,p=0,cr=0,cu=0,mis=0,r=0,dep=2,og=4,tim=3864619466
FETCH #494:c=0,e=0,p=0,cr=2,cu=0,mis=0,r=1,dep=2,og=4,tim=3864619466
```

Table 5-8 shows the clock-walk of these lines. In the walk for this excerpt, notice that I've assigned *k* labels only to database call lines (not the WAIT lines). It's okay to track the anticipated progress of the *tim* clock during wait events, but remember that the *e* value in a database call already includes the time recorded in *ela* values for wait events motivated by the database call. Therefore, the basis for predicting a tim_k value for a database call is always the tim_{k-1} from the prior database call line.

Table 5-8. Walking the tim clock for Oracle8i database calls and wait events

Line (k)	e	Predicted $tim_k = tim_{k-1} + e_k$	Actual tim_k	Error
1	5		3864619462	
	2	3864619462 + 2 = 3864619464		
	2	3864619464 + 2 = 3864619466		
2	4	3864619462 + 4 = 3864619466	3864619466	0
3	0	3864619466 + 0 = 3864619466	3864619466	0

Now for a tricky excerpt to make sure that you're paying attention. Can you explain why the actual *tim* value of 198360796 in the EXEC #8 line is so different from the value you might have expected, 198360795 + 19 = 198360814?

```
EXEC #9:c=0,e=0,p=0,cr=0,cu=0,mis=0,r=0,dep=2,og=3,tim=198360795
FETCH #9:c=0,e=0,p=0,cr=3,cu=0,mis=0,r=1,dep=2,og=3,tim=198360795
EXEC #9:c=0,e=0,p=0,cr=0,cu=0,mis=0,r=0,dep=2,og=3,tim=198360795
FETCH #9:c=0,e=0,p=0,cr=3,cu=0,mis=0,r=1,dep=2,og=3,tim=198360795
EXEC #8:c=4,e=19,p=16,cr=162,cu=0,mis=0,r=0,dep=1,og=4,tim=198360796
FETCH #8:c=0,e=5,p=4,cr=4,cu=0,mis=0,r=1,dep=1,og=4,tim=198360801
FETCH #8:c=0,e=0,p=0,cr=0,cu=0,mis=0,r=0,dep=1,og=0,tim=198360801
FETCH #7:c=0,e=0,p=0,cr=2,cu=0,mis=0,r=1,dep=1,og=4,tim=198360801
EXEC #8:c=0,e=0,p=0,cr=0,cu=0,mis=0,r=0,dep=1,og=4,tim=198360801
```

The answer is that the EXEC #8 database call is the dep=1 recursive parent of each of the dep=2 actions shown here on cursor #9. Therefore, the e=19 field contains all of the cursor #9 e values shown here plus some other time-consuming activities that

are *not* shown here. The EXEC #8 action probably began very near *tim* 198360796 −
19 = 198369777. Between *tim* values ...777 and ...796, lots of dep=2 actions took
place, each consuming time while the tim clock advanced. But remember, these
dep=2 actions all took place *during* the single EXEC #8 action.

Oracle Release 9

The microsecond output resolution of time statistics in Oracle9*i* is a helpful enhancement. The first thing you'll notice about SQL trace data when you upgrade to
Oracle9*i* is that the microsecond resolution feature provides real data for cases in
which Oracle8*i* would have emitted lots of zero values.

> However, do not hesitate to use extended SQL trace data with Version
> 8 or even Version 7 systems. The optimization method described in this
> book *does* work reliably for diagnostic data expressed in centiseconds.
> In the vast majority of real-life performance improvement projects, the
> microsecond output resolution of Oracle9*i* is merely a luxury.

The new resolution has allowed us to see a little more clearly into the Oracle kernel's behavior. This section describes a few cases in which we've been able to learn
more as a result of the Oracle kernel's improved output resolution.

Walking the clock in Oracle9*i* trace files requires a little more patience. The first difference you'll notice is that the numbers are all so much larger that it's quite a bit
more difficult to do the walk in your head. For example:

```
EXEC #1:c=0,e=1863,p=0,cr=0,cu=0,mis=0,r=0,dep=1,og=4,tim=1017039275956134
FETCH #1:c=0,e=2566,p=0,cr=23,cu=0,mis=0,r=1,dep=1,og=4,tim=1017039275958821
FETCH #1:c=0,e=50,p=0,cr=0,cu=0,mis=0,r=1,dep=1,og=4,tim=1017039275959013
FETCH #1:c=0,e=34,p=0,cr=0,cu=0,mis=0,r=1,dep=1,og=4,tim=1017039275959155
FETCH #1:c=0,e=34,p=0,cr=0,cu=0,mis=0,r=1,dep=1,og=4,tim=1017039275959293
FETCH #1:c=0,e=35,p=0,cr=0,cu=0,mis=0,r=1,dep=1,og=4,tim=1017039275959433
```

The next thing that you might notice is that the numbers don't add up. Observe the
large numbers that show up in the "Error" column of Table 5-9.

*Table 5-9. Walking the tim clock for Oracle9i database calls. Notice the apparently large error
values, but remember that the errors here are actually quite small because they're expressed in
microseconds*

Line (*k*)	*e*	Predicted $tim_k = tim_{k-1} + e_k$	Actual tim_k	Error
1	1863		...956134	
2	2566	...956134 + 2566 = ...958700	...958821	−121
3	50	...958821 + 50 = ...958871	...959013	−142
4	34	...959013 + 34 = ...959047	...959155	−108
5	34	...959155 + 34 = ...959189	...959293	−104
6	35	...959293 + 35 = ...959328	...959433	−105

The sensation produced by these large error values is quite horrific until you realize that the errors are expressed in microseconds. Small time gap errors like this have always been present in Oracle diagnostic data. They were usually invisible when measured with centisecond resolution. When we view microsecond timing data, the impact of another type of response time measurement error becomes apparent: the calls to gettimeofday and getrusage consume elapsed time that the calls themselves do not measure (see the Chapter 7 discussion of the *measurement intrusion effect*).

In Oracle9i trace files, you might notice the "disturbing" fact that not all trace lines are listed in ascending time order. Specifically, the tim value for a PARSING IN CURSOR section always occurs in the future relative to the tim value of the database call immediately following the PARSING IN CURSOR section. For example:

```
PARSING IN CURSOR #1 len=32 dep=0 uid=5 oct=42 lid=5 tim=1033050389206593
hv=1197935484 ad='50f93654'
alter session set sql_trace=true
END OF STMT
EXEC #1:c=0,e=33,p=0,cr=0,cu=0,mis=0,r=0,dep=0,og=4,tim=1033050389204497
```

You can confirm why this occurs by tracing the wait events of an Oracle kernel process with strace or a similar tool. The Oracle kernel finishes processing the EXEC call before it begins computing the information for the PARSING IN CURSOR section. But then the kernel *prints* the PARSING IN CURSOR section before it prints the EXEC line. Hence, the times appear out of order.

You'll find that the Oracle8i kernel does things in this order as well. You just didn't notice, because the centisecond statistics emitted by Oracle8i in most cases concealed the true time sequence information from you. With the microsecond statistics emitted by Oracle9i, the order becomes apparent.

Clock Walk Formulas

After having seen a few clock-walk examples, you have probably caught onto the formula. As long as you remember not to double-count in the presence of different levels of recursive database calls, then the values of the tim and e fields bear the following relationship:

$$tim_{k+1} \approx tim_k + e_{k+1}$$

That is, the following line's tim field value is approximately this line's tim field value plus the following line's e field value. Equivalently, you can write:

$$tim_k \approx tim_{k+1} - e_{k+1}$$

That is, the current line's tim field value approximately equals the following line's tim field value minus the following line's e field value.

Of course, a WAIT line has no tim field, so if you want to estimate what a WAIT line's *tim* value would be, you have to estimate it by walking the clock forward from the most recently available *tim* value, using the relationship:

$$tim_{k+1} \approx tim_k + ela_{k+1}$$

These formulas will come in handy when you learn how to correct for data collection error in Chapter 7.

Forward Attribution

When you identify a time-consuming wait event in an Oracle extended SQL trace file, your next task will be to determine which application action you might modify to reduce the time consumption. Doing this with extended SQL trace data is straightforward. You should attribute each WAIT #*n* duration to the first database call for cursor #*n* that *follows* the WAIT line in the trace file. I call this method *forward attribution*. Forward attribution helps you accurately identify which application SQL is responsible for motivating the wait time. Perhaps remarkably, forward attribution works both for events that are executed *within* database calls and for events that are executed *between* database calls.

Forward Attribution for Within-Call Events

For events executed *within* database calls, the reason for forward attribution is easy to understand. Because lines are written to the trace file as their corresponding actions complete, the wait events executed by a given database call appear in the trace stream *before* the call's trace file line. The following excerpt (snipped from Example 5-3) shows how the Oracle kernel emits within-call event lines:

```
=====================
PARSING IN CURSOR #4 len=132 dep=1 uid=0 oct=3 lid=0 tim=1033064137929238
hv=3111103299 ad='517ba4d8'
select /*+ index(idl_ub1$ i_idl_ub11) +*/ piece#,length,piece from idl_ub1$ where
obj#=:1 and part=:2 and version=:3 order by piece#
END OF STMT
PARSE #4:c=0,e=306,p=0,cr=0,cu=0,mis=0,r=0,dep=1,og=4,tim=1033064137929139
EXEC #4:c=0,e=146,p=0,cr=0,cu=0,mis=0,r=0,dep=1,og=4,tim=1033064137931262
```
❶ `WAIT #4: nam='db file sequential read' ela= 13060 p1=1 p2=53903 p3=1`
❷ `WAIT #4: nam='db file sequential read' ela= 6978 p1=1 p2=4726 p3=1`
❸ `FETCH #4:c=0,e=21340,p=2,cr=3,cu=0,mis=0,r=0,dep=1,og=4,tim=1033064137953092`

In this example, the db file sequential read events on lines ❶ and ❷ were executed within the context of the FETCH depicted on line ❸.

Forward Attribution for Between-Call Events

For events executed *between* database calls, the reason that forward attribution works is more subtle. The following Oracle8*i* example (snipped from Example 5-4) helps to illustrate the issue. Because of a database driver deficiency, this application actually submitted each parse call to the database *two* times.* Notice the identical PARSING IN CURSOR sections separated by a to/from SQL*Net message pair:

```
=====================
PARSING IN CURSOR #9 len=360 dep=0 uid=26 oct=2 lid=26 tim=1716466757 hv=2475520707
ad='d4c55480'
INSERT INTO STAGING_AREA (TMSP_LAST_UPDT, OBJECT_RESULT, USER_LAST_UPDT, DOC_OBJ_ID,
TRADE_NAME_ID, LANGUAGE_CODE) values(TO_DATE('11/05/2001 16:39:06', 'MM/DD/YYYY HH24:
MI:SS'), 'if ( exists ( stdphrase ( "PCP_MAV_1" ) ) , langconv ( "Incompatibility
With Other Materials" ) + ":  " , log_omission ( "Materials to Avoid:  " ) )', 'sa',
222, 54213, 'NO_LANG')
END OF STMT
PARSE #9:c=0,e=0,p=0,cr=0,cu=0,mis=1,r=0,dep=0,og=4,tim=1716466757
```
❶ `WAIT #9: nam='SQL*Net message to client' ela= 0 p1=1413697536 p2=1 p3=0`
❷ `WAIT #9: nam='SQL*Net message from client' ela= 3 p1=1413697536 p2=1 p3=0`
```
=====================
PARSING IN CURSOR #9 len=360 dep=0 uid=26 oct=2 lid=26 tim=1716466760 hv=2475520707
ad='d4c55480'
INSERT INTO STAGING_AREA (TMSP_LAST_UPDT, OBJECT_RESULT, USER_LAST_UPDT, DOC_OBJ_ID,
TRADE_NAME_ID, LANGUAGE_CODE) values(TO_DATE('11/05/2001 16:39:06', 'MM/DD/YYYY HH24:
MI:SS'), 'if ( exists ( stdphrase ( "PCP_MAV_1" ) ) , langconv ( "Incompatibility
With Other Materials" ) + ":  " , log_omission ( "Materials to Avoid:  " ) )', 'sa',
222, 54213, 'NO_LANG')
END OF STMT
```
❸ `PARSE #9:c=0,e=0,p=0,cr=0,cu=0,mis=0,r=0,dep=0,og=4,tim=1716466760`

Even though the parse calls were routinely inexpensive (note the two e=0 durations highlighted in the example), the response time for the overall user action suffered brutally from the tremendous number of unnecessary SQL*Net message from client executions, which consumed an average of over 0.027 seconds per call. The overall impact to response time was several minutes on a user action that should have consumed less than 10 seconds in total (see "Case 3: Large SQL*Net Event Duration" in Chapter 12). To eliminate the SQL*Net event executions shown on lines ❶ and ❷, you can eliminate the parse call depicted on line ❸ that follows it. In general, the database call that has "caused" a between-call event is the database call whose trace file line follows the WAIT.

---

* Lots of drivers provide an option to behave this way. The extra parse is used to produce a "describe" of the SQL being parsed, so that the driver can produce more informative error messages for the developer. Even the Perl DBI behaves this way by default. In Perl, you can deactivate this behavior by specifying the ora_check_sql=>0 attribute in prepare calls.

Detailed Trace File Walk-Through

At the beginning of this chapter, I promised you a detailed walk-through of the trace file displayed in Example 5-2. Now it is time for the full tour.

Each SQL trace file begins with a preamble that describes information about the file such as the file name, the Oracle release, and various elements describing the system environment and the session being traced. Here is the preamble from Example 5-2:

```
/u01/oradata/admin/V901/udump/ora_9178.trc
Oracle9i Enterprise Edition Release 9.0.1.0.0 - Production
With the Partitioning option
JServer Release 9.0.1.0.0 - Production
ORACLE_HOME = /u01/oradata/app/9.0.1
System name:    Linux
Node name:  research
Release:    2.4.4-4GB
Version:    #1 Fri May 18 14:11:12 GMT 2001
Machine:    i686
Instance name: V901
Redo thread mounted by this instance: 1
Oracle process number: 9
Unix process pid: 9178, image: oracle@research (TNS V1-V3)
```

After the preamble, the Oracle kernel emitted information that identifies the time and the session at which the first trace line was emitted:

```
*** SESSION ID:(7.6692) 2002-12-03 10:07:40.051
```

The next line reveals information about the module and action names that were set with DBMS_APPLICATION_INFO by the client program, which in my case was SQL*Plus:

```
APPNAME mod='SQL*Plus' mh=3669949024 act='' ah=4029777240
```

The first actual action that the kernel recorded in the trace file was the execution of the ALTER SESSION command. The kernel did not emit information about the parse of the ALTER SESSION command, because tracing wasn't enabled until after the parse had completed. Conveniently, the Oracle kernel emitted a section describing the cursor being acted upon by the execute call, before it emitted the information about the EXEC call itself. The execute call did very little work. The e=1 string indicates that the call consumed only 1 microsecond (1 μs = 0.000 001 seconds) of elapsed time.

```
=====================
PARSING IN CURSOR #1 len=69 dep=0 uid=5 oct=42 lid=5 tim=1038931660052098
hv=1509700594 ad='50d6d560'
alter session set events '10046 trace name context forever, level 12'
END OF STMT
EXEC #1:c=0,e=1,p=0,cr=0,cu=0,mis=0,r=0,dep=0,og=4,tim=1038931660051673
```

When the execution of the ALTER SESSION command completed, the Oracle kernel shipped the result back to the client program by writing to a socket controlled by the SQL*Net driver. The elapsed duration of this write call was 5 μs.

```
WAIT #1: nam='SQL*Net message to client' ela= 5 p1=1650815232 p2=1 p3=0
```

Upon completing the write call, the Oracle kernel issued a read upon the same socket (note that the p1 values for both the write and the read are the same), and the kernel awaited the next request from its client program. Approximately 1,262 µs after issuing the read call, the read call returned with another request for the kernel.

```
WAIT #1: nam='SQL*Net message from client' ela= 1262 p1=1650815232 p2=1 p3=0
```

The request received by the read of the socket was in fact the instruction to parse my "Hello, world" query. Note that before printing the PARSE statistics, the kernel helpfully emitted a section beginning with a sequence of "=" characters and ending with the string END OF STMT that describes the cursor being parsed. The parse call itself consumed 214 µs of elapsed time.

```
=====================
PARSING IN CURSOR #1 len=51 dep=0 uid=5 oct=3 lid=5 tim=1038931660054075
hv=1716247018 ad='50c551f8'
select 'Hello, world; today is '||sysdate from dual
END OF STMT
PARSE #1:c=0,e=214,p=0,cr=0,cu=0,mis=0,r=0,dep=0,og=4,tim=1038931660054053
```

The next database call is EXEC, which denotes the execution of the cursor that the kernel had parsed. Immediately preceding the EXEC line is an empty BINDS section, which indicates that although the SQL*Plus program requested a bind operation, there was nothing in the statement for the kernel *to* bind. Total elapsed time for the execution: 124 µs.

```
BINDS #1:
EXEC #1:c=0,e=124,p=0,cr=0,cu=0,mis=0,r=0,dep=0,og=4,tim=1038931660054311
```

At the conclusion of the EXEC call, the kernel shipped a result back to the client program (that is, the SQL*Plus program). The write to the socket consumed 5 µs of elapsed time.

```
WAIT #1: nam='SQL*Net message to client' ela= 5 p1=1650815232 p2=1 p3=0
```

Immediately following the write to the socket, the kernel's next action was a fetch operation. The FETCH statistics show an elapsed duration of 177 µs to return one row (r=1), which required three reads of the database buffer cache, one in consistent mode (cr=1) and two in current mode (cu=2).

```
FETCH #1:c=0,e=177,p=0,cr=1,cu=2,mis=0,r=1,dep=0,og=4,tim=1038931660054596
```

The next database call recorded in the trace file is another fetch, which took place after a 499-µs read from the SQL*Net socket. The fetch returned no rows and consumed only 2 µs of elapsed time.

```
WAIT #1: nam='SQL*Net message from client' ela= 499 p1=1650815232 p2=1 p3=0
FETCH #1:c=0,e=2,p=0,cr=0,cu=0,mis=0,r=0,dep=0,og=0,tim=1038931660055374
```

Next, the kernel shipped a result back to the client in a socket write operation that consumed 4 µs of elapsed time.

```
WAIT #1: nam='SQL*Net message to client' ela= 4 p1=1650815232 p2=1 p3=0
```

After shipping back the fetch result to the client, the kernel sat idle awaiting its next request. It didn't wait long. Only 1,261 μs after initiating the SQL*Net socket read, the read call was complete.

```
WAIT #1: nam='SQL*Net message from client' ela= 1261 p1=1650815232 p2=1 p3=0
```

The instruction that the read call delivered to the kernel resulted in the closing of the "Hello, world" cursor and finally the end of the read-only transaction. Upon cursor close, the kernel helpfully emitted a STAT line that indicates the execution plan that the query optimizer had chosen for executing my query. In this case, my query had motivated a full-table scan of DUAL.

```
STAT #1 id=1 cnt=1 pid=0 pos=0 obj=221 op='TABLE ACCESS FULL DUAL '
XCTEND rlbk=0, rd_only=1
```

As you can see, the Oracle kernel did quite a bit of work to fulfill the requirements of even my trivial SQL*Plus session. For performance problems on real-life systems, you can imagine the significant leap in trace file complexity. But even this simple example shows some of the actions that occur *within* database calls and some of the actions that occur *between* database calls. These actions are the building blocks that comprise the much larger and more complex trace files that you'll encounter in real life.

Exercises

1. In Example 5-8, which WAIT lines refer to wait events made *within* database calls, and which refer to wait events made *between* database calls? Describe how each c, e, and ela statistic shown fits into the relationship $e \approx c + \sum ela$.

Example 5-8. Extended SQL trace data file excerpt

```
...
Many WAIT #1 lines are omitted for clarity
...
=====================
PARSING IN CURSOR #1 len=253 dep=0 uid=18 oct=3 lid=18 tim=1024427939516845 hv=1223272015
ad='80cbc5b8'
...
SQL text is omitted for clarity
...
END OF STMT
PARSE #1:c=60000,e=55973,p=3,cr=44,cu=6,mis=1,r=0,dep=0,og=4,tim=1024427939516823
EXEC #1:c=0,e=140,p=0,cr=0,cu=0,mis=0,r=0,dep=0,og=4,tim=1024427939517471
WAIT #1: nam='SQL*Net message to client' ela= 15 p1=1650815232 p2=1 p3=0
WAIT #1: nam='db file sequential read' ela= 678 p1=7 p2=11146 p3=1
WAIT #1: nam='db file sequential read' ela= 815 p1=7 p2=11274 p3=1
FETCH #1:c=200000,e=259460,p=2,cr=12,cu=24,mis=0,r=1,dep=0,og=4,tim=1024427939777318
WAIT #1: nam='SQL*Net message from client' ela= 1450 p1=1650815232 p2=1 p3=0
WAIT #1: nam='SQL*Net message to client' ela= 5 p1=1650815232 p2=1 p3=0
FETCH #1:c=0,e=339,p=0,cr=0,cu=0,mis=0,r=12,dep=0,og=4,tim=1024427939779621
```

Example 5-8. Extended SQL trace data file excerpt (continued)

```
WAIT #1: nam='SQL*Net message from client' ela= 7828 p1=1650815232 p2=1 p3=0
...
STAT lines are omitted for clarity

...
=====================
PARSING IN CURSOR #1 len=55 dep=0 uid=18 oct=42 lid=18 tim=1024427939789693 hv=3381932903
ad='80c9e33c'
alter session set events '10046 trace name context off'
END OF STMT
PARSE #1:c=0,e=810,p=0,cr=0,cu=0,mis=1,r=0,dep=0,og=4,tim=1024427939789677
```

2. For Example 5-9, construct a graph like the one shown in Figure 5-3 that illustrates the recursive relationships among database calls. Compute the contribution to e of each database call. What type of application would perform the actions shown here?

Example 5-9. SQL trace file exhibiting recursive SQL behavior (level-1 output is shown to reduce clutter for the exercise)

```
/u01/oradata/admin/V901/udump/ora_23317_recursive.trc

*** TRACE DUMP CONTINUED FROM FILE  ***

Oracle9i Enterprise Edition Release 9.0.1.0.0 - Production
With the Partitioning option
JServer Release 9.0.1.0.0 - Production
ORACLE_HOME = /u01/oradata/app/9.0.1
System name:    Linux
Node name:  research
Release:    2.4.4-4GB
Version:    #1 Fri May 18 14:11:12 GMT 2001
Machine:    i686
Instance name: V901
Redo thread mounted by this instance: 1
Oracle process number: 9
Unix process pid: 23317, image: oracle@research (TNS V1-V3)

*** 2003-05-18 11:14:59.469
*** SESSION ID:(8.1578) 2003-05-18 11:14:59.469
APPNAME mod='SQL*Plus' mh=3669949024 act='' ah=4029777240
=====================
PARSING IN CURSOR #1 len=68 dep=0 uid=5 oct=42 lid=5 tim=1053274499469370 hv=1635464953
ad='51f65c00'
alter session set events '10046 trace name context forever, level 1'
END OF STMT
EXEC #1:c=0,e=1,p=0,cr=0,cu=0,mis=0,r=0,dep=0,og=3,tim=1053274499469133
=====================
PARSING IN CURSOR #2 len=175 dep=1 uid=0 oct=3 lid=0 tim=1053274499471797 hv=1491008679
ad='52107fa8'
```

Example 5-9. SQL trace file exhibiting recursive SQL behavior (level-1 output is shown to reduce clutter for the exercise) (continued)

```
select u.name,o.name, t.update$, t.insert$, t.delete$, t.enabled  from obj$ o,user$
u,trigger$ t  where t.baseobject=:1 and t.obj#=o.obj# and o.owner#=u.user#  order by o.
obj#
END OF STMT
PARSE #2:c=0,e=91,p=0,cr=0,cu=0,mis=0,r=0,dep=1,og=3,tim=1053274499471765
EXEC #2:c=0,e=160,p=0,cr=0,cu=0,mis=0,r=0,dep=1,og=3,tim=1053274499483293
FETCH #2:c=0,e=32228,p=1,cr=8,cu=0,mis=0,r=1,dep=1,og=3,tim=1053274499515571
FETCH #2:c=0,e=20,p=0,cr=0,cu=0,mis=0,r=0,dep=1,og=3,tim=1053274499515717
=====================
PARSING IN CURSOR #1 len=44 dep=0 uid=5 oct=2 lid=5 tim=1053274499516502 hv=2583883
ad='51f224f8'
insert into t values (1001, rpad(1001,1000))
END OF STMT
PARSE #1:c=0,e=45515,p=1,cr=8,cu=0,mis=1,r=0,dep=0,og=3,tim=1053274499516473
=====================
PARSING IN CURSOR #2 len=22 dep=1 uid=5 oct=3 lid=5 tim=1053274499535321 hv=4140187373
ad='521444c8'
SELECT count(*) from t
END OF STMT
PARSE #2:c=0,e=1003,p=0,cr=0,cu=0,mis=1,r=0,dep=1,og=3,tim=1053274499535287
EXEC #2:c=0,e=115,p=0,cr=0,cu=0,mis=0,r=0,dep=1,og=3,tim=1053274499535550
*** 2003-05-18 11:15:13.212
FETCH #2:
c=3730000,e=13676722,p=127292,cr=127894,cu=260,mis=0,r=1,dep=1,og=3,tim=1053274513212315
EXEC #1:
c=3730000,e=13695999,p=127293,cr=127897,cu=264,mis=0,r=1,dep=0,og=3,tim=1053274513212610
=====================
PARSING IN CURSOR #4 len=52 dep=0 uid=5 oct=47 lid=5 tim=1053274513254792 hv=1697159799
ad='51f59e44'
BEGIN DBMS_OUTPUT.GET_LINES(:LINES, :NUMLINES); END;
END OF STMT
PARSE #4:c=0,e=149,p=0,cr=0,cu=0,mis=0,r=0,dep=0,og=3,tim=1053274513254759
EXEC #4:c=0,e=38900,p=0,cr=0,cu=0,mis=0,r=1,dep=0,og=3,tim=1053274513293822
STAT #2 id=1 cnt=1 pid=0 pos=0 obj=0 op='SORT AGGREGATE '
STAT #2 id=2 cnt=1 pid=1 pos=1 obj=31159 op='TABLE ACCESS FULL T '
XCTEND rlbk=0, rd_only=0
```

3. Trace a DDL command, such as DROP TABLE. How many dictionary operations does the Oracle kernel perform implicitly for you when you drop a table? How does the number of operations change if the table being dropped has indexes? What if there are histograms in place on columns? What about constraints? What if the table is involved in a materialized view, or is subject to a security policy?

## CHAPTER 6

Collecting Extended SQL Trace Data

The process for collecting extended SQL trace data is somewhat of a moving target. For a while, Oracle appeared committed to the excruciatingly inefficient Oracle Trace mechanism. However, the Oracle9*i* release 2 documentation states flatly that Oracle trace will be deprecated in favor of SQL trace (presumably *extended* SQL trace) [Oracle (2002)]. Oracle describes the use of SQL trace in its standard documentation, but if you want to use *extended* SQL trace, you have to work to find the information. This chapter helps to solve that problem for Oracle releases 7 through 9. The architects of the Oracle kernel understand the value of response time data that can be attributed accurately to end-user business actions. Look for Oracle release 10 to contain several features that will simplify your data collection challenges.

 Note that when you generate SQL trace data, you are recording data about your application in an ASCII file. Each SQL trace file contains application SQL text. Many SQL trace files also contain application data. The use of this information is probably subject to strict rules within your company. You must ensure that your use of SQL trace files does not breach confidentiality or leak sensitive data to those who should not see it.

Understanding Your Application

As you learned in Chapter 3, you *want* to be able to trace exactly the actions motivated by a carefully specified user or batch program for a carefully specified time interval. As you'll see later in this chapter, the Oracle release 7, 8, and 9 kernels give you the ability to activate and deactivate extended SQL tracing only at the Oracle *session* level. Being able to control tracing only at the session level creates varying degrees of hardship for the data collection process, depending upon the architecture of your application. Before you can trace your application, unfortunately, you must understand its architecture.

The most difficult part of diagnosing performance problems in Oracle release 7, 8, or 9 applications is the collection of properly scoped diagnostic data. Once you collect properly scoped data, the diagnosis process runs very smoothly.

Let's begin with some definitions. A *user action* is a functional unit of work that some human being executes. A *user action* is the thing whose performance some user finds interesting (and therefore you find it interesting too). This action requires the execution of code that may exist on any or all of several architectural tiers (such as a client's browser, an application server, a database server, or various network devices).

The database server host is the tier on which this book focuses, because most performance problems can be diagnosed most efficiently by observing instrumentation produced by this tier. A user action may involve zero or many *processes* (or even threads) on the database server host. A *process* is an operating system object that is an instantiation of some executable program. You can identify an OS process by its unique OS process ID (PID), and you can monitor it with operating system tools. For example, the following Linux ps (report process status) output shows four processes (8233, 8325, 8326, and 8327) which are using only three different programs (ksh, ps, and two copies of t):

```
$ ps
  PID TTY          TIME CMD
 8233 pts/4    00:00:00 ksh
 8325 pts/4    00:00:00 t
 8326 pts/4    00:00:00 t
 8327 pts/4    00:00:00 ps
```

You will be interested primarily in two types of OS processes on your database server host. First and foremost, you will be interested in the Oracle *server* processes that share memory, access your Oracle database files, and do most of the work on most Oracle systems. These processes usually contain the string "oracle" in their names. The following Linux command produces a listing of all processes that contain the string "oracle" in the process table, but not the string "grep":

```
$ ps -ef | grep oracle | grep -v grep
oracle     756     1  0 Feb04 ?        00:00:19 ora_pmon_V816
oracle     758     1  0 Feb04 ?        00:00:04 ora_dbw0_V816
oracle     760     1  0 Feb04 ?        00:00:03 ora_lgwr_V816
oracle     762     1  0 Feb04 ?        00:00:43 ora_ckpt_V816
oracle     764     1  0 Feb04 ?        00:00:01 ora_smon_V816
oracle     766     1  0 Feb04 ?        00:00:00 ora_reco_V816
oracle    8834  8833  0 16:12 ?        00:00:00 oracleV816 (DESCRIPTION=(LO
oracle    8859  8858  0 16:13 ?        00:00:00 oracleV816 (DESCRIPTION=(LO
```

Note that this command has also displayed all of my system's Oracle *background* processes as well (because they're owned by the user called oracle).

You might hear *server* processes called many names, including:

Server processes
Shadow processes
Kernel processes
Foreground processes

The second interesting type of OS process that exists on your server host is any *client* process that makes database connections. For example, it is common to run database call-intensive application programs such as reports or batch uploads on the database server host itself. This configuration decision makes excellent sense for any client program that consumes most of its total elapsed time waiting for database calls. In such a case, the cost of executing the client program's CPU instructions on the server more than compensates for the cost of flooding a network with masses of SQL*Net chit-chat between the client and oracle server processes.

Examples of Oracle application client programs include:

sqlplus (SQL*Plus)
f60run (Oracle*Forms)
FNDLIBR (Oracle Financials Concurrent Manager program)
PYUGEN (An Oracle Human Resources program)

An *Oracle session* (or, in this book, simply a *session*) is a specific sequence of database calls that flow through a connection between a user process and an Oracle instance. You can identify a session by its unique identifier, the concatenation of V$SESSION.SID and V$SESSION.SERIAL#. For example, the following SQL*Plus output shows nine Oracle sessions:

```
SQL> select sid, serial#, username, type from v$session;

       SID    SERIAL# USERNAME                             TYPE
---------- ---------- ------------------------------------ ----------
         1          1                                      BACKGROUND
         2          1                                      BACKGROUND
         3          1                                      BACKGROUND
         4          1                                      BACKGROUND
         5          1                                      BACKGROUND
         6          1                                      BACKGROUND
         7         13 SYSTEM                               USER
         8         11 SYSTEM                               USER
         9        337 CVM                                  USER

9 rows selected.
```

Data collection is simple when a user action uses exactly one client process, one Oracle server process, and one Oracle session. Fortunately, this is what happens in many performance problem situations, such as long-running reports and batch jobs.

Complexity in data collection grows when a user action involves the participation of more Oracle processes or more Oracle sessions. For example:

Oracle Multithreaded Server (MTS)
> In an MTS configuration, several client processes share a smaller number of Oracle server processes. This configuration reduces the number of process instantiations required to run an application with a large number of constantly connected but mostly idle users.

Connection pooling
> In a connection pooling configuration, a single OS process (called a *service*) on the middle tier creates a single Oracle connection and establishes a single Oracle session on a single Oracle server process. The service then makes database calls on behalf of many users within its single session. This type of configuration permits even greater scalability for large user counts than MTS configurations.

My colleagues and I see mind-bogglingly complex combinations of these technologies and more in the field, especially in environments where a single user action requires work from services that are distributed across databases. As I mentioned previously, collecting properly scoped diagnostic data is usually the most difficult part of problem diagnosis methods today. The good news is that once you figure out how to do it for a given architecture, executing further data collection tasks for that architecture becomes much easier. Furthermore, I expect that the architectural changes planned for Oracle release 10 simplify the process of collecting properly scoped data for an individual user action.

The key to successful extended SQL trace data collection is to understand how to identify the right Oracle sessions. For connection pooling architectures, the key is to identify which database calls and wait events map to the user action that you're diagnosing.

Activating Extended SQL Trace

The first secret to the syntax of Oracle's extended SQL trace mechanism lies in the file *$ORACLE_HOME/rdbms/mesg/oraus.msg*. It's the error message file for the Oracle kernel. If you search for the first occurrence of the string "10000" that appears at the beginning of a line in the file (e.g., by issuing the command /^10000 in *vi*), you'll find yourself in the midst of the following file content:

```
/ Pseudo-error debugging events:
/    Error codes 10000 .. 10999 are reserved for debug event codes that are
/    not really errors.
/
// NLS_DO_NOT_TRANSLATE [10000,10999] - Tag to indicate messages should
// not be translated.
10000, 00000, "controlfile debug event, name 'control_file'"
// *Cause:
// *Action:
```

Oracle kernel developers have created debugging events with codes in the range 10000 through 10999 to assist them in testing and debugging the kernel.

 Oracle Corporation does not distribute *oraus.msg* on Microsoft Windows ports. To view the file, you'll need to find it on a non-Windows distribution.

The one-line descriptions of these debug event codes are quite educational. In them you can discover the existence of debug events that enable Oracle kernel developers to simulate events like memory errors or various types of file corruption, change the behavior of components like the query optimizer, or trace internal kernel operations like latch acquisitions. Debugging events that can assist you in your role as performance analyst include:

```
10032, 00000, "sort statistics (SOR*)"
10033, 00000, "sort run information (SRD*/SRS*)"
10053, 00000, "CBO Enable optimizer trace"
10079, 00000, "trace data sent/received via SQL*Net"
10104, 00000, "dump hash join statistics to trace file"
10241, 00000, "remote SQL execution tracing/validation"
```

Amid the list of over 400 debugging events is the one to activate extended SQL trace:

```
10046, 00000, "enable SQL statement timing"
```

This inconspicuous little capability, buried about 16,000 lines deep within an undocumented file, is one of the heroes of this book. It is the source of your ability to obtain a full account of how an Oracle application program consumes your users' response times.

 Prior to Oracle release 10, all pseudo-error debugging events are officially unsupported, unless you're acting specifically under the direction of Oracle Support. Later in this chapter, I describe the DBMS_SUPPORT.START_TRACE_IN_SESSION package, which is a fully supported way to use event 10046.

Tracing Your Own Source Code

Tracing a session is a very simple process when you have read-write access to the source code of the session to be traced. Activating and deactivating extended SQL trace requires only that the Oracle kernel execute the SQL statements shown in Example 6-1. The first line ensures that TIMED_STATISTICS is active for the session, regardless of the instance-wide value of TIMED_STATSITICS. Without activating Oracle timed statistics, all of your e, c, ela, and tim values will be zero and therefore of no value in your response time analysis.

Example 6-1. This code activates and deactivates extended SQL trace for a session

```
alter session set timed_statistics=true
alter session set max_dump_file_size=unlimited
alter session set tracefile_identifier='POX20031031a'
alter session set events '10046 trace name context forever, level 8'
/* code to be traced goes here */
alter session set events '10046 trace name context off'
```

The second line ensures that the Oracle kernel will not truncate your trace file against your wishes. The MAX_DUMP_FILE_SIZE parameter permits the Oracle database administrator to restrict the size of trace files generated by Oracle sessions. The feature is designed to prevent performance analysts from accidentally filling the filesystem(s) to which USER_DUMP_DEST and BACKGROUND_DUMP_DEST refer. However, forgetting to relax this file size restriction can be an expensive and frustrating mistake for a performance improvement project.* The last thing you want to see after three weeks of careful preparation to trace a long-running monthly batch job is a shorter-than-expected trace file with following line at its tail:

```
*** DUMP FILE SIZE IS LIMITED TO 1048576 BYTES ***
```

With the ability to relax the maximum dump file size limit comes the responsibility of not filling the filesystem to which your trace file will be written. If the Oracle kernel is writing to a filesystem that throws a "filesystem full" error, the result will be a truncated trace file. You'll end up with something that looks like this at the tail of the file:

```
WAIT #42: nam='db file sequential read' ela= 17101 p1=10 p2=2213 p3=1
WAIT #42: nam='db file se
```

Note that some Oracle ports (notably Oracle8*i* for Microsoft Windows) do not support the UNLIMITED keyword value. For these ports, simply set MAX_DUMP_FILE_SIZE to a large integer. On the 32-bit implementations of Oracle in our laboratory, the maximum value you can specify is $2^{31} - 1 = 2,147,483,647$. Note also that the parameters TIMED_STATISTICS and MAX_DUMP_FILE_SIZE have been session-modifiable since Oracle release 7.3. If you are using a release of Oracle prior to 7.3, the only way to set either of these parameters for a given session is to set them instance-wide.

It is possible that USER_DUMP_DEST may someday also become a session-settable parameter as well. This feature would be useful because it would allow you to redirect specific trace files to specific locations, based on motives of space economy, performance, or just ease of access. Oracle's release 9.2 documentation states that USER_DUMP_DEST is a session-settable parameter [Oracle (2002)]. However, it is not true at least on Oracle release 9.2.0.1.0 for Microsoft Windows.

The third line in Example 6-1 causes the resulting trace file to contain the string "POX20031031a" in its file name (this feature is available in 8.1.7). Inserting some

---

* The default setting is UNLIMITED on Oracle release 9.

kind of unique ID into the trace file name will make it easy later on to identify which file contains the information I've collected. Any unique ID will do. In this example, I've chosen a name that might make sense for run "a" of the "POX" report executed on 31 October 2003.

The fourth line in Example 6-1 activates the extended SQL trace mechanism itself, causing the Oracle kernel to write statistics into the kernel process' trace file. Note that in Example 6-1, I activated the extended SQL trace mechanism by setting the tracing level to 8. I deactivated SQL trace by specifying the OFF keyword, which set the tracing level to 0. The tracing levels are summarized in Table 6-1.

Table 6-1. Oracle's "pseudo-error debugging event" number 10046 tracing levels

Level	Implied bitmap	Function
0	0000	Emit no statistics.
1	0001	Emit ***, APPNAME, PARSING IN CURSOR, PARSE ERROR, EXEC, FETCH, UNMAP, SORT UNMAP, ERROR, STAT, and XCTEND lines.
2	0011	Apparently identical to level 1.
4	0101	Emit BINDS sections in addition to level-1 lines.
8	1001	Emit WAIT lines in addition to level-1 lines.
12	1101	Emit level-1, level-4, and level-8 lines.

Although you can deactivate tracing explicitly, it is often best not to. A session's tracing attribute dies with the session, so when a user disconnects from Oracle, the trace file closes gracefully. Allowing the disconnection to end the tracing is the best way to ensure that all of the session's STAT lines are emitted to the trace file, for the reasons described in Chapter 5. Of course, if you are tracing an application that uses a persistent Oracle connection, like processes configured as "linked internal" within the Oracle Applications Concurrent Manager, then you must deactivate tracing explicitly. Fortunately, it is easy enough to reproduce missing STAT data with Oracle's EXPLAIN PLAN facility or the new V$SQL_PLAN fixed view (available in release 9).

Tracing Someone Else's Source Code

You can trace *any* Oracle session you want, even background sessions. Do you suspect that writes to database files are taking too long? Trace DBWR and find out. Do you think that writing to the online redo log files is too slow? Trace LGWR and find out. Did you ever wonder what it costs for the Oracle kernel to automatically coalesce tablespaces for you? Trace SMON and find out.

 Do *not* trace PMON with extended SQL trace. Tracing PMON can cause instance failure (Oracle bug 2329767, reputedly fixed in Oracle release 10). The good news is that there are very few legitimate reasons why you might actually *want* to trace PMON.

Triggering a session to activate its own trace

The plot thickens a little bit when you need to trace a program to which you don't have write-access to the source code. It's often not much more difficult; you just have to use a little bit of imagination. For example, you can use the AFTER LOGON trigger function introduced in release 8.1 to activate level-8 tracing for any session with a particular attribute. The code in Example 6-2 creates a trigger that activates tracing for any session whose Oracle username has a suffix of _test.

Example 6-2. This code creates a trigger that activates tracing for any session whose Oracle username has the suffix _test

```
create or replace trigger trace_test_user after logon on database
begin
  if user like '%\_test' escape '\' then
    execute immediate 'alter session set timed_statistics=true';
    execute immediate 'alter session set max_dump_file_size=unlimited';
    execute immediate
        'alter session set events ''10046 trace name context forever, level 8''';
  end if;
end;
/
```

The implementation particulars of a trigger like this will vary widely from one application to the next. The important thing is that you understand your application well enough that you can think innovatively about how you might activate extended SQL tracing for the session of your choice.

Activating trace from a third-party session

Oracle provides several packaged procedures that allow you to manipulate attributes of a session to which you are not connected. Your first task is to identify the session that you want to trace. Many database administrators are already familiar with means for finding the SID and SERIAL# (from the V$SESSION fixed view) of a specific process from applications that they manage. Example 6-3 shows one example of a SQL statement that does this.

Example 6-3. This SQL statement lists attributes of a user session for which the session username is supplied in the Oracle placeholder variable :uname

```
select
  s.sid db_sid,
  s.serial# db_serial,
  p.spid os_pid,
  to_char(s.logon_time, 'yyyy/mm/dd hh24:mi:ss') db_login_time,
  nvl(s.username, 'SYS') db_user,
  s.osuser os_user,
  s.machine os_machine,
  nvl(decode(
    instr(s.terminal, chr(0)), 0,
    s.terminal, substr(s.terminal, 1, instr(s.terminal, chr(0))-1)
```

Example 6-3. This SQL statement lists attributes of a user session for which the session username is supplied in the Oracle placeholder variable :uname (continued)

```
), 'none') os_terminal,
  s.program os_program
from
  v$session s,
  v$process p
where
  s.paddr = p.addr
  and s.username like upper(:uname)
```

An application can greatly simplify the task of session identification by revealing some identifying information about the session to the end user. Imagine an application form that can list the values of V$SESSION.SID and V$SESSION.SERIAL# right on the user's form. Such a feature greatly assists the end-user in describing to the performance analyst how to identify a session that needs targeted performance analysis.

The package called DBMS_APPLICATION_INFO provides three useful procedures—SET_MODULE, SET_ACTION, and SET_CLIENT_INFO—for helping to identify targeted Oracle sessions. Each procedure inserts a value into the V$SESSION fixed view for the session executing the procedure. The attributes MODULE, ACTION, and CLIENT_INFO create a convenient hierarchy for identifying user actions. For example, Nikolas Alexander's application form might make the following settings:

```
dbms_application_info.set_module('Accounts Payable')
dbms_application_info.set_action('Pay Invoices')
dbms_application_info.set_client_info('Nikolas Alexander')
```

When an application "earmarks" itself by calling DBMS_APPLICATION_INFO procedures, it becomes trivial to target the Oracle session executed by an individual client, all Oracle sessions executing a particular action, or even all Oracle sessions participating in the actions of a given module. For example, the following query returns the session identification information for the set of all Oracle sessions running the Pay Invoices action of the Accounts Payable module:

```
select session, serial#
from v$session
where v$session.module = 'Accounts Payable'
  and v$session.action = 'Pay Invoices'
```

One problem with using the MODULE, ACTION, and CLIENT_INFO attributes through Oracle release 9 is that setting any of the attributes requires the overhead of a database call (which includes not just additional workload upon the Oracle kernel, but extra network capacity consumption as well). For small user actions, the overhead becomes a significant proportion of the action's total workload.

Once you have obtained the SID and SERIAL# identification for the session you want to trace, activating trace is straightforward. Example 6-4 shows how to use the

DBMS_SYSTEM package to activate TIMED_STATISTICS for a specific session and set its MAX_DUMP_FILE_SIZE to the desired value. Even if you don't have access to DBMS_SYSTEM, you can manipulate these Oracle system parameters system-wide without incurring outage with ALTER SYSTEM commands in any Oracle release since 7.3.

Example 6-4. Manipulating session parameters for a session identified by :sid and :serial

```
sys.dbms_system.set_bool_param_in_session(
  :sid, :serial,
  'timed_statistics', true
)
sys.dbms_system.set_int_param_in_session(
  :sid, :serial,
  'max_dump_file_size', 2147483647
)
```

There are several ways to activate extended SQL tracing for a given session. Two such ways are shown in Examples 6-5 and 6-6. Oracle encourages you to use the DBMS_SUPPORT package instead of DBMS_SYSTEM if you have a choice (Oracle *MetaLink* note 62294.1). However, Oracle does not ship *dbmssupp.sql* and *prvtsupp.plb* with some software distributions. If you cannot find DBMS_SUPPORT on your system, don't despair. My colleagues and I have used DBMS_SYSTEM.SET_EV in hundreds of performance improvement projects without negative incident. Friends in Oracle Support have informed me that the DBMS_SUPPORT.START_TRACE_IN_SESSION procedure is implemented as a call to SET_EV anyway.

The safety of using START_TRACE_IN_SESSION is that you're not susceptible to typographical errors in specifying event 10046. Accidentally typing the wrong event number could obviously lead to catastrophe.

Example 6-5. Activating extended SQL trace at level 8 with START_TRACE_IN_SESSION for a session identified by :sid and :serial

```
sys.dbms_support.start_trace_in_session(
  :sid, :serial,
  waits=>true, binds=>false
)
/* code to be traced executes during this time window */
sys.dbms_support.stop_trace_in_session(
  :sid, :serial
)
```

Do not use DBMS_SYSTEM.START_SQL_TRACE_IN_SESSION to activate extended SQL trace, because this procedure can activate SQL tracing *only* at level 1. You cannot activate *extended* SQL tracing with START_SQL_TRACE_IN_SESSION.

Example 6-6. Activating extended SQL trace at level 8 with SET_EV for a session identified by :sid and :serial

```
sys.dbms_system.set_ev(:sid, :serial, 10046, 8, '')
/* code to be traced executes during this time window */
sys.dbms_system.set_ev(:sid, :serial, 10046, 0, '')
```

Finding Your Trace File(s)

Once you have traced a session, your next task is to identify the one or more trace files into which your trace data were written. Each Oracle kernel process creates a single trace file; hence, depending upon an application's architectural configuration, there can be one or more trace files for each traced Oracle session. For example, Oracle Multi-Threaded Server can emit data for a single session into two or more trace files. Your first task will be to identify the directory in which your trace files reside. This step isn't difficult, because there are only two options. The answer is either the setting of the USER_DUMP_DEST Oracle parameter or the BACKGROUND_DUMP_DEST parameter.*

Next, you will need to identify the correct file (or files) within that directory. If you were able to tag your trace file name with a unique identifier by setting a session's TRACEFILE_IDENTIFIER attribute, then finding your trace file should be no problem. Simply search the trace file directory for a file name that contains your ID. However, if you were unable to tag your file name—for example, because you activated tracing for someone else's code from a third-party session—then your job is a little more difficult.

Trace File Names

One complication is that the various porting groups at Oracle Corporation have chosen different conventions for naming trace files. Table 6-2 illustrates some of the names we've seen in the field. Because there's no cross-platform naming standard, it can seem difficult to write a platform-independent tool that can predict the name of the trace file for a given session. But this isn't too difficult of a problem if your site uses only a few different environments. You simply figure out what pattern the Oracle kernel uses for its trace file names, and then you can predict the file names it will create. For example, on our Linux research server, trace files are named ora_*SPID*.trc, where *SPID* is the value of V$PROCESS.SPID for the session.

Table 6-2. Oracle trace file naming conventions vary by Oracle kernel porting group and by Oracle version

Oracle trace file name	Oracle version	Operating system
ora_1107.trc	8.1.6.0.0	Linux 2.2.15
ora_31641.trc	9.0.1.0.0	Linux 2.4.4

---

* I've heard reports of the occasional bug that causes the Oracle kernel to ignore the dump destination parameters and write trace files instead to *$ORACLE_HOME/rdbms/log*.

Oracle trace file name	Oracle version	Operating system
ora_31729.trc	8.1.5.0.0	OSF1 V4.0
proa021_ora_9452.trc	8.0.5.2.1	SunOS 5.6
cdap_ora_17696.trc	9.2.0.1.0	SunOS 5.8
ora_176344_crswp.trc	8.1.6.3.0	AIX 3
MERKUR_S7_FG_ORACLE_013.trc	8.1.7.0.0	OpenVMS 2-1
ora_3209_orapatch.trc	8.1.6.3.0	HP-UX B.11.00
ORA01532.TRC	8.1.7.0.0	Windows 2000 V5.0
v920_ora_1072.trc	9.2.0.1.0	Windows 2000 V5.1

Simple Client-Server Applications

Even in the modern age of complex multi-tier architectures, you probably execute many programs in simple client-server mode, especially batch jobs. Any time you isolate an application component for testing, you're likely to enjoy the same luxury. In such a configuration, any Oracle session creates a single trace file that contains data exactly for that session (Figure 6-1).

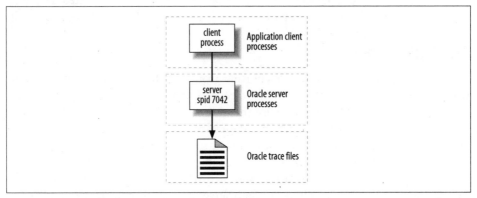

Figure 6-1. For simple client-server configurations, there is one server process per session and, therefore, one trace file per session

The absence of a cross-platform trace file naming standard made it difficult for our company to develop a portable software tool to find the right trace file. We considered maintaining a table of file naming patterns (i.e., regular expressions) that we could update as we learned about changes brought on by new ports and new Oracle releases. But we decided that maintaining such a table would be too error-prone. Instead, we landed upon the following algorithm:

1. Given the session ID and serial number for your chosen session (the values of V$SESSION.SID and V$SESSION.SERIAL#), determine the system process ID (SPID)

---

of your server process. The SPID is the value of V$PROCESS.SPID for your session, which you can find using a join like the one shown in Example 6-3.

2. Identify the directory in which your trace file resides. The directory is the value of USER_DUMP_DEST if V$SESSION.TYPE='USER'; it is BACKGROUND_DUMP_DEST if V$SESSION.TYPE='BACKGROUND'.

3. List the contents of that directory, ordered by descending file modification time (for example, using ls -lt in Unix). Note that a file modification time (or *mtime*) typically has resolution of one second. Hence, if two or more trace files are created in the same second, then it is impossible for you to know which one is newer by comparing their *mtimes*.

4. For each file in that list whose *mtime* is more recent than the time at which your data collection began (it is possible to be more precise than this, but comparing the *mtime* to the data collection begin time is a more conservative approach):

   a. Seek to the *final* preamble in the file. This is especially important on Microsoft Windows platforms, where the Oracle kernel tends to reuse trace file names frequently, and where the kernel *appends* to existing trace data. (Therefore, it is possible to have two or more preambles in a single trace file.)

   b. Search the preamble for the line containing the string "pid" (on Unix variants and OpenVMS) or "thread id" (on Windows). The preamble consists of all the lines up to the line that begins with the string "***".

   c. If the number following "pid" or "thread id" matches the SPID for your chosen session, then you have found your file, and you may stop searching.

   If you exhaust the list of files without finding a matching system process ID, then stop searching; the file or files you are looking for do not exist.

I have written portable Perl code that implements approximately these steps as a part of project *Sparky*, which you can read about at *http://www.hotsos.com*.

This method of peeking at file content may strike you as inelegant, especially if your shop uses only one or two operating systems. However, the algorithm has the advantage of reliability across platforms and across Oracle software upgrades. The algorithm scales well with respect to the number of trace files in the directory. It scales less well if the trace files being peeked at are very large and contain several preambles.

Oracle Parallel Execution

Using Oracle's Parallel Execution (PX) capabilities causes an Oracle kernel process to fork two or more child processes (called *PX slaves*) to fulfill the responsibilities of parallel reading and parallel sorting. PX slave processes inherit the tracing attributes of their query coordinator. Consequently, activating extended SQL trace for a session that uses PX features will generate several relevant trace files. The remaining task is to identify and analyze *all* of the relevant trace files. This task is usually simple enough to do by assessing the modification times of the most recently generated trace files. For queries using parallel degree p, the number n of relevant trace files will be in the range $1 \le n \le 2p + 1$ per enlisted instance.

Oracle Multi-Threaded Server

Using Oracle's Multi-Threaded Server (MTS) capability makes finding your trace data a little more complicated. MTS allows switched connections, which creates a one-to-many relationship between an Oracle session and the Oracle kernel processes that service database calls made by the session (Figure 6-2). Thus, the trace output from a single session can be scattered throughout two or more trace files. The Oracle kernel does provide complete session identification and timestamp data each time a session migrates to a new server process (and hence a new trace file). It is straightforward to create the logical equivalent of a single trace file for a given session. The modifications to the method for finding trace files detailed previously are:

- Depending upon your version of Oracle, your shared server trace files may reside in BACKGROUND_DUMP_DEST (my staff and I have seen this behavior on some release 7 and 8 platforms), or they may be in USER_DUMP_DEST (we've seen this behavior on release 9).

- Instead of quitting when you find *one* trace file with the correct session identification information within it, you must continue searching *all* the trace files with qualifying modification times.

- Once you've identified all the files that contain relevant trace data, you must discard the irrelevant data from sessions other than the one in which you're interested, and then you have to merge the resulting data. First, discard segments of trace data that correspond to sessions other than the specified session. You can determine easily which sections you want to keep by observing the session ID lines that begin with ***. Finally, merge the remaining segments of trace data into ascending time order. This is also an easy step because the *** lines contain times as well. The result is a "virtual" trace file containing only the session information that you require. You can perform this step by hand with a multi-window text editor, or you can purchase a tool that can do it for you. We have created such a tool at *hotsos.com*, which we sell as a commercial product.

Connection-Pooling Applications

As I described earlier, connection pooling is a valuable technique designed to reduce the number of database *connect* and *disconnect* calls. Connection-pooling applications are only as easy to diagnose as their design permits. If an application is instrumented in such a manner that the database calls executed on behalf of a user action can be identified, then your data collection job will be easy. Unfortunately, many connection-pooling applications are not instrumented in this way. I believe that the

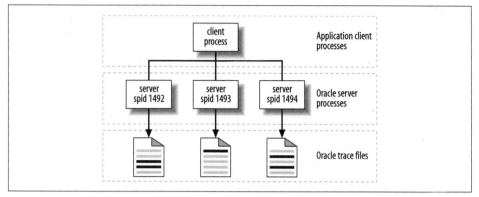

Figure 6-2. Oracle Multi-Threaded Server uses a one-to-many relationship between client and server processes; hence, MTS can stream data about a session into more than one trace file

release of Oracle release 10 will facilitate the creation of such instrumentation over the next several years.

The performance diagnostic problem of connection pooling occurs when the application server conceals the identity of the end user from the database. Because several users share a single session, it is impossible to determine from the trace file alone which user has motivated a given line of trace data (Figure 6-3).

 The best permanent solution to the connection-pooling diagnosis problem is an application design that facilitates the activation of extended SQL trace for any individual application user's experience.

If your application lacks instrumentation to facilitate tracing of an individual user's SQL, you are not alone. There are of course other ways you can make progress. Consider the following scenario: a user named Nancy at IP address 150.121.1.102 has reported a performance problem with the connection-pooling order entry application shown in Figure 6-3. The application does not facilitate the identification of Nancy's extended SQL trace data.

One simple strategy is to force all users other than Nancy to cease their use of the system temporarily. Then activate extended SQL tracing for Nancy's service and allow Nancy to execute her slow business function. When the function has completed, deactivate tracing and allow all the other users back onto the system. This strategy has proven effective in some limited cases, but in addition to the obvious business disruption, it has a profound diagnostic disadvantage. If Nancy's performance problem is the result of competition with other sessions, then the data collected with this method will be devoid of evidence of the problem's root cause.

A more powerful workaround is possible if you can alter the architecture temporarily to isolate Nancy's session. Figure 6-4 shows one way in which you might accomplish this modification. In this figure, I show the isolation of Nancy's session

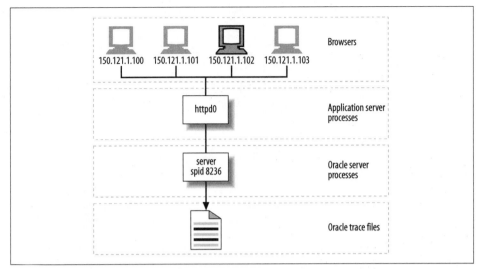

Figure 6-3. A connection-pooling architecture. Unless the middle tier records a mapping of end user identity to database call, there will be no way to determine which user motivated which lines of trace data

by supplying her with her own application server process and single dedicated Oracle server process. One way to accomplish this switch-over is to provide Nancy with a special "service identifier" (the application service layer analog of a special TNS alias) that provides connection to the special diagnostic application server process.

A commonly stated objection to this method is that the architecture change might itself influence the performance behavior of Nancy's session while it is being diagnosed. However, the change is more localized in this case than in the first workaround I described, because you haven't changed the workload that competes with Nancy. Certainly, you will need to investigate the changes you *have* made, especially if you notice that an architecture change does beget a performance change. For example, if the modified architecture shown in Figure 6-4 produces consistently faster performance than the one shown in Figure 6-3, then you might investigate whether the httpd0 application server process might be a significant participant in the problem.

A final strategy that I'll describe here is possible only if *all* the users who share one or more Oracle server processes with Nancy are doing approximately the same type of work as Nancy is doing. If all the connections that use the server processes are submitting the same kinds of workload, then each of the lines in the resulting trace file will be approximately representative of Nancy's workload, as illustrated in Figure 6-5.

Of course, it is true that you "cannot extrapolate detail from an average" and therefore, considering a single trace file as representative of Nancy's work bears a risk (see Chapter 3). However, in this case, our knowledge of session homogeneity is vital

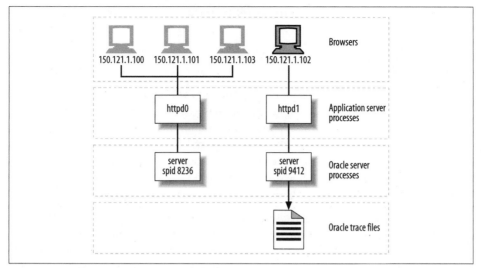

Figure 6-4. If you can isolate the user's workload so that no other user action's database call lines appear in its Oracle trace file, then the diagnostic data collection is no more difficult than in the simple client-server case

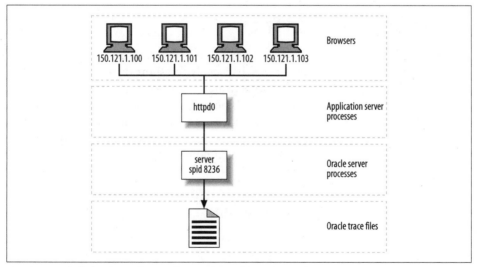

Figure 6-5. If all the users who use the Oracle server processes shown here are doing approximately the same type of work, then any of the workload depicted in the trace file is an approximate representation of any individual user action's workload

additional information. It's as if I had told you that the mean of a list of numbers is eleven *and that the numbers are all approximately the same.* That extra bit of information—that the numbers are all approximately the same—enables you to extrapolate legitimate conclusions about the data behind the mean. If all the users who share an Oracle server process are doing approximately the same type of work, then you can

consider any line of trace data in the resulting trace file as an approximate representation of any user's workload.

Some Good News

Data collection is more complicated for application configurations that allow a single
application user action to distribute its database calls across two or more distinct
Oracle kernel processes. Of course, this is the strategy employed by virtually all applications being built today. I hope that the problem of trace data identification is one
motivation behind Oracle Corporation's significant investment into diagnostic
changes scheduled for Oracle release 10. I do believe that the problem shall become
easier to manage in the future. There are two pieces of good news for today, however:

- Collecting extended SQL trace statistics for many batch jobs is easy, and it should
  continue to be so, even in the increasingly *n*-tier world, because the best configuration for many batch jobs is to run with a dedicated Oracle server process.
- Every data collection problem that my colleagues have encountered so far has a
  practical solution. I hope the *hotsos.com* web site is one of the first places you'll
  check for new developments as they occur.

Eliminating Collection Error

As you have seen in Chapter 3, it is of paramount importance to collect SQL trace
data *precisely* for a desired time scope. Especially for short-duration user response
time diagnosis projects, it is critical to activate and deactivate SQL trace at exactly
the right times. When trace for a session is activated or deactivated by a third-party
session, time scope violations can occur either at the head or the tail of the trace file.
The remainder of this chapter shows you how to determine how and why data collection errors occur and how to get the maximum possible information from your
trace data.

Time Scope Errors at Trace Activation

When a session activates its own SQL trace, the first thing you'll find in the session's
trace file is information pertaining to the ALTER SESSION SET EVENTS command. However, when a session's trace attribute is set by another session (with, for example,
DBMS_SYSTEM.SET_EV or DBMS_SUPPORT.START_TRACE_IN_SESSION), it's more difficult to
predict what the first event printed into the trace file will be.

Missing wait event data at trace activation

If tracing is activated in the midst of a wait event that occurs between database calls,
then there can be missing data at the head of the trace file. For example, consider the
sequence of actions depicted in Figure 6-6. In a test, I created two SQL*Plus sessions:

one identified as 7.10583 (the SID and SERIAL# for the session), and another called the "second" session. In the second session, I executed the following PL/SQL block, supplying the values 7 and 10583 in response to the prompts:

```
set serveroutput on
undef 1
undef 2

declare
  t varchar(20);
begin
  dbms_system.set_ev(&1,&2,10046,8,'');
  select to_char(sysdate, 'hh24:mi:ss') into t from v$timer;
  dbms_output.put_line('time='||t);
end;
/
```

Executing this block activated tracing for session 7.10583 and displayed that my trace activation time was 12:31:11. Therefore, I know that this time marked the beginning of my requested data collection interval.

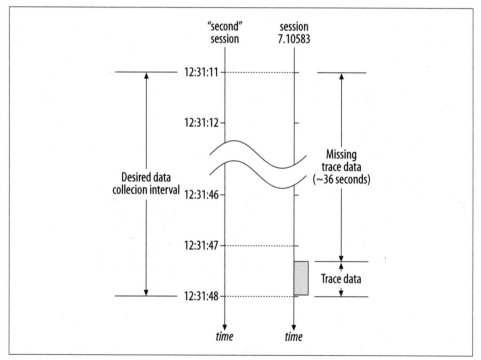

Figure 6-6. Although the SET_EV call was made in the second session at 12:31:11, the first entry into the session 7.10583 trace file didn't occur until 12:31:47.330, leaving an unaccounted-for duration of roughly 36 seconds

Within session 7.10583, I waited a few seconds and then executed a simple query for the current system time. The query result was 12:31:47. Then I exited session 7.10583. The trace file for the session is shown in Example 6-7. Notice that the trace file accounts for actions taking place between 12:31:47.330 and approximately 12:31:47.983 (I computed this second figure by walking the clock in the trace data), but it contains no data whatsoever for the approximately 36 seconds that elapsed between 12:31:11 and 12:31:47.330.

Example 6-7. This trace file was created by a query for the current system time. The query result was 12:31:47, which matches the first timestamp (highlighted) in the trace file

```
/u01/oradata/admin/V901/udump/ora_31262.trc
Oracle9i Enterprise Edition release 9.0.1.0.0 - Production
With the Partitioning option
JServer release 9.0.1.0.0 - Production
ORACLE_HOME = /u01/oradata/app/9.0.1
System name:    Linux
Node name:  research
Release:    2.4.4-4GB
Version:    #1 Fri May 18 14:11:12 GMT 2001
Machine:    i686
Instance name: V901
Redo thread mounted by this instance: 1
Oracle process number: 8
Unix process pid: 31262, image: oracle@research (TNS V1-V3)

*** 2003-01-28 12:31:47.330
*** SESSION ID:(7.10583) 2003-01-28 12:31:47.330
APPNAME mod='SQL*Plus' mh=3669949024 act='' ah=4029777240
====================
PARSING IN CURSOR #1 len=47 dep=0 uid=5 oct=3 lid=5 tim=1043778707330593 hv=2972477985
ad='51302734'
select to_char(sysdate, 'hh24:mi:ss') from dual
END OF STMT
PARSE #1:c=10000,e=1510,p=0,cr=0,cu=0,mis=1,r=0,dep=0,og=4,tim=1043778707330128
EXEC #1:c=0,e=97,p=0,cr=0,cu=0,mis=0,r=0,dep=0,og=4,tim=1043778707330810
WAIT #1: nam='SQL*Net message to client' ela= 5 p1=1650815232 p2=1 p3=0
FETCH #1:c=0,e=156,p=0,cr=1,cu=2,mis=0,r=1,dep=0,og=4,tim=1043778707331088
WAIT #1: nam='SQL*Net message from client' ela= 452 p1=1650815232 p2=1 p3=0
FETCH #1:c=0,e=2,p=0,cr=0,cu=0,mis=0,r=0,dep=0,og=0,tim=1043778707331819
WAIT #1: nam='SQL*Net message to client' ela= 4 p1=1650815232 p2=1 p3=0
WAIT #1: nam='SQL*Net message from client' ela= 650421 p1=1650815232 p2=1 p3=0
STAT #1 id=1 cnt=1 pid=0 pos=0 obj=221 op='TABLE ACCESS FULL DUAL '
XCTEND rlbk=0, rd_only=1
```

Because I had complete control over session 7.10583 for the duration of its existence, I know that the 36 seconds that are missing from the trace data should have been attributed to the kernel event called SQL*Net message from client. However, if I had not known this, there would have been no accurate way to account for the missing time. This is why the *Sparky* data collector (*http://www.hotsos.com*) queries V$SESSION_WAIT at trace activation (and deactivation). Had I executed the following query at the time of trace activation, I would have known which wait event was in-process at the time of trace activation (12:31:11):

```
select event from v$session_wait where sid=7 and state='WAITING'
```

Missing database call data at trace activation

A more difficult problem occurs when a session's tracing attribute is activated in the midst of a database call. For example, I activated the tracing attribute for session 8.1665 in the midst of a long-running fetch, resulting in the trace data shown in Example 6-8. The trace file is disturbing if you study it. In the over 87,700 lines of trace data that I've not shown here, there are thousands of centiseconds' worth of wait event time attributable to cursor #1 (the sum of the ela field values on WAIT #1 lines). However, the very first database call printed to the trace file is the UNMAP database call that is highlighted in Example 6-8. Notice that its total elapsed duration is only 3 centiseconds (e=3). We have thousands of centiseconds' worth of wait event time motivated by some database call, but the database call that accounts for all that time doesn't appear in the trace data!

Example 6-8. The trace file produced by activating trace in the midst of a long-running fetch call. The fetch call in-process when tracing was activated is completely absent from the trace data

```
Dump file C:\oracle\admin\ora817\udump\ORA02124.TRC
Tue Jan 28 02:13:21 2003
ORACLE V8.1.7.0.0 - Production vsnsta=0
vsnsql=e vsnxtr=3
Windows 2000 Version 5.0 Service Pack 3, CPU type 586
Oracle8i Enterprise Edition release 8.1.7.0.0 - Production
With the Partitioning option
JServer release 8.1.7.0.0 - Production
Windows 2000 Version 5.0 Service Pack 3, CPU type 586
Instance name: ora817

Redo thread mounted by this instance: 1

Oracle process number: 10

Windows thread id: 2124, image: ORACLE.EXE

*** 2003-01-28 02:13:21.520
*** SESSION ID:(8.1665) 2003-01-28 02:13:21.510
WAIT #1: nam='direct path write' ela= 0 p1=4 p2=1499 p3=1
WAIT #1: nam='direct path write' ela= 0 p1=4 p2=1501 p3=1
WAIT #1: nam='db file sequential read' ela= 0 p1=1 p2=3690 p3=1
WAIT #1: nam='db file sequential read' ela= 0 p1=1 p2=3638 p3=1
WAIT #1: nam='db file sequential read' ela= 12 p1=1 p2=3691 p3=1
WAIT #1: nam='db file sequential read' ela= 0 p1=1 p2=3692 p3=1
======================
PARSING IN CURSOR #2 len=36 dep=1 uid=0 oct=3 lid=0 tim=38025864 hv=1705880752
ad='39be068'
select file# from file$ where ts#=:1
```

```
END OF STMT
PARSE #2:c=0,e=0,p=0,cr=0,cu=0,mis=1,r=0,dep=1,og=0,tim=38025864
...
Approximately 87,700 lines are omitted here, none of which contains a dep=0 action.
...
WAIT #1: nam='direct path read' ela= 0 p1=4 p2=3710 p3=1
WAIT #1: nam='direct path read' ela= 0 p1=4 p2=3711 p3=3
WAIT #1: nam='direct path read' ela= 1 p1=4 p2=3586 p3=1
WAIT #1: nam='direct path read' ela= 0 p1=4 p2=3587 p3=4
WAIT #1: nam='direct path read' ela= 0 p1=4 p2=3591 p3=1
WAIT #1: nam='direct path read' ela= 0 p1=4 p2=3592 p3=2
=====================
PARSING IN CURSOR #1 len=32 dep=0 uid=5 oct=3 lid=5 tim=38037728 hv=3588977815
ad='39b3e88'
select count(*) from dba_source
END OF STMT
UNMAP #1:c=0,e=3,p=0,cr=0,cu=0,mis=0,r=0,dep=0,og=4,tim=38037728
WAIT #1: nam='SQL*Net message from client' ela= 2 p1=1111838976 p2=1 p3=0
FETCH #1:c=0,e=0,p=0,cr=0,cu=0,mis=0,r=0,dep=0,og=0,tim=38037730
WAIT #1: nam='SQL*Net message to client' ela= 0 p1=1111838976 p2=1 p3=0
```

Worse yet, where's the fetch that returned my count from DBA_SOURCE? The query consumed over ten seconds of elapsed time—I sat there and watched it—and it returned one row, yet the only FETCH line in the trace data says the query took practically no time and returned zero rows.

Example 6-9 shows what we wanted to see but couldn't in Example 6-8. This file was created by activating trace before parsing the query. Notice that instead of just two database calls (an UNMAP and a FETCH shown in Example 6-8), we can see *five* database calls in Example 6-9:

1. The PARSE for the query of DBA_SOURCE, which occurred in the first example before tracing was activated; hence this line was not emitted into Example 6-8.

2. The EXEC for the query, which also occurred in the first example before tracing was activated; hence this line was not emitted into Example 6-8.

3. The FETCH that consumed most of the query's response time. In the first example, this call began before tracing was activated; hence, this line was not emitted into Example 6-8 either.

4. The UNMAP that releases a sort segment used by one of the recursive views.

5. The final FETCH to ensure that there's no more data available from the cursor. Notice that this fetch call returned zero rows.

Finally, notice that activating trace before the query also graced Example 6-9 with the session's STAT lines, which is a nice bonus in itself.

Example 6-9. This trace file tail was created by tracing the same count of DBA_SOURCE rows, but this time, the tracing attribute was set by the session itself. Because tracing was active when the FETCH call began, the FETCH line appears in the trace data

```
Dump file C:\oracle\admin\ora817\udump\ORA01588.TRC
Tue Jan 28 10:23:25 2003
ORACLE V8.1.7.0.0 - Production vsnsta=0
vsnsql=e vsnxtr=3
Windows 2000 Version 5.0 Service Pack 3, CPU type 586
Oracle8i Enterprise Edition release 8.1.7.0.0 - Production
With the Partitioning option
JServer release 8.1.7.0.0 - Production
Windows 2000 Version 5.0 Service Pack 3, CPU type 586
Instance name: ora817

Redo thread mounted by this instance: 1

Oracle process number: 9

Windows thread id: 1588, image: ORACLE.EXE


*** 2003-01-28 10:23:25.791
*** SESSION ID:(8.1790) 2003-01-28 10:23:25.781
APPNAME mod='SQL*Plus' mh=3669949024 act='' ah=4029777240
=====================
PARSING IN CURSOR #1 len=69 dep=0 uid=5 oct=42 lid=5 tim=40966100 hv=589283212
ad='394821c'
alter session set events '10046 trace name context forever, level 8'
END OF STMT
EXEC #1:c=0,e=2,p=0,cr=0,cu=0,mis=1,r=0,dep=0,og=4,tim=40966101
WAIT #1: nam='SQL*Net message to client' ela= 0 p1=1111838976 p2=1 p3=0
*** 2003-01-28 10:23:36.267
WAIT #1: nam='SQL*Net message from client' ela= 1046 p1=1111838976 p2=1 p3=0
=====================
PARSING IN CURSOR #2 len=37 dep=1 uid=0 oct=3 lid=0 tim=40967147 hv=1966425544
ad='3afe9c4'
select text from view$ where rowid=:1
END OF STMT
PARSE #2:c=0,e=0,p=0,cr=0,cu=0,mis=0,r=0,dep=1,og=4,tim=40967147
EXEC #2:c=0,e=0,p=0,cr=0,cu=0,mis=0,r=0,dep=1,og=4,tim=40967147
WAIT #2: nam='db file sequential read' ela= 5 p1=1 p2=1669 p3=1
FETCH #2:c=0,e=5,p=1,cr=2,cu=0,mis=0,r=1,dep=1,og=4,tim=40967152
STAT #2 id=1 cnt=1 pid=0 pos=0 obj=59 op='TABLE ACCESS BY USER ROWID VIEW$ '
=====================
PARSING IN CURSOR #1 len=32 dep=0 uid=5 oct=3 lid=5 tim=40967154 hv=3588977815
ad='39b3e88'
select count(*) from dba_source
END OF STMT
PARSE #1:c=1,e=8,p=1,cr=2,cu=0,mis=1,r=0,dep=0,og=4,tim=40967155
EXEC #1:c=0,e=0,p=0,cr=0,cu=0,mis=0,r=0,dep=0,og=4,tim=40967155
WAIT #1: nam='SQL*Net message to client' ela= 0 p1=1111838976 p2=1 p3=0
WAIT #1: nam='db file sequential read' ela= 2 p1=1 p2=53 p3=1
WAIT #1: nam='db file sequential read' ela= 2 p1=1 p2=642 p3=1
WAIT #1: nam='db file sequential read' ela= 0 p1=1 p2=62 p3=1
```

Example 6-9. This trace file tail was created by tracing the same count of DBA_SOURCE rows, but this time, the tracing attribute was set by the session itself. Because tracing was active when the FETCH call began, the FETCH line appears in the trace data (continued)

```
...
Approximately 6,700 lines are omitted here, none of which contains a dep=0 action.
...
WAIT #1: nam='direct path read' ela= 0 p1=4 p2=1944 p3=2
WAIT #1: nam='direct path read' ela= 0 p1=4 p2=1834 p3=1
WAIT #1: nam='direct path read' ela= 0 p1=4 p2=1835 p3=4
WAIT #1: nam='direct path read' ela= 0 p1=4 p2=1839 p3=1
WAIT #1: nam='direct path read' ela= 1 p1=4 p2=1840 p3=2
FETCH #1:c=1449,e=3669,p=6979,cr=879863,cu=10,mis=0,r=1,dep=0,og=4,tim=40970824
UNMAP #1:c=0,e=0,p=0,cr=0,cu=0,mis=0,r=0,dep=0,og=4,tim=40970824
WAIT #1: nam='SQL*Net message from client' ela= 0 p1=1111838976 p2=1 p3=0
FETCH #1:c=0,e=0,p=0,cr=0,cu=0,mis=0,r=0,dep=0,og=0,tim=40970824
WAIT #1: nam='SQL*Net message to client' ela= 0 p1=1111838976 p2=1 p3=0
WAIT #1: nam='SQL*Net message from client' ela= 951 p1=1111838976 p2=1 p3=0
XCTEND rlbk=0, rd_only=1
STAT #1 id=1 cnt=1 pid=0 pos=0 obj=0 op='SORT AGGREGATE '
STAT #1 id=2 cnt=436983 pid=1 pos=1 obj=0 op='VIEW DBA_SOURCE '
STAT #1 id=3 cnt=436983 pid=2 pos=1 obj=0 op='SORT UNIQUE '
STAT #1 id=4 cnt=436983 pid=3 pos=1 obj=0 op='UNION-ALL '
STAT #1 id=5 cnt=436983 pid=4 pos=1 obj=0 op='NESTED LOOPS '
STAT #1 id=6 cnt=405 pid=5 pos=1 obj=0 op='NESTED LOOPS '
STAT #1 id=7 cnt=22 pid=6 pos=1 obj=22 op='TABLE ACCESS FULL USER$ '
STAT #1 id=8 cnt=425 pid=6 pos=2 obj=18 op='TABLE ACCESS BY INDEX ROWID OBJ$ '
STAT #1 id=9 cnt=3200 pid=8 pos=1 obj=34 op='INDEX RANGE SCAN '
STAT #1 id=10 cnt=436983 pid=5 pos=2 obj=64 op='TABLE ACCESS BY INDEX ROWID SOURCE$ '
STAT #1 id=11 cnt=437387 pid=10 pos=1 obj=109 op='INDEX RANGE SCAN '
STAT #1 id=12 cnt=0 pid=4 pos=2 obj=0 op='NESTED LOOPS '
STAT #1 id=13 cnt=1 pid=12 pos=1 obj=0 op='NESTED LOOPS '
STAT #1 id=14 cnt=1 pid=13 pos=1 obj=0 op='FIXED TABLE FULL X$JOXFT '
STAT #1 id=15 cnt=0 pid=13 pos=2 obj=18 op='TABLE ACCESS BY INDEX ROWID OBJ$ '
STAT #1 id=16 cnt=0 pid=15 pos=1 obj=33 op='INDEX UNIQUE SCAN '
STAT #1 id=17 cnt=0 pid=12 pos=2 obj=22 op='TABLE ACCESS CLUSTER USER$ '
STAT #1 id=18 cnt=0 pid=17 pos=1 obj=11 op='INDEX UNIQUE SCAN '
```

Activating extended SQL trace in the midst of any long-running database call is prone to causing problems with missing data, like the one you've just seen. It is important that you be able to recognize when you have committed a data collection error like this. Otherwise, if you promote data with this error from data collection into your problem diagnosis phase, you're going to be sent down a rat hole of having to deal with potentially massive amounts of *over*accounted-for time.

You can detect such a collection error by noticing that the sum of the ela values for a sequence of wait events (WAIT lines) drastically exceeds the confines of the total elapsed duration (e value) of the database call that motivated those wait events. In Example 6-8, you can see the problem by noticing that the more than 87,700 WAIT #1 lines accounted for far more than the e=3 centiseconds of elapsed duration for the UNMAP #1 call that immediately followed those WAIT lines.

The only cure for this type of collection error that I can recommend is prevention. Avoid activating SQL trace in the midst of a long-running database call. If an existing trace file contains such an error, then your best remedy is to begin your data collection procedure again.

 When you activate extended SQL trace from a third-party session, do your best never to execute the activation in the midst of a long-running database call. If you cannot avoid doing this, then it is probably best to use some of the techniques that I describe in Chapter 8.

Excess database call data at trace activation

Sometimes, the reported duration of a database call exceeds the duration for which the session's tracing attribute has been activated. This phenomenon has occurred whenever a database call's start time (value of $tim - e$) precedes the data collection start time (that is, when $tim - e < t_0$). We have observed this phenomenon in some cases when tracing has been activated by a third-party session in the midst of a long-running PL/SQL block. (The presence of a long-running PL/SQL block is what distinguishes this case from the one discussed previously, in which tracing is simply activated in the midst of a long-running database call.) The only actions in a trace file that can suffer from the excess time phenomenon are the first actions listed in the file for a given recursive depth (dep field value).

This phenomenon can be particularly difficult to notice if several thousand WAIT lines (which contain no tim fields) precede your first database call line that contains a tim field. In Chapter 5 you learned how to walk the clock backward from the first tim field value in the file through all of the ela field values until you reach the first line. However, that technique is prone to significant accumulation of systematic error as demonstrated during my explanation of clock-walking in Chapter 5.

A much better way to determine the "virtual" *tim* value for the first WAIT line in a trace file is to establish conversion functions that allow you to convert between Oracle tim field values and the system wall clock and back. You can establish a correlation between the Oracle *tim* clock and your system's wall clock by executing the following steps:

1. Execute the following commands in SQL*Plus on the system for which you are trying to establish the clock correlation:

   ```
   alter system set events '10046 trace name context forever, level 8';
   execute sys.dbms_system.ksdddt;
   exit
   ```

2. Examine the resulting trace data. It will contain lines like the following:

   ```
   *** 2003-01-28 14:30:56.513
   EXEC #1:c=0,e=483,p=0,cr=0,cu=0,mis=0,r=1,dep=0,og=4,tim=1043785856513829
   ```

3. From this information, you can establish the direct equivalence of the given tim field value to the given timestamp. In the example shown here, notice the match

in the seconds and milliseconds portions of the two times (highlighted). On our research system, the mapping is simple: each tim field value is simply a number of microseconds elapsed since the Unix Epoch (00:00:00 UTC, 1 January 1970). The program shown in Example 6-10 is the tool I use to convert back and forth between tim and wall clock values.

Example 6-10. A program that converts Oracle tim values to wall clock values and back

```perl
#!/usr/bin/perl

# $Header: /home/cvs/cvm-book1/sqltrace/tim.pl,v 1.3 2003/02/05 05:06:58 cvm Exp $
# Cary Millsap (cary.millsap@hotsos.com)

# Show the wall time that corresponds to a given tim value

use strict;
use warnings;
use Date::Format qw(time2str);
use Date::Parse  qw(str2time);

my $usage = "Usage: $0 wall-time\n        $0 tim-value\n\t";
my $arg = shift or die $usage;     # tim or wall-time value
# printf "arg =%s\n", $arg;
if ($arg =~ /^[0-9]+$/) {
    # input argument is a tim value
    my $sec  = substr($arg, 0, length($arg)-6);
    my $msec = substr($arg, -6);
    # printf "sec =%s\n", $sec;
    # printf "msec=%s\n", $msec;
    printf "%s\n", time2str("%T.$msec %A %d %B %Y", $sec);
}
else {
    # input argument is a wall time value
    my $frac = ($arg =~ /\d+:\d+\.(\d+)/) ? $1 : 0;
    if ((my $l = length $frac) >= 6) {
        # if length(frac) >=6, then round
        $frac = sprintf "%6.0f", $frac/(10**($l-6));
    } else {
        # otherwise, right-pad with zeros
        $frac .= ('0' x (6-$l));
    }
    printf "%s%s\n", str2time($arg), $frac;
}
```

Here is a simple example of a trace file whose initial lines contain data for events that occur before the moment of collection activation:

```
*** 2003-02-24 04:28:19.557
WAIT #1: ... ela= 20000000 ...
EXEC #1:c=10000000,e=30000000,...,tim= 1046082501582881
```

The problem is difficult to recognize until you convert the time values shown here into like units. Using the tool shown in Example 6-10 to convert the tim value on my Linux system to a more readable wall clock time, you can see that the execute call concluded only 2.025881 seconds after the moment tracing was activated:

```
$ perl tim.pl 1046082501582881
04:28:21.582881 Monday 24 February 2003
```

The twist is that the execute call consumed 30 seconds of elapsed time (e=30000000). Thus, part of the elapsed duration for this database call occurred prior to the time-stamp printed at the beginning of the trace file. I've already shown that this time-stamp doesn't always match the time at which the session's tracing attribute was actually set. You need to keep track of the tracing activation time (call it t_0) separately. The easiest way to do it is to mark the time in tim field units when you execute the command to activate SQL trace.

Once you have identified that there is excess time accounted for within a trace file, the next task is to eliminate it. Figure 6-7 shows how. In this figure, SQL trace is activated at time t_0, in the midst of some parse call that occurs within a long-running PL/SQL block. In this case, some of the parse call's duration e occurs within the desired observation interval, and some occurs before t_0. The excess time in this case is easy to compute, as long as you know the value of t_0 in tim units. You can compute the excess time T as:

$$T = t_0 - (t - e)$$

When the first several lines emitted into the trace file contain no tim field value, then you can compute the file's beginning t value by translating the initial timestamp value (on the *** line) into an equivalent tim value as I described previously. Remember, a timestamp is the ending time of action following that line in the trace file. The problem then reduces to the same situation as the one described in Figure 6-7, in which you know t, e, t_0 (and in fact all of the intervening ela values as well in case one of the wait event durations includes time t_0 as well).

Missing Time at Trace Deactivation

When a session terminates with extended SQL trace turned on, all of the time near the end of the session will be accounted for in the trace file. Likewise, when a session deactivates its own tracing with an ALTER SESSION SET EVENTS command, all of the session's time up to that execution will be accounted for. However, if tracing is deactivated by a third-party session, then it is likely that the deactivation will occur in the midst of either a wait event or a database call being performed by the session. When this occurs, some desirable data about the session will be missing from the trace file.

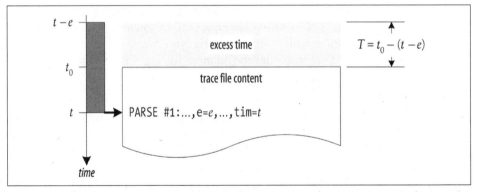

Figure 6-7. When SQL trace is activated by a third-party session at time t_0, tracing can begin in the midst of a database call. When this occurs, the trace file contains excess time that the database call consumed before SQL trace was activated

For example, I deactivated tracing for a given session at time `tim=1043788733690992`. However, the tail of trace file contains only the following data:

```
*** 2003-01-28 15:18:43.688
WAIT #1: nam='SQL*Net message from client' ela= 24762690 p1=1650815232 p2=1 p3=0
STAT #1 id=1 cnt=1 pid=0 pos=0 obj=0 op='MERGE JOIN '
STAT #1 id=2 cnt=1 pid=1 pos=1 obj=0 op='SORT JOIN '
STAT #1 id=3 cnt=1 pid=2 pos=1 obj=0 op='FIXED TABLE FULL X$KSUSE '
STAT #1 id=4 cnt=1 pid=1 pos=2 obj=0 op='SORT JOIN '
STAT #1 id=5 cnt=9 pid=4 pos=1 obj=0 op='FIXED TABLE FULL X$KSUPR '
=====================
PARSING IN CURSOR #1 len=39 dep=0 uid=5 oct=3 lid=5 tim=1043788723689828 hv=364789794
ad='512c8b5c'
select 'missing time at tail' from dual
END OF STMT
PARSE #1:c=0,e=871,p=0,cr=0,cu=0,mis=1,r=0,dep=0,og=4,tim=1043788723689794
EXEC #1:c=0,e=72,p=0,cr=0,cu=0,mis=0,r=0,dep=0,og=4,tim=1043788723690030
WAIT #1: nam='SQL*Net message to client' ela= 5 p1=1650815232 p2=1 p3=0
FETCH #1:c=0,e=118,p=0,cr=1,cu=2,mis=0,r=1,dep=0,og=4,tim=1043788723690276
WAIT #1: nam='SQL*Net message from client' ela= 445 p1=1650815232 p2=1 p3=0
FETCH #1:c=0,e=2,p=0,cr=0,cu=0,mis=0,r=0,dep=0,og=0,tim=1043788723690992
WAIT #1: nam='SQL*Net message to client' ela= 4 p1=1650815232 p2=1 p3=0
```

Notice the highlighted portion of the final `tim` field value: the trace file contains information about what happened up to time ...23.690992 (expressed in seconds), and in fact 4 ms afterward, but there's no record of what happened between times ...23.690992 and ...33.690992. There is unaccounted-for time of exactly 10 seconds.

Figure 6-8 shows how this happens. In this figure, SQL trace is deactivated at time t_1, in the midst of a wait event named z. But the Oracle kernel cannot emit a wait event's trace line until that wait event has completed. Since trace deactivation has occurred before the wait event's conclusion, nothing about the wait event is emitted to the trace file. Part of the wait event's duration occurs after t_1, but the portion of its duration that occurred before t_1 remains unaccounted for.

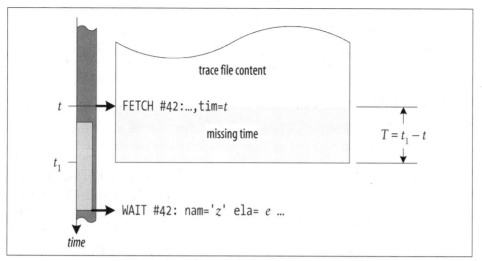

Figure 6-8. When SQL trace is deactivated by a third-party session at time t_1, tracing can end in the midst of an event. When this occurs, the time consumed by the event is never printed into the trace file, resulting in missing time

The missing time in this case is easy to compute as long as you know the value of t_1 in tim units. You can compute the missing time as:

$$T = t_1 - t$$

Again, the easiest way to keep track of t_1 is to mark the time when you execute the command to deactivate SQL trace. When you deactivate SQL trace, you also need to determine the name of the event that is in progress at time t_1. This is easy to accomplish from the third-party session with the following SQL:

```
select event from v$session_wait
where sid=:sid and state='WAITING'
```

In the Hotsos *Sparky* data collector, we execute a query that is similar to this one immediately prior to executing the command to activate tracing. If this query returns *no* event name, then you should attribute the missing time T to total CPU consumption. If this query does return an event name, then at least some of the missing time T is attributable to the event whose name is returned by the query. As you can see in Figure 6-8, some of the missing time may still be attributable to CPU consumption.

 It is also possible that some of the missing time is consumed by an uninstrumented sequence of Oracle kernel instructions, the concept of which is explained in Chapter 7.

It may be possible to determine approximately how much of T you should attribute to CPU consumption and how much to event. However, our field work has shown that when the V$SESSION_WAIT query returns an event name, attributing all of T to that event is a good approximation.

The presence of WAIT lines at the tail of the trace file complicates the computation of missing time slightly by introducing another walk-the-clock exercise. In this case, you must construct *t* by walking the clock forward through ela field values from the final tim field value in the file.

Incomplete Recursive SQL Data

Activating and deactivating SQL trace from a third-party session can also cause truncation of the trace data required to determine the nature of recursive SQL relationships. Activating SQL trace after the execution of recursive actions but before the completion of their parent action causes trace data that is absent the child data. For example, if you execute the following PL/SQL code, the resulting trace file will reveal several recursive relationships between the various elements of the block and the block itself:

```
alter session set events '10046 trace name context forever, level 8';
declare
    cursor lc is select count(*) from sys.source$;
    cnt number;
begin
    open lc;
    fetch lc into cnt;
    close lc;
    open lc;
    fetch lc into cnt;
    close lc;
end;
/
```

However, you change the trace data considerably if you omit the ALTER SESSION command and activate tracing from a third-party session (with, for example, DBMS_SUPPORT.START_TRACE_IN_SESSION) in the midst of the block's execution. What you'll find if you do this is that the kernel will omit a significant amount of detail for any of the recursive child actions whose executions began before tracing was activated. Activating SQL trace from a third-party session creates the possibility that the trace file will not contain child database calls for all the recursive parent actions listed in the trace file.

As in the missing database call data at trace activation case described previously, the best remedy to this type of data collection error is avoidance. And avoidance should come naturally if you are basing your data collection upon user actions, as you should be. However, even if you hit the "start collecting" button a little late, this type of data collection error is not nearly as severe as the database call-interruption type I described previously. Although there will be missing detail that would perhaps help explain why a session consumed the time it did, at least you'll typically have the parent database call data to help guide your analysis.

Similarly, *de*activating SQL trace from a third-party session creates the possibility that the trace file will not contain *parent* database calls for all the recursive (*dep* > 0) actions in the trace file. For example, imagine in Example 6-11 that tracing had been active for the beginning of the excerpt but then deactivated by a third-party session at the point labeled ❶. The result is shown in Example 6-12.

Example 6-11. This listing (a copy of Example 6-5) shows what really happened during the parse of the DBA_OBJECTS query: the parse motivated three recursive database calls upon a query of VIEW$

```
...
=====================
PARSING IN CURSOR #2 len=37 dep=1 uid=0 oct=3 lid=0 tim=1033174180230513 hv=1966425544
ad='514bb478'
select text from view$ where rowid=:1
END OF STMT
PARSE #2:c=0,e=107,p=0,cr=0,cu=0,mis=0,r=0,dep=1,og=4,tim=1033174180230481
BINDS #2:
 bind 0: dty=11 mxl=16(16) mal=00 scl=00 pre=00 oacflg=18 oacfl2=1 size=16 offset=0
   bfp=0a22c34c bln=16 avl=16 flg=05
   value=00000AB8.0000.0001
EXEC #2:c=0,e=176,p=0,cr=0,cu=0,mis=0,r=0,dep=1,og=4,tim=1033174180230878
FETCH #2:c=0,e=89,p=0,cr=2,cu=0,mis=0,r=1,dep=1,og=4,tim=1033174180231021
❶
STAT #2 id=1 cnt=1 pid=0 pos=0 obj=62 op='TABLE ACCESS BY USER ROWID VIEW$ '
=====================
PARSING IN CURSOR #1 len=85 dep=0 uid=5 oct=3 lid=5 tim=1033174180244680 hv=1205236555
ad='50cafbec'
select object_id, object_type, owner, object_name from dba_objects where object_id=:v
END OF STMT
PARSE #1:c=10000,e=15073,p=0,cr=2,cu=0,mis=1,r=0,dep=0,og=0,tim=1033174180244662
...
```

In Example 6-11, you have positive evidence of a recursive relationship among database calls, because there are three actions listed with the string dep=1 (highlighted in both Examples 6-11 and 6-12). The problem in Example 6-12 is that tracing was deactivated before the Oracle kernel emitted any information for the dep=0 recursive parent of these actions. Note that in Example 6-11, you can see the dep=0 action (highlighted) that serves as the parent, but in Example 6-12, the trace was deactivated before the dep=0 parent was emitted to the trace file.

Example 6-12. In this trace file tail, there is no database call following the dep=1 actions to act as these actions' parent

```
...
=====================
PARSING IN CURSOR #2 len=37 dep=1 uid=0 oct=3 lid=0 tim=1033174180230513 hv=1966425544
ad='514bb478'
select text from view$ where rowid=:1
END OF STMT
PARSE #2:c=0,e=107,p=0,cr=0,cu=0,mis=0,r=0,dep=1,og=4,tim=1033174180230481
```

Example 6-12. In this trace file tail, there is no database call following the dep=1 actions to act as these actions' parent (continued)

```
BINDS #2:
 bind 0: dty=11 mxl=16(16) mal=00 scl=00 pre=00 oacflg=18 oacfl2=1 size=16 offset=0
   bfp=0a22c34c bln=16 avl=16 flg=05
   value=00000AB8.0000.0001
EXEC #2:c=0,e=176,p=0,cr=0,cu=0,mis=0,r=0,dep=1,og=4,tim=1033174180230878
FETCH #2:c=0,e=89,p=0,cr=2,cu=0,mis=0,r=1,dep=1,og=4,tim=1033174180231021
STAT #2 id=1 cnt=1 pid=0 pos=0 obj=62 op='TABLE ACCESS BY USER ROWID VIEW$ '
End of file
```

From the truncated data of Example 6-12, you can know that there are three recursive SQL actions that have a parent somewhere, but you cannot know the identity of that parent. These database calls are thus "orphans." Deactivating SQL trace from a third-party session creates the possibility that the trace file will not contain parent database calls for all the recursive (*dep* > 0) actions listed in the trace file.

Once again, the best remedy for this type of collection error is avoidance. Avoidance of this type of error should come naturally if you are basing your data collection stop time upon the observation of a user action, as you should be.

Exercises

1. System administrators and database administrators can argue endlessly about whether the setting of the TIMED_STATISTICS Oracle parameter has a profound effect upon application performance. Research Oracle *MetaLink* to determine whether there are any bugs that induce an unacceptable penalty upon your implementation. Next, construct an experiment to reveal the response time impact of using a system-wide value of TIMED_STATISTICS=TRUE.

2. A trace file contains elapsed time data about significantly less time than the known duration of the attempted observation interval. Explain the types of data collection error that could have caused this phenomenon to occur.

Oracle Kernel Timings

Regardless of whether you access the Oracle kernel's timing statistics through extended SQL trace data, V$ fixed views, or even by hacking directly into the Oracle shared memory segment beneath those V$ fixed views, the time statistics you're accessing were obtained using a simple set of operating system function calls. Regardless of which interface you use to access them, those timing statistics are subject to the limitations inherent in the operating system timers that were used to produce them. This chapter explains those limitations and describes their true impact upon your work.

Operating System Process Management

From the perspective of your system's host operating system, the Oracle kernel is just an application. There's nothing mystical about how it works; it's just a huge, extremely impressive C program. To gain a full appreciation for the operational timing data that the Oracle kernel reveals, you need to understand a little bit about the services an operating system provides to the Oracle kernel.

In this section, I am going to focus my descriptions on the behavior of operating systems derived from Unix. If your operating system is a Unix derivative like Linux, Sun Solaris, HP-UX, IBM AIX, or Tru64, then the explanations you will see here will closely resemble the behavior of your system. You should find the descriptions in this section relevant even if you are studying a Microsoft Windows system. If your operating system is not listed here, then I suggest that you augment the descriptions in this section with the appropriate operating system internals documentation for your system.

The Design of the Unix Operating System, written by Maurice Bach, contains what is still my very favorite tool for describing what a process "does" in the context of a modern operating system. Bach's Figure 2-6, entitled "Process States and Transitions" [Bach 1986 (31)], serves as my starting point. I have reproduced it here as Figure 7-1. In this diagram, each *node* (rectangle) represents a state that a process can take on in the operating system. Each *edge* (directed line) represents a transition from one state to another. Think of states as nouns and transitions as verbs that motivate the passage of a process from one state to the next.

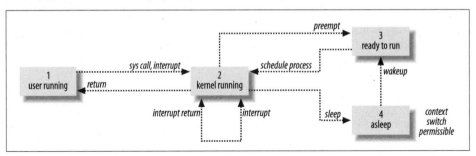

Figure 7-1. This simplified process state diagram illustrates the principal states that a process can assume in most modern time-sharing operating systems [Bach (1986) 31]

Most Oracle kernel processes spend most of their time in the *user running* state, also called *user mode*. Parsing SQL, sorting rows, reading blocks in the buffer cache, and converting data types are common operations that Oracle executes in user mode. There are two events that can cause a process to transition from the user running state to the *kernel running* state (also called *kernel mode*). It is important for you to understand both transitions from user mode to kernel mode. Let's follow each one in more detail.

The sys call Transition

When a process in user mode makes an operating system call (a *sys call*), it transitions to kernel mode. read and select are two typical system calls. Once in kernel mode, a process is endowed with special privileges that allow it to manipulate low-level hardware components and arbitrary memory locations. In kernel mode, a process is able, for example, to manipulate I/O devices like sockets and disk drives [Bovet and Cesati (2001) 8].

Many types of system call can be expected to wait on a device for many, many CPU cycles. For example, a read call of a disk subsystem today typically consumes time on the order of a few milliseconds. Many CPUs today can execute millions of instructions in the time it takes to execute one physical disk I/O operation. So during a single read call, enough time to perform on the order of a million CPU instructions will elapse. Designers of efficient read system calls of course realize this and design their code in a manner that allows another process to use the CPU while the reading process waits.

Imagine, for example, an Oracle kernel process executing some kind of read system call to obtain a block of Oracle data from a disk. After issuing a request from an expectedly "slow" device, the kernel code in the read system call will transition its calling process into the *sleep* state, where that process will await an interrupt signaling that the I/O operation is complete. This polite yielding of the CPU allows another *ready to run* process to consume the CPU capacity that the reading process would have been unable to use anyway.

When the I/O device signals that the *asleep* process's I/O operation is ready for further processing, the process is "awoken," which is to say that it transitions to *ready to run* state. When the process becomes ready to run, it becomes eligible for scheduling. When the scheduler again chooses the process for execution, the process is returned to *kernel running* state, where the remaining kernel mode code path of the read call is executed (for example, the data transfer of the content obtained from the I/O channel into memory). The final instruction in the read subroutine returns control to the calling program (our Oracle kernel process), which is to say that the process transitions back into *user running* state. In this state, the Oracle kernel process continues consuming user-mode CPU until it next receives an interrupt or makes a system call.

exit, by the way, is itself a system call, so even when an application finishes its work, the *only* ways out of the *user running* state are the *sys call* and *interrupt* transitions.

The interrupt Transition

The second path through the operating system process state diagram is motivated by an *interrupt*. An interrupt is a mechanism through which a device such as an I/O peripheral or the system clock can interrupt the CPU asynchronously [Bach (1986) 16]. I've already described why an I/O peripheral might interrupt a process. Most systems are configured so that the system clock generates an interrupt every 1/100th of a second (that is, once per centisecond). Upon receipt of a clock interrupt, each process on the system in *user running* state saves its *context* (a frozen image of what the process was doing) and executes the operating system *scheduler* subroutine. The scheduler determines whether to allow the process to continue running or to *preempt* the process.

Preemption essentially sends a process directly from *kernel running* state to *ready to run* state, clearing the way for some other *ready to run* process to return to *user running* state [Bach (1986) 148]. This is how most modern operating systems implement time-sharing. Any process in *ready to run* state is subject to treatment that is identical to what I have described previously. The process becomes eligible for scheduling, and so on. Your understanding of preemptions motivated by clock interrupts will become particularly important later in this chapter when I describe one of the most important causes of "missing data" in an Oracle trace file.

Other States and Transitions

I have already alluded to the existence of a more complicated process state transition diagram than I've shown in Figure 7-1. Indeed, after discussing the four process states and seven of the transitions depicted in Figure 7-1, Bach later in his book reveals a more complete process state transition diagram [Bach (1986) 148]. The more complicated diagram details the actions undertaken during transitions such as preempting, swapping, forking, and even the creation of zombie processes. If you run applications on Unix systems, I strongly encourage you to add Bach's book to your library.

For the purposes of the remainder of this chapter, however, Figure 7-1 is all you need. I hope you will agree that it is easy to learn the precise definitions of Oracle timing statistics by considering them in terms of the process states shown in Figure 7-1.

Oracle Kernel Timings

The Oracle kernel publishes only a few different types of timing information. Extended SQL trace output contains four important ones. You can see all four on the following two lines, generated by an Oracle release 9.0.1.2.0 kernel a Solaris 5.6 system:

```
WAIT #34: nam='db file sequential read' ela= 14118 p1=52 p2=2755 p3=1
FETCH #34:c=0,e=15656,p=1,cr=6,cu=0,mis=0,r=1,dep=3,og=4,tim=1017039276349760
```

The two adjacent lines of trace data shown here describe a single fetch database call. The timing statistics in these lines are the following:

ela= 14118

> The Oracle kernel consumed an elapsed time of 14,118 microseconds (or µs, where 1 µs = 0.000 001 seconds) executing a system call denoted db file sequential read.

c=0

> The Oracle kernel reports that a fetch database call consumed 0 µs of total CPU capacity.

e=15656

> The kernel reports that the fetch consumed 15,656 µs of elapsed time.

tim=1017039276349760

> The system time when the fetch concluded was 1,017,039,276,349,760 (expressed in microseconds elapsed since midnight UTC 1 January 1970).

The total elapsed duration of the fetch includes both the call's total CPU capacity consumption and any time that the fetch has consumed during the execution of Oracle wait events. The statistics in my two lines of trace data are related through the approximation:

$$e \approx c + ela$$

In this case, the approximation is pretty good on a human scale: $15656 \approx 0 + 14118$, which is accurate to within 0.001538 seconds.

A single database call (such as a *parse*, *execute*, or *fetch*) emits only one database call line (such as PARSE, EXEC, or FETCH) to the trace data (notwithstanding the *recursive* database calls that a single database call can motivate). However, a single database call may emit several WAIT lines representing system calls for each cursor action line. For example, the following trace file excerpt shows 6,288 db file sequential read calls executed by a single fetch:

```
WAIT #44: nam='db file sequential read' ela= 15147 p1=25 p2=24801 p3=1
...
6,284 similar WAIT lines are omitted here for clarity

...
WAIT #44: nam='db file sequential read' ela= 105 p1=25 p2=149042 p3=1
WAIT #44: nam='db file sequential read' ela= 18831 p1=5 p2=115263 p3=1
WAIT #44: nam='db file sequential read' ela= 114 p1=58 p2=58789 p3=1
FETCH #44:c=7000000,e=23700217,p=6371,cr=148148,cu=0,mis=0,r=1,dep=1,og=4,
tim=1017039304454213
```

So the true relationship that binds the values of c, e, and ela for a given database call must refer to the *sum* of ela values that were produced within the context of a given database call:

$$e \approx c + \sum_{db\ call} ela$$

This approximation is the basis for all response time measurement in the Oracle kernel.

How Software Measures Itself

Finding out how the Oracle kernel measures itself is not a terribly difficult task. This section is based on studies of Oracle8*i* and Oracle9*i* kernels running on Linux systems. The Oracle software for your host operating system might use different system calls than our system uses. To find out, you should see how *your* Oracle system behaves by using a software tool that traces system calls for a specified process. For example, Linux provides a tool called strace to trace system calls. Other operating systems use different names for the tool. There is truss for Sun Solaris (truss is actually the original system call tracing tool for Unix), sctrace for IBM AIX, tusc for HP-UX, and strace for Microsoft Windows. I shall use the Linux name strace to refer generically to the collection of tools that trace system calls.

 At the time of this writing, it is possible to find strace tools for several operating systems at *http://www.pugcentral.org/howto/truss.htm*.

The strace tool is easy to use. For example, you can observe directly what the Oracle kernel is doing, right when each action takes place, by executing a command like the following:

```
$ strace -p 12417
read(7,
```

In this example, strace shows that a Linux program with process ID 12417 (which happens to have been an Oracle kernel process on my system) has issued a read call and is awaiting fulfillment of that call (hence the absence of the right parenthesis in the output shown here).

It is especially instructive to view strace output and Oracle SQL trace output simultaneously in two windows, so that you can observe exactly *when* lines are emitted to both output streams. The write calls that the Oracle kernel uses to emit its trace data of course appear in the strace output exactly when you would expect them to. The appearance of these calls makes it easy to understand when Oracle kernel actions produce trace data. In Oracle9*i* for Linux (and Oracle9*i* for some other operating systems), it is especially easy to correlate strace output and SQL trace output, because values returned by gettimeofday appear directly in the trace file as tim values. By using strace and SQL trace simultaneously in this manner, you can positively confirm or refute whether your Oracle kernel behaves like the pseudocode that you will see in the following sections.

 Using strace will introduce significant *measurement intrusion effect* into the performance of the program you're tracing. I discuss the performance effects of measurement intrusion later in this chapter.

Elapsed Time

The Oracle kernel derives all of its timing statistics from the results of system calls issued upon the host operating system. Example 7-1 shows how a program like the Oracle kernel computes the durations of its own actions.

Example 7-1. How software measures its own response time

```
t0 = gettimeofday;    # mark the time immediately before doing something
do_something;
t1 = gettimeofday;    # mark the time immediately after doing it
t = t1 - t0;          # t is the approximate duration of do_something
```

The gettimeofday function is an operating system call found on POSIX-compliant systems. You can learn by viewing your operating system's documentation that gettimeofday provides a C language data structure to its caller that contains the number of seconds and microseconds that have elapsed since the Epoch, which is 00:00:00 Coordinated Universal Time (UTC), January 1, 1970.

Documentation for such system calls is usually available with your operating system. For example, on Unix systems, you can view the gettimeofday documentation by typing man gettimeofday at the Unix prompt. Or you can visit *http://www.unix-systems.org/single_unix_specification/* to view the POSIX definition.

Note that in my pseudocode, I've hidden many mechanical details that I find distracting. For example, gettimeofday doesn't really return a time; it returns 0 for success and −1 for failure. It writes the "returned" time as a two-element structure (a *seconds* part and a *microseconds* part) in a location referenced by the caller's first argument in the gettimeofday call. I believe that showing all this detail in my pseudocode would serve only to complicate my descriptions unnecessarily.

Imagine the execution of Example 7-1 on a timeline, as shown in Figure 7-2. In the drawing, the value of the gettimeofday clock is $t_0 = 1492$ when a function called do_something begins. The value of the gettimeofday clock is $t_1 = 1498$ when do_something ends. Thus the measured duration of do_something is $t = t_1 - t_0 = 6$ clock ticks.

I've used the time values 1492 through 1499 to keep our discussion simple. These values of course do not resemble the actual second and microsecond values that gettimeofday would return in the twenty-first century. Consider the values I'll discuss in this book to be just the final few digits of an actual clock.

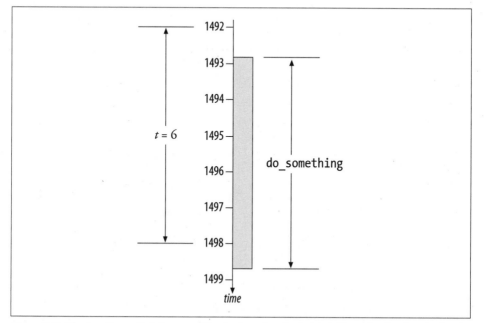

Figure 7-2. The function called do_something begins after clock tick 1492 and ends after clock tick 1498, resulting in a measured response time of 6 clock ticks

The Oracle kernel reports on two types of elapsed duration: the e statistic denotes the elapsed duration of a single database call, and the ela statistic denotes the elapsed duration of an instrumented sequence of instructions (often a system call) executed by an Oracle kernel process. The kernel performs these computations by executing code that is structured roughly like the pseudocode shown in Example 7-2. Notice that the kernel uses the method shown in Example 7-1 as the basic building block for constructing the e and ela metrics.

Example 7-2. Pseudocode showing how the Oracle kernel measures its own run times

```
procedure dbcall {
    e0 = gettimeofday;      # mark the wall time
    ...                     # execute the db call (may call wevent)
    e1 = gettimeofday;      # mark the wall time
    e = e1 - e0;            # elapsed duration of dbcall
    print(TRC, ...);        # emit PARSE, EXEC, FETCH, etc. line
}

procedure wevent {
    ela0 = gettimeofday;    # mark the wall time
    ...                     # execute the wait event here
    ela1 = gettimeofday;    # mark the wall time
    ela = ela1 - ela0;      # ela is the duration of the wait event
    print(TRC, "WAIT...");  # emit WAIT line
}
```

CPU Consumption

The Oracle kernel reports not only the elapsed duration e for each database call and ela for each system call, but also the amount of total CPU capacity c consumed by each database call. In the context of the process state transition diagram shown in Figure 7-1, the c statistic is defined as the approximate amount of time that a process has spent in the following states:

user running
kernel running

On POSIX-compliant operating systems, the Oracle kernel obtains CPU usage information from a function called getrusage on Linux and many other operating systems, or a similar function called times on HP-UX and a few other systems. Although the specifications of these two system calls vary significantly, I will use the name getrusage to refer generically to either function. Each function provides its caller with a variety of statistics about a process, including data structures representing the following four characteristics:

- Approximate time spent by the process in *user running* state
- Approximate time spent by the process in *kernel running* state
- Approximate time spent by the process's children in *user running* state
- Approximate time spent by the process's children in *kernel running* state

Each of these amounts is expressed in microseconds, regardless of whether the data are accurate to that degree of precision.

 You'll see shortly that, although by POSIX standard, getrusage returns information expressed in microseconds, rarely does the information contain detail at sub-centisecond resolution.

The Oracle kernel performs c, e, and ela computations by executing code that is structured roughly like the pseudocode shown in Example 7-3. Notice that this example builds upon Example 7-2 by including executions of the getrusage system call and the subsequent manipulation of the results. In a method analogous to the gettimeofday calculations, the Oracle kernel marks the amount of user-mode CPU time consumed by the process at the beginning of the database call, and then again at the end. The difference between the two marks (c0 and c1) is the approximate amount of user-mode CPU capacity that was consumed by the database call. Shortly I'll fill you in on exactly how approximate the amount is.

Example 7-3. Pseudocode showing how the Oracle kernel measures its own run times and CPU consumption

```
procedure dbcall {
    e0 = gettimeofday;          # mark the wall time
    c0 = getrusage;             # obtain resource usage statistics
    ...                         # execute the db call (may call wevent)
    c1 = getrusage;             # obtain resource usage statistics
    e1 = gettimeofday;          # mark the wall time
    e = e1 - e0;                # elapsed duration of dbcall
    c = (c1.utime + c1.stime)
      - (c0.utime + c0.stime);  # total CPU time consumed by dbcall
    print(TRC, ...);            # emit PARSE, EXEC, FETCH, etc. line
}

procedure wevent {
    ela0 = gettimeofday;        # mark the wall time
    ...                         # execute the wait event here
    ela1 = gettimeofday;        # mark the wall time
    ela = ela1 - ela0;          # ela is the duration of the wait event
    print(TRC, "WAIT...");      # emit WAIT line
}
```

Unaccounted-for Time

Virtually every trace file you'll ever analyze will have some mismatch between actual response time and the amount of time that the Oracle kernel accounts for in its trace file. Sometimes there will be an under-counting of time, and sometimes there will be an over-counting of time. For reasons you'll understand shortly, under-counting is more common than over-counting. In this book, I refer to both situations as *unaccounted-for time*. When there's missing time, there is a positive unaccounted-for duration. When there is an over-counting of time, there is a negative unaccounted-for duration. Unaccounted-for time in Oracle trace files can be caused by five distinct phenomena:

- Measurement intrusion effect
- CPU consumption double-counting
- Quantization error
- Time spent not executing
- Un-instrumented Oracle kernel code

I'll discuss each of these contributors of unaccounted-for time in the following sections.

Measurement Intrusion Effect

Any software application that attempts to measure the elapsed durations of its own subroutines is susceptible to a type of error called *measurement intrusion effect* [Malony et al. (1992)]. Measurement intrusion effect is a type of error that occurs because the execution duration of a measured subroutine is different from the execution duration of the subroutine when it is not being measured. In recent years, I have *not* had reason to suspect that measurement intrusion effect has meaningfully influenced any Oracle response time measurement I've analyzed. However, understanding the effect has helped me fend off illegitimate arguments against the reliability of Oracle operational timing data.

To understand measurement intrusion, imagine the following problem. You have a program called U, which looks like this:

```
program U {
    # uninstrumented
    do_something;
}
```

Your goal is to find out how much time is consumed by the subroutine called do_something. So you instrument your program U, resulting in a new program called I:

```
program I {
    # instrumented
    e0 = gettimeofday;  # instrumentation
    do_something;
    e1 = gettimeofday;  # instrumentation
    printf("e=%.6f sec\n", (e1-e0)/1E6);
}
```

You would expect this new program I to print the execution duration of do_something. But the value it prints is only an approximation of do_something's runtime duration. The value being printed, e1 – e0 converted to seconds, contains not just the duration of do_something, but the duration of one gettimeofday call as well. The picture in Figure 7-3 shows why.

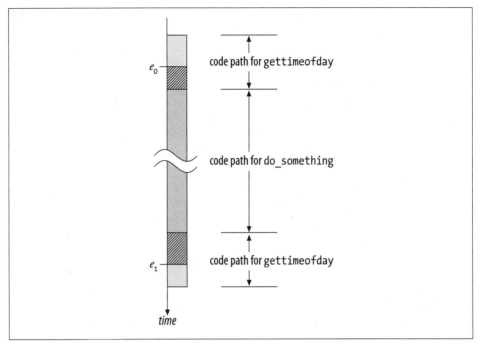

Figure 7-3. The elapsed time $e_1 - e_0$ is only an approximation of the duration of do_something; the duration also includes the total execution duration (shaded area) of one gettimeofday call

The impact of measurement intrusion effect upon program U is the following:

- Execution time of I includes two gettimeofday code paths more than the execution time of U.

- The measured duration of do_something in I includes one full gettimeofday code path more than do_something actually consumes.

This impact is minimal for applications in which the duration of one gettimeofday call is small relative to the duration of whatever do_something-like subroutine you are measuring. However, on systems with inefficient gettimeofday implementations (I believe that HP-UX versions prior to release 10 could be characterized this way), the effect could be meaningful.

Measurement intrusion effect is a type of *systematic error*. A systematic error is the result of an experimental "mistake" that is consistent across measurements [Lilja (2000)]. The consistency of measurement intrusion makes it possible to compute its influence upon your data. For example, to quantify the Oracle kernel's measurement intrusion effect introduced by gettimeofday calls, you need two pieces of data:

- The number of timer calls that the Oracle kernel makes for a given operation.

- The expected duration of a single timer call.

Once you know the frequency and average duration of your Oracle kernel's timer calls, you have everything you need to quantify their measurement intrusion effect. Measurement intrusion is probably one reason for the missing time that you will encounter when performing an Oracle9*i* clock-walk (Chapter 5).

Finding these two pieces of data is not difficult. You can use the strace tool for your platform to find out how many timer calls your Oracle kernel makes for a given set of database operations. To compute the expected duration of one timer call, you can use a program like the one shown in Example 7-4. This code measures the distance between adjacent gettimeofday calls and then computes their average duration over a sample size of your choosing.

Example 7-4. Measuring the measurement intrusion effect of calls to gettimeofday

```perl
#!/usr/bin/perl

# $Header: /home/cvs/cvm-book1/measurement\040intrusion/mef.pl,v 1.4 2003/03/19 04:38:48
cvm Exp $
# Cary Millsap (cary.millsap@hotsos.com)
# Copyright (c) 2003 by Hotsos Enterprises, Ltd. All rights reserved.

use strict;
use warnings;
use Time::HiRes qw(gettimeofday);

sub fnum($;$$) {
    # return string representation of numeric value in
    # %.${precision}f format with specified separators
    my ($text, $precision, $separator) = @_;
    $precision = 0   unless defined $precision;
    $separator = "," unless defined $separator;
    $text = reverse sprintf "%.${precision}f", $text;
    $text =~ s/(\d\d\d)(?=\d)(?!\d*\.)/$1$separator/g;
    return scalar reverse $text;
}

my ($min, $max) = (100, 0);
my $sum = 0;
print "How many iterations? "; my $n = <>;
print "Enter 'y' if you want to see all the data: "; my $all = <>;
for (1 .. $n) {
    my ($s0, $m0) = gettimeofday;
    my ($s1, $m1) = gettimeofday;
    my $sec = ($s1 - $s0) + ($m1 - $m0)/1E6;
    printf "%0.6f\n", $sec if $all =~ /y/i;
    $min = $sec if $sec < $min;
    $max = $sec if $sec > $max;
    $sum += $sec;
}
printf "gettimeofday latency for %s samples\n", fnum($n);
printf "\t%0.6f    seconds minimum\n", $min;
printf "\t%0.6f    seconds maximum\n", $max;
printf "\t%0.9f seconds average\n", $sum/$n;
```

On my Linux system used for research (800MHz Intel Pentium), this code reveals typical gettimeofday latencies of about 2 μs:

```
Linux$ mef
How many iterations? 1000000
Enter 'y' if you want to see all the data: n
gettimeofday latency for 1,000,000 samples
        0.000001    seconds minimum
        0.000376    seconds maximum
        0.000002269 seconds average
```

Measurement intrusion effect depends greatly upon operating system implementation. For example, on my Microsoft Windows 2000 laptop computer (also 800MHz Intel Pentium), gettimeofday causes more than 2.5 times as much measurement intrusion effect as our Linux server, with an average of almost 6 μs:

```
Win2k$ perl mef.pl
How many iterations? 1000000
Enter 'y' if you want to see all the data: n
gettimeofday latency for 1,000,000 samples
        0.000000    seconds minimum
        0.040000    seconds maximum
        0.000005740 seconds average
```

By experimenting with system calls in this manner, you can begin to understand some of the constraints under which the kernel developers at Oracle Corporation must work. Measurement intrusion effect is why developers tend to create timing instrumentation only for events whose durations are long relative to the duration of the measurement intrusion. The tradeoff is to provide valuable timing information without debilitating the performance of the application being measured.

CPU Consumption Double-Counting

Another inaccuracy in the relationship:

$$e \approx c + \sum_{db\ call} ela$$

is an inherent double-counting of CPU time in the right-hand side of the approximation. The Oracle kernel definition of the c statistic is all time spent in user running and kernel running states. Each ela statistic contains all time spent within an instrumented sequence of Oracle kernel instructions. When the instrumented sequence of instructions causes consumption of CPU capacity, that consumption is double-counted.

For example, imagine an Oracle database call that performs a disk read, such as the one shown in Figure 7-4. In this drawing, a database call begins its execution at time e_0. For the duration labeled A, the call consumes CPU capacity in the user running state. At time ela_0, the Oracle kernel process issues the gettimeofday call that precedes the execution of an Oracle wait event. Depending upon the operating system, the execution of the gettimeofday system call puts the Oracle kernel process into kernel running state for a few microseconds before retuning the process to user running state.

 Some Linux kernels allow the gettimeofday system call to execute entirely in user running state, resulting in a significant performance improvement (for one example, see *http://www-124.ibm.com/linux/patches/?patch_id=597*).

After some more CPU consumption in user running state for the duration labeled *B*, the process transitions into kernel running state for the duration labeled *C*. At the conclusion of duration *C*, the kernel process transitions to the asleep state and awaits the result of the request from the disk.

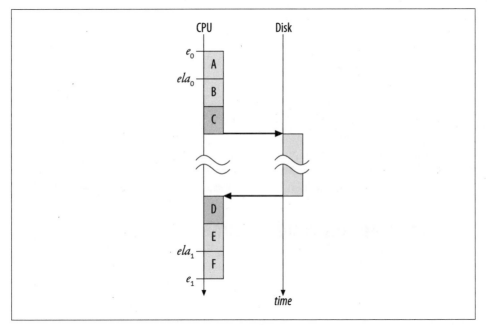

Figure 7-4. This Oracle database call consumes CPU in both user mode and kernel mode, and it waits for a read from disk

Upon completion of the request, the disk sends an interrupt that motivates the wakeup of the Oracle kernel process, which then transitions to the ready to run state. In Figure 7-4, the CPU is idle at this point in time, and the process is immediately scheduled and thus transitioned to kernel running state. While executing in this state, the Oracle process then wraps up the details of the disk I/O call, such as the copying of the data from the I/O channel to the Oracle process's user-addressable memory, which consumes the duration labeled *D*.

Finally at the end of duration D, the disk read call returns, and the Oracle process transitions to user running state for the duration labeled E. At time ela_1, the Oracle process marks the end of the disk read with a gettimeofday call. The Oracle process then proceeds to execute the remaining instructions (also in user running state) that are required to complete the database call. Finally, at time e_1, the database call processing is complete.

As the result of these actions, the Oracle kernel will produce the following statistics for the database call:

$$e = e_1 - e_0$$
$$ela = ela_1 - ela_0 = B + C + Disk + D + E$$
$$c = A + B + C + D + E + F$$

I shall describe, a little later, exactly how c is computed. The value that c will have is approximately the sum of the durations A, B, C, D, E, and F. At this point, it should be easy for you to see where the double-counting occurs. Both ela and c contain the durations B, C, D, and E. The segments of CPU consumption that have occurred within the confines of the wait event have been double-counted.

How big of a problem is the double-counting? Fortunately, the practical impact is usually negligible. Our experience with over a thousand trace files at *hotsos.com* indicates that the durations marked as B, C, D, and E in Figure 7-4 are usually small. It appears that most of the wait events instrumented in Oracle8*i* and Oracle9*i* have response times (that is, ela values) that are dominated by durations other than CPU consumption. In a few rare cases (I'll show you one shortly), the double-counting shows up in small sections of trace data, but in the overall scheme of Oracle response time accounting, the effect of *CPU consumption double-counting* seems to be generally negligible.

Quantization Error

A few years ago, a friend argued that Oracle's extended SQL trace capability was a performance diagnostic dead-end. His argument was that in an age of 1GHz CPUs, the one-centisecond resolution of the then-contemporary Oracle8*i* kernel was practically useless. However, in many hundreds of projects in the field, the extended SQL trace feature has performed with practically flawless reliability—even the "old one-centisecond stuff" from Oracle8*i*. The reliability of extended SQL trace is difficult to understand unless you understand the properties of *measurement resolution* and *quantization error*.

Measurement Resolution

When I was a kid, one of the everyday benefits of growing up in the Space Age was the advent of the digital alarm clock. Digital clocks are fantastically easy to read, even for little boys who don't yet know how to "tell the time." It's hard to go wrong when you can see those big red numbers showing "7:29". With an analog clock, a kid sometimes has a hard time knowing whether it's five o'clock and seven o'clock, but the digital difference between 5 and 7 is unmistakable.

But there's a problem with digital clocks. When you glance at a digital clock that shows "7:29", how close is it to 7:30? The problem with digital clocks is that you can't know. With a digital clock, you can't tell whether it's 7:29:00 or 7:29:59 or anything in-between. With an analog clock, even one without a second-hand, you can guess about fractions of minutes by looking at how close the minute hand is to the next minute.

All times measured on digital computers derive ultimately from *interval timers*, which behave like the good old digital clocks at our bedsides. An interval timer is a device that ticks at fixed time intervals. Times collected from interval timers can exhibit interesting idiosyncrasies. Before you can make reliable decisions based upon Oracle timing data, you need to understand the limitations of interval timers.

An interval timer's *resolution* is the elapsed duration between adjacent clock ticks. Timer resolution is the inverse of *timer frequency*. So a timer that ticks at 1 GHz (approximately 10^9 ticks per second) has a resolution of approximately $1/10^9$ seconds per tick, or about 1 nanosecond (ns) per tick. The larger a timer's resolution, the less detail it can reveal about the duration of a measured event. But for some timers (especially ones involving software), making the resolution too small can increase system overhead so much that you alter the performance behavior of the event you're trying to measure.

As a timing statistic passes upward from hardware through various layers of application software, each application layer can either degrade its resolution or leave its resolution unaltered. For example:

- The resolution of the result of the gettimeofday system call, by POSIX standard, is one microsecond. However, many Intel Pentium CPUs contain a hardware time stamp counter that provides resolution of one nanosecond. The Linux gettimeofday call, for example, converts a value from nanoseconds (10^{-9} seconds) to microseconds (10^{-6} seconds) by performing an integer division of the nanosecond value by 1,000, effectively discarding the final three digits of information.

- The resolution of the e statistic on Oracle8i is one centisecond. However, most modern operating systems provide gettimeofday information with microsecond accuracy. The Oracle8i kernel converts a value from microseconds (10^{-6} seconds) to centiseconds (10^{-2} seconds) by performing an integer division of the microsecond value by 10,000, effectively discarding the final four digits of information [Wood (2003)].

Heisenberg Uncertainty and Computer Performance Analysis

The problem of measuring computer event durations with a discrete clock is analogous to the famous *uncertainty principal* of quantum physics. The uncertainty principal, formulated by Werner Heisenberg in 1926, holds that the uncertainty in the position of a particle times the uncertainty in its velocity times the mass of the particle can never be smaller than a certain quantity, which is known as Planck's constant [Hawking (1988) 55]. Hence, for very small particles, it is impossible to know precisely both the particle's position and its velocity.

Similarly, it is difficult to measure some things very precisely in a computing system, especially when using software clocks. A smaller resolution yields a more accurate measurement, but using a smaller resolution on a clock implemented with software can have a debilitating performance impact upon the application you're trying to measure. You'll see an example later in this chapter when I discuss the resolution of the getrusage system function.

In addition to the influences of resolution upon computer application timings, the effects of measurement intrusion of course influence the user program's execution time as well. The total impact of such unintended influences of instrumentation upon an application's performance creates what Oracle performance analysts might refer to as a "Heisenberg-like effect."

Thus, each e and ela statistic emitted by an Oracle8*i* kernel actually represents a system characteristic whose actual value cannot be known exactly, but which resides within a known range of values. Such a range of values is shown in Table 7-1. For example, the Oracle8*i* statistic e=2 can refer to any actual elapsed duration e_a in the range:

$$2.000\ 000 \text{ cs} \le e_a \le 2.999\ 999 \text{ cs}$$

Table 7-1. A single e or ela statistic in Oracle8i represents a range of possible actual timing values

e, ela statistic (cs)	Minimum possible gettimeofday value (cs)	Maximum possible gettimeofday value (cs)
0	0.000 000	0.999 999
1	1.000 000	1.999 999
2	2.000 000	2.999 999
3	3.000 000	3.999 999
...	...	...

Definition of Quantization Error

Quantization error is the quantity E defined as the difference between an event's actual duration e_a and its measured duration e_m. That is:

$$E = e_m - e_a$$

Let's revisit the execution of Example 7-1 superimposed upon a timeline, as shown in Figure 7-5. In this drawing, each tick mark represents one clock tick on an interval timer like the one provided by gettimeofday. The value of the timer was $t_0 = 1492$ when do_something began. The value of the timer was $t_1 = 1498$ when do_something ended. Thus the measured duration of do_something was $e_m = t_1 - t_0 = 6$. However, if you physically measure the length of the duration e_a in the drawing, you'll find that the actual duration of do_something is $e_a = 5.875$ ticks. You can confirm the actual duration by literally measuring the height of e_a in the drawing, but it is not possible for an application to "know" the value of e_a by using only the interval timer whose ticks are shown in Figure 7-5. The quantization error is $E = e_m - e_a = 0.125$ ticks, or about 1.7 percent of the 5.875-tick actual duration.

Now, consider the case when the duration of do_something is much closer to the timer resolution, as shown in Figure 7-6. In the left-hand case, the duration of do_something spans one clock tick, so it has a measured duration of $e_m = 1$. However, the event's actual duration is only $e_a = 0.25$. (You can confirm this by measuring the actual duration in the drawing.) The quantization error in this case is $E = 0.75$, which is a whopping 300% of the 0.25-tick actual duration. In the right-hand case, the execution of do_something spans no clock ticks, so it has a measured duration of $e_m = 0$; however, its actual duration is $e_a = 0.9375$. The quantization error here is $E = -0.9375$, which is −100% of the 0.9375-tick actual duration.

To describe quantization error in plain language:

> Any duration measured with an interval timer is accurate only to within one unit of timer resolution.

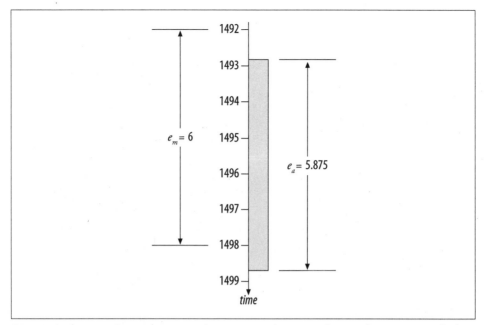

Figure 7-5. An interval timer is accurate for measuring durations of events that span many clock ticks

More formally, the difference between any two digital clock measurements is an elapsed duration with quantization error *whose exact value cannot be known,* but which ranges anywhere from almost −1 clock tick to almost +1 clock tick. If we use the notation r_x to denote the resolution of some timer called x, then we have:

$$x_m - r_x < x_a < x_m + r_x$$

The quantization error E inherent in any digital measurement is a uniformly distributed *random variable* (see Chapter 11) with range $-r_x < E < r_x$, where r_x denotes the resolution of the interval timer.

Whenever you see an elapsed duration printed by the Oracle kernel (or any other software), you must think in terms of the measurement resolution. For example, if you see the statistic e=4 in an Oracle8*i* trace file, you need to understand that this statistic does *not* mean that the actual elapsed duration of something was 4 cs. Rather, it means that *if* the underlying timer resolution is 1 cs or better, then the actual elapsed duration of something was between 3 cs and 5 cs. That is as much detail as you can know.

For small numbers of statistic values, this imprecision can lead to ironic results. For example, you can't actually even make accurate comparisons of event durations for events whose measured durations are approximately equal. Figure 7-7 shows a few ironic cases. Imagine that the timer shown here is ticking in 1-centisecond intervals. This is behavior that is equivalent to the Oracle8*i* practice of truncating digits of

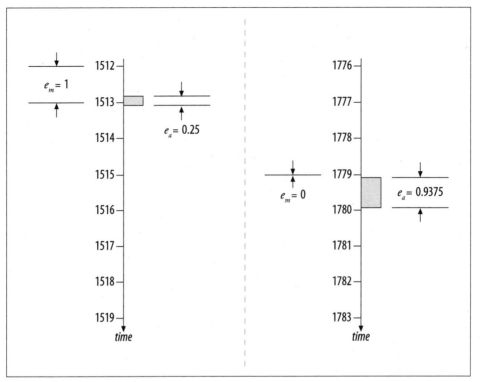

Figure 7-6. An interval timer is not accurate for measuring durations of events that span zero or only a few clock ticks

timing precision past the 0.01-second position. Observe in this figure that event *A* consumed more actual elapsed duration than event *B*, but *B* has a longer measured duration; *C* took longer than *D*, but *D* has a longer measured duration. In general, any event with a measured duration of *n* + 1 may have an actual duration that is longer than, equal to, *or even shorter than* another event having a measured duration of *n*. You cannot know which relationship is true.

An interval timer can give accuracy only to ±1 clock tick, but in practical application, this restriction does not diminish the usefulness of interval timers. Positive and negative quantization errors tend to cancel each other over large samples. For example, the sum of the quantization errors in Figure 7-6 is:

$$E_1 + E_2 = 0.75 + (-0.9375) = 0.1875$$

Even though the individual errors were proportionally large, the sum of the errors is a much smaller 16% of the sum of the two actual event durations. In a several hundred SQL trace files collected at *hotsos.com* from hundreds of different Oracle sites, we have found that positive and negative quantization errors throughout a trace file with hundreds of lines tend to cancel each other out. Errors commonly converge to magnitudes smaller than ±10% of the total response time measured in a trace file.

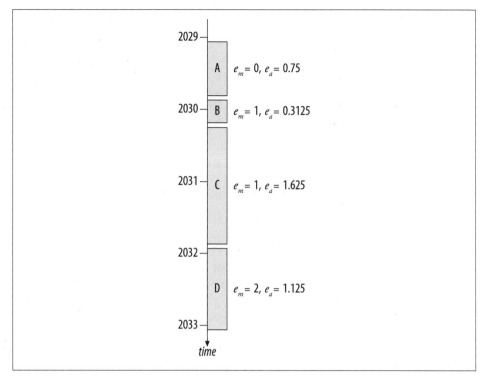

Figure 7-7. *Any duration measured with an interval timer is accurate only to within one unit of timer resolution. Notice that events measured as n clock ticks in duration can actually be longer than events measured as n + 1 ticks in duration*

Complications in Measuring CPU Consumption

You may have noticed by now that your gettimeofday system call has much better resolution than getrusage. Although the pseudocode in Example 7-3 makes it look like gettimeofday and getrusage do almost the same thing, the two functions work in profoundly different ways. As a result, the two functions produce results with profoundly different accuracies.

How gettimeofday works

The operation of gettimeofday is much easier to understand than the operation of getrusage. I'll use Linux on Intel Pentium processors as a model for explaining. As I mentioned previously, the Intel Pentium processor has a hardware time stamp counter (TSC) register that is updated on every hardware clock tick. For example, a 1-GHz CPU will update its TSC approximately a billion times per second [Bovet and Cesati (2001) 139–141]. By counting the number of ticks that have occurred on the TSC since the last time a user set the time with the date command, the Linux kernel can determine how many clock ticks have elapsed since the Epoch. The result returned by gettimeofday is the result of truncating this figure to microsecond resolution (to maintain the POSIX-compliant behavior of the gettimeofday function).

How getrusage works

There are two ways in which an operating system can account for how much time a process spends consuming user-mode or kernel-mode CPU capacity:

Polling (sampling)
> The operating system could be instrumented with extra code so that, at fixed intervals, each running process could update its own rusage table. At each interval, each running process could update its own CPU usage statistic with the estimate that it has consumed the entire interval's worth of CPU capacity in whatever state the processes is presently executing in.

Event-based instrumentation
> The operating system could be instrumented with extra code so that every time a process transitions to either *user running* or *kernel running* state, it could issue a high-resolution timer call. Every time a process transitions out of that state, it could issue another timer call and publish the microseconds' worth of difference between the two calls to the process' rusage accounting structure.

Most operating systems use polling, at least by default. For example, Linux updates several attributes for each process, including the CPU capacity consumed thus far by the process, upon every clock interrupt [Bovet and Cesati (2001) 144–145]. Some operating systems do provide event-based instrumentation. Sun Solaris, for example, provides this feature under the name *microstate accounting* [Cockroft (1998)].

With microstate accounting, quantization error is limited to one unit of timer resolution per state switch. With a high-resolution timer (like gettimeofday), the total quantization error on CPU statistics obtained from microstate accounting can be quite small. However, the additional accuracy comes at the cost of incrementally more measurement intrusion effect. With polling, however, quantization error can be significantly worse, as you'll see in a moment.

Regardless of how the resource usage information is obtained, an operating system makes this information available to any process that wants it via a system call like getrusage. POSIX specifies that getrusage must use microseconds as its unit of measure, but—for systems that obtain rusage information by polling—the true resolution of the returned data depends upon the clock interrupt frequency.

The clock interrupt frequency for most systems is 100 interrupts per second, or one interrupt every centisecond (operating systems texts often speak in terms of milliseconds; 1 cs = 10 ms = 0.010 s). The clock interrupt frequency is a configurable parameter on many systems, but most system managers leave it set to 100 interrupts per second. Asking a system to service interrupts more frequently than 100 times per second would give better time measurement resolution, but at the cost of degraded performance. Servicing interrupts even only ten times more frequently would intensify the kernel-mode CPU overhead consumed by the operating scheduler by a factor of ten. It's generally not a good tradeoff.

If your operating system is POSIX-compliant, the following Perl program will reveal its operating system scheduler resolution [Chiesa (1996)]:

```
$ cat clkres.pl
#!/usr/bin/perl
use strict;
use warnings;
use POSIX qw(sysconf _SC_CLK_TCK);
my $freq = sysconf(_SC_CLK_TCK);
my $f = log($freq) / log(10);
printf "getrusage resolution %.${f}f seconds\n", 1/$freq;
$ perl clkres.pl
getrusage resolution: 0.01 seconds
```

With a 1-cs clock resolution, getrusage may return microsecond data, but those microsecond values will never contain valid detail smaller than $1/100^{th}$ (0.01) of a second.

The reason I've explained all this is that the quantization error of the Oracle c statistic is fundamentally different from the quantization error of an e or ela statistic. Recall when I wrote:

> Any duration measured with an interval timer is accurate only to within one unit of timer resolution.

The problem with Oracle's c statistic is that the statistic returned by getrusage is *not really a duration*. That is, a CPU consumption "duration" returned by getrusage is not a statistic obtained by taking the difference of a pair of interval timer measurements. Rather:

- On systems with microstate accounting activated, CPU consumption is computed as potentially very many short durations added together.
- On systems that poll for rusage information, CPU consumption is an estimate of duration obtained by a process of polling.

Hence, in either circumstance, the quantization error inherent in an Oracle c statistic can be *much worse* than just one clock tick. The problem exists even on systems that use microstate accounting. It's worse on systems that don't.

Figure 7-8 depicts an example of a standard polling-based situation in which the errors in user-mode CPU time attribution add up to cause an over-attribution of time to a database call's response time. The sequence diagram in this figure depicts both the user-mode CPU time and the system call time consumed by a database call. The *CPU* axis shows clock interrupts scheduled one cs apart. Because the drawing is so small, I could not show the 10,000 clock ticks on the *non-CPU time consumer* axis that occur between every pair of ticks on the *CPU* axis.

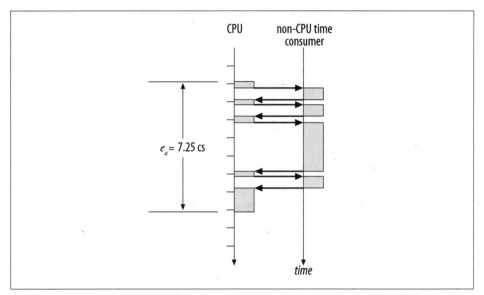

Figure 7-8. The way getrusage polls for CPU consumption can cause over-attributions of response time to an individual database call

In response to the actions depicted in Figure 7-8, I would expect an Oracle9i kernel to emit the trace data shown in Example 7-5. I computed the expected e and ela statistics by measuring the durations of the time segments on the *sys call* axis. Because of the fine resolution of the gettimeofday clock with which e and ela durations are measured, the quantization error in my e and ela measurements is negligible.

Example 7-5. The Oracle9i timing statistics that would be generated by the events depicted in Figure 7-8

```
WAIT #1: ...ela= 6250
WAIT #1: ...ela= 6875
WAIT #1: ...ela= 32500
WAIT #1: ...ela= 6250
FETCH #1:c=60000,e=72500,...
```

The actual amount of CPU capacity consumed by the database call was 2.5 cs, which I computed by measuring durations physically in the picture. However, getrusage obtains its CPU consumption statistic from a process's resource usage structure, which is updated by polling at every clock interrupt. At every interrupt, the operating system's process scheduler tallies one full centisecond (10,000 µs) of CPU consumption to whatever process is running at the time. Thus, getrusage will report that the database call in Figure 7-8 consumed six full centiseconds' worth of CPU time. You can verify the result by looking at Figure 7-8 and simply counting the number of clock ticks that are spanned by CPU consumption.

It all makes sense in terms of the picture, but look at the unaccounted-for time that results:

$$\Delta = e - \left(c + \sum_{\text{db call}} ela \right)$$
$$= 72500 - \left(60000 + \left(6250 + 6875 + 32500 + 6250 \right) \right)$$
$$= -39375$$

Negative unaccounted-for time means that there is a negative amount of "missing time" in the trace data. In other words, there is an *over*-attribution of 39,375 μs to the database call. It's an alarmingly large-looking number, but remember, it's only about 4 cs. The actual amount of user-mode CPU that was consumed during the call was only 25,000 μs (which, again, I figured out by cheating—by measuring the physical lengths of durations depicted in Figure 7-8).

Detection of Quantization Error

Quantization error $E = e_m - e_a$ is the difference between an event's actual duration e_a and its measured duration e_m. You cannot know an event's actual duration; therefore, you cannot detect quantization error by inspecting an individual statistic. However, you can prove the existence of quantization error by examining *groups* of related statistics. You've already seen an example in which quantization error was detectable. In Example 7-5, we could detect the existence of quantization error by noticing that:

$$c + \sum_{\text{db call}} ela > e$$

It is easy to detect the existence of quantization error by inspecting a database call and the wait events executed by that action on a *low-load* system, where other influences that might disrupt the $e \approx c + \sum ela$ relationship are minimized.

The following Oracle8*i* trace file excerpt shows the effect of quantization error:

```
WAIT #103: nam='db file sequential read' ela= 0 p1=1 p2=3051 p3=1
WAIT #103: nam='db file sequential read' ela= 0 p1=1 p2=6517 p3=1
WAIT #103: nam='db file sequential read' ela= 0 p1=1 p2=5347 p3=1
FETCH #103:c=0,e=1,p=3,cr=15,cu=0,mis=0,r=1,dep=2,og=4,tim=116694745
```

This fetch call motivated exactly three wait events. We know that the c, e, and ela times shown here should be related by the approximation:

$$e \approx c + \sum_{\text{db call}} ela$$

On a low-load system, the amount by which the two sides of this approximation are unequal is an indication of the total quantization error present in the five measurements (one c value, one e value, and three ela values):

$$E \approx e_m - \left(c_m + \sum_{\text{db call}} ela_m \right)$$
$$= 1 - \left(0 + \left(0 + 0 + 0 \right) \right)$$
$$= 1$$

Given that individual gettimeofday calls account for only a few microseconds of measurement intrusion error on most systems, quantization error is the prominent factor contributing to the 1-centisecond (cs) "gap" in the trace data.

The following Oracle8i trace file excerpt shows the simplest possible over-counting of elapsed time, resulting in a negative amount of unaccounted-for time:

```
WAIT #96: nam='db file sequential read' ela= 0 p1=1 p2=1691 p3=1
FETCH #96:c=1,e=0,p=1,cr=4,cu=0,mis=0,r=1,dep=1,og=4,tim=116694789
```

Here, we have $E = -1$ cs:

$$E \approx e_m - \left(c_m + \sum_{\text{db call}} ela_m \right)$$
$$= 0 - \left(1 + \left(0 \right) \right)$$
$$= -1$$

In this case of a "negative gap" like the one shown here, we cannot appeal to the effects of measurement intrusion for explanation; the measurement intrusion effect can create only *positive* unaccounted-for time. It might have been possible that a CPU consumption double-count had taken place; however, this isn't the case here, because the value ela= 0 means that no CPU time was counted in the wait event at all. In this case, quantization error has had a dominating influence, resulting in the over-attribution of time within the fetch.

Although Oracle9i uses improved output resolution in its timing statistics, Oracle9i is by no means immune to the effects of quantization error, as shown in the following trace file excerpt with $E > 0$:

```
WAIT #5: nam='db file sequential read' ela= 11597 p1=1 p2=42463 p3=1
FETCH #5:c=0,e=12237,p=1,cr=3,cu=0,mis=0,r=1,dep=2,og=4,tim=1023745094799915
```

In this example, we have $E = 640 \ \mu s$:

$$E \approx e_m - \left(c_m + \sum_{\text{db call}} ela_m \right)$$
$$= 12237 - \left(0 + \left(11597 \right) \right)$$
$$= 640$$

Some of this error is certainly quantization error (it's impossible that the total CPU consumption of this fetch was *actually* zero). A few microseconds are the result of measurement intrusion error.

Finally, here is an example of an $E < 0$ quantization error in Oracle9*i* trace data:

```
WAIT #34: nam='db file sequential read' ela= 16493 p1=1 p2=33254 p3=1
WAIT #34: nam='db file sequential read' ela= 11889 p1=2 p2=89061 p3=1
FETCH #34:c=10000,e=29598,p=2,cr=5,cu=0,mis=0,r=1,dep=3,og=4,tim=1017039276445157
```

In this case, we have $E = -8784$ μs:

$$
\begin{aligned}
E \approx e_m - \left(c_m + \sum_{\text{db call}} ela_m \right) \\
= 29598 - \left(10000 + \left(16493 + 11889 \right) \right) \\
= -8784
\end{aligned}
$$

It is possible that some CPU consumption double-counting has occurred in this case. It is also likely that the effect of quantization error is a dominant contributor to the attribution of time to the fetch call. The 8,784-μs over-attribution is evidence that the actual total CPU consumption of the database call was probably only about $(10,000 - 8,784)$ μs $= 1,216$ μs.

Bounds of Quantization Error

The amount of quantization error present in Oracle's timing statistics cannot be measured directly. However, the statistical properties of quantization error can be analyzed in *extended* SQL trace data. First, there's a limit to how much quantization error there can be in a given set of trace data. It is easy to imagine the maximum quantization error that a set of elapsed durations like Oracle's e and ela statistics might contribute. The worst total quantization error for a sequence of e and ela statistics occurs when all the individual quantization errors are at their maximum magnitude *and* the signs of the quantization errors all line up.

Figure 7-9 exhibits the type of behavior that I'm describing. This drawing depicts eight very-short-duration system calls that happen to *all* cross an interval timer's clock ticks. The actual duration of each event is practically zero, but the measured duration of each event is one clock tick. The total actual duration of the system calls shown is practically zero, but the total measured duration is 8 clock ticks. For this set of $n = 8$ system calls, the total quantization error is essentially nr_x, where r_x is, as described previously, the resolution of the interval timer upon which the x characteristic is measured.

It shouldn't take you long to notice that the situation in Figure 7-9 is horribly contrived to suit my purpose of illustrating a point. For things to work out this way in reality is extremely unlikely. The probability that n quantization errors will all have

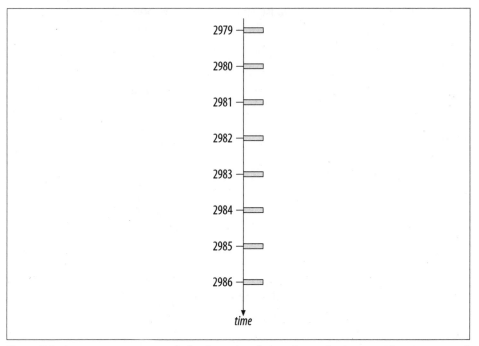

Figure 7-9. A worst-case type scenario for the accumulation of quantization error for a sequence of measured durations

the same sign is only 0.5^n. The probability of having $n = 8$ consecutive negative quantization errors is only 0.00390625 (that's only about four chances in a thousand). There's less than one chance in 10^{80} that $n = 265$ statistics will all have quantization errors with the same sign.

For long lists of elapsed duration statistics, it is virtually impossible for all the quantization errors to "point in the same direction." Yet, my contrivance in Figure 7-9 goes even further. It assumes that the *magnitude* of each quantization error is maximized. The odds of this happening are even more staggeringly slim than for the signs to line up. For example, the probability that the magnitude of each of n given quantization error values exceeds 0.9 is only $(1 - 0.9)^n$. The odds of having each of $n = 265$ quantization error magnitudes exceed 0.9 are one in 10^{265}.

For n quantization errors to all have the same sign and all have magnitudes greater than m, the probability is the astronomically unlikely product of both probabilities I've described:

$$P(n \text{ quantization error values are}$$
$$\text{all greater than } m \text{ or all less than } -m)$$
$$= (0.5)^n (1 - m)^n.$$

What Does "One Chance in Ten to [Some Large Power]" Mean?

To put the probability "one chance in 10^{80}" into perspective, realize that scientists estimate that there are only about 10^{80} atoms in the observable universe (source: *http://www.sunspot.noao.edu/sunspot/pr/answerbook/universe.html*, *http://www.sciencenet.org.uk/database/Physics/0107/p01539d.html*, and others). This means that if you could print 265 uniformly distributed random numbers between −1 and +1 on every atom in our universe, you should expect that only *one* such atom would have all 265 numbers on it with all the same sign.

The other probability, "one chance in 10^{265}," is even more mind-boggling to imagine. To do it, imagine nesting universes three levels deep. That is, imagine that every one of the 10^{80} atoms in our universe is itself a universe with 10^{80} universes in it, and that each of those universes contains 10^{80} atoms. At that point, you'd have enough atoms to imagine one occurrence of a "one chance in 10^{240}" atom. Even in universes nested three levels deep, the odds of finding an atom with all 265 of its random numbers exceeding 0.9 in magnitude would still be only one chance in 10,000,000,000,000,000,000,000,000.

Quantization errors for elapsed durations (like Oracle e and ela statistics) are random numbers in the range:

$$-r_x < E < r_x$$

where r_x is the resolution of the interval timer from which the x statistic (where x is either e or ela) is obtained.

Because negative and positive quantization errors occur with equal probability, the average quantization error for a given set of statistics tends toward zero, even for large trace files. Using the *central limit theorem* developed by Pierre Simon de Laplace in 1810, you can even predict the probability that quantization errors for Oracle e and ela statistics will exceed a specified threshold for a trace file containing a given number of statistics.

I've begun work to compute the probability that a trace file's *total* quantization error (including the error contributed by c statistics) will exceed a given threshold; however, I have not yet completed that research. The problem in front of me is to calculate the distribution of the quantization error produced by c, which, as I've said already, is complicated by the nature of how c is tallied by polling. I intend to document my research in this area in a future project.

Happily, there are several pieces of good news about quantization error that make not yet knowing how to quantify it quite bearable:

- In the many hundreds of Oracle trace files that we have analyzed at *hotsos.com*, it has been extremely uncommon for a *properly collected* (see Chapter 6) file's total unaccounted-for duration to exceed about 10% of total response time.

- In spite of the possibilities afforded by both quantization error and CPU consumption double-counting, it is apparently *extremely* rare for a trace file to contain negative unaccounted-for time whose magnitude exceeds about 10% of total response time.

- In cases where unaccounted-for time accounts for more than 25% of a properly collected trace file's response time, the unaccounted-for time is *almost always* caused by one of the two remaining phenomena that I'll discuss in the following sections.

- The presence of quantization error has not yet hindered our ability to properly diagnose the root causes of performance problems by analyzing only Oracle extended SQL trace data, even in Oracle8*i* trace files in which all statistics are reported with only one-centisecond resolution.

- Quantization error becomes even more of a non-issue in Oracle9*i* with the improvement in statistical resolution.

Sometimes, the effect of quantization error can cause loss of faith in the validity of Oracle's trace data. Perhaps nothing can be more damaging to your morale in the face of a tough problem than to gather the suspicion that the data you're counting on might be lying to you. A firm understanding of the effects of quantization error is possibly your most important tool in keeping your faith.

Time Spent Not Executing

To understand a fourth cause of unaccounted-for time in a properly collected Oracle trace file, let's perform a brief thought experiment. Imagine a program P that consumes exactly ten seconds of user-mode CPU time and produces an output on your terminal. Imagine that you were to run this program in a loop on a system with one CPU. If you were the only user connected to this system, you should expect response time of ten seconds for each execution of P.

If you were to observe the CPU utilization of this single-CPU system during your single-user repetitive execution of P, you would probably notice your CPU running at 100% utilization for the duration of your job. But what if you were to add a second instance of the P loop on the single-CPU system? In any ten-second elapsed time interval, there is only ten seconds' worth of CPU capacity available on the single-CPU machine. We thus cannot expect to accomplish two complete executions of a program that consumes ten seconds of capacity in one ten-second interval. We would expect that the response time of each P would increase to roughly 20 seconds each. That's how long it would take for one CPU to provide ten seconds' worth of CPU capacity to each of two competing processes, if its capacity were to be dispensed fairly and in small time slices to the two competing processes.

Instrumenting the Experiment

Let's assume that we had instrumented our code in a manner similar to how the Oracle kernel does it, as I've shown in Example 7-6.

Example 7-6. The program P instrumented to report on its own response time and total CPU capacity consumption

```
e0 = gettimeofday;
c0 = getrusage;
P;                       # remember, P makes no system calls
c1 = getrusage;
e1 = gettimeofday;
e = e1 - e0;
c = (c1.stime + c1.utime) - (c0.stime + c0.utime);
printf "e=%.0fs, c=%.0fs\n", e, c;
```

Then we should expect approximately the timing output shown in Table 7-2 for each given concurrency level on a single-CPU system. You should expect our program P to consume the same amount of total CPU capacity, regardless of how busy the system is. But of course, since the CPU capacity of the system is being shared more and more thinly across users as we increase the concurrency level, you should expect for the program to execute for longer and longer elapsed times before being able to obtain the ten seconds of CPU time that it needs.

Table 7-2. Expected output from running the timing-instrumented program P (which consumes ten seconds of user-mode CPU time) at varying concurrency levels

Number of users running P concurrently	Timing output
1	e=10s, c=10s
2	e=20s, c=10s
3	e=30s, c=10s
4	e=40s, c=10s

The table shows what we expected to see, but notice that we now have created a "problem with missing time" in some of our measurements. Remember our performance model: the elapsed time of a program is supposed to approximately equal the time spent consuming CPU capacity plus the time spent executing instrumented "wait events," as in:

$$e \approx c + \sum_{db\ call} ela$$

However, even in the two-user case, this works out to:

$$20 \approx 10 + 0$$

We can use the substitution *ela* = 0 because we know our program executes no instrumented "wait events" whatsoever. All our program does is consume some CPU capacity and then print the result. (And even the `printf` statement can be eliminated as a suspect because the call to it occurs *outside* of the domain of the timer calls.) As you can plainly see, $c + \sum ela = 10$ is a really lousy approximation of $e = 20$. Where did the "missing time" go? In our Table 7-2 cases, the problem just keeps getting worse as user concurrency increases. Where have we gone wrong in our instrumentation of *P*?

Process States and Transitions Revisited

The answer is easy to understand after looking again at Figure 7-1. Recall that even when a process is executing happily along in user running state, a system clock interrupt occurs on most systems every 1/100th of a second. This regularly scheduled interrupt transitions each running process into the kernel running state to service the interrupt. Once in kernel running state, the process saves its current *context* and then executes the scheduler subroutine (see "The interrupt Transition" earlier in this chapter). If there is a process in the ready to run state, then the system's scheduling policy may dictate that the running process must be preempted, and the ready to run process be scheduled and given an opportunity to consume CPU capacity itself.

When this happens, note what happens to our originally running process. When it is interrupted, it is transitioned immediately to kernel running state. Note in particular that the process does not get the chance to execute any application code to see what time it is when this happens. When the process is preempted, it is transitioned to ready to run state, where it waits until it is scheduled. When it is finally scheduled (perhaps only a mere 10 milliseconds later), it spends enough time in kernel running state to reinstate its context, and then it returns to user running state, right where it left off.

How did the preemption activity affect the timing data for the process? The CPU time spent in kernel running state while the scheduler was preparing for the process's preemption counts as CPU time consumed by the process. But time spent in ready to run state did *not* count as CPU time consumed by the process. However, when the process had completed its work on *P*, the difference e=e1−e0 of course included *all* time spent in *all* states of the process state transition diagram. The net effect is that all the time spent in ready to run state continues to tally on the e clock, but it's not accounted for as CPU capacity consumption, or for anything else that the application is aware of for that matter. It's as if the process had been conked on the head and then awoken, with no way to account for what happened to the time spent out of consciousness.

This is what happens to each process as more concurrent processes were added to the mix shown in Table 7-2. Of course, the more processes there were waiting in ready to run state, the more each process had to wait for its turn at the CPU. The longer the wait, the longer the program's elapsed time. For three and four users, the unaccounted-for time increases proportionally. It's simply a problem of a constant-sized pie (CPU capacity) being divvied up among more and more pie-eaters (users running *P*). There's really nothing in need of "repair" about the instrumentation upon *P*. What you need is to understand how to estimate how much of the unaccounted-for time is likely to be due to time spent not executing.

The existence and exact size of this gap is of immense value to the Oracle performance analyst. The size of this gap permits you to use extended SQL trace data to identify when performance problems are caused by excessive swapping or time spent in the CPU run queue, as you shall see in one of the case studies in Chapter 12.

Un-Instrumented Oracle Kernel Code

The final cause of missing time in a trace file that I'll cover is the category consisting of *un-instrumented Oracle kernel code*. As you've now seen, Oracle provides instrumentation for database calls in the form of c and e data, which represent total CPU consumption and total elapsed duration, respectively. For segments of Oracle kernel code that can consume significant response time but not much CPU capacity, Oracle Corporation gives us the "wait event" instrumentation, complete with an elapsed time and a distinguishing name for the code segment being executed.

Chapter 12 lists the number of code segments that are instrumented in a few popular releases of the Oracle kernel since 7.3.4. Notice that the number grows significantly with each release listed in the table. There are, for example, 146 more instrumented system calls in release 9.2.0 than there are in release 8.1.7. Certainly, some of these newly instrumented events represent new product features. It is possible that some new names in V$EVENT_NAME correspond to code segments that were present but just not yet instrumented in an earlier Oracle kernel release.

Effect

When Oracle Corporation leaves a sequence of kernel instructions un-instrumented, the missing time becomes apparent in one of two ways:

Missing time within a database call
   Any un-instrumented code that occurs within the context of a database call will leave a gap between the database call's elapsed duration (*e*) and the value of *c* + $\sum ela$ for the call. Within the trace file, the phenomenon will be indistinguishable from the *time spent not executing* problem that I described earlier. On systems that do not exhibit much paging or swapping, the presence of a large gap

(Δ) in the following equation for an entire trace file is an indicator of an un-instrumented time problem:

$$\Delta = \sum_{dep=0} e - \left[\sum_{dep=0} c + \sum_{\substack{within \\ calls}} ela \right]$$

To envision this problem, imagine what would happen if a five-second database file read executed by a fetch were un-instrumented. The elapsed time for the fetch (e) would include the five-second duration, but neither the total CPU consumption for the fetch (c) nor the wait event durations (ela values) would be large enough to account for the whole elapsed duration.

Missing time between database calls

Any un-instrumented code that occurs outside of the context of a database call cannot be detected in the same manner as un-instrumented code that occurs within a database call. You can detect missing time between calls in one of two ways. First, a sequence of between-call events with no intervening database calls is an indication of un-instrumented Oracle kernel code path. Second, you can detect un-instrumented calls by inspecting tim statistic values within a trace file. If you see "adjacent" tim values that are much farther apart in time than the intervening database call and wait event lines can account for, then you've discovered this problem. A trace file exhibits this issue if it has a large Δ value in the formula in which R denotes the known response time for which the trace file was supposed to account:

$$\Delta = R - \sum_{dep=0} e$$

Oracle bug number 2425312 is one example of this problem. It is a case in which entire database calls executed through the PL/SQL remote procedure call (RPC) interface emit no trace data whatsoever. The result is a potentially enormous gap in the time accounting within a trace file.

In practice you may never encounter a situation in which un-instrumented system calls will consume an important proportion of a program's elapsed time. We encounter the phenomenon at a rate of fewer than five per thousand trace files at *hotsos.com*. One case of un-instrumented database activity is documented as bug number 2425312 at Oracle *MetaLink*. You may encounter this bug if you trace Oracle Forms applications with embedded (client-side) PL/SQL. You will perhaps encounter other cases in which un-instrumented time materially affects your analysis, but those cases will be rare.

Trace Writing

You will encounter at least one un-instrumented system call every time you use SQL trace, although its performance impact is usually small. It is the `write` call that the Oracle kernel uses to write SQL trace output to the trace file. Using `strace` allows you to see quite plainly how the Oracle kernel writes each line of data to a trace file. Of the several hundred extended SQL trace files collected at *hotsos.com* by the time of this writing, fewer than 1% exhibit accumulation of unaccounted-for time that might be explained by slow trace file writing. However, you should follow these recommendations to reduce the risk that the very act of tracing an application program will materially degrade the performance of an application:

- Check with Oracle *MetaLink* to ensure that your system is not susceptible to Oracle kernel bugs that might unnecessarily impede the performance of trace file writing. For example, bug number 2202613 affects the performance of trace file writing on some Microsoft Windows 2000 ports. Bug number 1210242 needlessly degrades Oracle performance while tracing is activated.

- Place your USER_DUMP_DEST and BACKGROUND_DUMP_DEST directories on efficient I/O channels. Don't write trace data to your root filesystem or the oldest, slowest disk drive on your system. Although the outcome of the diagnostic process will often be significant performance improvement, no analyst wants to be accused of even temporarily degrading the performance of an application.

- Keep load that competes with trace file I/O as low as possible during a trace. For example, avoid tracing more than one session at a time to the same I/O device. Exceptions include application programs that naturally emit more than one trace file, such as parallel operations or any program that distributes workload over more than one Oracle server processes.

Don't let the overhead of writing to trace files deter you from using extended SQL trace data as a performance diagnostic tool. Keep the overhead in perspective. The potential overhead is not noticeable in most cases. Even if the performance overhead were nearly unbearable, the overhead of tracing a program *once* is a worthwhile investment if the diagnosis results in either of the following outcomes:

- You can repair the program under analysis, resulting in significant conservation of system capacity and a significant reduction in end-user response time.

- You can prove that the program under analysis performs as well as it can, and thus that further optimization investment will be futile.

Exercises

1. Install a system call trace utility like `strace` on your system. Use it to trace an Oracle kernel process. In a separate window, view the SQL trace output as it is emitted (using `tail -f` or a similar command). What timing calls does the

Oracle kernel make on your system? In what sequence are the timing calls made? Does your system's behavior resemble the behavior described in Example 7-2?

2. Run the program listed in Example 7-4 on your system. What is the average measurement intrusion effect of one gettimeofday call on your system?

3. The Perl program in Example 7-7 saves the values returned from a rapid-fire sequence of times system calls. It traverses the list of saved values and prints a value only if it differs from the prior value in the list. What, if anything, does running this program indicate about the resolution of CPU resource accounting on your system?

Example 7-7. A Perl program that executes a rapid-fire sequence of times system calls

```perl
#!/usr/bin/perl
use strict;
use warnings;
use IO::File;
autoflush STDOUT 1;
my @times = (times)[0];
while ((my $t = (times)[0]) - $times[0] < 1) {
    push @times, $t;
}
print scalar @times, " distinct times\n";
my $prior = '';
for my $time (@times) {
    print "$time\n" if $time ne $prior;
    $prior = $time;
}
```

4. At *hotsos.com*, we have several millions of lines of Oracle8*i* trace data that resemble the following:

```
FETCH #1:c=1,e=0,p=0,cr=0,cu=0,mis=0,r=10,dep=0,og=3,tim=17132884
```

Explain how this can occur.

5. In Oracle9*i*, trace file lines like the following occur as frequently as the phenomenon described in the previous exercise:

```
PARSE #7:c=10000,e=2167,p=0,cr=0,cu=0,mis=1,r=0,dep=1,og=0,tim=1016096093915846
```

Explain how this can occur. How different is this phenomenon from the one described in the previous exercise?

6. Write a program to test the thought experiment shown in Example 7-6. Explain any major differences between its output and the output of the thought experiment shown in Table 7-2.

7. Trace client programs that use different Oracle interfaces on your system, such as:
   - PL/SQL RPC calls issued by client-side PL/SQL within Oracle Forms applications
   - Java RMI calls between the client VM and server VM

   Do they result in unexpectedly large amounts of unaccounted-for time?

## CHAPTER 8

Oracle Fixed View Data

Chances are that before you picked up this book, you had spent far more time assessing V$ data than you ever spent looking at raw trace data. Each of us is taught either overtly or covertly that to be competent Oracle performance analysts, we have to know lots of things about Oracle's *fixed views*. Fixed views are pseudo-tables that begin with a prefix like V$ or GV$, or better yet X$. A whole cottage industry seems to exist with the sole purpose of providing updated posters that depict the complicated relationships among the almost 500 views described in V$FIXED_VIEW_DEFINITION.

Some people who inquire about *hotsos.com* courses find it strange that we devote comparatively little time to discussion of Oracle's fixed views in those courses. Oracle fixed views indeed provide useful data that we need on occasion to supplement our performance improvement projects. But in hundreds of cases in which my staff and I have resolved performance problems since 1999, we have used properly scoped extended SQL trace data and nothing else.

Throughout the year 2000, *hotsos.com* invested into two concurrent research projects. One was to construct an optimized performance improvement method based upon extended SQL trace data. The other was to create an optimized performance improvement method based upon fixed view data. The results of the two projects surprised me. I entered the two projects assuming that of course a method based upon Oracle fixed view data would be superior to any method based upon "mere" trace data. However, we ran into roadblock after roadblock with the fixed view data. I heavily invested my own time into designing workarounds for various deficiencies inherent in Oracle V$ data, in an effort to bring analysis quality to par with our method based upon trace data.

One day in June 2000, I consulted Oracle's extended SQL trace file for about the umpteenth time to confirm or refute whether my hundred-line fixed view analyzer workaround-of-the-day was working correctly. Until that day, we had used our trace file analysis software as a yardstick for our fixed view analysis software. But on that day, we promoted the trace file analyzer to our primary analysis tool. We dropped our fixed view analyzer project, and we've never looked back. This chapter begins with a description of some of the difficulties that Oracle's fixed view data imposes upon you. The latter part of the chapter reviews some common fixed view queries and assesses some of their strengths and weaknesses.

Deficiencies of Fixed View Data

Oracle's fixed views are invaluable. You'll see several good uses of V$ queries soon. For example, for every line of data that the Oracle kernel emits to a trace file, there can be thousands of operations that you'll never discover unless you examine your V$ data. However, Oracle's V$ fixed views contain several deficiencies which many Oracle performance analysts are not aware of. The following sections describe the deficiencies that my colleagues and I have encountered in attempts to use Oracle fixed view data as our primary performance-diagnostic data source.

Too Many Data Sources

It is possible to construct an approximate resource profile for a specified session with queries of fixed data. This chapter shows how. However, the resource profile is just the tip of the data you really need, and you won't know what drill-down you'll need next until after you've assessed the resource profile. Consequently, the only way to ensure that you'll have everything you might need is to collect everything you might need for the targeted time scope and action scope. Doing this with fixed view data is virtually impossible.

Lack of Detail

The documented Oracle fixed views make it intensely difficult to acquire several types of detailed data that are easy to acquire from extended SQL trace data. Using only Oracle's fixed views, for example, it is very difficult to:

- Observe trends in durations of individual Oracle kernel actions
- Attribute individual I/O calls to their target devices
- Attribute capacity consumption to individual database calls
- Determine recursion relationships among database calls

The vast majority of Oracle's fixed views reveal only statistics that are aggregated either by session (for example, V$SESSTAT) or by instance (for example, V$SYSSTAT). Aggregate statistics introduce unnecessary analysis complexity, because of course aggregates conceal details.

X$TRACE and V$SESSION_WAIT are notable exceptions that reveal in-process data. However, using X$TRACE at least through Oracle9i release 2 is a bad idea because it is undocumented, unsupported, and unreliable. V$SESSION_WAIT is of course supported, but to acquire the same level of detail from V$SESSION_WAIT as you can get from an Oracle7 extended SQL trace file, you would have to poll the view at a rate of more than 100 queries per second. You can't do this with SQL (see "Measurement Intrusion Effect of Polling"). To acquire the same level of detail from V$SESSION_WAIT as you can get from an Oracle9i extended SQL trace file, you would have to poll at a rate of 1,000,000 queries per second.

Measurement Intrusion Effect of Polling

Using SQL to poll Oracle fixed views imposes an overwhelming measurement intrusion effect upon the system. It is simply impossible to use SQL to acquire fine granularity operational statistics in real time. Example 8-1 illustrates the problem. Typical behavior on our 800-MHz Linux server is fewer than 50 polls per second on a 50-row V$SESSION fixed view:

```
$ perl polling.pl --username=system --password=manager
        sessions        50
           polls      1000
         elapsed    21.176
   user-mode CPU    14.910
 kernel-mode CPU     0.110
       polls/sec    47.223
```

The verdict: you can't use SQL to poll even one small V$ view a hundred times per second.

Example 8-1. A Perl program that demonstrates a fundamental limitation of polling with SQL. Note that the program carefully parses only once and also uses array fetching instead of fetching one row at a time

```perl
#!/usr/bin/perl

# $Header: /home/cvs/cvm-book1/polling/polling.pl,v1.6 2003/04/23 03:49:37
# Cary Millsap (cary.millsap@hotsos.com)

use strict;
use warnings;
use DBI;
use DBD::Oracle;
use Getopt::Long;
use Time::HiRes qw(gettimeofday);

my @dbh;      # list of database connection handles
my $dbh;      # "foreground" session database connection handle
my $sth;      # Oracle statement handle

my $hostname = "";
my $username = "/";
my $password = "";
my %attr = (
    RaiseError => 1,
    AutoCommit => 0,
```

Example 8-1. A Perl program that demonstrates a fundamental limitation of polling with SQL. Note that the program carefully parses only once and also uses array fetching instead of fetching one row at a time (continued)

```perl
);
my %opt = (
    sessions    => 50,      # number of Oracle sessions
    polls       => 1_000,   # number of polls on the v$ object
    hostname    => "",
    username    => "/",
    password    => "",
    debug       => 0,
);

# Get command line options and arguments.
GetOptions(
    "sessions=i"    => \$opt{sessions},
    "polls=i"       => \$opt{polls},
    "debug"         => \$opt{debug},
    "hostname=s"    => \$opt{hostname},
    "username=s"    => \$opt{username},
    "password=s"    => \$opt{password},
);

# Fill v$session with "background" connections.
for (1 .. $opt{sessions}) {
    push @dbh, DBI->connect("dbi:Oracle:$opt{hostname}", $opt{username}, $opt{password}, \
%attr);
    print "." if $opt{debug};
}
print "$opt{sessions} sessions connected\n" if $opt{debug};

# Execute the query to trace.
$dbh = DBI->connect("dbi:Oracle:$opt{hostname}", $opt{username}, $opt{password}, \%attr);
$sth = $dbh->prepare(q(select * from v$session));
my $t0 = gettimeofday;
my ($u0, $s0) = times;
for (1 .. $opt{polls}) {
    $sth->execute();
    $sth->fetchall_arrayref;
}
my ($u1, $s1) = times;
my $t1 = gettimeofday;
$dbh->disconnect;
print "$opt{polls} polls completed\n" if $opt{debug};

# Print test results.
my $ela = $t1 - $t0;
my $usr = $u1 - $u0;
my $sys = $s1 - $s0;
printf "%15s %8d\n", "sessions", $opt{sessions};
printf "%15s %8d\n", "polls", $opt{polls};
printf "%15s %8.3f\n", "elapsed", $ela;
printf "%15s %8.3f\n", "user-mode CPU", $usr;
```

Example 8-1. A Perl program that demonstrates a fundamental limitation of polling with SQL. Note that the program carefully parses only once and also uses array fetching instead of fetching one row at a time (continued)

```
printf "%15s %8.3f\n", "kernel-mode CPU", $sys;
printf "%15s %8.3f\n", "polls/sec", $opt{polls}/$ela;

# Disconnect "background" connections from Oracle.
for my $c (@dbh) {
    $c->disconnect;
    print "." if $opt{debug};
}
print "$opt{sessions} sessions disconnected\n" if $opt{debug};

__END__

=head1 NAME

polling - test the polling rate of SQL upon V$SESSION


=head1 SYNOPSIS

polling
  [--sessions=I<s>]
  [--polls=I<p>]
  [--hostname=I<h>]
  [--username=I<u>]
  [--password=I<p>]
  [--debug=I<d>]


=head1 DESCRIPTION

B<polling> makes I<s> Oracle connections and then issues I<p> queries of
B<V$SESSION>. It prints performance statistics about the polls, including
the elapsed duration, the user- and kernel-mode CPU consumption, and the
number of polls per second exeucted. The program is useful for
demonstrating the polling capacity of an Oracle system.


=head2 Options

=over 4

=item B<--sessions=>I<s>

The number of Oracle connections that are created before the polling
begins. The default value is 50.

=item B<--polls=>I<p>

The number of queries that sill be executed. The default value is 1,000.
```

Example 8-1. A Perl program that demonstrates a fundamental limitation of polling with SQL. Note that the program carefully parses only once and also uses array fetching instead of fetching one row at a time (continued)

```
=item B<--hostname=>I<u>

The name of Oracle host. The default value is "" (the empty string).

=item B<--username=>I<u>

The name of the Oracle schema to which B<polling> will connect. The
default value is "/".

=item B<--password=>I<p>

The Oracle password that B<polling> will use to connect. The default value
is "" (the empty string).

=item B<--debug=>I<d>

When set to 1, B<polling> dumps its internal data structures in addition
to its normal output. The default value is 0.

=back


=head1 EXAMPLES

Use of B<polling> will resemble the following example:

    $ perl polling.pl --username=system --password=manager
            sessions      50
               polls    1000
             elapsed  15.734
       user-mode CPU   7.111
     kernel-mode CPU   0.741
           polls/sec  63.557


=head1 AUTHOR

Cary Millsap (cary.millsap@hotsos.com)


=head1 COPYRIGHT

Copyright (c) 2003 by Hotsos Enterprises, Ltd. All rights reserved.
```

Difficulty of Proper Action-Scoping

Most V$ data sources have no session label attribute. To see why this is a problem, imagine that the resource profile reveals that waits for latch free dominate its response time. V$LATCH shows that two different latches were accessed heavily during the user action's time scope. Which latch is responsible for the user action's response time? It could be one, the other, or even both. How will you determine whether the session you are monitoring is responsible for motivating the activity, or if it's just some other session that happened to be running at the same time? Learning the answers with only properly time-scoped V$ data at your disposal consumes significantly more analysis time than learning the answers from extended SQL trace data.

A similar argument cuts the other way as well. The Oracle kernel emits a latch free wait event only when a latch acquisition attempt spins and fails, resulting in a system call in which the Oracle kernel process voluntarily yields the CPU to some other process. Nothing appears in the trace file when a latch acquisition attempt results in an acquisition, even if the Oracle kernel process had to execute many spin iterations to acquire it [Millsap (2001c)].

The combination of extended SQL trace data and good V$ tools like Tom Kyte's test harness (described later in this chapter) provide much more capability than either a trace file or V$ output by itself.

Difficulty of Proper Time-Scoping

One of the nagging problems that motivated me to abandon the big *hotsos.com* fixed view diagnosis project was the incessant difficulty in acquiring properly time-scoped data. If an observation interval boundary occurs in the middle of an event, it is important to know how much of the event's duration should be included within the interval and how much should be discarded. For example, if you query V$SESSION_ WAIT at time t and find a db file scattered read event in progress, then how can you determine how long the event has been executing? It appears impossible to know to within 0.01 seconds unless you can poll at a rate of 100 or more times per second.

Another annoyance is the problem of what to do if a session disconnects before you can collect all the fixed view data you needed at the end of the desired observation interval. If you don't query the various V$ views that contain session information before the disconnect takes place, then the data you need are lost forever. Again, fine-resolution polling would help solve this problem, but fine-resolution requires that you access Oracle shared memory contents through means other than SQL.

Susceptibility to Overflow and Other Errors

Another nagging problem is fixed views' susceptibility to overflow errors. The problem is that an n-bit counter variable can store only 2^n-1 distinct values. When an n-bit unsigned integer in the Oracle kernel takes on the value 2^n-1, then the next time it is incremented, its value becomes zero. Overflow errors cause a supposed "accumulator" statistic to have a smaller value than it had at some time in the past. If an Oracle kernel developer has chosen to regard a counter variable as a *signed* integer, then you may notice values that turn negative after getting very large. To repair overflow data is not complicated, but it's one more thing that analyses of V$ data sometimes require and that analyses of extended SQL trace data don't.

Other aggravations with erroneous statistics include issues with the Oracle statistic called CPU used by this session, including Oracle bug numbers 2327249, 2707060, 1286684, and others. When you can't trust your system's measurements of what should be the dominant consumer of response time on an optimized system, it puts a big dent in your progress.

Lack of Database Call Duration Data

Search Oracle's V$ view definitions and I believe you won't find an equivalent of the e statistic anywhere. Without knowing a database call's elapsed duration, it is impossible even to detect the *existence* of unaccounted-for time that should be attributed to the call. Of course, if you can't prove that unaccounted-for time even exists, then you certainly can't measure its duration. As I describe in Chapters 6, 9, and 12, quantifying a user action's unaccounted-for time is the key to being able to positively identify, for example, paging or swapping problems from viewing only operating system-*independent* Oracle data.

The absence of database call duration data from Oracle's V$ data creates an irony that I hope you'll enjoy with me. Some analysts regard the "problem of missing time" in trace files as proof that V$ data provide superior value to the performance analyst. But, remember, Oracle V$ data come from the same system calls that extended SQL trace data come from (the ones I explained in Chapter 7). Thus, Oracle V$ data suffer from the same "missing time" problems from which extended SQL trace files allegedly "suffer." Proving that V$ data are superior to extended SQL trace data because of the "missing time" issue is analogous to proving that it's safer to be in a room with a hungry bear if you'll just close your eyes.

Lack of Read Consistency

As if the problems you've read about so far weren't enough, the problem of read consistency was something of a technical sword in the heart of our ambition to create the "mother of all V$ analyzers." The root of the read consistency problem is that Oracle makes performance data available via peeks into shared memory, not through standard tables. Thus, Oracle fixed views don't use the standard Oracle read consistency model that uses undo blocks to construct a read-consistent image of a block at a specified point in the past.

 Oracle Corporation can't impose the overhead of read consistency upon its fixed views. To do so would intensify the overhead of accessing those views so much that it would render the V$ views practically useless.

You have two choices for obtaining Oracle V\$ data: either you can peek into shared memory yourself, or you can use SQL to peek via Oracle's published V\$ fixed views. The peek-into-shared-memory yourself approach has the much touted benefit of avoiding a tremendous amount of extra SQL processing workload on your Oracle server (which is presumably already burdened with a performance problem). However, neither approach provides a read-consistent image of your performance data. When we query a V\$ view, the output does not represent the system at a point in time. Rather, the output slurs over the duration of the query.

Reading a large chunk of memory is not an atomic operation. To construct a read-consistent image of a memory segment, you must either lock the segment for the duration of the query, or you must use a more complicated read consistency mechanism like the one the Oracle kernel uses for real tables. Otherwise, the output of the query may represent a system state that has never actually existed. Figure 8-1 illustrates the problem. A scan of a memory segment begins at time t_0 and concludes at time t_3. A dark box indicates a memory location whose contents are being changed at a given time. A lightly shaded box indicates the memory location whose contents are being copied to the output stream at a given time. Because reading a large chunk of memory is not an atomic operation, the output stream can contain a state that has never actually existed in memory at any time in the past.

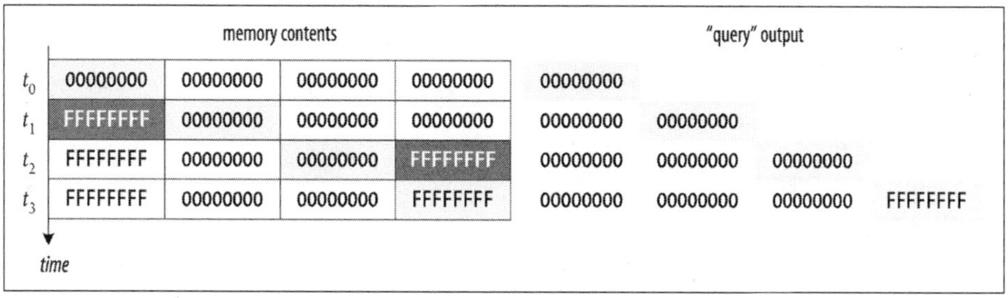

Figure 8-1. The problem caused by lack of read consistency: an output stream can contain a state that has never actually existed in memory at any time in the past

The magnitude of the read consistency problem increases with the execution duration of a snapshot. Imagine that fetching data for 2,000 Oracle sessions from a simple query upon V\$SESSION motivates the sequence of events depicted in Table 8-1. The query's result set is not a snapshot, but a collection of rows that all represent slightly different system states smeared across the 0.40 seconds of the query's total elapsed time.

Table 8-1. The sequence of events motivated by a query of V\$SESSION

Time	Event
0:00:00.00	select sid from v$session; there are 2,000 sessions connected
0:00:00.01	First row of output is returned

Table 8-1. The sequence of events motivated by a query of V$SESSION (continued)

Time	Event
0:00:00.12	Session number 1297 disconnects
0:00:00.26	The location in shared memory that contained information for session number 1297 no longer contains information about session 1297; hence, no data about session number 1297 (which was active at 10:00:00.00) is returned
0:00:00.40	Final row of output is returned

Of course, the result of a query without a read-consistency guarantee is prone to be incorrect. The problem compounds when you attempt to include multiple data sources in your snapshots. Imagine that you have decided that each operational data snapshot you need contains data from each of the following Oracle fixed views:

```
V$BH
V$DB_OBJECT_CACHE
V$FILESTAT
V$LATCH
V$LIBRARYCACHE
V$LOCK
V$OPEN_CURSOR
V$PARAMETER
V$PROCESS
V$ROLLSTAT
V$ROWCACHE
V$SESSION
V$SESSION_EVENT
V$SESSION_WAIT
V$SESSTAT
V$SQL
V$SQLTEXT
V$TIMER
V$TRANSACTION
V$WAITSTAT
```

You would love to believe that all of the data collected during a single snapshot actually represent a single instant in time. However, it's not true. For fixed views with only a small number of relatively nonvolatile rows, this is not a big problem. But for fixed views with thousands of rows, you can create strange results with simple SELECT statements. The problem is even worse if you have such a long list of fixed views across which you wish to construct a snapshot. If these were real Oracle tables, you would probably use the following technique to force several queries to behave as though they were participants in a single atomic event:

```
set transaction readonly;
select * from v$bh;
```

```
select * from v$db_object_cache;
...
select * from v$waitstat;
commit;
```

However, this strategy won't work for V$ fixed views because they're not real tables. Regardless of how you collect the data for your snapshot, the data will be slurred over the duration of the snapshot collection query set. The time-state of the first row of the V$BH query will differ from the time-state of the last row of the V$WAITSTAT query by the accumulated duration of these statements' executions. The duration in this example will likely be more than a whole second. No program can scan gigabytes or even hundreds of megabytes of memory in a single atomic operation.

It is very difficult to do time-based correlation among data sources, even for data collected within a single snapshot. The problem, of course, takes on even more complexity if you introduce operating system statistics into the collected data set.

Fixed View Reference

In spite of their deficiencies, Oracle's fixed views provide value to the performance analyst in many situations. For this section, I describe a few Oracle fixed views that are important for you to understand in your role of performance analyst. All object descriptions shown were taken from an Oracle release 9.0.1.0.0 system.

V$SQL

Probably the most important fixed view for the performance analyst is V$SQL. This view shows several important attributes of the SQL statements whose header information currently reside in the shared pool. The columns in this view are as follows:

```
SQL> desc v$sql
 Name                                      Null?    Type
 ----------------------------------------- -------- ----------------------------
 SQL_TEXT                                           VARCHAR2(1000)
 SHARABLE_MEM                                       NUMBER
 PERSISTENT_MEM                                     NUMBER
 RUNTIME_MEM                                        NUMBER
 SORTS                                              NUMBER
 LOADED_VERSIONS                                    NUMBER
 OPEN_VERSIONS                                      NUMBER
 USERS_OPENING                                      NUMBER
 EXECUTIONS                                         NUMBER
 USERS_EXECUTING                                    NUMBER
 LOADS                                              NUMBER
 FIRST_LOAD_TIME                                    VARCHAR2(19)
 INVALIDATIONS                                      NUMBER
 PARSE_CALLS                                        NUMBER
 DISK_READS                                         NUMBER
 BUFFER_GETS                                        NUMBER
```

ROWS_PROCESSED	NUMBER
COMMAND_TYPE	NUMBER
OPTIMIZER_MODE	VARCHAR2(10)
OPTIMIZER_COST	NUMBER
PARSING_USER_ID	NUMBER
PARSING_SCHEMA_ID	NUMBER
KEPT_VERSIONS	NUMBER
ADDRESS	RAW(4)
TYPE_CHK_HEAP	RAW(4)
HASH_VALUE	NUMBER
PLAN_HASH_VALUE	NUMBER
CHILD_NUMBER	NUMBER
MODULE	VARCHAR2(64)
MODULE_HASH	NUMBER
ACTION	VARCHAR2(64)
ACTION_HASH	NUMBER
SERIALIZABLE_ABORTS	NUMBER
OUTLINE_CATEGORY	VARCHAR2(64)
CPU_TIME	NUMBER
ELAPSED_TIME	NUMBER
OUTLINE_SID	NUMBER
CHILD_ADDRESS	RAW(4)
SQLTYPE	NUMBER
REMOTE	VARCHAR2(1)
OBJECT_STATUS	VARCHAR2(19)
LITERAL_HASH_VALUE	NUMBER
LAST_LOAD_TIME	VARCHAR2(19)
IS_OBSOLETE	VARCHAR2(1)

With V$SQL, you can rank SQL statements in your system by the amount of work they do, or by whatever measure of efficiency you like (see "Finding Inefficient SQL" later in this chapter). By querying V$SQLTEXT_WITH_NEWLINES, you can see the entire text of a SQL statement, not just the first 1,000 bytes that are stored in V$SQL.SQL_TEXT:

```
select sql_text from v$sqltext_with_newlines
where hash_value=:hv and address=:addr
order by piece
```

You can even sense the presence of how distinct SQL texts might have been able to make more effective use of bind variables:

```
select count(*), min(hash_value), substr(sql_text,1,:len) from v$sql
group by substr(sql_text,1,:len)
having count(*)>=:threshold
order by 1 desc, 3 asc
```

In this query, :len specifies a SQL text prefix length that defines whether two distinct statements are "similar" or not. For example, if :len=8, then the strings **select s**alary,... and **select s**.program,... are similar, because their first eight characters are the same. Values like 32, 64, and 128 usually produce interesting results. The value of :threshold determines your threshold of tolerance for similar statements in your library cache. You'll normally want to set :threshold to at least three, because having only two similar SQL statements in your library cache is not really a problem. If your system is running amok in unshared SQL, then you'll want to set : threshold to a larger value so that you can focus on fixing a few unshared statements at a time.

V$SESS_IO

V$SESS_IO is a simple fixed view that allows you to measure the logical and so-called physical I/O that has been generated for a session:

```
SQL> desc v$sess_io
Name                                    Null?    Type
------------------------------------    -------- --------------------------
SID                                              NUMBER
BLOCK_GETS                                       NUMBER
CONSISTENT_GETS                                  NUMBER
PHYSICAL_READS                                   NUMBER
BLOCK_CHANGES                                    NUMBER
CONSISTENT_CHANGES                               NUMBER
```

The statistics in V$SESS_IO map nicely to extended SQL trace statistics:

BLOCK_GETS
> The equivalent of the cu statistic in raw trace data.

CONSISTENT_GETS
> The equivalent of the cr statistic in raw trace data.

PHYSICAL_READS
> The equivalent of the p statistic in raw trace data.

The number of logical I/Os (LIOs) is the sum of the values of BLOCK_GETS and CONSISTENT_GETS. When an Oracle session consumes massive amounts of CPU capacity with only intermittent executions of instrumented Oracle wait events, the session's trace will appear to "sit still." With repeated executions of the following query, you can observe whether a session that is running but emitting no trace data is executing LIO calls:

```
select block_gets, consistent_gets from v$sess_io where sid=:sid
```

V$SYSSTAT

V$SYSSTAT is one of the first fixed views I remember using. Its structure is simple:

```
SQL> desc v$sysstat
Name                                    Null?    Type
------------------------------------    -------- --------------------------
STATISTIC#                                       NUMBER
NAME                                             VARCHAR2(64)
CLASS                                            NUMBER
VALUE                                            NUMBER
```

Each row in V$SYSSTAT contains an instance-wide statistic. Most statistics are tallies of operations that have occurred since the most recent instance startup. V$SYSSTAT rows are subject to overflow errors.

The denormalized structure of V$SYSSTAT makes it easy to find out what the system has done since the most recent instance startup, without having to do a join. The following query executed in Oracle9i displays roughly 250 statistics that describe what the entire instance has done over its lifespan:

```
select name, value from v$sysstat order by 1
```

The following query lists the values of several statistics related to parsing:

```
select name, value from v$sysstat where name like 'parse%'
```

V$SESSTAT

As I described in Chapter 3, the system-wide scope is probably the incorrect action scope for your diagnostic data collection. V$SESSTAT contains the same statistics as V$SYSSTAT, except at the session level:

```
SQL> desc v$sesstat
 Name                                      Null?    Type
 ----------------------------------------- -------- ---------------------------
 SID                                                NUMBER
 STATISTIC#                                         NUMBER
 VALUE                                              NUMBER
```

Each row in V$SESSTAT contains a tally of how many times a statistic has been incremented since the creation of a specified session.

V$SESSTAT is not denormalized like V$SYSSTAT, so finding a statistic by name requires a join with V$STATNAME. The following query lists all the statistics that have aggregated for a session since its birth:

```
select name, value
from v$statname n, v$sesstat s
where sid=:sid and n.statistic#=s.statistic#
and s.value>0
order by 2
```

The following query lists the approximate number of centiseconds' worth of CPU capacity consumed by a given session:

```
select name, value
from v$statname n, v$sesstat s
where sid=:sid and n.statistic#=s.statistic#
and n.name='CPU used by this session'
```

V$SYSTEM_EVENT

The V$SYSTEM_EVENT fixed view records aggregated statistics about instrumented code paths that the Oracle kernel has executed since its most recent instance startup:

```
SQL> desc v$system_event
Name                                      Null?    Type
----------------------------------------  -------- -------------------------
EVENT                                              VARCHAR2(64)
TOTAL_WAITS                                        NUMBER
TOTAL_TIMEOUTS                                     NUMBER
TIME_WAITED                                        NUMBER
AVERAGE_WAIT                                       NUMBER
TIME_WAITED_MICRO                                  NUMBER
```

Each row in V$SYSTEM_EVENT contains information about the calls of a given event for the lifespan of the instance.

> You might notice that there is no MAX_WAIT column in V$SYSTEM_EVENT. You can add this useful column to the definition of V$SYSTEM_EVENT, if you like, by following the instructions presented in [Lewis (2001b) 577–581].

On Oracle7 and Oracle8i kernels, you can obtain resource consumption statistics about everything but CPU consumption with following query:

```
select event, total_waits, time_waited/100 t
from v$system_event
order by 3 desc
```

With Oracle9i kernels, you can obtain the same statistics displayed with microsecond precision by using the following query:

```
select event, total_waits, time_waited_micro/1000000 t
from v$system_event
order by t desc
```

V$SESSION_EVENT

Once again, the system-wide scope is often the incorrect scope for diagnostic data collection. V$SESSION_EVENT provides the ability to collect properly session-scoped diagnostic data for Oracle kernel code paths:

```
SQL> desc v$session_event
Name                                      Null?    Type
----------------------------------------  -------- -------------------------
SID                                                NUMBER
EVENT                                              VARCHAR2(64)
TOTAL_WAITS                                        NUMBER
TOTAL_TIMEOUTS                                     NUMBER
TIME_WAITED                                        NUMBER
AVERAGE_WAIT                                       NUMBER
MAX_WAIT                                           NUMBER
TIME_WAITED_MICRO                                  NUMBER
```

Each row in V$SESSION_EVENT contains information about the executions of a given segment of Oracle kernel code (a "wait event") for a given session since its birth.

Thus, the information in V$SESSION_EVENT is an aggregation of the data that appears in extended SQL trace output:

EVENT

The name of an Oracle wait event. Note that each EVENT value corresponds to a nam value in the WAIT lines of Oracle's extended SQL trace data.

TOTAL_WAITS

The number of WAIT lines with nam='x', where x is the value of the row's EVENT.

TIME_WAITED

The sum of the ela values for all WAIT lines with nam='x', where x is the value of the row's EVENT.

The V$SESSION_EVENT fixed view contains no record of a session's CPU capacity consumption. You have to go to V$SESSTAT for that.

The following query will display information about the wait events that a given Oracle8i session has executed over its lifespan:

```
select event, total_waits, time_waited/100 t
from v$session_event
where sid=:sid
order by t desc
```

The following query will display information about the wait events that a given Oracle9i session has executed over its lifespan:

```
select event, total_waits, time_waited_micro/1000000 t
from v$session_event
where sid=:sid
order by t desc
```

V$SESSION_WAIT

Ask people what the "wait interface" is, and most will probably mention V$SESSION_WAIT. Unlike the V$SYSTEM_EVENT and V$SESSION_EVENT fixed views, V$SESSION_WAIT does not contain an aggregation of historical events. Instead, it provides a view into what a specified session is doing *right now*:

```
SQL> desc v$session_wait
 Name                                      Null?    Type
 ----------------------------------------- -------- ----------------------------
 SID                                                NUMBER
 SEQ#                                               NUMBER
 EVENT                                              VARCHAR2(64)
 P1TEXT                                             VARCHAR2(64)
 P1                                                 NUMBER
 P1RAW                                              RAW(4)
 P2TEXT                                             VARCHAR2(64)
 P2                                                 NUMBER
 P2RAW                                              RAW(4)
 P3TEXT                                             VARCHAR2(64)
```

```
P3                              NUMBER
P3RAW                           RAW(4)
WAIT_TIME                       NUMBER
SECONDS_IN_WAIT                 NUMBER
STATE                           VARCHAR2(19)
```

Each row in V$SESSION_WAIT contains information about a session's present state. The statistics revealed by V$SESSION_WAIT include:

SEQ#

Each time an event completes, the Oracle kernel increments this sequence number.

WAIT_TIME

At the beginning of an instrumented wait event, the Oracle kernel sets the value of WAIT_TIME to zero. The value remains zero until the wait event is complete, when the kernel sets its value to one of those shown in Table 8-2. Note that the unit of measure is the centisecond, even in Oracle9*i*. There is no WAIT_TIME_MICRO column at least through release 9.2.0.2.1, although the value of WAIT_TIME is derived from a microsecond value in its underlying X$ view.

SECONDS_IN_WAIT

At the beginning of an instrumented wait event, the Oracle kernel sets the value of SECONDS_IN_WAIT to zero. The session itself never updates the value again until the next instrumented wait event, whereupon the session resets the value back to zero again. The value of SECONDS_IN_WAIT is incremented by 3 approximately every three seconds by the log writer (LGWR) process. Note that the unit of measure is seconds, not centiseconds or microseconds.

Events that "time out" complicate matters somewhat. For example, an enqueue wait event times out roughly every two seconds, even for enqueue waits that last considerably longer. Upon each timeout, the Oracle kernel increments SEQ#, but it does not reset the value of SECONDS_IN_WAIT.

STATE

At the beginning of an instrumented wait event, the value of STATE becomes WAITING. The value remains WAITING until the wait event is complete, when the kernel sets its value to one of the values described in Table 8-2.

Table 8-2. Meanings of the values of the STATE and WAIT_TIME columns in V$SESSION_WAIT

STATE	WAIT_TIME	Implication
WAITED UNKNOWN TIME	−2	The value of TIMED_STATISTICS was FALSE for the session when the event completed, so the actual duration is unknown.
WAITED SHORT TIME	−1	The wait event has completed, but it began and ended within the same gettimeofday clock tick.
WAITING	0	The wait event is in process, pending completion.
WAITED KNOWN TIME	$t \geq 0$	The wait event has completed, and it consumed $t = t_1 - t_0$ centiseconds of elapsed execution time (Chapter 7).

The following query will display information about the wait events that are presently executing on a given Oracle system:

```
select sid, event, wait_time/100 t, seconds_in_wait w, state
from v$session_wait
order by 1
```

The following query will show a histogram of which activity your system's sessions are doing right now:

```
select event, count(*) from v$session_wait
where state='WAITING'
group by event
order by 2 desc
```

Don't write V$SESSION_WAIT queries with WAIT_TIME=0 in your where clause if what you really mean is STATE='WAITING'. Some analysts got into the habit of assuming that the predicates WAIT_TIME=0 and STATE='WAITING' are equivalent, because in Oracle7 and Oracle8i kernels, they were. However, in Oracle9i kernels, the two predicates are not equivalent.

Oracle9i kernels compute WAIT_TIME as round(x$ksusecst.ksusstim/10000), but the STATE value is a DECODE of the *un-rounded* value of KSUSSTIM. Therefore, WAIT_TIME can appear to be zero when its base data value is actually not. Hence, Oracle9i kernels produce situations in which WAIT_TIME is zero, but STATE is something other than WAITING.

Useful Fixed View Queries

Almost every database administrator has a tool kit of V$ queries that she uses to help with database performance analysis work. This section discusses some of my favorites and I'm sure some of yours as well. Be prepared though. Chances are good that some of the reports you count on for information today are feeding you misleading data. Practically every V$ query you can run is susceptible to one or more serious interpretation fallacies. This section illustrates several.

Tom Kyte's Test Harness

One of my favorite fixed view–based tools ever is Tom Kyte's test harness that allows an application developer to compare the performance of two competing application development approaches. You can see a complete description online at *http://asktom.oracle.com/~tkyte/runstats.html*. This URL contains instructions about how to use the simple harness, including an example of using the harness to demonstrate the horrifyingly bad scalability of applications that do not use bind variables (*http://asktom.oracle.com/pls/ask/f?p=4950:8:::::F4950_P8_DISPLAYID:2444907911913*).

Tom's test harness is especially valuable for developers of Oracle applications to use *early* in their SQL development cycles. Developers usually write code that users will

Oracle's Inauspicious Early Attempt to Document V$SESSION_WAIT

The kernel instrumentation described in this book and published back in 1992 has taken many years to catch on. Oracle Corporation's earliest documentation about the new capability didn't exactly hasten the feature's acceptance. For example, the *Oracle7 Server Tuning* guide shows the following V$SESSION_WAIT query output [Oracle (1996)]:

```
SQL> SELECT sid, event, wait_time
  2    FROM v$session_wait
  3    ORDER BY wait_time, event;
 SID EVENT                   WAIT_TIME
---- ----------------------- ----------

...
 205 latch free             4294967295
 207 latch free             4294967295
 209 latch free             4294967295
 215 latch free             4294967295
 293 latch free             4294967295
 294 latch free             4294967295
 117 log file sync          4294967295
 129 log file sync          4294967295
  22 virtual circuit status 4294967295
```

The guide then provides the following advice: "The unusually large wait times for the last several events signify that the sessions are currently waiting for that event [sic]. As you can see, there are currently several sessions waiting for a latch to be free and for a log file sync."

If the implication in the document were true, then the events pictured in this example had been waiting for 1.36193 years. Oops.

The problem began with omitting the STATE column from the query's select list. As it happens, the 32-bit hexadecimal representation of the decimal integer -1 is ffffffff. Print this value as an unsigned 32-bit integer, and you get $2^{32} - 1$, or 4294967295.

The WAIT_TIME values shown here are actually -1. This value corresponds to the STATE value WAITED SHORT TIME (Table 8-2). Each of the "unusually large wait times" actually represents an event that had already completed, and that had in fact completed so quickly that it was measured as having a zero-centisecond duration.

Lots of authors made similar mistakes during the early years in their attempts to explain how to use the new "wait" and "event" data. To their credit, they were the pioneers who stimulated many early adopters of a new technology. But mistakes like the one described here, especially in the official Oracle Corporation documentation, did retard the rate of acceptance of Oracle's amazing new diagnostic features.

later execute on a busy system. However, the systems on which developers write that code are usually *not* busy—at least not in the same way that their users' systems are. Tom's test harness measures an application's use of the Oracle resources that scale the worst (including, perhaps most notably, Oracle latches). The results are simple to interpret. The fewer serialized resources that an approach requires, the better you can expect it to scale when it becomes a part of your production workload. The best thing about Tom's harness is that it's so easy to use that developers actually *will* use it. Once developers start thinking in the terms of the resource consumption data that the harness provides, they write more scalable code.

Finding a Fixed View Definition

It can be difficult to find the information you need about a V$ fixed view from publications about Oracle. Sometimes the information you want is simply not published. Other times you find the information that you think you're looking for, but it's just plain wrong. Publications about Oracle are particularly unreliable in areas of the Oracle kernel that evolve quickly. Fortunately, the kernel is somewhat self-documenting in the domain of fixed views. One secret lies within knowing how to use V$FIXED_VIEW_DEFINITION. The hardest part is knowing its name:

```
SQL> desc v$fixed_view_definition
 Name                                     Null?    Type
 ---------------------------------------- -------- --------------------------
 VIEW_NAME                                         VARCHAR2(30)
 VIEW_DEFINITION                                   VARCHAR2(4000)
```

V$FIXED_VIEW_DEFINITION is the means through which I learned, for example, the detailed definitions of the STATE and WAIT_TIME columns of V$SESSION_WAIT. You can reproduce the result in just a few simple steps. Begin by executing the following query to return the definition of the V$SESSION_WAIT view:

```
SQL> select * from v$fixed_view_definition
  2  where view_name='V$SESSION_WAIT';

VIEW_NAME
------------------------------
VIEW_DEFINITION
--------------------------------------------------------------------------
V$SESSION_WAIT
select sid,seq#,event,p1text,p1,p1raw,p2text,p2,p2raw,p3text, p3,p3raw,wait
_time,seconds_in_wait,state from gv$session_wait where inst_id = USERENV('I
nstance')
```

Notice, by the way, that the VIEW_NAME value for this view is stored using uppercase letters. So now you know that V$SESSION_WAIT is simply a projection of GV$SESSION_WAIT. That doesn't tell you very much yet, however. The next step is to figure out the definition of GV$SESSION_WAIT:

```
SQL> desc gv$session_wait
 Name                                     Null?    Type
 ---------------------------------------- -------- --------------------------
 INST_ID                                           NUMBER
 SID                                               NUMBER
 SEQ#                                              NUMBER
 EVENT                                             VARCHAR2(64)
```

```
P1TEXT                          VARCHAR2(64)
P1                              NUMBER
P1RAW                           RAW(4)
P2TEXT                          VARCHAR2(64)
P2                              NUMBER
P2RAW                           RAW(4)
P3TEXT                          VARCHAR2(64)
P3                              NUMBER
P3RAW                           RAW(4)
WAIT_TIME                       NUMBER
SECONDS_IN_WAIT                 NUMBER
STATE                           VARCHAR2(19)

SQL> select * from v$fixed_view_definition
  2 where view_name='GV$SESSION_WAIT';


VIEW_NAME
------------------------------
VIEW_DEFINITION
--------------------------------------------------------------------------
GV$SESSION_WAIT
select s.inst_id,s.indx,s.ksussseq,e.kslednam, e.ksledp1,s.ksussp1,s.ksussp
1r,e.ksledp2, s.ksussp2,s.ksussp2r,e.ksledp3,s.ksussp3,s.ksussp3r, round(s.
ksusstim / 10000), s.ksusewtm, decode(s.ksusstim, 0, 'WAITING', -2, 'WAITED
 UNKNOWN TIME',  -1, 'WAITED SHORT TIME', 'WAITED KNOWN TIME')  from x$ksus
ecst s, x$ksled e where bitand(s.ksspaflg,1)!=0 and bitand(s.ksuseflg,1)!=0
 and s.ksussseq!=0 and s.ksussopc=e.indx
```

Voilà! Here you can see the rounding operation used to compute WAIT_TIME. From what you see here, you can also determine the unit of measure in which this thing called X$KSUSECST.KSUSSTIM is expressed. We know that WAIT_TIME is reported in centiseconds, and we know that the Oracle kernel divides this value by 10^4 to produce a centisecond value. Therefore, there are 10^k KSUSSTIM units in one second, where $10^k/10^4 = 10^2$. Hence, there are 10^6 KSUSSTIM units in a second. In other words, the Oracle kernel computes the wait time in microseconds, but the public API (V$SESSION_WAIT) provides it in centiseconds.

Finding Inefficient SQL

Jeff Holt's *htopsql.sql* script, shown in Example 8-2, is what *hotsos.com* staff use when we wish to get a fast overview of which SQL statements presently in the library cache have contributed the most to recent workload. The query has no direct relationship to response time, but there is a strong correlation between a query's LIO count and the total execution time for most SQL statements. The new columns CPU_TIME and ELAPSED_TIME, available in Oracle9*i*, reveal in V$SQL some of the data previously available only in SQL trace data.

Example 8-2. This script reports on the apparent efficiency of SQL statements whose information presently resides in the shared pool

```
rem $Header: /usr/local/hostos/RCS/htopsql.sql,v 1.6 2001/11/19 22:31:35
rem  Author: jeff.holt@hotsos.com
rem          Copyright (c) 1999 by Hotsos Enterprises, Ltd.
             All rights reserved.
rem  Usage: This script shows inefficient SQL by computing the ratio
rem          of logical_reads to rows_processed.  The user will have
rem          to press return to see the first page.  The user should
rem          be able to see the really bad stuff on the first page and
rem          therefore should press ^C and then press [Return] when the
rem          first page is completely displayed.
rem          SQL hash values are really statement identifiers. These
rem          identifiers are used as input to a hashing function to
rem          determine if a statement is in the shared pool.
rem          This script shows only statement identifiers. Use hsqltxt.sql
rem          to display the text of interesting statements.
rem  Notes: This will return data for select,insert,update, and delete
rem          statements. We don't return rows for PL/SQL blocks because
rem          their reads are counted in their underlying SQL statements.
rem          There is value in knowing the PL/SQL routine that executes
rem          an inefficient statement but it's only important once you
rem          know what's wrong with the statment.

col stmtid      heading 'Stmt Id'          format    9999999999
col dr          heading 'PIO blks'         format    999,999,999
col bg          heading 'LIOs'             format    999,999,999
col sr          heading 'Sorts'            format        999,999
col exe         heading 'Runs'             format    999,999,999
col rp          heading 'Rows'             format  9,999,999,999
col rpr         heading 'LIOs|per Row'     format    999,999,999
col rpe         heading 'LIOs|per Run'     format    999,999,999

set termout   on
set pause     on
set pagesize  30
set pause     'More: '
set linesize  95

select  hash_value stmtid
       ,sum(disk_reads) dr
       ,sum(buffer_gets) bg
       ,sum(rows_processed) rp
       ,sum(buffer_gets)/greatest(sum(rows_processed),1) rpr
       ,sum(executions) exe
       ,sum(buffer_gets)/greatest(sum(executions),1) rpe
  from v$sql
where command_type in ( 2,3,6,7 )
group by hash_value
order by 5 desc
/

set pause off
```

The query sorts its output by the number of LIO calls executed per row returned. This is a rough measure of statement efficiency. For example, the following output should bring to mind the question, "Why should an application require more than 174 million memory accesses to compute 5 rows?"

```
SQL> @htopsql
More:
```

Stmt Id	PIO blks	LIOs	Rows	LIOs per Row	Runs	LIOs per Run
2503207570	39,736	871,467,231	5	174,293,446	138	6,314,980
1647785011	10,287,310	337,616,703	3	112,538,901	7,730,556	44
4085942203	45,748	257,887,860	8	32,235,983	138	1,868,753
3955802477	10,201	257,887,221	8	32,235,903	138	1,868,748
1647618855	53,136	5,625,843	0	5,625,843	128,868	44
3368205675	35,666	3,534,374	0	3,534,374	1	3,534,374
3722360728	54,348	722,866	1	722,866	1	722,866
497954690	54,332	722,779	0	722,779	1	722,779
90462217	361,189	4,050,206	8	506,276	137	29,564
299369270	1,268	382,211	0	382,211	42,378	9

...

The output shown here was used in 1999 to identify a single SQL statement that was consuming almost 50% of the total daily CPU capacity of an online system. However, as with any ratio, the *LIOs per row* definition of statement efficiency can motivate false conclusions. For example, consider a SQL statement like this one:

```
select cust, sum(bal)
from colossal_order_history_table
where cust_id=:id
group by cust
```

This query may legitimately visit a very large number of Oracle blocks (even using a primary key index on CUST_ID), but it will at most return only one row. An *htopsql.sql* report would thus imply that this query is inefficient, when in fact this might be a false negative implication.

Many analysts use a query like *htopsql.sql* as the beginning step in each of their performance improvement projects. However, basing a performance improvement method upon any report upon V$SQL suffers from deficiencies induced by time scope and program scope errors. Like most information you learn from V$ fixed views, it is difficult to exercise control over the time scope and program scope of data obtained from V$SQL. For example, consider the following situations:

- The SQL statement that most needs your attention is one that has not been run since last month's month-end close. The statement is no longer in the library cache, so it will not be revealed in today's V$SQL report.

- The SQL statement that appears "most inefficient" is an element of an interface upload program that your company will never run again.

- The SQL statement that appears "most inefficient" is one that runs from midnight to 3:00 a.m. Since its window of permissible execution time extends until 6:00 a.m., and since all the nightly batch work finishes long before that deadline, nobody cares that the inefficient SQL statement is slow.

- The SQL statement whose performance is most hurting the business's ability to improve net profit, cash flow, and return on investment is not listed near the top of any of your V$SQL reports. Its ranking is mediocre because none of its statistics is particularly remarkable, but from the business's perspective, this is clearly the statement that is most hurting the system's economic value.

Without obtaining information from the *business*, there is no way to know whether the performance of a SQL statement that rises to the top of the report is actually even critical to the business. I believe that V$SQL is any performance analyst's most valuable V$ fixed view in the database. However, the power of using V$SQL is far less than the power of a performance improvement project that follows Method R.

Finding Where a Session Is Stuck

From time to time, we all get that call. It's Nancy on the phone, and her session is "stuck." She's asked her colleagues already if the system is down, and everyone else around her seems to be working fine. Perhaps the reason Nancy's calling is because in last week's brown-bag lunch event,* you explained to your users why they should not reboot their personal computer when this kind of thing happens. If you know how to find Nancy's session ID (Chapter 6), then it is easy to determine what's going on with her session. Imagine that we had found out that Nancy's session ID is 42. Then you use the following query to determine why she's stuck:

```
SQL> col sid format 999990
SQL> col seq# format 999,990
SQL> col event format a26
SQL> select sid, seq#, event, state, seconds_in_wait seconds
  2  from v$session_wait
  3  where sid=42

    SID    SEQ# EVENT                      STATE                SECONDS
------- -------- -------------------------- -------------------- ----------
     42  29,786 db file sequential read    WAITED SHORT TIME         174
```

Does this mean that Nancy's session is stuck waiting for I/O? No; actually this query indicates the contrary. The most recent wait event that Nancy's Oracle kernel process executed was in fact a file read operation, but the operation completed approximately 174 seconds ago (plus or minus roughly 3 seconds). Furthermore, the operation completed in less than one unit of Oracle timer resolution. (On an

---

* A *brown-bag lunch* is an event at which employees eat lunch they've brought while they discuss a work-related topic.

Oracle8*i* system, this means that the elapsed time of the read operation was less than 0.01 seconds.) So what is Nancy's session waiting on?

The answer is that her session (really, her Oracle kernel process) is either working its brains out consuming CPU capacity, or her session is waiting its turn in the *ready to run* queue for its next opportunity to work its brains out consuming CPU capacity. You can watch what the session is doing by issuing successive queries of V$SESS_IO:

```
SQL> col block_gets format 999,999,999,990
SQL> col consistent_gets format 999,999,999,990
SQL> select to_char(sysdate, 'hh:mi:ss') "TIME",
  2  block_gets, consistent_gets
  3  from v$sess_io where sid=42;

TIME           BLOCK_GETS  CONSISTENT_GETS
--------  ----------------  ----------------
05:20:27            2,224        22,647,561

SQL> /

TIME           BLOCK_GETS  CONSISTENT_GETS
--------  ----------------  ----------------
05:20:44            2,296        23,382,994
```

By incorporating a timestamp into your query, you can get a feel for the rate at which your Oracle system can process LIO calls. The system shown here processed 735,505 LIO calls in about 17 seconds, which yields a rate of 43,265 LIOs per second. With this information, you can begin to appreciate what Nancy is going through. The more than 22,000,000 LIOs executed by her program when you first began looking at it had already consumed almost nine minutes of execution time. It's time now for you to find out what SQL Nancy's program is running so that you can get it fixed. You can do that job by joining V$OPEN_CURSOR and V$SQL. I'd rather have extended SQL trace data for Nancy's program if I could get it, but if you don't have that luxury, smart use of Oracle's fixed views can help you find the problem.

Finding Where a System Is Stuck

Sometimes the phone rings, and before Nancy finishes describing her problem, you notice another incoming call on line two. Then within two minutes, you've heard complaints from four users, and you have seven new voicemails containing ones you haven't heard yet. What should you do? If your system permits the execution of a query, here's the one I'd suggest that you run:

```
SQL> break on report
SQL> compute sum of sessions on report
SQL> select event, count(*) sessions from v$session_wait
  2  where state='WAITING'
  3  group by event
  4  order by 2 desc;
```

```
EVENT                                                             SESSIONS
----------------------------------------------------------    ----------
SQL*Net message from client                                         211
log file switch (archiving needed)                                  187
db file sequential read                                              27
db file scattered read                                                9
rdbms ipc message                                                     4
smon timer                                                            1
pmon timer                                                            1
                                                              ----------
sum                                                                 440
```

The report shown here depicts 440 connected sessions. At the time of the query, over 200 of the Oracle kernel processes are blocked on a read of the SQL*Net socket while their end-user applications execute code path between database calls. Many of these 211 processes are probably sitting idle while their users use non-Oracle applications, talk with colleagues, or attend to one or more of our species' many physiological needs. More disturbing is that 187 sessions are blocked waiting for log file switch (archiving needed). This message indicates that the Oracle ARCH process is not able to keep pace with the generation of online redo.

A few other users on the system are actually getting work done (36 are engaged in reading database files), but as each user attempts to execute a database COMMIT call, she'll get caught waiting for a log file switch (archiving needed) event. The longer the problem goes uncorrected, the more users will get stuck waiting for the event. On the system where this output was obtained, the database administrator had neglected to anticipate that on this particular day, the ARCH process's destination file system would fill.

Approximating a Session's Resource Profile

The program *vprof*, shown in Example 8-3, is something that I cobbled together to collect Oracle timing data for a specified Oracle session for a specified time interval. I designed *vprof* not for production use (I don't consider it worthy for production use), but to illustrate some of the complexities of trying to use SQL upon fixed views to perform well-scoped diagnostic data collection. I find *vprof* to be useful in educational environments to help explain points including:

- The union of data from V$SESSTAT and V$SESSION_EVENT approximately accounts for the total response time of a user action.

- Attempts to obtain user action timing data from Oracle V$ fixed views are plagued by difficult time scope challenges.

- Diagnosing the performance problem of a targeted user action is a much bigger job than just creating the action's resource profile.

Example 8-3. A Perl program that uses SQL to approximate a session's resource profile for a specified time interval

```perl
#!/usr/bin/perl

# $Header: /home/cvs/cvm-book1/sqltrace/vproP.pl,v 1.8 2003/04/08 14:27:30
# Cary Millsap (cary.millsap@hotsos.com)
# Copyright (c) 2003 by Hotsos Enterprises, Ltd. All rights reserved.

use strict;
use warnings;
use Getopt::Long;
use DBI;
use Time::HiRes  qw(gettimeofday);
use Date::Format qw(time2str);

sub nvl($;$) {
    my $value   = shift;
    my $default = shift || 0;
    return $value ? $value : $default;
}

# fetch command-line options
my %opt = (
    service      => "",
    username     => "/",
    password     => "",
    debug        => 0,
);
GetOptions(
    "service=s"  => \$opt{service},
    "username=s" => \$opt{username},
    "password=s" => \$opt{password},
    "debug"      => \$opt{debug},
);

# fetch sid from command line
my $usage = "Usage: $0 [options] sid\n\t";
my $sid = shift or die $usage;

# connect to Oracle and prepare snapshot SQL
my %attr = (RaiseError => 1, AutoCommit => 0);
my $dbh = DBI->connect(
    "dbi:Oracle:$opt{service}", $opt{username}, $opt{password}, \%attr
);
my $sth = $dbh->prepare(<<'END OF SQL', {ora_check_sql => 0});
select
  'CPU service' ACTIVITY,
  value TIME,
  (
    select
      value
    from
      v$sesstat s,
```

*Example 8-3. A Perl program that uses SQL to approximate a session's resource profile for a
specified time interval (continued)*

```
      v$statname n
    where
      sid = ?
      and n.statistic# = s.statistic#
      and n.name = 'user calls'
  ) CALLS
from
  v$sesstat s,
  v$statname n
where
  sid = ?
  and n.statistic# = s.statistic#
  and n.name = 'CPU used by this session'
union
select
  e.event ACTIVITY,
  e.time_waited TIME,
  e.total_waits CALLS
from
  v$session_event e
where
  sid = ?
END OF SQL

# wait for signal and collect t0 consumption snapshot
print "Press <Enter> to mark time t0: "; <>;
my ($sec0, $msec0) = gettimeofday;
$sth->execute($sid, $sid, $sid);
my $h0 = $sth->fetchall_hashref("ACTIVITY");

# wait for signal and collect t1 consumption snapshot
print "Press <Enter> to mark time t1: "; <>;
my ($sec1, $msec1) = gettimeofday;
$sth->execute($sid, $sid, $sid);
my $h1 = $sth->fetchall_hashref("ACTIVITY");

# construct profile table
my %prof;
for my $k (keys %$h1) {
    my $calls = $h1->{$k}->{CALLS} - nvl($h0->{$k}->{CALLS}) or next;
    $prof{$k}->{CALLS} = $calls;
    $prof{$k}->{TIME} = ($h1->{$k}->{TIME} - nvl($h0->{$k}->{TIME})) / 100;
}

# compute unaccounted-for duration
my $interval = ($sec1 - $sec0) + ($msec1 - $msec0)/1E6;
my $accounted = 0; $accounted += $prof{$_}->{TIME} for keys %prof;
$prof{"unaccounted-for"} = {
    ACTIVITY => "unaccounted-for",
    TIME     => $interval - $accounted,
    CALLS    => 1,
```

Example 8-3. A Perl program that uses SQL to approximate a session's resource profile for a specified time interval (continued)

```perl
};

# print debugging output if requested
if ($opt{debug}) {
    use Data::Dumper;
    printf "t0 snapshot:\n%s\n", Dumper($h0);
    printf "t1 snapshot:\n%s\n", Dumper($h1);
    print "\n\n";
}

# print the resource profile
print "\nResource Profile for Session $sid\n\n";
printf "%24s = %s.%06d\n", "t0", time2str("%T", $sec0), $msec0;
printf "%24s = %s.%06d\n", "t1", time2str("%T", $sec1), $msec1;
printf "%24s = %15.6fs\n", "interval duration", $interval;
printf "%24s = %15.6fs\n", "accounted-for duration", $accounted;
print "\n";
my ($c1, $c2, $c4, $c5) = (32, 10, 10, 11);
my ($c23) = ($c2+1+7+1);
printf "%-${c1}s %${c23}s %${c4}s %${c5}s\n",
    "Response Time Component", "Duration (seconds)", "Calls", "Dur/Call";
printf "%-${c1}s %${c23}s %${c4}s %${c5}s\n",
    "-"x$c1, "-"x$c23, "-"x$c4, "-"x$c5;
for my $k (sort { $prof{$b}->{TIME} <=> $prof{$a}->{TIME} } keys %prof) {
    printf "%-${c1}s ", $k;
    printf "%${c2}.2f ", $prof{$k}->{TIME};
    printf "%7.1f%% ", $prof{$k}->{TIME}/$interval*100;
    printf "%${c4}d ", $prof{$k}->{CALLS};
    printf "%${c5}.6f\n",
        ($prof{$k}->{CALLS} ? $prof{$k}->{TIME}/$prof{$k}->{CALLS} : 0);
}
printf "%-${c1}s %${c23}s %${c4}s %${c5}s\n",
    "-"x$c1, "-"x$c23, "-"x$c4, "-"x$c5;
printf "%-${c1}s %${c2}.2f %7.1f%%\n",
    "Total", $interval, $interval/$interval*100;

# wrap up
$dbh->disconnect;

__END__

=head1 NAME

vprof - create an approximate resource profile for a session


=head1 SYNOPSIS

vprof
  [--service=I<h>]
  [--username=I<u>]
```

Example 8-3. A Perl program that uses SQL to approximate a session's resource profile for a specified time interval (continued)

```
[--password=I<p>]
[--debug=I<d>]
I<session-id>


=head1 DESCRIPTION

B<vprof> uses queries from B<V$SESSTAT> and B<V$SESSION_EVENT> to
construct an approximate resource profile for the Oracle session whose
B<V$SESSION.SID> value is given by I<session-id>. The time scope of the
observation interval is defined interactively by the user's response to
the prompts to mark the times I<t0> and I<t1>, where I<t0> is the
observation interval start time, and I<t1> is the observation interval end
time.


=head2 Options

=over 4

=item B<--service=>I<h>

The name of the Oracle service to which B<vprof> will connect. The default
value is "" (the empty string), which will cause B<vprof> to connect
using, for example, the default Oracle TNS alias.

=item B<--username=>I<u>

The name of the Oracle schema to which B<vprof> will connect. The default
value is "/".

=item B<--password=>I<p>

The Oracle password that B<vprof> will use to connect. The default value
is "" (the empty string).

=item B<--debug=>I<d>

When set to 1, B<vprof> dumps its internal data structures in addition to
its normal output. The default value is 0.

=back


=head1 EXAMPLES

Use of B<vprof> will resemble something like the following case in which I
used B<vprof> to report on statistics generated by B<vprof>'s own Oracle
connection:

  $ vprof --username=system --password=manager 8
```

Example 8-3. A Perl program that uses SQL to approximate a session's resource profile for a
specified time interval (continued)

```
Press <Enter> to mark time t0:
Press <Enter> to mark time t1:

Resource Profile for Session 8

                       t0 = 14:59:12.596000
                       t1 = 14:59:14.349000
         interval duration =     1.753000s
    accounted-for duration =     1.670000s

Response Time Component       Duration (seconds)   Calls   Dur/Call
---------------------------   ------------------   -----   ----------
SQL*Net message from client      1.38    78.7%         1   1.380000
CPU service                      0.29    16.5%         1   0.290000
unaccounted-for                  0.08     4.7%         1   0.083000
SQL*Net message to client        0.00     0.0%         1   0.000000
---------------------------   ------------------   -----   ----------
Total                            1.75   100.0%


=head1 AUTHOR

Cary Millsap (cary.millsap@hotsos.com)


=head1 BUGS

B<vprof> suffers from several severe limitations, including:

=over 2

=item -

If a wait event is pending at time I<t0>, then the profile will contain
excess time, which will manifest as negative "unaccounted-for" time. This
situation happens frequently for the event 'SQL*Net message from client'.
This is the wait event whose execution is pending while an application user
is idle.

=item -

If a wait event is pending at time I<t1>, then the profile will be absent
some missing time, which will manifest as positive "unaccounted-for" time.
This situation is likely to happen if you choose time I<t1> to occur
during a long-running program.

=item -

The limitations listed above can combine to offset each other, on occasion
resulting in small "unaccounted-for" duration. This produces a false
positive indication that everything is alright when actually there are two
```

Example 8-3. A Perl program that uses SQL to approximate a session's resource profile for a specified time interval (continued)

```
problems.

=item -

If the specified sid does not exist at time I<t0>, then the program will
return a profile filled with unaccounted-for time.

=item -

If a session with the specified sid terminates between time I<t0> and
I<t1>, then the resulting resource profile will contain only
unaccounted-for time. ...Unless a new session with the specified B<sid>
(but of course a different B<serial#>) is created before I<t1>. In this
case, the output will look appropriate but be completely erroneous.

=back


=head1 COPYRIGHT

Copyright (c) 2000-2003 by Hotsos Enterprises, Ltd. All rights reserved.
```

The output of *vprof* looks like this for a session on my system with V$SESSION.SID=8:

```
$ perl vprof.pl --username=system --password=manager 8
Press <Enter> to mark time t0: ↵
Press <Enter> to mark time t1: ↵

Resource Profile for Session 8

                  t0 = 09:08:00.823000
                  t1 = 09:08:01.103000
      interval duration =      0.280000s
  accounted-for duration =      0.280000s


Response Time Component       Duration (seconds)     Calls  Dur/Call
-----------------------       ------------------     -----  --------
CPU service                     0.27    96.4%            1  0.270000
SQL*Net message from client     0.01     3.6%            1  0.010000
unaccounted-for                 0.00     0.0%            1  0.000000
SQL*Net message to client       0.00     0.0%            1  0.000000
-----------------------       ------------------     -----  --------
Total                           0.28   100.0%
```

The chief benefit of *vprof* is how it puts CPU service, unaccounted-for time, and the actual Oracle wait events on an equal footing to create a real resource profile. The output of *vprof* gets really interesting when you experiment with the timing of the two interactive inputs. For example, if you mark the time t_0 several seconds before the session under diagnosis does anything, then *vprof* will produce a large negative unaccounted-for duration, as follows:

```
$ perl vprof.pl --username=system --password=manager 58
Press <Enter> to mark time t0: ↵
Press <Enter> to mark time t1: ↵

Resource Profile for Session 58

                       t0 = 23:48:18.072254
                       t1 = 23:49:09.992339
          interval duration =    51.920085s
     accounted-for duration =    86.990000s

Response Time Component        Duration (seconds)     Calls    Dur/Call
------------------------------  -------------------  ---------  ----------
SQL*Net message from client        54.04   104.1%          2   27.020000
CPU service                        31.98    61.6%          3   10.660000
db file sequential read             0.93     1.8%      29181    0.000032
async disk IO                       0.03     0.1%       6954    0.000004
direct path read                    0.01     0.0%       1228    0.000008
SQL*Net message to client           0.00     0.0%          2    0.000000
db file scattered read              0.00     0.0%          4    0.000000
direct path write                   0.00     0.0%          2    0.000000
unaccounted-for                    -35.07   -67.5%          1  -35.069915
------------------------------  -------------------  ---------  ----------
Total                              51.92   100.0%
```

At the time t_0, a long SQL*Net message from client event was in-process, so none of its total duration had yet been tallied to V$SESSION_EVENT. By the arrival of time t_1, the entire long SQL*Net message from client event had tallied to V$SESSION_EVENT, but part of that event duration occurred prior to the beginning of the observation interval. The *vprof* program computed the interval duration correctly as $t_1 - t_0$, but the total Oracle event time accounted for between times t_1 and t_0 exceeded the quantity $t_1 - t_0$, so *vprof* introduced a negative unaccounted-for pseudo-event to true up the profile.

This is a nice example of *collection error* that can taint your diagnostic data (see Chapter 6 for more on the topic of collection error). If you were to improve the production-worthiness of *vprof*, you could check V$SESSION_WAIT for an in-process event execution at t_0 and then correct for it based on what you found. This is the kind of thing we did in the year 2000 for our big V$ data analysis project. It was after figuring out how to correct several problems like this that we discovered all the other limitations described earlier in this chapter and decided to cut our losses on the project. For example, what if enqueue waits had shown up at the top of your resource profile? How would you go about determining which lock it was that your program under diagnosis had *waited* on (past tense) when it was running? Performing further diagnosis of such a problem without properly time- and action-scoped data is a non-deterministic process that can easily result in one of the project catastrophes described in Chapter 1.

Viewing Waits System-Wide

One of the most popular reports on system performance executed since the mid-1990s is probably the system-wide events report. Just about the simplest decent version of the report looks something like this:

```
SQL> col event format a46
SQL> col seconds format 999,999,990.00
SQL> col calls format 999,999,990
SQL> select event, time_waited/100 seconds, total_waits calls
  2  from v$system_event
  3  order by 2 desc;
```

EVENT	SECONDS	CALLS
rdbms ipc message	13,841,814.91	3,671,093
pmon timer	3,652,242.44	1,305,093
smon timer	3,526,140.14	12,182
SQL*Net message from client	20,754.41	12,627
control file parallel write	2,153.49	1,218,538
db file sequential read	91.61	547,488
log file parallel write	55.66	23,726
db file scattered read	26.26	235,882
control file sequential read	8.12	365,643
control file heartbeat	3.99	1
latch activity	2.93	30
buffer busy waits	1.41	72
resmgr:waiting in end wait	0.93	44
latch free	0.80	39
resmgr:waiting in check	0.53	36
log file sync	0.28	19
process startup	0.22	6
rdbms ipc reply	0.14	9
db file parallel read	0.11	4
async disk IO	0.10	19,116
db file parallel write	0.09	24,420
SQL*Net more data to client	0.09	2,014
resmgr:waiting in check2	0.06	2
SQL*Net message to client	0.06	12,635
direct path read	0.05	5,014
log file sequential read	0.03	4
refresh controlfile command	0.00	1
log file single write	0.00	4
SQL*Net break/reset to client	0.00	23
direct path write	0.00	10

```
30 rows selected.
```

This type of report is supposed to help the performance analyst instantly determine the nature of a "system's" performance problem. However, the report has many problems living up to that job description. Reports like this can help you solve *some types* of performance problems, but they fail to help you solve many of the problems I've illustrated throughout this book, such as:

- Problems with user actions whose performance characteristics do not resemble the system-wide average performance characteristics. You cannot extrapolate detail from an aggregate. Not realizing this can lead to accidental performance degradation for important user actions for the reasons described in Chapter 4.

- Problems with user actions whose performance problems can be diagnosed quickly by observing SQL*Net message from client durations that should be counted as user action response time. Does the SQL*Net message from client duration shown in a V$SYSTEM_EVENT report indicate a network I/O inefficiency, or that an application is issuing an excessive number of database calls? You simply can't tell from V$SYSTEM_EVENT data. Big numbers might indicate problems like these. And big numbers might indicate simply that users spend a lot of time connected but not doing anything productive.

Relying on V$SYSTEM_EVENT reports thus returns me to the topic I addressed in Chapter 3 about whether it makes sense to use different methods for different problems. Using different methods to diagnose different problem types presupposes that you can guess what the problem is before you begin your diagnosis. This is the method deficiency that causes many of the project catastrophes that I describe in Chapter 1.

The following sections illustrate some of the reasons why V$SYSTEM_EVENT reports fail to help you solve certain performance problem types.

The "idle events" problem

From looking at the system-wide events report shown previously, a naïve analyst would surely identify rdbms ipc message as far and away the top problem on the system. However, this diagnosis would probably be incorrect. As most analysts experienced with the "Oracle wait interface" know, rdbms ipc message is one of the so-called *idle wait events*. The event is in fact where Oracle DBWn, LGWR, CKPT, and RECO processes log all the time they spend not doing anything. For similar reasons, pmon timer, smon timer, and SQL*Net message from client are regarded as idle events as well.

The standard advice is that you should ignore Oracle idle events. However, there's a big problem with this advice: considering some events to be "idle" eliminates your ability to diagnose certain whole problem classes. Some of the case studies shown in Chapter 12 illustrate this point. In targeted user actions that my colleagues and I have diagnosed since the year 2000, in a significant proportion of cases SQL*Net message from client is the dominant contributor to end-user response time.

Why, then, is SQL*Net message from client considered an "idle event"? It is because in a profile with *whole-instance* action scope and *since-startup* time scope, most sessions in fact sit idle awaiting user input. The whole time you spend connected but not making Oracle database calls while you're on a coffee break is tallied to the event

SQL*Net message from client. So in a system-wide wait event report, you really *must* ignore all the idle events. More "sophisticated" applications that produce system-wide wait data reports use a table of idle events to filter "idle event" rows completely out of the report.

The denominator problem

If you study a simple V$SYSTEM_EVENT report for a while, you might start wondering how the statistics relate to total instance uptime. Just about the fanciest program I've ever seen to help answer this question is shown in Example 8-4. This SQL*Plus program is an attempt to produces a true resource profile that depicts each event's total duration as a percentage of total instance uptime.

Example 8-4. A SQL program that displays a system's wait events

```
/* $Header: /home/cvs/cvm-book1/sql/sysprof.sql,v 1.2 2003/04/24 05:19:20
Cary Millsap (cary.millsap@hotsos.com)
Copyright (c) 2002 by Hotsos Enterprises, Ltd. All rights reserved.

This program creates an approximate resource profile for a system. Note,
however, that the very concept of attributing time_waited as a proportion
of instance uptime makes no sense, because it doesn't take into account
the varying number of sessions that are active at different times in the
history of the instance.
*/

set echo off feedback on termout on linesize 75 pagesize 66
clear col break compute
undef instance_uptime cpu_consumption event_duration delta

/* compute total instance uptime */
col td format 999,999,999,990 new_value instance_uptime
select (sysdate-startup_time)*(60*60*24) td from v$instance;

/* compute total Oracle kernel CPU consumption */
col cd format 999,999,999,990 new_value cpu_consumption
select value/100 cd from v$sysstat
where name = 'CPU used by this session';

/* compute total event duration */
col ed format 999,999,999,990 new_value event_duration
select sum(time_waited)/100 ed from v$system_event;

/* compute unaccounted-for duration */
col dd format 999,999,999,990 new_value delta
select &instance_uptime - (&cpu_consumption + &event_duration) dd
from dual;

/* compute the resource profile */
col e format a30              head 'Event'
col t format 99,999,990.00    head 'Duration'
col p format 990.9            head '%'
```

Example 8-4. A SQL program that displays a system's wait events (continued)

```
col w format 999,999,999,999,990 head 'Calls'
break on report
compute sum label TOTAL of w t p on report
select
  'CPU service' e,
  &cpu_consumption t,
  (&cpu_consumption)/(&instance_uptime)*100 p,
  (select value from v$sysstat where name = 'user calls') w
from dual
union
select
  'unaccounted for' e,
  &delta t,
  (&delta)/(&instance_uptime)*100 p,
  NULL w
from dual
union
select
  e.event e,
  e.time_waited/100 t,
  (e.time_waited/100)/(&instance_uptime)*100 p,
  e.total_waits w
from v$system_event e
order by t desc
/
```

Does printing event wait time as a percentage of total instance uptime sound like a nice theory to you? Here's a report that does it:

Event	Duration	%	Calls
rdbms ipc message	13,848,861.00	369.6	3,672,850
pmon timer	3,653,991.35	97.5	1,305,718
smon timer	3,527,940.29	94.2	12,188
CPU service	89,365.37	2.4	12,807
SQL*Net message from client	23,209.05	0.6	12,655
control file parallel write	2,154.32	0.1	1,219,121
db file sequential read	91.66	0.0	547,493
log file parallel write	55.68	0.0	23,739
db file scattered read	26.66	0.0	236,079
control file sequential read	8.12	0.0	365,817
control file heartbeat	3.99	0.0	1
latch activity	2.93	0.0	30
buffer busy waits	1.41	0.0	72
resmgr:waiting in end wait	0.93	0.0	44
latch free	0.80	0.0	39
resmgr:waiting in check	0.53	0.0	36
log file sync	0.28	0.0	19
process startup	0.22	0.0	6
rdbms ipc reply	0.14	0.0	9
db file parallel read	0.11	0.0	4
async disk IO	0.10	0.0	19,116

SQL*Net more data to client	0.09	0.0	2,018
db file parallel write	0.09	0.0	24,436
SQL*Net message to client	0.06	0.0	12,663
resmgr:waiting in check2	0.06	0.0	2
direct path read	0.05	0.0	5,014
log file sequential read	0.03	0.0	4
SQL*Net break/reset to client	0.00	0.0	25
direct path write	0.00	0.0	10
log file single write	0.00	0.0	4
refresh controlfile command	0.00	0.0	1
unaccounted for	-17,398,633.00	-464.3	
	---------------	------	---------------------
TOTAL	3,747,082.32	100.0	7,472,020

Notice the percentage for the rdbms ipc message event. Weird, right? How can a single event's total duration be 369.6% of total instance uptime? This one's actually easy. It's because on the system behind this report, there are four processes logging time to rdbms ipc message, and each is logging nearly 100% of its time to the event (my test system behind this report is a mostly idle instance). Next, what's up with the −17,398,633.00 seconds of unaccounted-for time? It's a simple artifact of my program's attempt to "true up" the accounting of all the time that is attributed to an observation interval that is known to be 3,747,082.32 seconds long (our instance has been running for about 43 days).

Perhaps a great idea would be to create a report that shows consumption for each type of resource as a percentage of total capacity for that resource? It's a nice idea, but even this introduces several surprises. You've already seen that the "capacity" for a system's rdbms ipc message consumption is the uptime for the instance times the number of processes that might log time to the event. Consider some other events:

CPU service

A system's CPU service capacity is the number of CPUs times the uptime for the instance.

*SQL*Net message from client*

A system's capacity for logging "between db call" time is the sum of all the Oracle session durations that have occurred since instance startup. One might calculate this figure using operational data available from connect-level auditing.

db file scattered read

A system's disk read capacity is the number of disk drives times the uptime for the instance, right? Not so fast. The Oracle kernel includes more than just disk service time in an Oracle wait event duration. Remember from Chapter 7 that, in addition to resource service time, there's also (most significantly) queueing for the resource and time spent in the operating system's ready to run state. A system's db file scattered read capacity is thus *also* the sum of all the Oracle session durations that have occurred since instance startup.

As far as I can tell, there's no denominator by which you can divide to make a V$SYSTEM_EVENT report into a legitimate resource profile.

Infinite capacity for waiting

A big part of the problem is a principal that I can best illustrate with a brief thought experiment. Imagine that a hundred users stand in line to connect to an Oracle instance on a desktop personal computer with one very slow CPU and one very slow disk drive. When a user reaches the head of the queue, she opens a new SQL*Plus session, connects to Oracle, minimizes the session, and then leaves the room. After all 100 users had performed this task, imagine that you could see exactly how the resulting 100 Oracle sessions had consumed their time for a one-minute interval.

You would find that there had been 100 minutes of time spent by the Oracle kernel waiting on 100 different blocking read calls of a SQL*Net socket. An instance-wide resource profile for that minute would reveal that the system had consumed 100 minutes of elapsed time "executing an event." How can this be? The system has only one CPU and one disk. How could it have enough capacity for 100 users to have consumed 100 minutes of elapsed time? The answer is simple:

> Any system has an infinite capacity for waiting.

Of course, this example proves only a weak little point, because the event I've asked you to consider is widely acknowledged as an "idle event." Even a single-CPU system could wait for a million idle events at the same time and never use the CPU or disk at all.

The stunning thing is that the example works equally well if we modify it to integrate quite an obviously non-idle event into the starring role. Imagine that through some trick of coordination, all 100 users were able to simultaneously request different database blocks from the single very slow disk drive on this desktop PC. Let's say for the sake of simplicity that this very slow disk was able to fulfill the read requests at a rate of one block per second.

At first, all 100 sessions would be waiting for a single-block db file sequential read event. After one second, the first session to have its read request fulfilled would switch to waiting for SQL*Net message from client, and the other 99 would continue to wait for db file sequential read. After two seconds, there would be two sessions waiting on socket reads, and 98 sessions waiting on file reads. Finally, after 100 seconds, all 100 sessions would again be waiting on SQL*Net socket reads.

After 100 seconds, there would be $1 + 2 + 3 + ... + 100$ seconds' worth of waiting on file reads, for a grand total of 5,050 seconds of waiting. And there would be $99 + 98 + 97 + ... + 0$ seconds' worth of waiting on socket reads, for a grand total of 4,950 seconds of waiting. A system-wide resource profile for the 100-seconds interval during fulfillment of the 100 file reads would look like this:

```
Event                          Duration       %            Calls
-----------------------------  -------------- --------  --------------------
db file sequential read         5,050.00  5,050.0               100
SQL*Net message from client     4,950.00  4,950.0                99
unaccounted for                -9,900.00 -9,900.0
                               -------------- --------  --------------------
TOTAL                             100.00    100.0               200
```

Now, it appears that our single-CPU system with one very slow disk has provided 5,050 seconds' worth of disk service to its users in a 100 second interval. How can this be possible? It is because there were only 100 seconds' worth of disk *service* provided to end users' sessions. The remainder of the "wait time" (which is actually a *response time* in queueing theory terms, as you'll see in Chapter 11) is actually *queueing delay*—time spent waiting for the busy disk device. Again, you see, any system has an infinite capacity for waiting.

Idle events in background sessions

User sessions (sessions for which V$SESSION.TYPE = 'USER') tend to tally time to SQL*Net message from client when their human end-users are idle. On Oracle systems with a lot of user logons executed over the life of an instance, this time commonly sorts to the top of any query on V$SYSTEM_EVENT that sorts by descending TIME_WAITED order.

However, the Oracle background processes (sessions for which V$SESSION.TYPE = 'BACKGROUND') stay connected for an instance's entire lifespan, and background processes do very little when they're not required to. Consequently, background processes contribute heavily to the body of "idle events." The following query shows why:

```
SQL> col program format a23
SQL> col event format a18
SQL> col seconds format 99,999,990
SQL> col state format a17
SQL> select s.program, w.event, w.seconds_in_wait seconds, w.state
  2  from v$session s, v$session_wait w
  3  where s.sid = w.sid and s.type = 'BACKGROUND'
  4  order by s.sid;

PROGRAM                  EVENT                SECONDS STATE
------------------------ ------------------ --------- -----------------
oracle@research (PMON)   pmon timer         1,529,843 WAITING
oracle@research (DBW0)   rdbms ipc message        249 WAITING
oracle@research (LGWR)   rdbms ipc message        246 WAITING
oracle@research (CKPT)   rdbms ipc message          0 WAITING
oracle@research (SMON)   smon timer             1,790 WAITING
oracle@research (RECO)   rdbms ipc message    208,071 WAITING

6 rows selected.
```

You can see in this report that the PMON session has been "waiting" on an event called pmon timer for roughly 17.7 days (we don't do much work on our research instance). The DBW0, LGWR, CKPT, and RECO sessions are waiting on an event called rdbms ipc message. And SMON has its own timer event called smon timer. It is completely fair to call these events "idle," because the sessions that log time to them are literally sitting idle, awaiting demand to arrive upon some communication device.

However, ignoring idle events is a poor workaround to the fundamental problem of botching either the time scope or the action scope of the data collection process. Unless you are concerned that the performance of a background session requires improvement, you should never encounter `pmon timer`, `rdbms ipc message`, or `smon timer` events in an analysis. If you actually *are* working on improving the performance of a background session, and your well-scoped diagnostic data contain large contributions of one of these events, then the right question for you to answer is:

> Why is this session sitting idle when I expect it to be doing its work more quickly than it is right now?

If a so-called idle event is consuming end-user response time, then it *is* something to worry about.

Targeting revisited

Why have I waited until this late in the book to tell you about the horrible complications caused by these "idle events"? Actually, I haven't. I described Oracle idle events in Chapter 5. However, I called them "events that occur between database calls," and I never once described them in a manner that makes them seem like a problem. The between-call events aren't a problem at all if you are using *properly scoped* diagnostic data. Without proper scoping, you lose data. With proper scoping, a between-call event has every bit as much diagnostic value as any other event.

> Proper scoping during the data collection phase of a performance improvement project makes *all* Oracle wait events relevant. With properly scoped data, there is no such thing as an "idle event" that can be ignored.

Targeting is the key to economically efficient performance improvement.

The Oracle "Wait Interface"

In conferences held around the turn of this century, it was apparent that the popular fashion in Oracle "tuning" had taken a dramatic turn. In the year 2001, Oracle conference papers about the new "wait interface" equaled or outnumbered papers about the traditional utilization-based approaches. What is the "wait interface?"

Many performance analysts define the wait interface narrowly as the set of four new fixed views introduced to the public in Oracle 7.0.12:

```
V$SYSTEM_EVENT
V$SESSION_EVENT
V$SESSION_WAIT
V$EVENT_NAME
```

These fixed views indeed provide significantly important performance information, but they do not *replace* other information in the database, nor do they constitute a complete new interface to performance measurement. These fixed views merely provide more information to the performance analyst, helping us improve our response time model from the unreliable $e = c + \Delta$ model that we had to use in the 1980s, to the complete response time accounting model that we can use today:

$$e = c + \sum_{\text{db call}} ela + \Delta$$

The new fixed views do not contain *any* information about CPU capacity consumption or an Oracle kernel program's motives for such consumption (LIO calls, sorts, hashes, and so on). But of course that's okay, because this information already exists in V$SESSTAT and V$SYSSTAT. The new fixed views are designed to be used in union with the existing ones.

Defining the wait interface narrowly as the collection of four new V$ tables leads to unfairly restrictive propositions like this one:

> You can't find some kinds of performance problems with the Oracle wait interface: CPU consumers like LIO hogs, sessions that wait for CPU, and sessions that wait for paging or swapping.

Of course you can no more find LIO hogs in V$SESSION_EVENT than you can find the names of your online redo log files in V$PROCESS. But, as you have seen, you *can* find CPU consumers like LIO hogs by using Oracle's fixed views or extended SQL trace data. You can even find sessions that wait for CPU, and sessions that wait for paging and swapping by understanding Oracle's extended SQL trace data.

When you use the term "wait interface," just make sure that you and the person you're talking to both know what you mean. When I use the term, I'm typically thinking about *all* of the Oracle operational timing data that I describe in Chapter 7. However, if the person you're talking to has a narrower definition, then you might have to do a little extra work to explain that what you mean is really a union of "working" and "waiting" data that can be obtained, for example, either from views like V$SESSTAT and V$SESSION_EVENT, or from extended SQL trace data.

Exercises

1. If the thought experiment in the section "Infinite capacity for waiting" had specified that each of the 100 users had simultaneously requested one second of CPU capacity, what would the resource profile look like for the 100-second interval?

2. Using V$SQL consumes less server capacity than using V$SQLAREA. Use extended SQL trace data to explain why.

3. Experiment with *vprof*. Try the following time scope experiments:

   - Mark t_0 and then wait several seconds before executing the first database call in the targeted session.
   - Mark t_0 immediately preceding the first database call in the targeted session.

- Mark t_0 in the midst of a long-running SQL statement's execution in the targeted session.
- Mark t_1 immediately after the conclusion of the final database call in the targeted session.
- Mark t_1 several seconds after the conclusion of the final database call in the targeted session.
- Mark t_1 in the midst of a long-running SQL statement's execution in the targeted session.

4. Describe the challenges that prevent us from constructing a utilization report that shows utilization by Oracle kernel wait event. For example, imagine a system with the following three indications:

- There have been 1,000,000 seconds of waiting for disk I/O events since instance startup.
- The instance startup occurred 500,000 seconds ago.
- The system has six disks, so how much can we know about per-disk utilization since instance startup?

What conclusions can you draw from these observations?

CHAPTER 9
Queueing Theory for the Oracle Practitioner

Professionals can argue forever about how best to improve system performance unless there's a way to prove who's right. One way to validate performance improvement conjectures is by trial and error. The problem with trial-and-error performance optimization is that, on average, it's hugely expensive. It costs so much money and time to try each scenario that, frequently, the number of scenarios that a company can afford to test is very small. Often, a company runs out of time or money before finding a satisfactory solution.

Trial and error has hope of being efficient only if some kind of intelligence guides the process of choosing which trial to try next. Such choices are usually based upon some combination of experience, intuition, and luck. However, experience, intuition, and luck are what drive those endless debates:

> *Analyst*: We upgraded to faster CPUs at my former client, and everything became 50% faster overnight. We should upgrade CPUs here immediately, and just cut out the performance problem at its knees.

> *Other analyst*: Well, I think that's a waste of time and money. The last seven projects that I've seen upgrade to faster CPUs regretted the investment, because the upgrade didn't produce any real impact. One of my recent clients upgraded to faster CPUs, and parts of the application actually got *slower*.

So, who's right? It is certainly possible that each of the phenomena described here did in fact happen the way the teller is telling it. But which one of these experiences might best describe *your* near future? I'll answer in the form of a more blatantly comical hypothetical dialogue amidst two well-meaning but incompetent analysts who are trying to figure out whether a particular glass is large enough to hold a quantity of water that is stored in a pitcher:

> *Analyst*: We poured water from a pitcher into a glass at my former client, and I can assure you that the glass quite comfortably held the entire content of the pitcher. I say we should dump the water into the glass.

> *Other analyst*: Well, I think it's a disaster waiting to happen. The last seven times I've watched people try to empty pitchers into glasses, the glasses weren't big enough to hold all the water. One of my recent clients poured water from a pitcher into a glass, and the results were horrific. Water went everywhere.

The solution to this argument is clear: stop guessing. Measure how much water is in the pitcher. Measure the capacity of the glass. If the quantity in the pitcher exceeds the capacity of the glass, then don't pour. Otherwise, pour away.

As long as you can measure the quantity of water in the pitcher and the capacity of the glass, you don't have to try the experiment to be reasonably certain of how it would turn out. It's an extremely simple example of a mathematical *model*. The benefit of the model is an ability to predict the future without having to actually try it first. Of course, we could complicate the model by integrating factors such as the likelihood of spills depending upon the shape of the pitcher's mouth, the steadiness of the pourer, and so on. The smartest solution is to choose the simplest model that produces results that meet our accuracy requirements.

 Maybe the analogy would have been more accurate if I had used moon rocks instead of water. Like application workload, moon rocks have irregular shapes that are difficult to model, and they are incredibly expensive to obtain for testing.

Performance Models

Computer performance models are more complicated than the water problem model, but not so complicated as to be inaccessible. The difficult part of performance modeling is that constructing the model requires some mathematical sophistication. But the hardest work has already been done for you. Over the course of nearly a century, scientists have developed a branch of mathematics called *queueing theory* to model the performance of systems like yours. This chapter describes how to use one particular queueing theory model that reliably answers questions like these:

- How much faster will the application function f perform for n users if I add k CPUs to my system? What if I replace my existing CPUs with units that are p percent faster?

- How much slower will application function f become if I add n users of f into my system's current workload?

- How many CPUs will my system need if we require that p percent of executions of f must complete in r seconds or less?

- How much faster will f perform for n users if we can eliminate p percent of the code path for f?

- Which is better suited to my needs, a system with m really fast CPUs? Or a system with $m + n$ slower CPUs?

This book contains no derivations of queueing theory formulas. A number of excellent resources are available to help you if you would like to study *why* queueing theory works. My aim in this chapter is to explain *how* to use queueing theory as a tool in real-world Oracle performance improvement projects. To this end, this textbook includes a field-tested queueing theory model implemented in Microsoft Excel. This chapter describes the model and how to use it.

 If you are interested in the study of queueing theory, there are several excellent references available. My favorites include [Gross and Harris (1998); Gunther (1998); Jain (1991); Allen (1994); and Kleinrock (1975)].

Queueing

Computer applications are all about requesters that demand things and providers that supply them. Oracle performance analysis is all about the relationships between the suppliers and demanders, especially when competition for shared resources gets intense.

Queueing is what happens when a requester demands service from a resource that happens to be busy serving another request. Most of us queue every day for busy resources. It's simple: you wait until it's finally your turn. Different cultures engage different queue disciplines. Many cultures engage the egalitarian discipline of granting service in the same order as the arrivals occurred, which is called a *first-come, first-served* discipline. Other cultures engage a priority discipline in which, for example, the status of the request affects the order of service. Examples of other queue disciplines include: insiders-first, royalty-first, sharpest-elbows-first, and meekest-last.

"Queueing" Versus "Queuing"

All queueing theorists who write about queueing must decide about whether to spell the word with two occurrences of the letter "e" or just one. My word processor's spell-check tool originally informed me (as did many dictionaries) that "queueing" is supposed to be spelled without the extra "e", as queuing. However, the accepted standard in the field of queueing theory (see *http://www2.uwindsor.ca/~hlynka/qfaq.html* for details) is to spell the word as "queueing." Happily, this spelling is a prescribed alternate in both the *Oxford English Dictionary* and the *Oxford American Dictionary*.

After you've "waited your turn," then you receive the service you asked for, which of course takes a bit more time. Then you get out of the way, and the person that was behind you in the queue gets service for his request. People queue for things like dinner tables, tellers, ticket agents, elevators, freeways, and software support hotlines. Computer programs queue for resources like CPU, memory, disk I/O, network I/O, locks, and latches.

Queueing Economics

Queueing of course gives you the distinct feeling that you're wasting your time. One way to reduce your queuing time is for your service provider to upgrade the quality or number of the resources that you're using. With faster resources or more resources, or both, your time in the queue would decrease. But, of course, the people providing your service would typically pass the cost of those improved resources on to you through higher prices for their service. In the end, it's *your* decision where to set the economic tradeoff between faster service and cheaper service.

We optimize to economic and response time constraints every day of our lives. For example, many of us pay thousands of dollars to own an automobile. Although bicycles are much cheaper to own and operate than automobiles, we buy cars in part because they are so much faster, thus providing significantly better response times for our travels. (We Americans are of course famously prone to using automobiles even in circumstances in which using a bicycle would be not only cheaper, but actually faster.)

Once we own a car, we find that further optimizations are necessary. For routine errands, a car that goes 200 mph (about 325 km/h) is no more time-efficient than a car with a 60-mph top speed (about 100-km/h), because traffic laws and safety concerns constrain your velocity more than your car's performance limitations do. Consequently, even people with fast cars plan their errands so they won't have to compete with rush-hour traffic. Some of our optimization tactics reduce service time. Some of our optimization tactics reduce queueing delay. The best win-win for you and your users occurs when you can convert a minimal investment into a reduction in service time, queueing delay, or both.

Queueing Visualized

In Chapter 1 I explained that a *sequence diagram* is a convenient way to denote how a user action consumes time as it visits different layers in a technology stack. Figure 9-1 shows a sequence diagram for a system with one CPU and one disk. A user making a request of the system motivates the consumption of CPU and disk capacity, arranged in time as shown in the drawing. In a sequence diagram, each line represents the capacity of a resource through time. Each shaded block on a resource's timeline represents a request's use of that resource. The length of each shaded block is proportional to the amount of time consumed at the resource. Portions of a timeline that do not contain a shaded block represent idle time. Read a sequence diagram from top to bottom. A left-to-right arrow represents demand for service, and a right-to-left arrow represents supply. Response time is the duration that elapses from the initiation of a request until fulfillment of the request.

In Figure 9-1, an application user makes a request for service of a CPU. In this drawing, the CPU is unoccupied at the time it receives the request, so CPU service begins

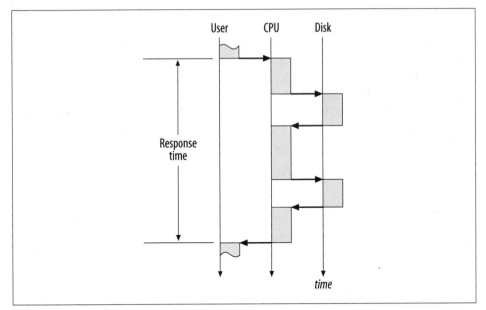

Figure 9-1. A sequence diagram is a convenient way to denote how an operation consumes time

immediately upon receipt. As the request consumes CPU time, the system computes that a disk request must be fulfilled in order to continue. The CPU issues a service demand of the disk. The disk is unoccupied at the time it receives the request, and so the disk service begins immediately upon receipt. Upon completion of the disk service request, the disk returns the desired result back to the CPU, which continues as before. After the third CPU request, the original user demand has been satisfied, and the CPU supplies the result back to the user.

The response time from the user's perspective is the time that elapses from the user's request until fulfillment of that request. Note that Figure 9-1 depicts several other response times as well. For example, the length of the first (i.e., topmost) shaded bar on the *Disk* timeline is the response time, from the CPU's perspective, of the first disk I/O call.

The sequence diagram is an especially useful tool for understanding the impact of competition for shared resources on a multitasking system. For example, Figure 9-2 shows why response time can degrade if we add workload onto the system shown in Figure 9-1. Requests for CPU service are fulfilled without delay on the system in its unloaded state (case *a*).

When we add load to the system (case *b*), some of our requests for CPU service must wait because the CPU is busy servicing other workload at the time of the request. Figure 9-2 shows two such queueing delays. The second request for CPU service after control returns from the disk must wait because the CPU is already occupied with the lighter-shaded workload element. And the third request for CPU service

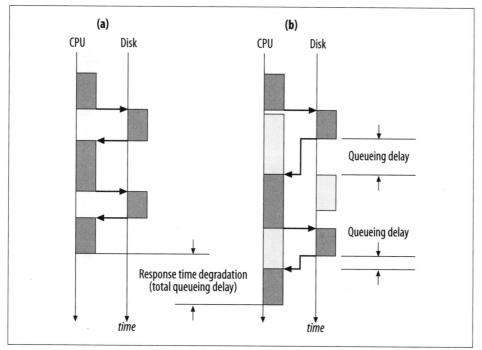

Figure 9-2. Executing only one application function on an unloaded system leaves idle CPU capacity (case a). The presence of other workload (case b) results in fewer wasted CPU cycles, but at the expense of degraded response time for our original application function

waits again for the same reason. The amount of total response time degradation from the system in its unloaded state (case *a*) to the system in its loaded state (case *b*) is precisely the total duration that our service requests have spent queued for a busy resource.

How much response time degradation can we expect to incur as we add load to a system? The tool that is designed to answer this important question and many others is called *queueing theory*.

Queueing Theory

Queueing theory is a branch of mathematics dedicated to explaining the behavior of queueing systems. The sequence diagram demonstrates a fundamental relationship of queueing theory:

$$R = S + W$$

Response time equals service time plus queueing delay. *Service time* is the amount of time spent actually consuming a requested resource, and *queueing delay* is the duration that a request spends waiting in a queue.

Figure 9-3 shows the $R = S + W$ relationship in a graph. Response time on the vertical axis responds to changes in system utilization on the horizontal axis. As you have already seen in the sequence diagram example, service time remains constant for all system load levels. However, queueing delay degrades (that is, increases) exponentially in response to increases in workload. Adding the variant queueing delay to the constant service time for each possible system utilization value produces the famous response time curve that is shaped like an ice hockey stick (Figure 9-4).

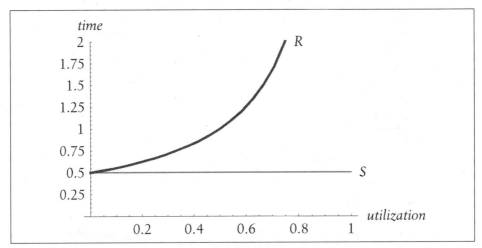

Figure 9-3. The fundamental relationship of queueing theory: $R = S + W$. Service time (S) remains constant at all load levels; however, response time (R) degrades under high loads because queueing delay (the distance from S to R) degrades exponentially as utilization increases

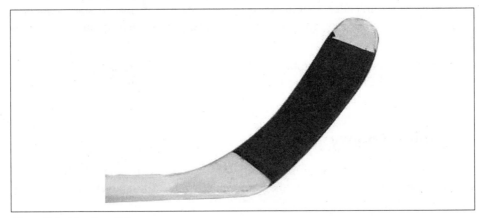

Figure 9-4. A hockey stick

Model Input and Output Values

Queueing theory provides enormous value to the performance analyst by allowing us to predict system response times in hypothetical situations. Sensibly applied queueing models can reveal future performance problems very nicely, without incurring the cost of actually trying different system configurations. For example, if a CPU upgrade is destined not to improve your performance, it's a lot cheaper to figure it out in Excel than to learn by actually implementing and testing a hardware upgrade.

But perhaps even more important is how queueing theory structures our thinking about response time. It highlights the very important distinction between time spent working and time spent waiting. The competent use of queueing theory forces us to understand the interrelationships and sensitivities of various performance optimization parameters. It forces us to see more clearly what is relevant and what is not.

You have already seen the fundamental result of queueing theory: response time equals service time plus queueing delay, or $R = S + W$. You have seen that when response time degrades as loads increase, the degradation is due to changes in W, not changes in S. The following sections explain the meanings of the formulas that will enable you to predict the performance characteristics of a specified system configuration, whether that configuration exists yet or not. (The entire list of queueing theory formulas used in this book is printed in Appendix D.) I'll begin by explaining the input parameters that drive these formulas.

Arrivals and completions

Most of the things you need to know about queueing theory are very simple to understand. You can think of a queueing system as a black box that takes input, processes it, and produces output that presumably represents some improvement upon the input. The number of arrivals that come into the system is denoted as A. The number of completed requests that exit the system is denoted as C. For any stable queueing system, $A = C$. That is, in a stable system, everything that goes into the box comes out, and nothing comes out of the box that didn't go in. If we consider a specific time period called T, then the ratio $\lambda = A/T$ (λ is the Greek letter lambda) yields the system's *arrival rate*, and $X = C/T$ yields the system's *completion rate* (or *throughput*). The *mean interarrival time* $\tau = T/A = 1/\lambda$ (τ is the Greek letter tau) is the average duration between adjacent arrivals into a system. Figure 9-5 shows the relationships among A, T, λ, and τ.

Service channels, utilization, and stability

Inside a queueing system—the "black box" that I mentioned before—there can be one or more *service channels*. Each service channel operates independently of other service channels to provide service in response to requests arriving at a given queue. For example, a symmetric multiprocessing (SMP) computer system with 8 CPUs servicing a single CPU run queue can be modeled as a single system with eight parallel

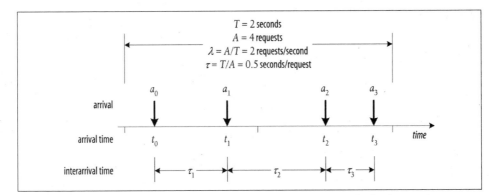

Figure 9-5. This two-second interval illustrates the relationships among the fundamental parameters A, T, λ, and τ, which describe a queueing system's arrivals

service channels. The number of parallel service channels inside the system is denoted as m, c, and s in various texts. In this text, I have chosen to use m as in [Kleinrock (1975)].

The Motive for the Greek Letters

One aspect of queueing theory that makes the field inaccessible to a lot of Oracle performance analysts is that the formulas look really difficult. It doesn't help that a lot of the basic concepts are expressed in Greek letters. Many colleagues asked me during the preparation of this text to consider converting each Greek letter used in this chapter to something chosen from the Latin alphabet. (If I'm not mistaken, the event at which they pleaded with me to do this is called an "intervention.")

I've chosen to remain faithful to the notation used in the well-established literature of queueing theory. I believe that creating a "new" notation for this text would be pretentious of me, and in the long term it wouldn't help you either. Assuming that I would have converted all the Greek symbols to something "more comfortable" without introducing new errors in the notation, I would have left you with a notation that wouldn't match anything else you'd ever study. The formulas would still be ugly, even "in English"—trust me. If I had converted Greek letters to Latin letters, I would have only penalized readers who actually wanted to study queueing theory by making them learn the technology in two different languages.

The Greek letter problem really isn't that bad anyway. In this chapter, you'll encounter only the Greek letters λ (lambda), μ (mu), ρ (rho), τ (tau), θ (theta), and Σ (which is the letter sigma, but which should be read as "sum of"). Other chapters of course include the letter Δ (delta) and maybe others. A complete list of Greek symbols and their English names is included in Appendix B.

The total amount of time that service channels inside the system spent actually fulfilling service requests is denoted as B, for busy time. *Total system utilization* for a given time interval is the proportion of the interval that the system was busy, $U = B/T$. If you have more than one service channel inside your system (if $m > 1$), then U can be greater than 1.0. Most people find this statistic disturbing until they normalize it to produce a per-channel average utilization. The *mean utilization per channel* is then $\rho = U/m$ (ρ is the Greek letter rho). The quantity ρ is also called a system's *traffic intensity*. Notice that having a mean utilization per channel of ρ does *not* mean that every channel has a mean utilization of ρ. For example, an eight-channel system can achieve $\rho = 0.5$ in any way between the extremes of four channels running at 100% and four others at 0%, to all eight channels running at exactly 50%.

A queueing system is said to be *stable* if and only if its per-server utilization is in the range $0 \le \rho < 1$. As you use queueing models, you will find it possible to model hypothetical systems for which $\rho \ge 1$. For example, as you drive arrival rates higher and higher, you can make it so that the system can't keep up unless it could operate at a utilization in the domain $\rho \ge 1$. However, it is impossible to drive a system at $\rho \ge 1$ in reality.

Service time and service rate

We have already discussed the service time for a system. More formally, a system's *expected service time* is the average amount of time that a service channel spends busy per completion, or $S = B/C$. Computing service time is usually easy, because on most systems it is easy to measure busy time and completion counts. Sometimes it is more convenient to discuss the service *rate* instead of service *time*. The *service rate* is the number of requests that a single service channel can complete per time unit, $\mu = C/B$ (μ is the Greek letter mu), or equivalently, $\mu = 1/S$.

Queueing delay and response time

As you have seen, a system's *expected queueing delay* (W) is simply the amount of time that you should expect to elapse between a request's arrival into the system and the time at which service begins. For your request, queueing delay is thus the sum of the expected service times of the requests that arrived at the queue ahead of you. Predicting queueing delay is one of the wondrous rewards of queueing theory. Queueing delay depends not only upon the average service time at the device in which you're interested, it also depends upon the number of people that are expected to be waiting when you get there.

The formula for predicting queueing delay is difficult to understand without a good bit of study, but fortunately the hard work of constructing the formula has been done for us. For an M/M/*m* queueing system (the exact definition of which appears later in this chapter), the answer is:

$$W = \frac{C(m, \rho)}{m\mu(1-\rho)},$$

where:

$$C(m, \rho) = P(\geq m \text{ jobs}) = \frac{\dfrac{(m\rho)^m}{m!}}{(1-\rho)\displaystyle\sum_{k=0}^{m-1}\frac{(m\rho)^k}{k!} + \frac{(m\rho)^m}{m!}}$$

The hardest part was the formula for C(*m*, ρ), which was completed in 1917 by a Danish mathematician named Agner Erlang [Erlang (1917)]. The *Erlang C formula* produces the probability that an arriving request will queue for service.

 Don't confuse the *C* used to denote the Erlang C formula with the *C* that denotes the number of completions in a system. It is usually easy to tell the two C's apart by context, because the Erlang C formula is always depicted as a function with two arguments.

Programming Erlang C requires a bit more mathematical sophistication than most of us bring to the game. However, in 1974, a research scientist named David Jagerman developed a fast algorithm for computing Erlang C [Jagerman (1974)] that makes it easy to calculate a system's expected queueing delay. I have used Jagerman's algorithm in Example 9-1.

Example 9-1. This Visual Basic code uses Jagerman's algorithm to compute Erlang C

```
Function ErlangC(m, Rho) As Double
' Erlang's C formula, adapted from [Gunther (1998), 65]
    Dim i As Integer
    Dim traffic, ErlangB, eb As Double
    ' Jagerman's algorithm
    traffic = Rho * m
    ErlangB = traffic / (1 + traffic)
    For i = 2 To m
        eb = ErlangB
        ErlangB = eb * traffic / (i + eb * traffic)
    Next i
    ErlangC = ErlangB / (1 - Rho + Rho * ErlangB)
End Function
```

Once you know a system's expected service time and its expected queueing delay, computing the expected response time is trivial, as we have already explored. A system's *expected response time* is simply its expected service time plus its expected queueing delay, $R = S + W$.

Figure 9-6 depicts an *m*-channel queueing system. Requests arrive at an average rate of λ requests per time unit. The duration between successive request arrivals is the interarrival time τ. Each of *m* parallel channels completes service requests at an average service rate of μ requests per time unit, consuming an average service time of *s* time units per request.

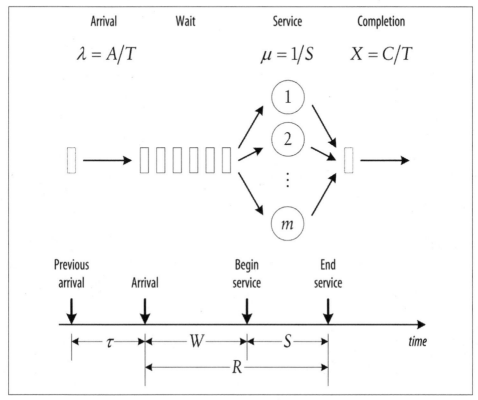

Figure 9-6. *This drawing of a multi-channel queueing system illustrates the fundamental relationships among several queueing theory parameters (adapted from [Jain (1991) 511])*

Maximum effective throughput

The *maximum effective throughput* of a system is the largest arrival rate that we can ask that system to process without exceeding a user's response time tolerance r_{max}. The maximum effective throughput for the system shown in Figure 9-7 is the quantity λ_{max}. As the rate of arrivals into the system increases, the average queueing delay increases, and system response time degrades. The throughput value at which the system's response time degrades beyond the users' threshold for response time degradation is the system's maximum effective throughput, λ_{max}. It's the most work you can ask of a system without driving average response times too high.

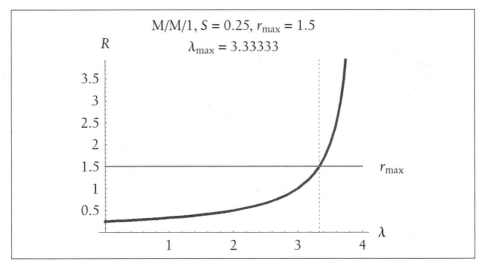

Figure 9-7. Response time is a function of arrival rate. Specifying an average response time tolerance r_{max} determines the location of λ_{max}, which is the largest completion rate value that this system can sustain without driving the average response time above the users' tolerance

To maintain satisfactory response times, you have to keep your system's arrival rate less than λ_{max}, so of course it is important that you know how to compute its value. There is no closed form solution for computing the value of λ_{max}, but estimating the value using interval bisection is fast and straightforward. Example 9-2 provides Visual Basic code to perform the computation.

Example 9-2 refers to objects such as the variable q and the function *ResponseTime* that are defined in the Microsoft Excel workbook provided on the catalog page for this book: *http://www.oreilly.com/ catalog/optoraclep.*

Example 9-2. This Visual Basic code uses interval bisection to compute maximum effective throughput

```
Function LambdaMax(Rmax, q, m, mu) As Double
' Maximum effective throughput of queueing system
' ASSUMPTION: ResponseTime() is a monotonically increasing continuous
' function
    Const error = 0.005      ' interval bisection halts when
                             ' abs(lambda1-lamba0) <= error*lambda0
    Dim lambda0 As Double    ' lambda value for which R < Rmax
    Dim lambda1 As Double    ' lambda value for which R >= Rmax
    Dim lambdaM As Double    ' arithmetic mean of {lambda0, lambda1}
    ' Seek an interval [lambda0, lambda1] for which R(lambda0)<Rmax and
    ' R(lambda1)>=Rmax
    lambda0 = 0
    lambda1 = 1
    While ResponseTime(m, mu, Rho(lambda1 / q, m, mu)) < Rmax
```

Example 9-2. This Visual Basic code uses interval bisection to compute maximum effective throughput (continued)

```
        lambda0 = lambda1
        lambda1 = 2 * lambda1
    Wend
    ' Narrow the interval by iterative bisection
    While Abs(lambda1 - lambda0) > error * lambda0
        lambdaM = (lambda0 + lambda1) / 2
        If ResponseTime(m, mu, Rho(lambdaM / q, m, mu)) < Rmax Then
            lambda0 = lambdaM
        Else
            lambda1 = lambdaM
        End If
    Wend
    LambdaMax = (lambda0 + lambda1) / 2
End Function
```

Cumulative distribution function (CDF) of response time

There is a problem with using maximum effective throughput as a performance measure, however. The problem is that users don't usually have a tolerance in mind for *average* response time; what they really have in mind is a tolerance for *worst-case* response time. The word "tolerance" connotes attention to some maximum value more often than it connotes attention to an average. For example, imagine the following dialog:

> *User*: My order entry form is too slow. We agreed that my response time tolerance for the commit at the end of the form would be 1.5 seconds, but my response time is less than 1.5 seconds in only about 63.2% of cases.[*]
>
> *System manager*: Actually, that's exactly what we agreed. We agreed only that your *average* response time for your order entry form would not exceed 1.5 seconds, and you have just admitted that we are meeting that goal.

The information provider has abided by the letter of the service level agreement, but the system is not meeting the spirit of the user's wishes. The response time goal that the users really *wish* they had specified is probably something like this:

> The commit at the end of the order entry form must complete in 1.5 seconds or less, for at least 95 out of every 100 user executions.

Or, to generalize:

> Function *f* must complete in *r* seconds or less in at least *p* percent of executions of the function.

Functionally, a statement of this form is a very useful basis for a contract between an information consumer and the information provider. The statement reminds the

---

[*] I selected the number 63.2% carefully for this example. It happens to be the CDF of the exponential distribution at its mean. By constructing my example dialog this way, the user is observing the behavior of a system whose mean response time is roughly 1.5 seconds.

provider that users are intolerant of response times for the function that are in excess of a specific value. The statement reminds the consumer that it is impossible to guarantee that *no* user will *ever* be dissatisfied with the performance of a given function, but that the provider has committed to limit the disappointment to some negotiated percentage of executions.

As you might expect, queueing theory gives us the mathematical means to compute the things we need in order to make service level agreements in this useful format. One final queueing theory formula gives the means to compute the minimum level of investment into system resources that is required to satisfy the system's performance requirements within its owner's economic constraints. The *cumulative distribution function* (CDF) *of response time* allows us to compute the probability $P(R \leq r)$, which is the likelihood that a given request will be fulfilled with total response time less than or equal to some response time tolerance r. This quantity is perhaps the most useful statistic emitted from a queueing model, because it is a direct measure of user satisfaction with response time.

The formula for the CDF of response time is complicated. For the particular queueing model (called M/M/*m*) that I shall describe later in this chapter, the formula is the following [Gross and Harris (1998) 72–73]:

$$P(R \leq r) = F(r) = \frac{m(1-\rho) - W_q(0)}{m(1-\rho) - 1}\left(1 - e^{-\mu r}\right) - \frac{1 - W_q(0)}{m(1-\rho) - 1}\left(1 - e^{-(m\mu - \lambda)r}\right),$$

where $W_q(0)$ is:

$$W_q(0) = 1 - \frac{(m\rho)^m p_0}{m!(1-\rho)},$$

and p_0 is:

$$p_0 = \left(\sum_{n=0}^{m-1} \frac{(m\rho)^n}{n!} + \frac{(m\rho)^m}{m!(1-\rho)}\right)^{-1}, \quad \rho < 1$$

Example 9-3 shows how you can accomplish all this in plain old Visual Basic.

Example 9-3. This Visual Basic code computes the cumulative distribution (CDF) of response time of an M/M/m queueing system

```
Function p0(m, Rho) As Double
' Compute P(zero jobs in system) [Jain (1991), 528]
    Dim i, n As Integer
    Dim t, term2, term3 As Double
    term2 = 1 / (1 - Rho)
    For i = 1 To m
        term2 = term2 * (m * Rho) / i
    Next i
    term3 = 0
```

Example 9-3. This Visual Basic code computes the cumulative distribution (CDF) of response time of an M/M/m queueing system (continued)

```
    For n = 1 To m - 1
        t = 1
        For i = 1 To n
            t = t * (m * Rho) / i
        Next i
        term3 = term3 + t
    Next n
    p0 = (1 + term2 + term3) ^ (-1)
End Function

Function Wq0(m, Rho) As Double
' Compute Wq(0) [Gross & Harris (1998) 72]
' Note that r = m*rho, c = m in G&H's notation
    Dim i As Integer
    Dim f As Double        ' (r^c)/(c!) factor
    f = 1
    For i = 1 To m
        f = f * (m * Rho) / i
    Next i
    Wq0 = 1 - f * p0(m, Rho) / (1 - Rho)
End Function

Function CDFr(r, m, mu, Rho) As Double
' CDF of the response time. This wrapper function is necessary because
' the formula in [Gross & Harris (1998), 73] contains a singularity.
    Const epsilon As Double = 0.000000001
    If (Abs(m * (1 - Rho) - 1) < epsilon) Then
        CDFr = (CDFr2(r, m, mu, Rho - epsilon) + CDFr2(r, m, mu, Rho + epsilon)) / 2
    Else
        CDFr = CDFr2(r, m, mu, Rho)
    End If
End Function

Function CDFr2(r, m, mu, Rho) As Double
' CDF of the response time, adapted from [Gross & Harris (1998), 73]
' Note that r = m*rho, c=m, lambda=rho*m*mu, t=r in G&H's notation
    Dim w As Double            ' Wq(0) value
    Dim cdf1, cdf2 As Double    ' complicated terms of CDF formula
    If (Rho >= 1 Or r <= 0) Then
        CDFr2 = 0
        Exit Function
    End If
    w = Wq0(m, Rho)
    cdf1 = (m * (1 - Rho) - w) / (m * (1 - Rho) - 1) * (1 - Exp(-mu * r))
    cdf2 = (1 - w) / (m * (1 - Rho) - 1) * (1 - Exp(-(m * mu - Rho * m * mu) * r))
    CDFr2 = cdf1 - cdf2
End Function
```

How I Figured Out That Jain's CDF Formula Is Incorrect

The Jain formula for the CDF of response time [Jain (1991), 528, 531] has bothered me for a long time. The formula contains the expression:

$$1 - e^{-\mu r} - \frac{C(m, \rho)}{1 - m + m\rho} e^{-m\mu(1-\rho)r} - e^{-\mu r}$$

Without even understanding what this formula means, the presence of the two identical terms $-e^{-\mu r}$ is the thing that has worried me. Why would the author or his copyeditor not catch the two identical terms and combine them into the single term $-2e^{-\mu r}$? The most likely explanation, I figured, was that the formula suffered from a typographical error of some sort.

So I created a test. I began by choosing an arbitrary integer value for m. Using *Mathematica*, I generated a random service time s_1 from an exponential distribution with some arbitrarily chosen mean $1/\mu$. Next, I generated a random interarrival time t_1 from an exponential distribution with an arbitrarily chosen mean $1/\lambda$. Using the $R = S + W$ formula described earlier, I computed the expected response time of the system whose service time and interarrival time were the two random numbers I generated. Using the input values $m, \mu = 1/s_1$, and $\lambda = 1/t_1$, the calculation of R was easy.

I repeated this test several millions of times (for several millions of random service time s_i values chosen from the exponential distribution with mean $1/\mu$, and the same number of random interarrival rate t_i values chosen from the exponential distribution with mean $1/\lambda$). I stored the results. Then, for some arbitrarily chosen response time value r, I simply counted the number of response times generated by my test that were less than r. The proportion of response time numbers that were less than r should have approximately matched the value of Jain's CDF. (This is the definition of how the CDF should behave.)

But Jain's formula consistently *failed* to match the results of my test. By contrast, the Gross and Harris CDF formula [Gross and Harris (1998) 72–73] consistently *succeeded* in matching the result of my test. I have attempted to contact Dr. Jain with the results of my testing, but as of the time of this writing, I have not yet received a response.

Random Variables

One tricky thing about real queueing systems is that arrivals don't enter the system at completely predictable times. (In fact, if requests arrive into a system at uniform intervals and if service times are constant, there will be *no* queueing unless the system is unstable.) For example, we may have evidence that the requests of a telephone system arrive at an average rate of 2.0 requests per second, but in real-life systems, it is almost never reasonable to expect that requests will arrive at a rate of *exactly* one every 0.5 seconds. Indeed, in most real systems we expect arrivals to be scattered randomly through time. We expect behaviors averaged across large numbers of requests to be predictable, but we expect individual arrival times to be *un*predictable.

Expected value

Mathematicians use the term "random variable" to describe the behavior of an unpredictable process. A *random variable* is simply a function whose value is a random number. The *expected value E[X]* of a random variable *X* is the mean (or average) of the values that *X* takes on. In many probability and statistics texts, a bare uppercase letter like *X* refers to a random variable, which has several properties, among which are its expected value and its distribution (defined in a moment). Queueing theory texts often use an uppercase letter to denote both a random variable and its expected value. The readers of those books are expected to understand by context which concept is being referenced. This book follows the same convention. For example, I use $R = S + W$ instead of the more technically precise but cumbersome $E[R] = E[S] + E[W]$.

Probability density function (pdf)

Although a random variable has, by definition, a random number value, the process through which values appear in nature is usually endowed with some sort of order. For example, on the telephone system whose average rate of arrivals is 2.0 requests per second, it may be possible for 200 requests to arrive in a given second, but it may be very unlikely. The mathematical function that models a random variable's likelihood of taking on a given value is called that random variable's *distribution*. Specifically, the probability that a discrete random variable *X* will take on a specified value *x* is called that variable's *probability density function* (or pdf), denoted $f(x) = P(X = x)$ [Hogg and Tanis (1977) 51–58].

Using the pdf

Because the exact arrival time for the next incoming request cannot be predicted exactly, a system's interarrival time is a random variable. Thus, the arrival rate (the reciprocal of arrival time) is a random variable as well. Agner Erlang showed in 1909 that the arrival rate of phone calls in a telephone system often has a *Poisson distribution* [Erlang (1909)]. Specifically, if telephone calls arrive randomly at an average rate of $\lambda > 0$, then the pdf of the arrival rate has the form:

$$f(x) = \frac{\lambda^x e^{-\lambda}}{x!}, \quad x = 0, 1, 2, \ldots.$$

Thus, if telephone calls arrive at an average rate of $\lambda = 2$ calls per second, then the probability that there will be 200 calls in a given second is only $f(200) = 2.7575 \times 10^{-316}$; in other words, if the telephone call arrival process is truly Poisson distributed with $\lambda = 2$, then it is more likely that you could deal fifty-four straight royal flush poker hands than to ever observe a one-second interval in which 200 calls would occur. On the other hand, there's a much greater probability that a one-second interval will contain exactly zero, one, two, three, or four arrivals. The pdf of the Poisson distribution with mean $\lambda = 2$ is shown in Figure 9-8. Conveniently, arrival rates in many computer applications, including many aspects of Oracle systems, also have a Poisson distribution.

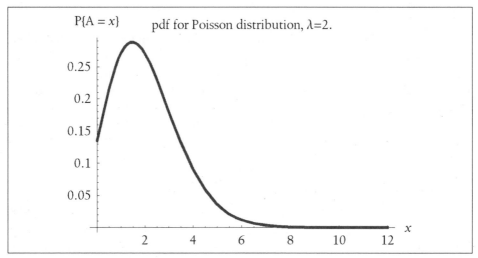

Figure 9-8. The probability density function (pdf) for the Poisson distribution with $\lambda = 2$ shows the probability P(A = x) that there will be exactly x arrivals in a one-second observation interval

It is, of course, no coincidence that the symbol λ (lambda) chosen to denote the average arrival rate of a queueing system is the same symbol used to denote the mean of a Poisson distribution. It's actually the other way around. As I shall divulge shortly, the specific M/M/m queueing theory model that is covered later in this chapter works only if a system's arrival process is Poisson distributed with mean λ. The arrival rate in queueing theory is called λ because it *is* the mean of a Poisson distribution.

A system's service time is also a random variable. For example, the time it takes a bank teller to count your money is predictable in the aggregate, but unpredictable in a specific case. Even the CPU time required to process an Oracle LIO is unpredictable. An Oracle *logical I/O* (LIO) is the operation that the Oracle kernel uses to fetch a single block from the Oracle database buffer cache. For example, a CPU might service an average of 40,000 LIO requests per second (that is, $\mu = 40000$), but from one second to the next, a CPUs service rate might vary significantly. Randomizing factors include the type and complexity of an Oracle block (e.g., whether the block is an index block or a table block), the varying number of rows in each Oracle block, and the varying column widths of data within those blocks.

Why understanding distribution is important

It is crucial to know a random variable's distribution before you can use that random variable's mean (expected value) in any predictive formulas. For example, you might say that customers arrive at a restaurant at an average rate of two customers per minute during lunchtime; thus, the expected interarrival time is 30 seconds.

However, the average doesn't tell the whole story. If you know only the expected interarrival time, then you can't tell, for example, whether individual customers are really arriving exactly 30 seconds apart, or if they're arriving in groups. If you know only that requests have an expected interarrival time of 30 seconds, then for example we *cannot* know which—if either—of the cases in Table 9-1 has occurred.

Table 9-1. *Two very different scenarios both lead to an expected interarrival time of $\tau = 30$ seconds*

Time interval	Number of arrivals	
	Case I	Case II
11:30 a.m. to 11:45 a.m.	0	34
11:45 a.m. to 12:00 noon	0	28
12:00 noon to 12:15 p.m.	240	31
12:15 p.m. to 12:30 p.m.	0	37
12:30 p.m. to 12:45 p.m.	0	24
12:45 p.m. to 1:00 p.m.	0	30
1:00 p.m. to 1:15 p.m.	0	32
1:15 p.m. to 1:30 p.m.	0	24
Average per 0:15 bucket	**30**	**30**

If reality consistently resembles Case I, then you shouldn't expect a mathematical formula to produce a reliable prediction of what happens between 1:00 p.m. and 1:15 p.m., if you tell the formula that your "average arrival rate is 120 arrivals per hour." For a queueing model to produce reliable results, you need to tell it something more about the properties of its random variable input parameters than just an average. You must also tell the model about each random variable's *distribution*.

Queueing Theory Versus the "Wait Interface"

Now that you've seen the definition for each of the formulas of queueing theory, how do Oracle operational data fit in? Specifically, how does information obtained from the so-called wait interface fit into queueing theory? Unfortunately, Oracle Corporation teaches inaccurate information on this topic. Oracle *MetaLink* article 223117.1 is an example:

Performance tuning is based on the following fundamental equation:

Response Time = Service Time + Wait Time

In the context of an Oracle database, "Service Time" is measured using the statistic "CPU used by this session" *and "Wait Time" is measured using Wait Events* [my emphasis].

The emphasized portion of this statement is false. A so-called Oracle wait event is *not* what this statement says it is.

Oracle wait times

The confusion begins with the name "wait event." It's an unfortunate choice of terminology, because the mere name encourages people to believe that the duration of an Oracle kernel event is a queueing delay. However, it is not. As you learned in Chapter 7, the elapsed time of a wait event actually includes lots of individual components. The response time components for a single OS read call are depicted in Figure 9-9.

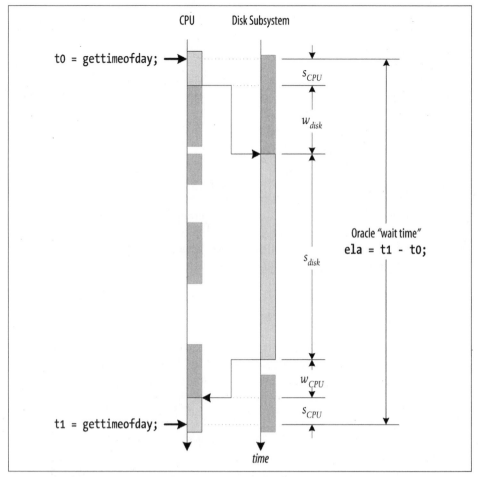

Figure 9-9. An Oracle wait time for a system call (like the disk I/O call shown here) is really a response time that is measured from the Oracle kernel's perspective. The duration ela=t1–t0 is not a queueing delay; it consists of service times and queueing delays

The Oracle wait time recorded for a system call execution is the total wall clock time that elapses from the final instruction before the OS call execution until the first instruction after the return of the OS call. Everything that happens in that interval between times t_0 and t_1 is an Oracle wait time. In Figure 9-9, a single Oracle wait time includes all of the following components:

s_{CPU}

CPU service time consumed to set up the system call. For a disk read call, most of this time is consumed in kernel running state. However, some system calls may consume CPU in user running state as well.

w_{disk}

Queueing delay for the disk device, which in this picture includes the transmission latency required for the request to reach the disk device from the CPU device.

s_{disk}

Service time for the disk device, including the seek latency, rotational latency, and data transfer latency from the I/O device back to the memory that is addressable by the CPU.

w_{CPU}

Queueing delay for the CPU, consumed with the process in the *ready to run* state.

s_{CPU}

Another segment of CPU service time required to complete the system call. Again for different system calls, some of this CPU capacity may be consumed in kernel running state, and some may be consumed in user running state.

I hope you can see clearly now that an Oracle wait time for an OS read call is definitely not a measure of w_{disk}. Other system calls behave similarly.

Differences in queueing theory notation

Studying different queueing theory books tends to even further confuse the issue of what kind of quantity an Oracle wait time really is. While most of the Greek letters retain consistent meaning across different texts, different authors use different notation for their fundamental queueing theory formula, as shown in Table 9-2.

Table 9-2. A sample of queueing theory notations

Notation	Source
$R = S + W$	Oracle *MetaLink*, [Gunther (1998) 84]
$T = S + T_q$	[Gross and Harris (1998) 11]
$W = 1/\mu + W_q$	[Gross and Harris (1998) 71]
$s_n = x_n + w_n$	[Kleinrock (1975) 198]

I have rearranged the terms on the right-hand side of each of these equations so that all of the equations represent exactly the same concept. In other words, Gunther's and my W is exactly the same thing as Gross and Harris's T_q and W_q, which are exactly the same thing as Kleinrock's w_n. It can be especially confusing when different books use the same words to mean completely different things. For example:

> Expected steady-state system waiting time W equals service time $1/\mu$ plus line delay W_q [Gross and Harris (1998) 64].

> Response time R equals service time S plus time spent waiting in the queue W [Gunther (1998) 52].

Gross and Harris use the term "waiting time" to mean what Gunther calls "response time." Furthermore, notice that the two sets of authors use the term "wait" to mean two completely different things. Considering the $R = S + W$ notation for a moment, Gross and Harris are calling R a *wait*, while Gunther calls W a wait. An Oracle wait time is closer in spirit to the Gross and Harris definition than to the Gunther definition.

Who's right? The choice of words doesn't matter, as long as the concepts represented by those words aren't intermingled. I've chosen notation that resembles what Jain and Gunther use, principally because those were the first two books on queueing theory that I studied. However, it's fine to call R, S, and W by any name that you like. It is *not* correct to regard an Oracle wait time as any single component in the right-hand side of an equation like $R = S + W$. An Oracle wait time is really the response time for an operating system call as viewed from the Oracle kernel's perspective. The Oracle kernel publishes wait times in several places, including the ela statistic in the WAIT lines of extended trace data, and the following fixed views:

```
V$SESSION_WAIT.WAIT_TIME
V$SESSION_EVENT.TIME_WAITED
V$SESSION_EVENT.AVERAGE_WAIT
V$SESSION_EVENT.MAX_WAIT
V$SESSION_EVENT.TIME_WAITED_MICRO
V$SYSTEM_EVENT.TIME_WAITED
V$SYSTEM_EVENT.AVERAGE_WAIT
V$SYSTEM_EVENT.TIME_WAITED_MICRO
```

Each of these statistics refers to a quantity of time that does include a queueing delay for the device being requested, but an Oracle wait time includes many other response time components as well. Specifically, an Oracle wait time is *not* the W of an $R = S + W$ equation from queueing theory.

The M/M/m Queueing Model

The M/M/*m* model is a set of mathematical formulas that can predict the performance of queueing systems that meet five very specific criteria. The notation M/M/*m* is actually shorthand for the longer notation M/M/*m*/∞/FCFS, which completely describes all five criteria:

M/M/*m*/∞/FCFS *(exponential interarrival time)*
> The request interarrival time is an exponentially distributed random variable. I shall discuss the meaning of this statement later in this section.

M/**M**/*m*/∞/FCFS *(exponential service time)*
> The service time is an exponentially distributed random variable.

M/M/**m**/∞/FCFS *(m homogeneous, parallel, independent service channels)*
> There are *m* parallel service channels, all of which have identical functional and performance characteristics, and all of which are identically capable of providing service to any arriving service request. For example, in an M/M/1 system, there is a single service channel. In an M/M/32 system, there are 32 parallel service channels.

M/M/*m*/**∞**/FCFS *(no queue length restriction)*
> There is no restriction on queue length. No request that enters the queue exits the queue until that request receives service.

M/M/*m*/∞/**FCFS** *(first-come, first-served queue discipline)*
> The queue discipline is first-come, first-served (FCFS). The system honors requests for service in the order in which they were received.

Why "M" Means Exponential

You might wonder why queueing theorists use the letter "M" instead of "E" to denote the exponential distribution. It is because "E" denotes another distribution, the Erlang distribution. Faced with the choice of letters other than "E" to denote the exponential distribution, mathematicians chose the letter "M" because the exponential distribution has a unique "Markovian" (or "memoryless") property. Other letters used in this slot for other models include "G" for general, "D" for deterministic, and "H_k" for *k*-stage hyperexponential distributions.

M/M/m Systems

These five criteria happen to be remarkably fitting descriptions of real phenomena on Oracle systems. M/M/*m* queueing systems occur abundantly in the human experience. Examples include:

- An airport ticket counter where six ticket agents service customers selected from the head of one long, winding queue. This is an M/M/6 system.

- A four-lane toll road where one toll booth services the cars and trucks selected from the head of a queue that forms in each lane. This is four separate M/M/1 systems, each with an average arrival rate chosen appropriately for each lane.

- A symmetric multiprocessing (SMP) computer system where twelve CPUs provide service to requests selected from the head of the ready-to-run queue. For reasons of operating system scalability imperfections that I shall discuss later, an appropriate model for this system is M/M/m, with m chosen in the range $0 < m < 12$.

It is clear that all of these examples meet the m, ∞, and FCFS criteria of the M/M/m/∞/FCFS model. But it is less clear without further analysis whether the examples meet the M/M criteria. In the next section, we shall explore what it means to say that a random variable is exponentially distributed.

Non-M/M/m Systems

Even before learning about the M/M criteria, it is easy to see that not all queueing systems are M/M/m. For example, the following applications are *not* M/M/m systems:

- An airport ticket counter where five ticket agents service airline passengers, but first-class and business class passengers are permitted to cut into the front of the queue. This system violates the FCFS criterion required for the system to be considered M/M/m.

- An array of six independent computer disks where each disk services I/O requests from the head of its dedicated queue. This system violates the M/M/6 assumption that all the participating parallel service channels are identically capable of providing service to any arriving service request. For example, a request to read disk D can be fulfilled only by disk D, regardless of what other disks happen to be idle. It is possible to model this system with six independent M/M/1 systems.

- Oracle latch acquisition. Oracle latches are not allocated to requests in the order the requests are made [Millsap (2001c)]. Therefore Oracle's latch acquisition system violates the FCFS assumption of M/M/m.

Many systems that fit the .../m/∞/FCFS criteria of queueing systems fail to meet the M/M criteria because their arrival and service processes don't fit the exponential distribution. In the next sections, I shall reveal how to test your operational data for fit to the exponential distribution.

Exponential Distribution

Previously I pointed out that in the early 1900s, Agner Erlang observed that the arrival rate in a telephone system "is Poisson distributed." The phrase "is such-and-such distributed" means only that the probability density function (pdf) of the random variable in question fits a particular mathematical form—in this case, the Poisson form. Once we know the pdf of a random variable, we can compute the probability that this random variable will take on any specific value in which we might be interested. To say that a random variable is *exponentially distributed* with mean $\theta > 0$ (the Greek letter theta) is to say that the variable's pdf is of the form:

$$f(x) = \frac{1}{\theta} e^{-x/\theta}, \quad 0 \le x < \infty$$

Figure 9-10 shows the pdf for an exponentially distributed random variable.

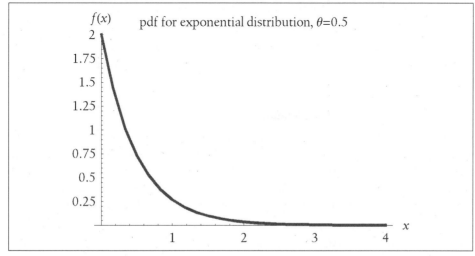

Figure 9-10. The pdf for an exponentially distributed random variable with mean $\theta = 0.5$

It so happens that many real-life systems have exponentially distributed interarrival times and service times, but we cannot reliably model a system with M/M/m until we test the system's arrival and service processes. This book provides everything you need to test whether your system's operational characteristics suit the M/M/m model.

Poisson-exponential relationship

Agner Erlang observed that the arrival rate of phone calls in a telephone system obeys a Poisson distribution. Earlier in this section, I commented that many arrival processes in computer systems, including Oracle systems, are Poisson distributed as well. Why, then, would I have chosen to show you the M/M/m queueing model, which works only if interarrival times and service times are *exponentially* distributed? Why did I not choose a model in which arrival and service processes were Poisson distributed?

The answer is that, actually, I *did* choose a model in which arrivals and services were Poisson. The exponential and Poisson distributions bear a reciprocal relationship [Gross and Harris (1998) 16-22]:

- For a system to suit the criterion defined by the first "M" in "M/M/*m*," its *request interarrival times* must be exponentially distributed. Remember, however, that the average interarrival time τ is the reciprocal of the average arrival rate ($\tau = 1/\lambda$). As it happens, an arrival rate with a mean of λ is Poisson if and only if the corresponding interarrival time is exponential with mean $\theta = \tau = 1/\lambda$.

- For a system to suit the criterion defined by the second "M" in "M/M/*m*," its *service times* must be exponentially distributed. Of course, the average service time S is the reciprocal of the average service rate ($S = 1/\mu$). A service rate with a mean of μ is Poisson if and only if the corresponding service time is exponential with mean $\theta = S = 1/\mu$.

This is why authors sometimes refer to the M/M/*m* model as the model for Poisson input and Poisson service.

Testing for fit to exponential distribution

The two "M"s of the M/M/*m* queueing model notation specify that we can use the model only if the interarrival time and service time are exponentially distributed. That is, we can use M/M/*m* to model that system's performance *only* if the histogram for a system's interarrival times *and* the histogram for its service rates both resemble the exponential distribution pdf curve shown in Figure 9-10. Figure 9-11 shows some examples.

The trick is, how can we tell whether a set of interarrival times or service rates sufficiently "resembles" Figure 9-10? Statisticians use the *chi-square goodness-of-fit test* to determine whether a list of numbers is sufficiently likely to belong to a specified distribution. The Perl program in Example 9-4 tests whether the numbers stored in a file are likely to be members of an exponential distribution. It produces the verdict "Accept," "Almost suspect," "Suspect," or "Reject" using the procedure recommended in [Knuth (1981) 43-44]. If you have too few data points to perform the chi-square test, the program will tell you. If your operationally measured interarrival times and service times receive a verdict of "Accept" or "Almost suspect," then you can be reasonably certain that the M/M/*m* model will produce reliable results.

M/M/*m* will make reliable predictions only if interarrival times and service times are both exponentially distributed random variables. Other queueing models produce accurate forecasts for systems with interarrival and service times that are not exponential. I focus here on the M/M/*m* model because it is so often well-suited for Oracle performance analysis projects. On Oracle performance projects, it is normally possible to define useful subsets of system workload that meet the M/M criteria. For example:

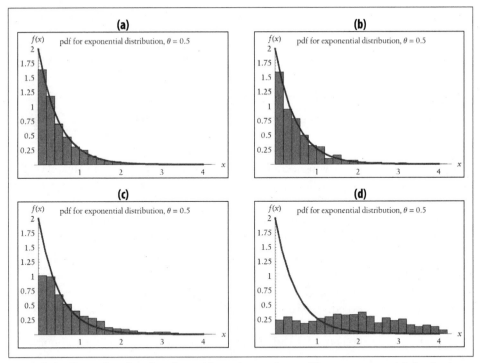

Figure 9-11. Examples of random data with varying goodness of fit to an exponential distribution with mean θ = 0.5

- Executions of batch jobs are easy to test for exponentially distributed interarrival times and service times. A good batch queue manager records job request times, job start times, and job completion times for later analysis. A job's interarrival time is simply the difference between the job's request time and the previous job's request time. A job's service time is merely the difference between the job's completion time and the job's start time. By collecting 50 or more interarrival times and 50 or more service times, you can determine whether a given subset of your batch jobs obeys the M/M/m model's M/M criteria.

  The important task here is to use M/M/m only for a properly behaved subset of your batch data. For example, the interarrival times of your batch jobs over a 24-hour period are likely *not* to be exponentially distributed: your nighttime interarrival times will likely be much larger than your daytime figures. Likewise, the service times for all of your batch jobs are likely not to be exponentially distributed. However, the service times for all your jobs that execute in less than one minute likely *will* be approximately exponentially distributed.

- The Oracle logical I/O (LIO) is a useful unit of measure for service requests. It is not possible to measure LIO interarrival times or service times directly in Oracle, but intuition and a track record of successes using M/M/m to model LIO performance indicate that LIO interarrival times and service times are indeed exponentially distributed. As long as the execution of each business function can be expressed in terms of an LIO count, you can translate the queueing model's output into terms of business function response time and throughput. Forcing yourself to think of application functions in terms of LIO count is a Very Good Thing.

A program to test for exponential distribution

All good queueing theory books inform their readers of the requirement that before you can use the M/M/*m* model, you must ensure that the system you're modeling has exponential interarrival times and exponential service times. The problem is that most of these books give you no practical means by which to ensure this. The Perl program shown in Example 9-4 performs the task for you. The idea for the program was inspired by [Allen (1994) 224-225]. Implementation was guided principally by [Knuth (1981) 38-45], with supplemental assistance from *Mathematica*, [Olkin et al. (1994)], [CRC (1991)], and *http://www.cpan.org*.

To use this program, download the source code to a system on which Perl is installed. On a Unix (Linux, HP-UX, Solaris, AIX, etc.) system, you'll probably want to name the file *mdist*. On Microsoft Windows, you'll probably want to call it *mdist.pl*. On Unix, you may have to edit the top line of the code to refer properly to your Perl executable (e.g., maybe your Perl executable is called */usr/local/bin/perl*). Then type perldoc mdist (or perldoc mdist.pl) to your command prompt to view the manual page for the program.

Example 9-4. This Perl program tests the likelihood that a random variable is exponentially distributed

```
#!/usr/bin/perl

# $Header: /home/cvs/cvm-book1/mdist/mdist.pl,v 1.7 2002/09/05 23:03:57 cvm
# Cary Millsap (cary.millsap@hotsos.com)
# Copyright (c) 2002 by Hotsos Enterprises, Ltd. All rights reserved.

use strict;
use warnings;

use Getopt::Long;
use Statistics::Distributions qw(chisqrdistr chisqrprob);

my $VERSION = do { my @r=(q$Revision: 1.20 $=~/\d+/g); sprintf "%d."."%02d"x$#r,@r };
my $DATE    = do { my @d=(q$Date: 2003/08/29 16:01:37 $=~/\d{4}\D\d{2}\D\d{2}/g); sprintf
$d[0] };
my $PROGRAM = "Test for Fit to Exponential Distribution";

my %OPT;

sub x2($$) {
    my ($mu, $p) = @_;
    # The p that &Statistics::Distributions::chisqrdistr expects is the
    # complement of what we find in [Knuth (1981) 41], Mathematica, or
```

Example 9-4. This Perl program tests the likelihood that a random variable is exponentially distributed (continued)

```perl
    # [CRC (1991) 515].
    return chisqrdistr($mu, 1-$p);
}

sub CDFx2($$) {
    my ($n, $x2) = @_;
    # The p that &Statistics::Distributions::chisqrprob returns is the
    # complement of what we find in [Knuth (1981) 41], Mathematica, or
    # [CRC (1991) 515].
    return 1 - chisqrprob($n, $x2);
}

sub mdist(%) {
    my %arg = (
        list        => [],               # list of values to test
        mean        => undef,            # expected mean of distribution
        quantiles   => undef,            # number of quantiles for test
        @_,                              # input args override defaults
    );

    # Assign the list. If there aren't at least 50 observations in the
    # list, then the chi-square test is not valid [Olkin et al. (1994)
    # 613].
    my @list = @{$arg{list}};
    die "Not enough data (need at least 50 observations)\n" unless @list >= 50;

    # Compute number of quantiles and the number of expected observations
    # for each quantile. If there aren't at least 5 observations expected
    # in each quantile, then we have too many quantiles [Knuth (1981) 42]
    # and [Olkin et al. (1994) 613].
    my $quantiles = $arg{quantiles} ? $arg{quantiles} : 4;
    my $m = @list/$quantiles;            # we expect quantiles to have identical areas
    die "Too many quantiles (using $quantiles quantiles reqiures at least ". 5*$quantiles
." observations)\n" unless $m >= 5;

    # Assign the mean and chi-square degrees of freedom. If no mean was
    # passed in, then estimate it. But if we estimate the mean, then we
    # lose an additional chi-square degree of freedom.
    my $mean = $arg{mean};
    my $n_loss = 1;                      # lose one degree of freedom for guessing
quantiles
    if (!defined $mean) {
        my $s = 0; $s += $_ for @list;   # sum the observed values
        $mean = $s/@list;                # compute the sample mean
        $n_loss++;                       # lose additional d.o.f. for estimating the
mean
    }
    my $n = $quantiles - $n_loss;        # chi-square degrees of freedom
    die "Not enough quantiles for $n_loss lost degrees of freedom (need at least ". ($n_
loss+1) ." quantiles)\n" unless $n >= 1;

    # Dump values computed thus far.
```

Example 9-4. This Perl program tests the likelihood that a random variable is exponentially distributed (continued)

```perl
if ($OPT{debug}>=1) {
    print  "list      = (", join(", ", @list), ")\n";
    printf "quantiles = %d\n", $quantiles;
    printf "mean      = %s\n", $mean;
}

# Compute interior quantile boundaries. N.B.: The definition of
# quantile boundaries is what makes this test for exponential
# distribution different from a test for some other distribution.  If
# the input list is exponentially distributed, then we expect for
# there to be $m observations in each quantile, with quantile
# boundaries defined at -$mean*log(1-$i/$quantiles) for each
# i=1..$quantiles-1.
my @q;                                 # list of interior quantile boundaries
for (my $i=1; $i<=$quantiles-1; $i++) {
    $q[$i] = -$mean*log(1-$i/$quantiles);
}

# Compute frequency of observed values [Knuth (1981) 40]. Setting
# $Y[0]=undef makes array content begin at $Y[1], which simplifies
# array indexing throughout.
my @Y = (undef, (0) x $quantiles);
for my $e (@list) {
    print "e=$e\n" if $OPT{debug}>=3;
    for (my $i=1; $i<=$quantiles; $i++) {
        print "  i=$i (before): q[$i]=$q[$i]\n" if $OPT{debug}>=3;
        if ($i == $quantiles) { $Y[-1]++; print "    Y[-1]->$Y[-1]\n" if $OPT{debug}>
=3; last }
        if ($e <= $q[$i])      { $Y[$i]++; print "    Y[$i]->$Y[$i]\n" if $OPT{debug}>
=3; last }
    }
}

# Populate list containing frequency of expected values per quantile
# [Knuth (1981) 40]. Using a data structure for this is unnecessarily
# complicated for this test, but it might make the program easier to
# adapt to tests for other distributions in other applications. (We
# could have simply used $m anyplace we mention $np[$anything].)
my @np = (undef, ($m) x $quantiles);

# Dump data structure contents if debugging.
if ($OPT{debug}>=1) {
    print "mean = $mean\n";
    print "q  = (", join(", ",  @q[1 .. $quantiles-1]), ")\n";
    print "Y  = (", join(", ",  @Y[1 .. $quantiles]  ), ")\n";
    print "np = (", join(", ", @np[1 .. $quantiles]  ), ")\n";
}

# Compute the chi-square statistic [Knuth (1981) 40].
my $V = 0;
$V += ($Y[$_] - $np[$_])**2 / $np[$_] for (1 .. $quantiles);
```

Example 9-4. This Perl program tests the likelihood that a random variable is exponentially distributed (continued)

```perl
    # Compute verdict as a function of where V fits in the appropriate
    # degrees-of-freedom row of the chi-square statistical table. From
    # [Knuth (1981) 43-44].
    my $verdict;
    my $p = CDFx2($n, $V);
    if     ($p <  0.01) { $verdict = "Reject" }
    elsif ($p <  0.05) { $verdict = "Suspect" }
    elsif ($p <  0.10) { $verdict = "Almost suspect" }
    elsif ($p <= 0.90) { $verdict = "Accept" }
    elsif ($p <= 0.95) { $verdict = "Almost suspect" }
    elsif ($p <= 0.99) { $verdict = "Suspect" }
    else               { $verdict = "Reject" }

    # Return a hash containing the verdict and key statistics.
    return (verdict=>$verdict, mean=>$mean, n=>$n, V=>$V, p=>$p);
}

%OPT = (                                # default values
    mean           => undef,
    quantiles      => undef,
    debug          => 0,
    version        => 0,
    help           => 0,
);
GetOptions(
    "mean=f"       => \$OPT{mean},
    "quantiles=i"  => \$OPT{quantiles},
    "debug=i"      => \$OPT{debug},
    "version"      => \$OPT{version},
    "help"         => \$OPT{help},
);
if ($OPT{version}) { print "$VERSION\n"; exit }
if ($OPT{help})    { print "Type 'perldoc $0' for help\n"; exit }
my $file = shift; $file = "&STDIN" if !defined $file;
open FILE, "<$file" or die "can't read '$file' ($!)";
my @list;
while (defined (my $line = <FILE>)) {
    next if $line =~ /^#/;
    next if $line =~ /^\s*$/;
    chomp $line;
    for ($line) {
        s/[^0-9.]/ /g;
        s/^\s*//g;
        s/\s*$//g;
    }
    push @list, split(/\s+/, $line);
}
close FILE;
print join(", ", @list), "\n" if $OPT{debug};

my %r = mdist(list=>[@list], mean=>$OPT{mean}, quantiles=>$OPT{quantiles});
print " Hypothesis: Data are exponentially distributed with mean $r{mean}\n";
```

Example 9-4. This Perl program tests the likelihood that a random variable is exponentially distributed (continued)

```
printf "Test result: n=%d V=%.2f p=%.3f\n", $r{n}, $r{V}, $r{p};
print  "    Verdict: $r{verdict}\n";

__END__

=head1 NAME

mdist - test data for fit to exponential distribution with specified mean

=head1 SYNOPSIS

mdist [--mean=I<m>] [--quantiles=I<q>] [I<file>]

=head1 DESCRIPTION

B<mdist> tests whether a random variable appears to be exponentially
distributed with mean I<m>. This information is useful in determining, for
example, whether a given list of operationally collected interarrival
times or service times is suitable input for the M/M/m queueing theory
model.

B<mdist> reads I<file> for a list of observed values. If no input file is
specified, then B<mdist> takes its input from STDIN. The input must
contain at least 50 observations.

The program prints the test hypothesis, the test results, and a verdict:

  $ perl mdist.pl 001.d
    Hypothesis: Data are exponentially distributed with mean 0.000959673232
  Test result: n=2 V=0.72 p=0.302
       Verdict: Accept

The test result statistics [Knuth (1981) 39-45] include:

=over 4

=item I<n>

Degrees of freedom from the chi-square test.

=item I<V>

The "chi-square" statistic.

=item I<p>

The probability at which I<V> is expected to occur in a chi-square
distribution with degrees of freedom equal to I<n>.

=back

B<mdist> uses a I<q>-quantile chi-square test for exponential
```

Example 9-4. This Perl program tests the likelihood that a random variable is exponentially distributed (continued)

distribution, adapted from [Allen (1994) 224-225] and [Knuth (1981) 39-40]. Allen provides the strategy for divvying the data into quantiles and testing whether the frequency in each quantile matches our expectation of the exponential distribution. Knuth provides the general chi-square testing strategy that produces a verdict of "Accept", "Almost suspect", "Suspect", or "Reject".

=head2 Options

=over 4

=item B<--mean=>I<m>

The hypothesized expected value of the random variable (i.e., the hypothesized mean of the exponential distribution). If no I<m> is specified, then B<mdist> will use the sample mean of the input and adjust the chi-square degrees of freedom parameter appropriately.

=item B<--quantiles=>I<q>

The number of quantiles to use in the chi-square test for goodness-of-fit. The number of quantiles must equal at least 2 if a mean is specified, and 3 if the mean will be estimated. The number of quantiles must be small enough that the number of observations divided by I<q> must be at least 5. The default is I<q>=4.

=back

=head1 AUTHOR

Cary Millsap (cary.millsap@hotsos.com)

=head1 BUGS

Instead of estimating the distribution mean by computing the sample mean, we should probalby use the minimum chi-squared estimation technique described in [Olkin et al. (1994) 617-623].

=head1 SEE ALSO

Allen, A. O. 1994. Computer Performance Analysis with Mathematica. Boston MA: AP Professional

CRC 1991. Standard Mathematical Tables and Formulae, 29ed. Boca Raton FL: CRC Press

Knuth, D. E. 1981. The Art of Computer Programming, Vol 2: Seminumerical Algorithms. Reading MA: Addison Wesley

Olkin, I.; Gleser, L. J.; Derman, C. 1994. Probability Models and Applications, 2ed. New York NY: Macmillan

Example 9-4. This Perl program tests the likelihood that a random variable is exponentially distributed (continued)

```
Wolfram, S. 1999. Mathematica. Champaign IL: Wolfram

=head1 COPYRIGHT

Copyright (c) 2002 by Hotsos Enterprises, Ltd. All rights reserved.
```

Behavior of M/M/m Systems

The beauty of M/M/*m* is that using the model makes it possible to experiment with parameters that would be very expensive to manipulate in the real world. In this section, we'll examine a few interesting behaviors of M/M/*m*. These model behaviors will help explain how to avoid some of the undesirable performance behaviors that plague real multi-channel queueing systems. The result will be a clearer understanding of the Oracle system you're probably thinking about right now.

Multi-channel scalability

Of course, two CPUs are better than one. But why? And under what circumstances? An easy way to conceptualize the answer is to use a sequence diagram. Figure 9-12 reveals the answer. On the system shown in case *a*, the first disk I/O call cannot return immediately to the single CPU because that CPU is occupied doing other work. Thus, the CPU request queues, which of course increases response time. The system shown in case *b* has two CPUs. When the disk I/O call returns, it finds CPU_1 busy, but CPU_2 is ready and able to service the request, which results in the elimination of a queueing delay, which improves response time for the business function. Note the interesting effect of creating a new bottleneck on the disk in case *b*.

This phenomenon of reduced queueing in systems with larger *m* manifests itself clearly in the output of M/M/*m*. Figure 9-13 shows the performance effect of increasing the number of parallel service channels. Although the service time (*S*) remains constant across all the systems represented by the figure, response times (*R*) are smaller at higher arrival rates (*λ*) on systems with more service channels (*m*), because there is less queueing delay ($W = R - S$).

So, which is better, a system with a single very fast CPU? Or a system with $m > 1$ slower CPUs? Most consultants have the correct answer programmed into their RNA: "It depends." But with M/M/*m* you have the tools to answer the very good question, "On *what?*"

Figure 9-14 shows very clearly that the "it depends" depends only upon one variable: the arrival rate. For low arrival rates, an $m = 1$ system with the fast CPU will provide superior performance. For high arrival rates, the $m > 1$ system will be faster. You can estimate the break-even point λ_{eq} by inspection if you plot the response time curves in a tool like you can find at *http://www.hotsos.com*. If you want a more

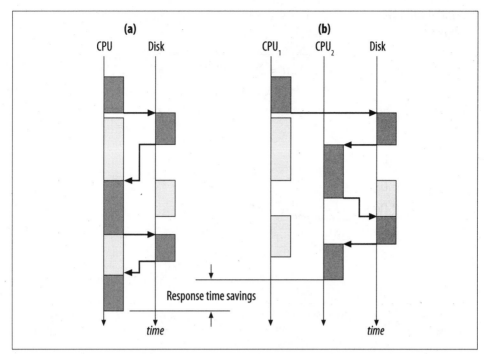

Figure 9-12. More service channels (in this drawing, CPUs) improve response times on busy systems by reducing queueing delays

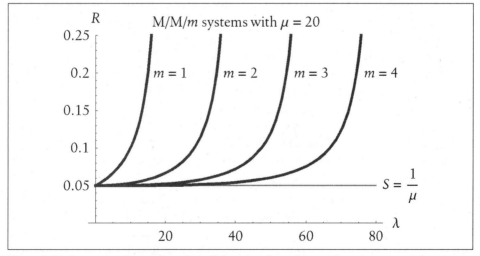

Figure 9-13. Increasing the number of parallel service channels provides greater capacity to arrivals requesting service, which reduces response time at higher arrival rates

detailed answer, you could find the λ value for which the two systems' response times are equal by using the interval bisection method shown earlier in the

LambdaMax function of Example 9-2. Or you can compute λ_{eq} symbolically with a tool like *Mathematica*.

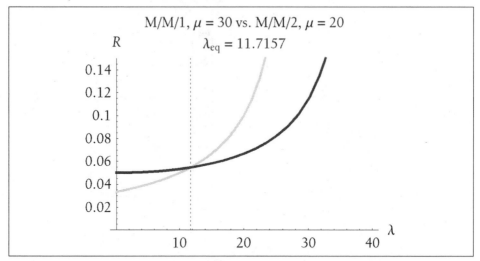

Figure 9-14. A computer with a single fast CPU produces better response times for low arrival rates, but a computer with four slower CPUs produces better response times for high arrival rates

People who have tried both types of system notice the behavior depicted in Figure 9-14 in very practical terms:

- A long nightly batch job runs faster on the system with the single fast CPU. This result often surprises people who "upgrade" from the single-CPU system to the multi-CPU system. But when a single-threaded job runs solo on a system, the arrival rate is low. It will run the fastest on a fast CPU. The multi-CPU system doesn't provide reduction in queueing delay on a system with a low arrival rate, because on such a system there is no queueing to begin with.

- The multi-CPU system provides better response times to online users during their busiest work hours. This result is due to the reduction in queueing that a multi-channel system provides. Multi-CPU systems scale better to high arrival rates (such as those induced by high concurrent user counts) than single-CPU systems.

Naturally, the better system to purchase depends upon an array of both technical and non-technical factors, including price, hardware reliability, dealer service, upgrade flexibility, and compatibility with other systems. But the expected peak arrival rate of workload into your system, which is profoundly influenced by your system's concurrency level, should definitely factor into your decision.

The knee

The most interesting part of the performance curve is its "knee." Intuitively, the location of the "knee in the curve" is the utilization value at which the curve appears to starting going *up* faster than it goes *out*. Unfortunately, this intuitive definition doesn't work, because the *apparent* location of the knee changes, depending on how you draw the curve. Figure 9-15 illustrates the problem. The graphs shown here are two different plots of the same response time curve. The only difference between the two plots is the scale of the vertical axis. The visual evidence presented here is overwhelming: clearly "these two systems have different knees." But remember, they are not two systems, they are plots of the *same* system using different vertical scales.

To visually seek the utilization at which the "greatest bend occurs" is thus an unreliable method for locating the knee. Obviously, a useful definition of a system's "knee" cannot rely upon an arbitrary selection of which drawing unit an artist chooses for a plot of the system's response time curve.

One author gets this point terribly wrong in his paper *Performance Management: Myths & Facts* [Millsap (1999) 8]. The points he was trying to make are indeed relevant—there in fact *is* a knee in the response time curve, and in fact the knee *does* move rightward as you add service channels.

However, the author's definition of *knee* (the ρ value "at which the curve begins to go 'up' faster than it goes 'out') is unfortunately the intuitive one that is debunked above. And the manner in which he suggested that the knee might be found (calculating the value of ρ for which $\partial R/\partial \rho = 1$, and so on) is just completely wrong. I'm sure that the author would be very sorry if he knew.

A more suitable technical definition for the "knee" is this: the *knee* of the response time curve occurs at the utilization value ρ^* (rho-star) at which the ratio R/ρ achieves its minimum value. Graphically, the location of the knee is the utilization (ρ) value at which a straight line drawn through the origin touches the response time curve in exactly one point, as shown in Figure 9-16. Many analysts consider the value ρ^* the optimal utilization for an M/M/m system, because...

> ...it is usually desirable to simultaneously minimize R (to satisfy users) and maximize ρ (to share resource cost among many users) [Vernon(2001)].

As we have seen, for utilization values to the left of the knee (for $\rho < \rho^*$), we waste system capacity. After all, if we're running at low utilization, we can add workload without appreciably degrading response times. For utilization values to the right of the knee (for $\rho > \rho^*$), we risk inflicting serious response time degradation upon our users even for tiny fluctuations in workload.

The location of the knee in an M/M/m system is a function solely of m, the number of parallel service channels. As we've seen, adding parallel service channels will allow

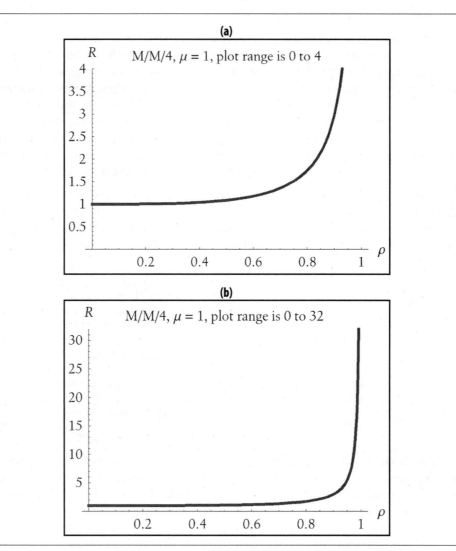

Figure 9-15. Two views of the exact same graph plotted using two different vertical scales. Intuitively, it appears that the knee in the top curve occurs at ρ ≈ 0.8 and that the knee in the bottom curve occurs to the right of ρ = 0.9

a system to run at higher utilization values without appreciable response time degradation. Figure 9-17 shows how the location of the knee moves rightward in the utilization domain as we increase the value of m.

The location of the knee for a given value of m is constant, regardless of service rate. This phenomenon is demonstrated in Figure 9-18. In this figure, changes to the service rate (μ) motivate changes to response times (note the differing labels on the R axis), but the shape of the performance curve and location of the knee are the same

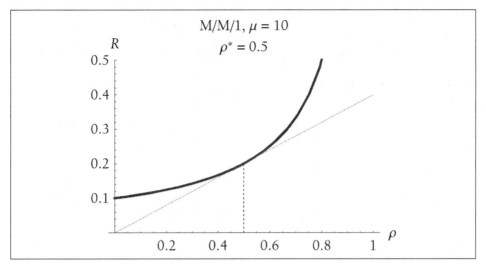

Figure 9-16. The knee is the utilization value ρ* at which R/ρ achieves its minimum value. Equivalently, the knee is the ρ value at which a line through the origin is tangent to the response time curve

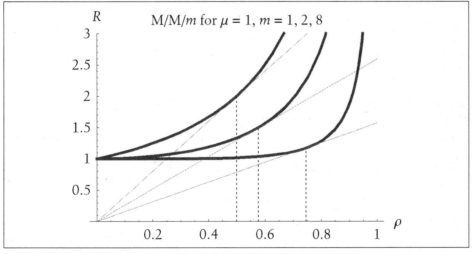

Figure 9-17. The knee value moves rightward in the utilization domain (ρ) as the number of parallel service channels (m) increases

for all M/M/1 systems. Similarly, all M/M/2 curves share a single shape and a single knee value. All M/M/3 curves share a single shape and a single knee value, and so on.

Two curves f_1 and f_2 can be said to have the *same shape* if $f_1(x) = k\, f_2(x)$ at every x for some constant k. That is, two curves have the same shape if they can be made to look identical by scaling one curve's vertical axis by a constant.

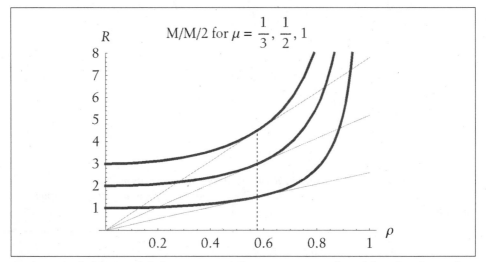

Figure 9-18. The location of the knee is constant for a given m, regardless of the value of μ. Under conditions of service rate changes, the vertical position of the curve moves, but neither the curve's shape nor its knee location changes

Because all M/M/m systems with a fixed value of m have an identical knee utilization, it is possible to create a table that lists the location of the knee for interesting values of m. Table 9-3 shows the location of the knee for various M/M/m systems.

Table 9-3. The utilization value ρ^* at which the knee occurs in an M/M/m system depends upon the value of m

m	ρ^*	m	ρ^*
1	0.5	32	0.86169
2	0.57735	40	0.875284
3	0.628831	48	0.885473
4	0.665006	56	0.893482
5	0.692095	64	0.899995
6	0.713351	80	0.910052
7	0.730612	96	0.917553
8	0.744997	112	0.923427
16	0.810695	128	0.928191
24	0.842207		

Table 9-4 gives further insight into the performance of M/M/m systems. It illustrates how average response time degrades relative to utilization on various M/M/m systems. For example, if the average response time on an unloaded M/M/1 system is $R = S$ seconds, then the average response time will degrade to $R = 2S$ seconds (twice the unloaded response time) when utilization reaches 50%. Response time will degrade to four times the unloaded response time when utilization reaches 75%, and to *ten* times the unloaded response time when utilization reaches 90%. On an M/M/8 system, response time will degrade to $R = 4S$ seconds only when system utilization reaches 96.3169%. These figures match the intuition acquired by studying the effects of adding service channels upon response time scalability.

Table 9-4. *The utilization on M/M/m systems at which response time becomes k times worse than the service time (that is, at which R = kS)*

k	m				
	1	2	4	8	16
1	0.	0.	0.	0.	0.
2	0.5	0.707107	0.834855	0.909166	0.950986
3	0.666667	0.816497	0.901222	0.947673	0.97263
4	0.75	0.866025	0.929336	0.963169	0.980984
5	0.8	0.894427	0.944954	0.971569	0.985426
6	0.833333	0.912871	0.954907	0.976844	0.988184
7	0.857143	0.92582	0.961807	0.980467	0.990064
8	0.875	0.935414	0.966874	0.983109	0.991427
9	0.888889	0.942809	0.970753	0.985121	0.992462
10	0.9	0.948683	0.973818	0.986704	0.993273

Response time fluctuations

Online system users who execute the same task over and over are very sensitive to fluctuations in response time. Given a choice, most users would probably prefer a consistent two-second response time for an online form over response time that averages two seconds per form but does so by providing sub-second response for 75% of executions and seven-second response time for 25% of executions. You have perhaps noticed that on low-load systems, response times are mostly stable, but on very busy systems, response times can fluctuate wildly. The queueing model explains why.

Figure 9-19 depicts the very small degradation in response time (from R_1 to R_2) of a multi-channel (i.e., $m > 1$) system as its utilization increases from ρ_1 to ρ_2. Notice how the R_1 and R_2 values are so close together that their labels overlap. However, to right of the knee, even a very tiny change in utilization from ρ_3 to ρ_4 produces a profound degradation in response time (from R_3 to R_4).

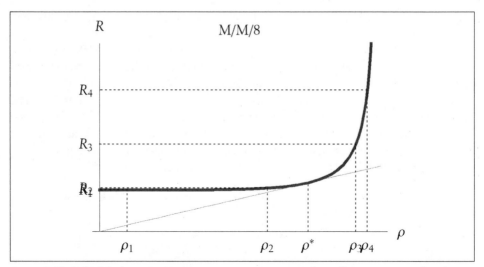

Figure 9-19. Left of the knee, response time is insensitive even to large fluctuations in utilization, but right of the knee, even tiny fluctuations in utilization create huge response time variances

As we learned in the previous section, multi-channel systems can provide stable response times for higher arrival rates than single-channel systems can handle. The excellent scalability shown in Figure 9-19 is another illustration of this phenomenon. However, the capacity of even the largest multi-channel system is finite, and when the arrival rate begins to encroach upon that finite limit of capacity, performance degrades quickly.

By contrast, performance of single-channel systems degrades more smoothly, as shown in Figure 9-20. In this picture, response time clearly degrades faster to the right of the knee. However, in systems with few parallel service channels (i.e., with small m), the degradation is distributed more uniformly throughout the entire range of utilization values than it is for systems with many parallel service channels (i.e., with large m).

A single-channel queueing system is less scalable than a similarly loaded queueing system with multiple service channels. That is, its knee is nearer to the low end of the utilization domain. But every system has a knee. Especially on highly scalable multi-channel systems, once you drive workload past the knee, the system's users are in for a wild ride of fluctuating response times.

Parameter sensitivity

Spreadsheet-based systems like Microsoft Excel allow you to test what-if situations at a pace that Agner Erlang would have envied. Such what-if tests can save countless iterations through emotional roller coaster rides with end users. For example, on very many occasions in my career, customers have engaged my services to determine why a performance improvement project has failed. Application of the M/M/m queueing model in several of these occasions has enabled me to explain quickly and

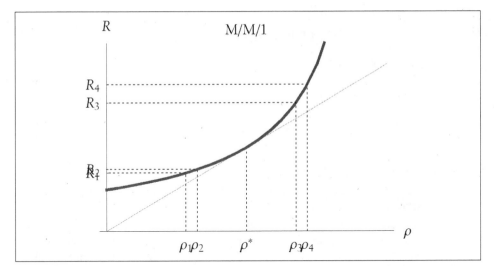

Figure 9-20. Response time degrades more uniformly throughout the domain of utilization values on single-channel (and small-m) systems

concisely why some hardware upgrade didn't produce the desired overall performance improvement. The queueing model has often led to proofs of assertions in forms like:

> ...This is why upgrading to 100% faster CPUs did not produce the desired performance improvement. Furthermore, even if you could have quadrupled the number of these faster CPUs, you *still* would not have achieved the desired performance improvement. The *only* way to produce the desired performance improvement is either to reduce the number of times you use this function, or to reduce the length of the code path that is executed when you use it.

In cases like this, earlier use of the queueing model might have averted the catastrophe that had motivated my presence.

Using the M/M/m queueing model in a spreadsheet teaches you that every input parameter and every output parameter of the model is negotiable. The key to optimizing the performance of a system is to understand how the parameters relate to each other, and to understand the economic impact of the choices you can make about each parameter. Each of the following items describes a negotiable parameter and some of the choices you can make about it:

λ

The arrival rate λ is a negotiable parameter that can provide significant leverage to the performance analyst. Many analysts fail even to consider negotiating workload with end users; they assume that the amount of work that the business needs from the system is fixed. But in many cases, a principal cause of system performance trauma is unnecessary workload. Examples include:

- An application sends scheduled alerts via email to each user every two minutes, but each end user reads alerts only twice a day. Thus, the arrival

Bad CPU Utilization Targets

I am reluctant to express a "*good* CPU utilization target" because CPU utilization is a side-effect of the metric to which you really *should* be targeting: response time. However, avoiding some *bad* utilization values can help keep you out of system performance trouble.

- On batch-only application systems, CPU utilization of less than 100% is bad if there's work waiting in the job queue. The goal of a batch-only system user is *maximized throughput*. If there's work waiting, then every second of CPU capacity left idle is a second of CPU capacity gone wasted that can never be reclaimed. But be careful: pegging CPU utilization at 100% over long periods often causes OS scheduler thrashing, which can *reduce* throughput.

- On interactive-only application systems, CPU utilization that stays to the right of the knee over long periods is bad. The goal of an interactive-only system user is *minimized response time*. When CPU utilization exceeds the knee in the response time curve, response time fluctuations become unbearable. By leaving idle capacity on the system, the system manager effectively purchases better response time stability.

- On systems with a mixture of batch and interactive workload, your job is much more difficult, because your users' performance goals are contradictory. On mixed-workload systems, it is important for you to *prioritize* your workloads. If interactive response time is more important, then you'll want to ensure that you don't drive CPU utilization too far to the right of the knee. If batch throughput is more important, then you'll not want to waste as much CPU capacity to provide response time stability to your less important users.

I discuss a method for determining the optimal mixture of batch and interactive workload in [Millsap (2000b)].

rate for alerts could be reduced by a factor of 120, from 30 alerts per hour to 0.25 alerts per hour.

- A system with eight CPUs becomes extremely slow for its online users from 2:00 p.m. to 3:00 p.m. A prominent workload element during this time period is a set of 16 reports (batch jobs), each of which consumes about 30 minutes of CPU time. The reports will not be read until 8:00 a.m. the next day. Thus, scheduling the 16 batch jobs to run at midnight instead of online business hours would reduce the arrival rate of CPU service requests by enough to conserve about eight CPU-hours of capacity during the 2:00 p.m. to 3:00 p.m. window.

- Accountants generate 14 aged trial balance reports each day to determine whether debits properly match credits in a set of books. Each 200-page report requires the execution of 72,000,000 Oracle logical read calls (LIOs), which consume about 30 minutes of CPU time. However, unbeknownst to the users, the application provides a web page that can tell them everything they need to know about out-of-balance accounts with fewer than 100 LIOs. Thus, the arrival rate of LIOs for this business requirement can be reduced from about one billion per day to about 1,400.

What is the fastest way to do something? Find a way to not do it at all. Many times, you can accomplish this goal with no functional compromise to the business.

r_{max}

It is possible that users will agree to compromise on their tolerance for spikes in response time, especially if a small compromise in response time tolerance might save their company a lot of money. However, users will quickly tire of attempts to convince them that they should be more tolerant of poor system performance. Unless it is absolutely necessary to find more breathing room, negotiating r_{max} is one of the last places you should seek relief.

p

As with negotiations about r_{max}, users are likely to find negotiations about p, the proportion of response times that must not exceed r_{max}, to be counterproductive and frustrating.

q

Although the number q of M/M/m queueing systems is technically a negotiable parameter, scaling an Oracle application system across more than one database server is, even with Oracle9i Real Application Clusters (RAC), still a technologically challenging endeavor that is almost certain to cost more than a configuration in which the database runs on only a single host.

m

The number m of parallel service channels in a system is negotiable, subject to physical constraints and scalability constraints that are imposed chiefly by the operating system. For example, a given system may require that CPUs be installed in multiples of two, up to 32 CPUs, but a 32-CPU system may be only as powerful as a theoretical system with 24 perfectly scalable CPUs. Benchmarks and discussions with vendor scientists can reveal these types of data.

μ

The service rate μ is a negotiable parameter that provides immense leverage to the performance analyst. Many analysts' first impulse for optimizing a system is to improve (increase) μ by providing faster hardware. For example, upgrading to 20% faster CPUs should produce a CPU service rate increase on the order of 20%, which can be enormously beneficial for CPU constrained applications.

However, what many analysts overlook is the even more important idea that service rate can be improved by reducing the amount of code path required to perform a given business function. In Oracle application systems, performance analysts can often achieve spectacular code path reduction by engaging in the task of *SQL optimization.* SQL optimization consists of manipulating some combination of schema definitions, database or instance statistics, configuration parameters, query optimizer behavior, or application source code to produce equivalent output with fewer instructions on the database server.

Code path reduction has several advantages over capacity upgrades, including:

Cost
> Capacity upgrades frequently motivate not only the procurement cost of the upgraded components, but also increased maintenance costs and software license fees. For example, some software licenses cost more for systems with $n + 1$ CPUs than they do for systems with n CPUs. Code path reduction for inefficient SQL statements generally requires no more than a few hours of labor per SQL statement.

Impact
> Code path reduction often provides far greater leverage to the performance analyst than capacity upgrades. For example, it may be possible to double CPU speeds only once every two years. It is frequently possible to reduce code path length by factors of 105 or more with just a few hours of labor.

Risk
> Code path reduction carries very little risk of unintended negative side effects that sometimes accompany a capacity upgrade. One possible side effect of a capacity upgrade is performance *degradation* of programs that were bottlenecked on a device other than one to which the upgrade was applied [Millsap (1999)].

Working even briefly with a queueing model reveals why eliminating unnecessary workload creates such spectacular system-wide performance leverage. The two ways to eliminate work are to eliminate business functions that do not legitimately add value to the business, and to eliminate unnecessary code path. These "two" endeavors are really a single waste-elimination task executed at different layers in the technology stack.

Using M/M/m: Worked Example

A worked example provides a good setting for exploring how to use the model and interpret its results. I encourage you to step through the problem that follows while using the M/M/*m* queueing theory model (a Microsoft Excel workbook) that is available at *http://www.hotsos.com.* The problem is a conceptually simple one, but its solution requires an understanding of queueing theory.

Here is the problem statement:

> An important SQL statement consumes 0.49 seconds of CPU service time to execute. We anticipate that each of 100 users will execute this statement at a rate of four times per minute during the system's peak load. The Linux server is equipped with boards that allow installation of up to 16 CPUs. How many CPUs will be required on this Linux server if our goal is to provide sub-second CPU response times in at least 95% of users' executions during peak load?

Let's go.

Suitability for modeling with M/M/m

The first thing you need to do is check whether the system under analysis is suitable for modeling with the M/M/m/∞/FCFS (or M/M/m for short) queueing model:

M/M/m/∞/FCFS *(exponential interarrival time)*
   If request interarrival times (the duration between arrivals) are operationally measurable, then your first step is to test whether the interarrival times are exponential by using the program shown in Example 9-4. If your interarrival times are not exponential, then consider modeling a smaller time window. For example, in Case I of the restaurant example I described earlier (reproduced here as Table 9-5), interarrival times are clearly *not* exponential when regarded over the observation period from 11:30 a.m. to 1:30 p.m. However, interarrival times are much more likely to be exponential over the period from 12:00 noon to 12:15 p.m.

Table 9-5. Two very different scenarios both lead to an expected interarrival time of
$\tau = 30$ seconds

	Number of arrivals	
Time interval	Case I	Case II
11:30 a.m. to 11:45 a.m.	0	34
11:45 a.m. to 12:00 noon	0	28
12:00 noon to 12:15 p.m.	240	31
12:15 p.m. to 12:30 p.m.	0	37
12:30 p.m. to 12:45 p.m.	0	24
12:45 p.m. to 1:00 p.m.	0	30
1:00 p.m. to 1:15 p.m.	0	32
1:15 p.m. to 1:30 p.m.	0	24
Average per 0:15 bucket	**30**	**30**

If request interarrival times are *not* operationally measurable (for example, because the system has not yet been designed), then you have to use your imagination. It is almost always possible to construct a time window in which you can confidently assume that interarrival times will be exponential (or, equivalently, that the rate of arrivals will be Poisson). Let's assume for this example that the arrivals can be confirmed operationally as being Poisson.

M/M/m/∞/FCFS *(exponential service time)*

Similarly, you must ensue that service times are exponentially distributed, using the program shown in Example 9-4 or by some other means. If your service times are not exponentially distributed, then consider redefining your service unit of measure. For example, if you define your service unit of measure as a *report*, but your reports range in service duration from 0.2 seconds to 1,392.7 seconds, the report service times are probably not exponential. Change your service unit of measure to a particular type of report whose service times have less fluctuation. Or reduce your unit of measure to a more "sub-atomic" level, by choosing a unit of measure like the Oracle LIO.

In this example, let's assume that we have confirmed by using operational measurements upon a test system that the "important SQL statement" produces service times that are exponentially distributed.

M/M/m/∞/FCFS *(m homogeneous, parallel, independent service channels)*

The problem statement specifies that our service channel of interest is the CPU on a computer running the Linux operating system. Because Linux is a fully symmetric multiprocessing (SMP) operating system, then we know our service channels to be homogenous, parallel, and independent. Some operating system configurations, such as those that use processor affinity, violate the CPU homogeneity constraint. As you shall soon see, we will also have to account for scalability imperfections when we use the model. We will end up using an M/M/m model to forecast the performance of a system with more than m CPUs.

M/M/m/∞/FCFS *(no queue length restriction)*

A Linux CPU run queue has no relevant depth constraints, so we're clear for takeoff on the "∞" attribute of the M/M/m definition.

M/M/m/∞/FCFS *(first-come, first-served queue discipline)*

The standard Linux process scheduling policy is *approximately* first-come, first-served. Even though the scheduling algorithm permits process prioritization and selection from different policies (FCFS and round-robin), the M/M/m model has proven suitable for predicting performance of Linux systems.

Computing the required number of CPUs

The problem statement specifies that our job is to determine the number of CPUs required to meet a particular performance goal. We can set up the problem in the input cells of the Excel M/M/m workbook as shown in Table 9-6. You will enter the values from the *Value* column into the yellow cells of the *Multiserver Model* worksheet of the *MMm.xls* workbook.

Table 9-6. Queueing model input parameters

Name	Value$_a$	Explanation
jobunit	stmt	The focal unit of work specified in the problem statement is "an important SQL statement."
timeunit	sec	Both the response time tolerance and the SQL statement's CPU service time are expressed in seconds.
queueunit	system	The problem specifies that we are searching for the number of CPUs that we will need to install in a single system.
serverunit	CPU	The server unit in the problem statement is the CPU.
λ	=100*4/60	"We anticipate that each of 100 users will execute this statement at a rate of four times per minute during the system's peak load."
r_{max}	1	The goal is to provide response times less than 1.0 second ("...provide sub-second CPU response times").
q	1	The problem statement specifies that we are to assess a single system.
m	1	The number of CPUs per system is the value that we are seeking. We can enter the value 1 into this cell, because we shall seek shortly for a suitable value.
μ	=1/0.49	"An important SQL statement consumes 0.49 seconds of CPU service time to execute." Therefore, the service rate is 1/0.49 statements per second.

Once we load these values into the workbook, we see that a configuration with only one CPU (*m* = 1) will definitely *not* handle the required workload (Figure 9-21).

The model predicts that if we equip our system with only one CPU, then keeping up with the 6.67 statements per second coming into the system would require an average CPU utilization of 326.7%. It is of course impossible to run CPU utilization to more than 100%. In reality, such a system would sit at 100% utilization forever. Arrivals would enter the system faster than it can process them, causing the system's queue length to grow continuously and without bound. However, this statistic does give us a clue that we would need to configure our system with at least four CPUs just to provide any chance of the system's keeping up with its workload.

The *MMm* workbook conveniently provides two columns (*value*$_a$ and *value*$_b$) that enable us to see the behavior of two systems side-by-side. If you try the model using *m* = 4, you'll see the results shown in Figure 9-22.

An ideal four-CPU system would produce an average response time of 0.908787 sec/stmt. However, we're still in trouble, because this configuration will provide sub-second response time in only 64.922% of executions of the statement. The original specification required sub-second response time in 95% of executions during peak load.

Let's see the theoretical best performance that could happen with the number of CPUs in the machine set to the maximum of *m* = 16, as shown in Figure 9-23. It turns out that this project is in big, big trouble. Even with the number of CPUs set to *m* = 16, it is impossible to create user satisfaction with a sub-second response time expectation in more than about 87% executions of the statement. You can try the

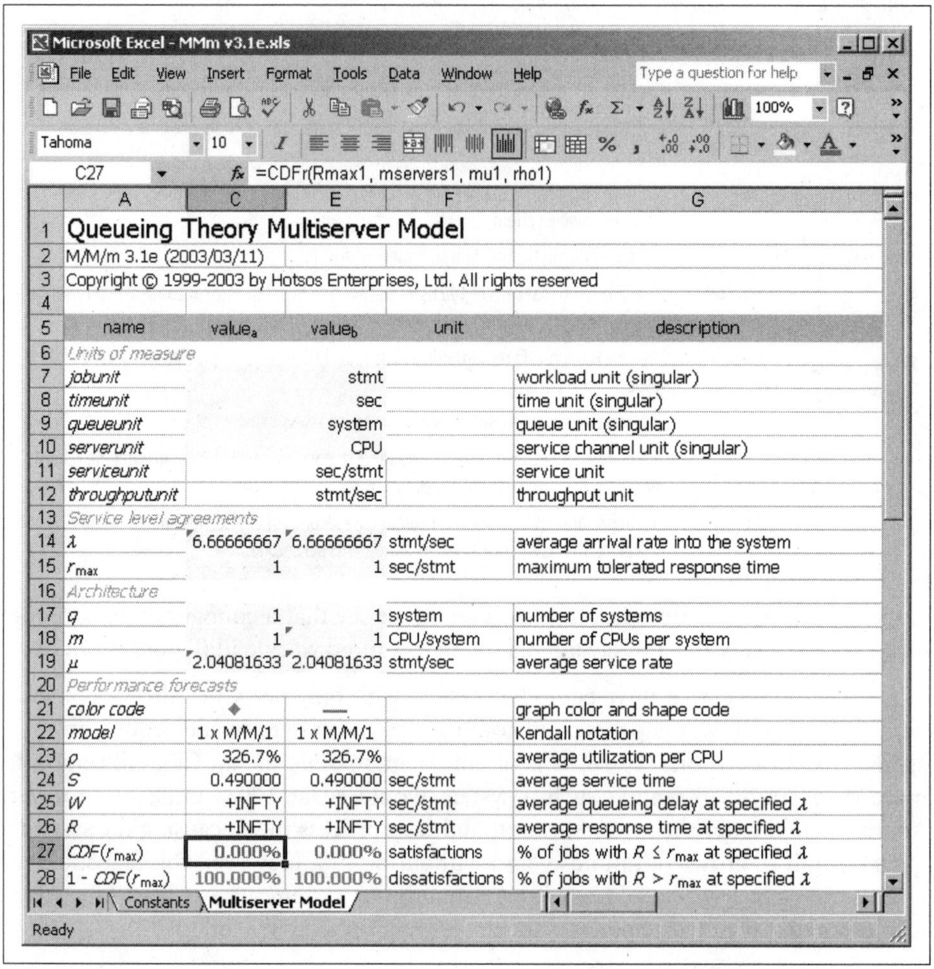

Figure 9-21. A one-CPU system will produce sub-second response times in zero percent of cases on a system with $\lambda = 6.667$ stmt/sec and $\mu = 2.041$ stmt/sec. Note that the high arrival rate and comparatively low service rate would drive CPU utilization to 326.7%, a value that is possible only in theory

model yourself: even if we could crank up the configuration to $m = 1000$, this system *still* wouldn't be able to provide satisfactory performance in more than about 87% of executions.

What we can learn from an optimistic model

Note that the M/M/m model will allow you to hypothesize the existence of systems that cannot exist in reality. You could, for example, model a perfectly scalable 1,000-CPU Linux system, or even a perfectly scalable 4-CPU Microsoft Windows NT system. No matter how preposterous the input values you enter, the queueing model

	A	C	E	F	G
1	**Queueing Theory Multiserver Model**				
2	M/M/m 3.1e (2003/03/11)				
3	Copyright © 1999-2003 by Hotsos Enterprises, Ltd. All rights reserved				
4					
5	name	value$_a$	value$_b$	unit	description
6	*Units of measure*				
7	*jobunit*		stmt		workload unit (singular)
8	*timeunit*		sec		time unit (singular)
9	*queueunit*		system		queue unit (singular)
10	*serverunit*		CPU		service channel unit (singular)
11	*serviceunit*		sec/stmt		service unit
12	*throughputunit*		stmt/sec		throughput unit
13	*Service level agreements*				
14	λ	6.66666667	6.66666667	stmt/sec	average arrival rate into the system
15	r_{max}	1	1	sec/stmt	maximum tolerated response time
16	*Architecture*				
17	q	1	1	system	number of systems
18	m	1	4	CPU/system	number of CPUs per system
19	μ	2.04081633	2.04081633	stmt/sec	average service rate
20	*Performance forecasts*				
21	*color code*	◆	—		graph color and shape code
22	*model*	1 x M/M/1	1 x M/M/4		Kendall notation
23	ρ	326.7%	81.7%		average utilization per CPU
24	S	0.490000	0.490000	sec/stmt	average service time
25	W	+INFTY	0.418787	sec/stmt	average queueing delay at specified λ
26	R	+INFTY	0.908787	sec/stmt	average response time at specified λ
27	$CDF(r_{max})$	0.000%	64.922%	satisfactions	% of jobs with $R \leq r_{max}$ at specified λ
28	$1 - CDF(r_{max})$	100.000%	35.078%	dissatisfactions	% of jobs with $R > r_{max}$ at specified λ

```
I◄ ◄ ► ►I \ Constants \ Multiserver Model /        | ◄ |        ► |
Ready
```

Figure 9-22. *Using four perfectly scalable CPUs would cause the system to meet the performance target in 64.9% of cases*

will faithfully report to you how a perfectly scalable hypothetical system of this configuration would perform. In fact, the model doesn't actually even know whether you are modeling computer systems, grocery stores, or toll booths. It is up to you to decide whether the system you're hypothesizing is feasible to construct. The M/M/*m* queueing theory model, used like we have described here, is *optimistic* because it omits any understanding of real-life barriers to scalability other than the effects of queueing.

The upshot of this understanding is significant. If this queueing theory model tells you that something *can* be done, then it's possible that you still might *not* be able to do that thing. You can, after all, tell the model that you can cram 1,000 CPUs into a Linux box, and that all this capacity will operate full-strength, no problem. However,

File   Edit   View   Insert   Format   Tools   Data   Window   Help   Type a question for help

Tahoma   10

E27 f_x =CDFr(Rmax2, mservers2, mu2, rho2)

Queueing Theory Multiserver Model

M/M/m 3.1e (2003/03/11)

Copyright © 1999-2003 by Hotsos Enterprises, Ltd. All rights reserved

name	value$_a$	value$_b$	unit	description
Units of measure				
jobunit			stmt	workload unit (singular)
timeunit			sec	time unit (singular)
queueunit			system	queue unit (singular)
serverunit			CPU	service channel unit (singular)
serviceunit			sec/stmt	service unit
throughputunit			stmt/sec	throughput unit
Service level agreements				
λ	6.66666667	6.66666667	stmt/sec	average arrival rate into the system
r_{max}	1	1	sec/stmt	maximum tolerated response time
Architecture				
q	1	1	system	number of systems
m	4	16	CPU/system	number of CPUs per system
μ	2.04081633	2.04081633	stmt/sec	average service rate
Performance forecasts				
color code	◆	—		graph color and shape code
model	1 x M/M/4	1 x M/M/16		Kendall notation
ρ	81.7%	20.4%		average utilization per CPU
S	0.490000	0.490000	sec/stmt	average service time
W	0.418787	0.000000	sec/stmt	average queueing delay at specified λ
R	0.908787	0.490000	sec/stmt	average response time at specified λ
$CDF(r_{max})$	64.922%	87.008%	satisfactions	% of jobs with $R \leq r_{max}$ at specified λ
$1 - CDF(r_{max})$	35.078%	12.992%	dissatisfactions	% of jobs with $R > r_{max}$ at specified λ

Constants \ **Multiserver Model**

Ready

Figure 9-23. Even with sixteen perfectly scalable CPUs, this system can meet the performance target in only 87% of cases

if this queueing theory model tells you that something *cannot* be done, you can take that advice all the way to the bank. If an optimistic model advises you that something is impossible, then it *is* impossible.

The M/M/*m* model implemented in my Excel workbook is *optimistic* because it omits any understanding of real-life barrier to scalability other than the effects of queueing. Consequently, for the model to advise you that something *can* be done does *not* constitute a proof that your project will succeed. However, for the model to advise you that something *cannot* be done *is* sufficient evidence that you cannot do it, as long as your input assumptions are valid.

Our model has told us that no matter how many CPUs we might add to our hypothetical configuration, we will never be able to meet the performance criterion that 95% of statement executions must finish in sub-second time. This might sound like bad news for the project, but it's immensely better to find out such an unpleasant truth using an inexpensive queueing model than to watch a project fail in spite of vast investments in attempt to make it succeed.

Negotiating the negotiable parameters

So, confronted with news that our project is doomed, what can we do? One more hidden beauty of queueing theory is that it reveals exactly which system manipulations (modeled as M/M/m parameter changes) might make a positive performance impact. I listed the negotiable parameters for you earlier in the "Parameter sensitivity" section. An analysis of those negotiable parameters for this example should include:

Number of systems q, and number of CPUs per system m

First, we can investigate a curious output of the model to understand why adding CPUs doesn't seem to increase the response time CDF beyond about 87%. The model shows that even a hundred systems with a hundred CPUs each will not produce satisfactory response times for the statement more than about 87% of the time.

The reason is that the service time in an M/M/m model is a random variable. Although the *average* service time is a constant, actual service times for a given type of function fluctuate from one function to the next. For example, two identical SQL queries with differing bind values in a where clause predicate might motivate slightly different LIO counts, which will motivate different CPU service times. By increasing the number of CPUs on a system, we reduce only the average queueing delay (W) component of response time ($R = S + W$). If the average service time alone is sufficiently near the response time tolerance, then random fluctuations in service times will be enough to cause response time to exceed the specified tolerance for a potentially significant proportion of total executions.

There is virtually no benefit to be gained by using more than about six CPUs for this problem's important SQL statement.

Average arrival rate λ

Does the business really *need* 100 users each running the important statement four times a minute? It is a legitimate question. In many situations, the best system optimization step to perform first is to realize that the users are asking the machine to do more work than the users could even use. For example, polling a manufacturing process and generating a user alert up to four times a minute is senseless if the user is getting his job done perfectly well by reviewing alerts only once an hour.

If the average arrival rate at peak load in our problem could be reduced similarly, from:

$$\lambda = 100\frac{4}{60} \approx 6.666667$$

statements per second to:

$$\lambda = 100\frac{1}{60 \times 60} \approx 0.027778$$

statements per second, it would reduce the workload generated by this statement by a factor of 240. The result would be a significant scalability benefit. The system would require only one CPU to produce satisfactory response times for 87% of the statement's executions.

Because the arrival rate $\lambda = A/T$ is a ratio, there are *two* ways that you can reduce its value. One way is to reduce the numerator A, the number of arrivals into the system, as I've suggested already. Another way is to increase the denominator T, the time period in which the system is required to absorb the specified number of arrivals.

Reducing the average arrival rate can enable us to use a less expensive system, but we would still have some work to do. None of the changes described so far will increase the proportion of satisfactory experiences with the important statement to 95%.

Response time tolerance r_{max}, and success percentile p

Does the business really need for the important statement to deliver response times less than one second? Does the success percentile really need to be 95%? Beware asking these questions out loud, because these particular inquiries breed suspicion. Users often consider these questions to be non-negotiable, but it is important to understand that making these questions non-negotiable imposes some cost constraints upon your system that your business might consider non-negotiable. For example, enduring 100 additional seconds of response time delay per day to save $100,000 per year is probably a good trade-off. If the business in this problem can afford to relax its 95th percentile response time tolerance to $r_{max} = 1.5$ seconds, then you could deliver the required performance for the originally stated arrival rate ($\lambda \approx 6.666667$ stmt/sec) with six CPUs. If we could also negotiate the arrival rate reduction mentioned previously, to $\lambda \approx 0.027778$ statements per second, then you would need only one CPU.

Average service rate μ

Here is where you can achieve the most extraordinary possible performance leverage without requiring the users to compromise their functional or performance constraints. You've probably heard that SQL tuning offers high payoffs, but it would be nice to know how high before you embark upon a SQL tuning expedition. The model can tell you the answer.

If you could, for example, improve the service time of the important statement from 0.49 seconds to 0.3125 seconds, you would improve the service rate for the statement from $\mu = 2.04$ stmt/sec to $\mu = 3.2$ stmt/sec. If you could improve your service rate just this much, then you could meet the original $r_{max} = 1.0$ requirement in 95% of statement executions, with just four CPUs. If you could improve average service rate to $\mu = 10$ statements per second (for example, by optimizing SQL to reduce average service time to 0.1 seconds), then you could meet the original performance requirements with just *one* CPU.

I believe that the greatest value of the M/M/*m* queueing model is that it stimulates you to ask the right questions. In this example, you've learned that it is futile to even *think* about using more than six CPUs' worth of capacity to run the important statement. You have learned that by negotiating a more liberal r_{max} value with your users, you can gain a little bit of headspace. But until you can reduce either the rate at which people run the important statement (λ), or reduce the service time of the statement ($S = 1/\mu$), you're going to be stuck with a system that at best barely meets its performance target.

Using Goal Seek in Microsoft Excel

Microsoft Excel provides a *Goal Seek* tool that makes it simple to answer many of the questions we've discussed in this section. It allows you to treat any model output value as an input parameters. For example, assume that you want to determine what average service rate would be required to drive response time satisfactions into the 95th percentile for a fixed value of *m*.

You can set up the problem this way. First, enter an arbitrary constant value for μ. In Figure 9-24, I have entered the value 1. Next, select the *Tools → Goal Seek* menu option to activate the goal seek dialog, as shown in Figure 9-25. The goal is to set $CDF(r_{max})$ to the value 95% by changing μ. After accepting the result of the goal seek operation, Figure 9-26 shows that using the value $\mu \approx 10$ produces the desired result.

Sensitivity analysis

The quality of your response time predictions will vary in proportion to the quality of the feedback loop that you use to refine your forecasts. Lots of people get the key numbers right when I present them with a queueing model and ask them to solve a carefully prepared story problem. But you need to resist the temptation to stop thinking, which begins when your model "produces the answer." When the answer comes out, you need to devote a bit more time to the very important task of sensitivity analysis that 99% of people trying models for the first time will habitually fail to do. The remainder of this section illustrates some key points of error analysis for my continuing example.

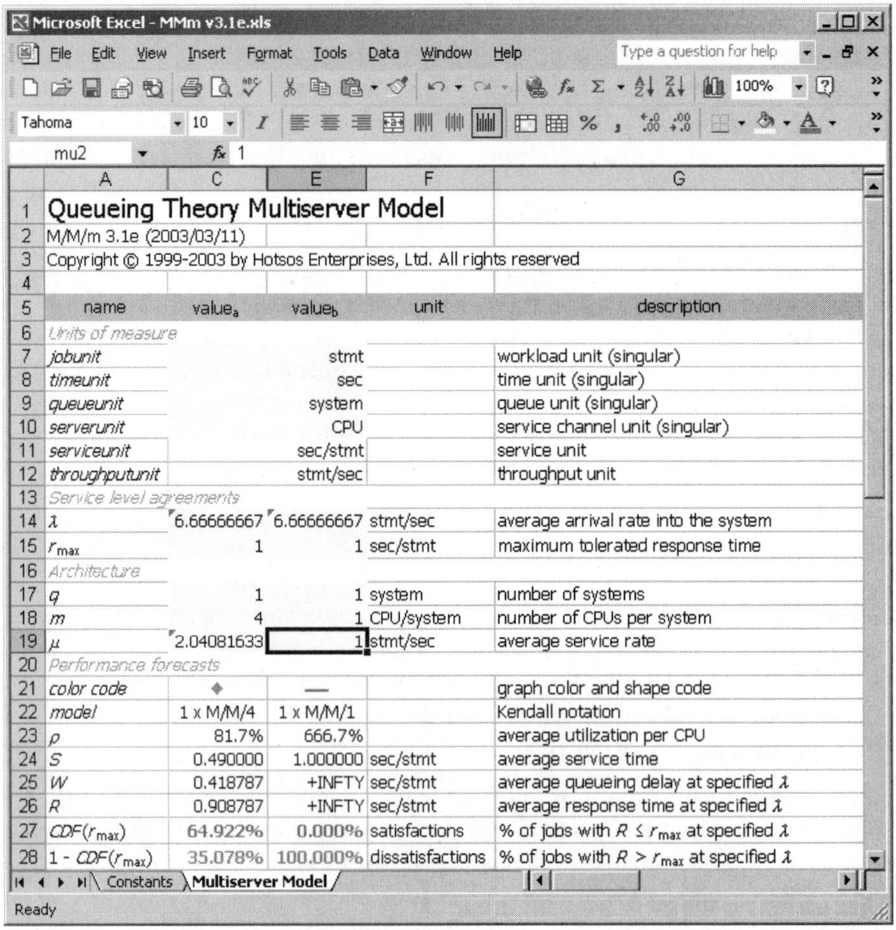

Figure 9-24. To find what μ value we need to drive CDF(r_{max}) $\geq$ 95%, we first enter an arbitrary constant value for μ

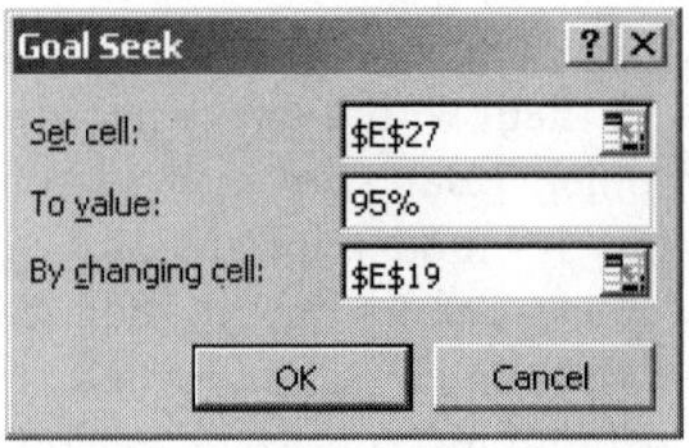

Figure 9-25. Our goal is to set CDF(r_{max}) to the value 95% by changing μ

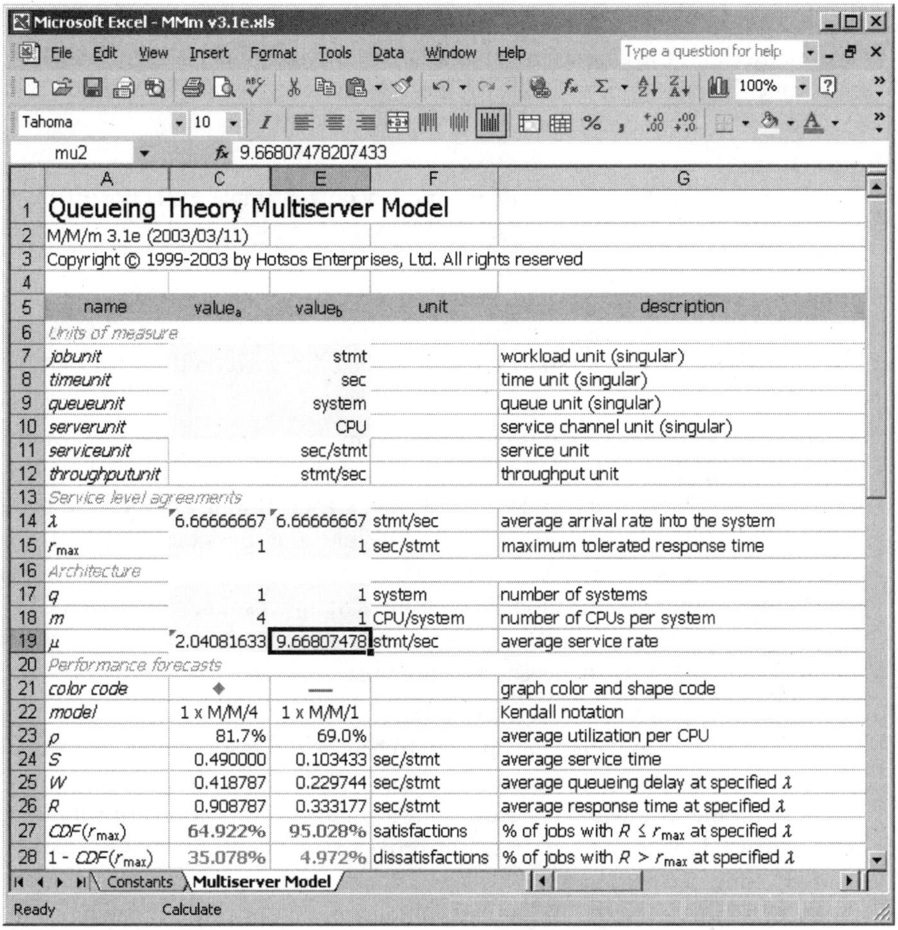

Figure 9-26. After accepting the goal seek solution, our worksheet shows that the value $\mu \approx 10$ produces the desired CDF(r_{max}) value

In addition to the model's output, you must consider several other factors:

Physical constraints

Of course, it is not possible to install part of a CPU. The number of CPUs you install in a system must be a whole number. Some systems may require a whole number of *pairs* of CPUs. Physical constraints of course also restrict the maximum number of CPUs that can be installed in a system.

Scalability imperfections

The queueing model knows nothing about scalability imperfections that might prevent a system with *m* CPUs from delivering the full *m* CPUs' worth of processing capacity. For example, to get six full CPUs' worth of processing from a Linux server, we might need to install eight or more CPUs. Using the Microsoft

Windows NT operating system, it might be impossible to configure a system that provides more than two full CPUs' worth of processing capacity, no matter how many CPUs the chassis might accept. It is up to the performance analyst to determine the impact of scalability imperfections that prevent a real m-CPU system from actually delivering m CPU's worth of system capacity.

Other workload

Although the problem statement mentioned only a single SQL statement, the system will almost certainly require the execution of several other workload components. Thus, the way to interpret this model's output for this particular problem statement is to conclude that, "The processing capacity required to support the response time requirements of this SQL statement is about 5 more than the number of CPUs required to support all the other load on the system."

Other bottlenecks

The problem statement focuses our attention exclusively upon the *CPU capacity* required to fulfill our response time expectations. But what about other potential bottlenecks? What if our SQL statement's total response time is impacted materially by disk or network latencies? While it is possible to model every resource that participates in a given function, minimizing the complexity of the model often maximizes the model's usefulness. If any resource other than CPU is expected to consume the bulk of a function's response time, then it is reasonable to inquire whether the reason is legitimate.

Changes in input parameters

In school, students are often encouraged to believe the assumptions set forth in a neatly packaged problem statement. Successful professionals quickly learn that errors in problem statements account for significant proportions of subsequent project flaws. How can we protect our project from the untrustworthy assumptions documented in the project plan? By assessing the impact of assumption variances upon our model. What is the impact upon our result if one or more of the assumptions laid out in the problem statement is inaccurate or is simply bound to evolve over time?

Overall system performance is very sensitive to even very small variances in average service rate (μ) and average arrival rate (λ). The model reflects this. The very property that endows these parameters with such leverage upon overall performance makes the model highly susceptible to errors in estimating them. For example, overestimating a function's average service rate by just 1% can result in a 10% or worse underestimate in a loaded system's average response times. Factors that are likely to cause variances in μ or λ include:

- Invalid testing. Classic examples include tests presumably designed to emulate production database behavior, but which are conducted using unrealistically simple product setups or unrealistically miniscule table sizes.

- Changes in data volume, especially for SQL queries whose performance scales linearly (or worse) to the sizes of the segments being queried [Millsap (2001a)].

- Changes in physical data distribution that might make an index become more or less useful (or attractive to the Oracle query optimizer) over time [Millsap (2002)].

- Changes to function code path, such as SQL changes or schema changes motivated by upgrades, performance improvement projects, and so on.

- Changes in business function volume motivated by acquisitions or mergers, unanticipated successes or failures in marketing projects, and so on.

If uncontrolled variances in sensitive input parameters are likely, then you should take special care to ensure that the system configuration you choose will permit inexpensive capacity upgrades (or downgrades). With knowledge of input parameter sensitivity, you will know which input parameters to manage the most carefully.

Perspective

Performance modeling is a complicated subject. I hope that this chapter helps you understand the technology. But even more importantly, I hope that you can more understand the constraints of performance. I've met many performance analysts that pitted themselves in a losing battle against immutable laws of nature. I have constructed this chapter to help prevent you from falling into the same traps. For a reasonably complete final perspective on the chapter, I offer you the following points:

- Trial-and-error is an inherently inefficient, expensive, and unreliable performance optimization method. When a system meets the constraints required for using a mathematical model, it is much more efficient to base performance optimization decisions upon the model.

- Response time is virtually the only performance metric that end users care about. To the user, response time is the duration between the issuance of a request and the return of the first byte fulfilling that request. To the queueing theorist, response time equals service time plus queueing delay. We can reduce response time either by reducing service time, or by reducing queueing delay.

- On busy systems, response time degrades because of queueing. You can reduce queueing either by reducing workload, or by reducing service times. Performance analysts often forget that workload reduction is often a legitimate business option. A mathematical queueing model helps the analyst understand the economic tradeoffs required to meet both the functional and performance goals of a business.

- The M/M/m queueing model is a well-researched, well-tested model for predicting performance of systems whose interarrival times and service rates are exponentially distributed. Many Oracle systems meet these criteria. This chapter provides a full Microsoft Excel implementation of M/M/m, a Perl program to test whether a sample appears to be taken from an exponential distribution, and detailed instructions for using the model in an Oracle project.

- One of the most important virtues of using a queueing model is that it structures our thinking about response time. It reveals the concrete mathematical relationship among the parameters of workload, service rate, and expectations. Furthermore, it highlights the notion that the way to optimize the *business value* of a system is to consider *all* of these parameters to be negotiable.

- Our worked example showed a common business case: a scenario in which even though CPU is the system's bottleneck, adding CPU capacity doesn't help the analyst meet the system's performance requirements. The model in this example reveals what it often reveals in reality: that the most economically efficient way to improve the performance of a system is to eliminate unnecessary workload. The two principal ways to eliminate unnecessary workload are to avoid unnecessary business functions, and to reduce application code path lengths.

- The M/M/m queueing model ignores a number of factors that the performance analyst must take into consideration. For example, the model assumes perfect scalability across all m service channels. The model is in several ways optimistic. An optimistic model that forecasts poor system performance is a *proof* that the modeled configuration will suffer poor performance in reality. However, an optimistic model that produces a positive verdict does not prove that the modeled configuration will perform well in reality; some un-modeled scalability barrier can still ruin the performance of your project.

Exercises

1. Use the M/M/m queueing model to verify all of the results of our worked example.

2. The designers of the new international terminal at the Millsap International Airport (MQP) in Millsap, Texas have solicited your help in optimizing customer response time. Each new state-of-the-art ticket counter will host six ticket agents. The airport designers need your help determining whether they should set up one long snaking queue to feed customers to all six ticket agents (an M/M/6 configuration), or six shorter straight queues that each feeds one agent (a configuration of six independent M/M/1 systems). Use the M/M/m queueing model to determine which configuration would provide faster customer response times.

3. A customer has a choice between purchasing two different types of computers. Model H has one CPU that's capable of executing 40,000 Oracle logical reads (LIOs) per second. Model L has four CPUs arranged in a symmetric multiprocessing (SMP) organization, but each CPU is capable of executing only 15,000 Oracle LIOs per second. Which computer should the customer buy?

4. Write a program to retrieve interarrival times from your batch queue manager. Are the numbers exponentially distributed? Can you find exponentially distributed subsets of your data by restricting the programs for which you collect interarrival times? Can you find exponentially distributed subsets of your data by restricting the times of the day for which you collect interarrival times?

5. Does your batch queue manager allow you to measure true service times for your jobs? For example, for a given job, can you determine how much CPU time the job has consumed? If it is possible, write a program to retrieve service times from your batch queue manager. Are the numbers exponentially distributed? Can you find subsets of the data that are exponentially distributed? If your batch queue manager does not reveal true service times, how might you go about collecting them?

6. An investments brokerage firm has purchased an Oracle Server license and plans to design and build a custom application to manipulate investment trade transactions. No code has yet been written, but the business requirements dictate that an end-user receive a query result or transaction confirmation within three seconds of pressing a key to execute the action. The firm expects to process 30,000 transactions per continental USA business day, with a peak processing rate of 650 transactions in a five-minute period. A business day in the continental USA spans from 8:00 a.m. Eastern time through 5:00 p.m. Pacific time (8:00 a.m. Pacific time is 11:00 a.m. Eastern time). There are an estimated 2,000 brokers who will have online access to the new system.

All users are connected to the database server via a complicated system involving LAN links, terminal servers, and a transaction processing monitor. After deducting time for client-side presentation management, network response time, and TP-monitor processing, the system designers estimate that out of the three-second response time tolerance, the time left over for Oracle Server operations for each transaction is about a second and a half, as shown in Table 9-7.

Table 9-7. Response time requirement for an investments brokerage firm

Max. allowable response time (sec)	Execution phase
1.500	Oracle Server response time
	Parse, bind, execute, fetch, etc.
1.500	Total non-Oracle response time
	Client-side presentation management
	Network response time
	Transaction processing monitor
3.000	Total response time

7. The client needs advice about hardware and application architecture. Specify a hardware architecture and a corresponding transaction performance target that will guide the design and development of application SQL that will meet this brokerage firm's performance requirements.

8. Use M/M/m to model response times of an important business function in your system. Manipulate the model parameters until the model reliably forecasts measurable present-day performance behavior. For example, if you have a 10-CPU system with over 100 distinct business functions, experiment with the model as if you had only a part of one CPU dedicated to a single specific business function. What happens when you double the arrival rate of that function? What if you could improve the service rate for that function by a factor of 10%? What would happen to the performance of that function if you could double the amount of CPU capacity you could dedicate to it? Aside from hardware upgrades, what are some ways that you can increase the amount of CPU that could be dedicated to a given business function?

## PART III

Deployment

## CHAPTER 10

Working the Resource Profile

As I illustrate in Chapter 1, response time optimization is a routine part of humans' everyday lives. The foundation of response time optimization is the commonsense notion, formalized by Gene Amdahl, that improving the largest component of response time creates the greatest opportunity for response time improvement.

Recall the resource profile format, also introduced in Chapter 1, which is shown again in Example 10-1. Response time optimization is so "built into us" that most people—including users and business managers with no performance analysis training—can understand a resource profile with very little effort. Technical and non-technical audiences alike never fail to respond correctly to Example 10-1 within ten seconds of seeing the data:

> I don't know what those two "SQL*Net" things are, but whatever they are, they're consuming nearly three quarters of the report's total duration. What causes SQL*Net message from client and SQL*Net more data from client?

This is exactly the right way to attack the problem. Business managers and users to whom I show this example are routinely confused about how professional performance analysts could have gone for three months believing that latch contention and CPU capacity were the root causes of this performance problem. (Example 10-1 is the same Oracle Payroll performance problem that I describe in Chapter 1.) Of course the answer is that the performance analysts on this project spent three months looking at the wrong diagnostic data.

Example 10-1. Technical and non-technical audiences alike make sense quickly of the resource profile format

Response Time Component	Duration		# Calls	Dur/Call
SQL*Net message from client	984.0s	49.6%	95,161	0.010340s
SQL*Net more data from client	418.8s	21.1%	3,345	0.125208s
db file sequential read	279.3s	14.1%	45,084	0.006196s
CPU service	248.7s	12.5%	222,760	0.001116s
unaccounted-for	27.9s	1.4%		
latch free	23.7s	1.2%	34,695	0.000683s

```
log file sync                    1.1s   0.1%        506    0.002154s
SQL*Net more data to client      0.8s   0.0%     15,982    0.000052s
log file switch completion       0.3s   0.0%          3    0.093333s
enqueue                          0.3s   0.0%        106    0.002358s
SQL*Net message to client        0.2s   0.0%     95,161    0.000003s
buffer busy waits                0.2s   0.0%         67    0.003284s
db file scattered read           0.0s   0.0%          2    0.005000s
SQL*Net break/reset to client    0.0s   0.0%          2    0.000000s
----------------------------   --------------   -----------  -----------
Total                         1,985.4s 100.0%
```

My favorite performance improvement epigraph comes from, of all places, an instructional book about golf [Pelz (2000) 215]:

> There's nothing worse than working hard on the wrong thing, expecting improvement from it, then ending up with nothing.

Resource profiles are superb at telling you *what* you need to fix whether you know *how* to fix it or not. They help you avoid the common Oracle tuning pitfall of fixing the thing you know how to fix without regard to whether your work will make any difference.

How to Work a Resource Profile

Although most people seem to innately understand the resource profile format, some formal guidelines usually help people make the most efficient use of the information. After analyzing several hundred resource profiles since the year 2000, my colleagues and I have refined our approach into the following guiding principles:

- Work the resource profile in descending order of response time contribution.
- Eliminate unnecessary calls before attempting to reduce per-call latency.
- If a response time component is still prominent after you have eliminated unnecessary calls to the resource, then eliminate unnecessary competition for the resource.
- Only after eliminating unnecessary calls to a resource and eliminating unnecessary competition for the resource should you consider increasing the capacity of the resource.

These guidelines have consistently helped us to produce effective optimizations quickly. The following sections describe the guidelines in detail.

Work in Descending Response Time Order

It is easy to work with a resource profile that is sorted in descending order of response time contribution. You simply use the data in top-down order. The top-line response time consumer is the resource that provides the greatest performance improvement leverage. Remember Amdahl's Law: the lower an item appears in the profile, the less opportunity that item provides for overall response time improvement.

Example 10-2 shows a resource profile that was created for a targeted user action on a system with "an obvious disk I/O problem." The I/O subsystem was occasionally providing single-block I/O latencies in excess of 0.600 seconds. Most technicians would deem single-block I/O latencies greater than 0.010 seconds to be unacceptable. The ones produced by this system were fully *sixty times worse* than this threshold.

Example 10-2. A resource profile created for a targeted user action on a system with a known disk I/O performance problem

Response Time Component	Duration		# Calls	Dur/Call
CPU service	37.7s	68.9%	214	0.175981s
unaccounted-for	8.4s	15.4%		
db file sequential read	5.5s	10.1%	568	0.009630s
db file scattered read	2.1s	3.8%	89	0.024157s
latch free	0.9s	1.6%	81	0.011605s
log file sync	0.1s	0.2%	3	0.026667s
SQL*Net more data to client	0.0s	0.0%	4	0.002500s
file open	0.0s	0.0%	12	0.001667s
SQL*Net message to client	0.0s	0.0%	58	0.000000s
Total	54.7s	100.0%		

However, the resource profile for this targeted user action indicates strongly that addressing the disk I/O problem is not the first thing you should do to improve response time for the action. The only response time components that better I/O performance will impact are the db file sequential read and db file scattered read line items. Even if you could totally *eliminate* both these lines from the resource profile, response time would improve by only about 14%.

 Ironically the I/O subsystem "problem" *did* impact the performance of the program profiled in Example 10-2. Evidence in the raw trace data revealed that some single-block I/O calls issued by this user action consumed as much as 0.620 seconds apiece. But even this knowledge is irrelevant. For this user action, the upside of fixing any I/O subsystem problem is so severely limited that your analysis and repair time will be better spent somewhere else.

Why targeting is vital

Now is a good time to test your commitment to Method R. You might ask, "But fixing such a horrible I/O problem would surely provide *some* benefit to system performance...." The answer is that yes, fixing the I/O problem will in fact provide *some* benefit to system performance. But it is *vital* for you to understand that fixing the I/O problem will not materially benefit *this* user action (the one corresponding to the resource profile in Example 5-2, and that the business was desperate to improve). Understanding this is vital for two reasons:

- Any time or materials that you might invest into fixing the "I/O problem" will be resources that you cannot invest into making material performance improvements to the user action profiled in Example 10-2. If you have correctly targeted the user action, then working on an I/O problem will be at best an unproductive distraction.

- Fixing the I/O problem can actually *degrade* the performance of the user action profiled in Example 10-2. This is not just a theoretical possibility; we see this type of phenomenon in the field (see Chapter 12). Here's one way it can happen: imagine that at the same time as the user action profiled in Example 10-2 runs, several other programs are running on the system as well. Further imagine that these programs consume a lot of CPU capacity, but they presently spend a lot of time queued for service from the slow disk. To remove the disk queueing delay for these slow processes will actually intensify competition for the CPU capacity consumption that presently dominates our targeted user action's response time. In this case, fixing the I/O problem will actually degrade the performance of the targeted user action.

Yes, fixing the I/O problem will provide some performance benefit to those other programs. But if you have properly targeted the user action of Example 10-2 for performance improvement, then fixing the I/O problem will degrade performance in an important action in trade for improving the performance of user actions that are less important. This result is contrary to the priorities of the business.

For both reasons, *if* you have properly targeted the user action depicted in Example 10-2, then working on the "I/O problem" is a mistake. If the user action is not a proper target for performance improvement, then you have not correctly done the job that I described in Chapter 2.

Possible benefits of low-return improvements

Having said this, it is possible that the most economically advantageous first response to a resource profile is to address an issue that is not the top-line issue. For example, imagine that the I/O subsystem problem of Example 10-2 could be "repaired" simply by deactivating a particular long-running, disk-I/O intensive report that runs every day during the targeted user action's execution. Imagine that the fix is to simply eliminate the report from the system's workload, because you discover that absolutely nobody in the business ever reads it. Then the problem's repair—simply turning off the report—is so inexpensive that you'd be crazy not to implement it.

Mathematically, the return on investment (ROI) of some repair activities can be extremely high because even though the return R is small, the investment I is so small that R/I is large. It happens sometimes. However, realize that high ROI is not your only targeted goal. My finance professor, Michel Vetsuypens, once illustrated this concept by tossing a five-cent coin to a student in our classroom. The student who kept the nickel enjoyed a nearly infinite ROI for the experience—it cost virtually nothing to catch the coin, and the return was five cents. Although it was probably the highest-ROI event in the student's whole life, of course adding five cents to his net worth produced an overall impact that was completely inconsequential. This story illustrates why it is so important that your performance improvement goal include the notions of *net profit* and *cash flow* in addition to ROI, as I describe in Chapter 2.

This story also illustrates the fundamental flaw of ratios: they conceal information about magnitude.

Eliminate Unnecessary Calls

A well-worn joke in our Hotsos Clinic classrooms is this one:

Question: What's the fastest way to do *x*? (In our classes, *x* can be virtually anything from executing database calls to flying from one city to another, to going to the bathroom.)

Answer: Don't.

The fastest way to do *anything* is to avoid doing it at all. (This axiom should hold until someone invents a convenient means of human-scale time travel. Until we can figure out how to make task durations negative, the best we're going to be able to do is make them zero.)

The most economically efficient way to improve a system's performance is usually to eliminate workload waste. *Waste* is any workload that can be eliminated from a system with no loss of functional value to its owner. Analysts who are new to Method R are often shocked to find the following maxim alive and well within their systems:

> Many systems' workloads consist of more than 50% waste.

It's been true for almost every system I've measured since 1989, and chances are that it's true for your system as well. It's true for good reason: throughout the 1980s and 1990s, when many Oracle performance analysts were trained, we were actually taught principals that encouraged waste. For example, the once-popular belief that higher database buffer cache hit ratios are better encourages many application inefficiencies. Several sources illustrate this fallacy, including [Millsap (2001b; 2001c); Lewis (2001a); Vaidyanatha et al. (2001); McDonald (2000)].

Why workload elimination works so well

Eliminating unnecessary work has an obvious first-order impact upon the performance of the job formerly doing the work. However, many people fail to understand the fabulous collateral benefit of workload elimination. Every time you eliminate unnecessary requests for a resource, it reduces the probability that other users of that resource will have to queue for it. It's easy to appreciate the second-order benefits of workload reduction. Imagine, for example, a program that consumes CPU capacity pretty much non-stop for about 14 hours (the resource profile in Example 1-4 shows such a program). Further imagine that the program's performance could be repaired so that it would consume only ten minutes of CPU capacity. (Such repairs usually involve manipulation of a critical SQL statement's query execution plan.)

It's easy to see why the user of the report that now takes ten minutes instead of fourteen hours will be delighted. However, imagine also the benefits that the other users on the system will enjoy. Before the repair, users who were competing for CPU service had to fight for capacity against a process that consumed a whole CPU for *more than half of a day*. In the post-repair scenario, the report competes for CPU only for ten minutes. The probability of queueing behind the report for CPU service drops to a mere sliver of its original value. For the 14-hour period, the benefit to the system will approximate the effect of installing another CPU into the system.

 The benefit of reducing workload in this case will actually be *more* than the benefit of adding a new CPU because adding a new chip would have incrementally increased the operating system overhead required to schedule the additional capacity. Plus, reducing workload in fact cost less than actually installing another CPU would have.

The collateral benefits of workload reduction can be stunning. Chapter 9 explains the mathematics of why.

Supply and demand in the technology stack

So how does one eliminate unnecessary workload? The answer varies by level in the technology stack. I introduced the concept of a system's *technology stack* in Chapter 1 when I described the sequence diagram notation of depicting response time for a user action. The technology stack consists of layers that interact with each other through a supply-and-demand relationship, as shown in Figure 10-1. The relationship is simple. Demand goes in; supply comes out; and everything takes time (hence, the demand and supply arrows are tilted downward).

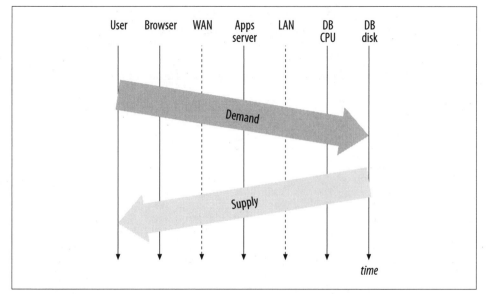

Figure 10-1. *This sequence diagram illustrates the supply and demand relationships among technology stack layers as time moves forward (downward on the page)*

Considering your technology stack in this way will help you to understand a fundamental axiom of performance improvement:

> Almost every performance problem is caused by *excessive demand* for one or more resources.

Virtually any performance problem can be solved by reducing demand for some resource. You will accomplish the task of demand reduction by looking "upward" from a high-demand device in the technology stack. (To look *upward* in the stack actually means to look *leftward* in the sequence diagram shown in Figure 10-1.) The question that will guide your performance improvement effort is this:

> Is the apparent requirement to use so much of this resource actually a *legitimate* requirement?

Consider the resource profile shown in Example 10-3. Almost 97% of the targeted user action's 1.3-hour response time was consumed waiting for disk I/O calls. The resource profile suggests two possible solutions:

- Reduce the number of calls to some number smaller than 12,165.
- Reduce the duration per call from 0.374109 seconds.

Notice that any improvement to either of these two numbers will translate linearly into the duration for the response time component. For example, if you can cut the number of calls in half, you will cut the duration in half. Similarly, if you can cut the per-call duration in half, you will cut the duration in half. Although reductions in call count and duration per call translate with equal potency to the duration column, it is generally much easier to achieve spectacular call count reductions than to achieve spectacular per-call latency reductions. I specifically chose the left-to-right column order of the resource profiles shown in this book to encourage you to see the better solution first.

Example 10-3. A targeted user action whose response time is dominated by read calls of the disk I/O subsystem

Response Time Component	Duration		# Calls	Dur/Call
db file scattered read	4,551.0s	96.9%	12,165	0.374109s
CPU service	78.5s	1.7%	215	0.365023s
db file sequential read	64.9s	1.4%	684	0.094883s
SQL*Net message from client	0.1s	0.0%	68	0.001324s
log file sync	0.0s	0.0%	4	0.010000s
SQL*Net message to client	0.0s	0.0%	68	0.000000s
latch free	0.0s	0.0%	1	0.000000s
Total	4,694.5s	100.0%		

How to eliminate calls

How do you reduce the number of events executed by a user action? First, figure out what the resource that's being consumed *does*. What causes the Oracle process profiled in Example 10-3 to execute 12,165 multiblock read calls? Then figure out whether there's any way you can meet your functional requirements with fewer calls to that resource. In Chapter 11, I explain how to do this for a few commonly occurring Oracle events. You proceed by assessing whether you can reduce demand for the busy resource at each level as you move throughout the technology stack. For example:

- Many analysts assume that by increasing the size of the database buffer cache (that is, by allocating more memory to an Oracle system), they can ensure that fewer of their memory lookups will motivate visits to disk devices.
- However, moving up the stack a little farther often provides better results without motivating a system memory upgrade. By improving the query execution

plan that your SQL uses to fetch rows from the database, you can often eliminate even the memory accesses.

- Moving even farther up the stack reveals potential benefits that cost even less to implement. For example, perhaps running the targeted user action less frequently, or perhaps even not at all (maybe something else instead), would not at all diminish the business value of the system.

Thinking in a bigger box

Technicians sometimes confine their work to a zone of comfort within the bottom layers of the technology stack. Such behavior increases the risk of missing significant performance improvement opportunities. For example, at one customer site I visited in the mid-1990s, the accounting department generated a three-foot-deep stack of General Ledger (GL) Aged Trial Balance reports every day. Upon learning why the users were running this report so frequently, the GL implementation leader from Oracle Consulting taught the users how they could acquire the information they needed more efficiently by running a fast online form. As a result, we were able to eliminate billions of computer instructions per day from the system's overall workload, with absolutely no "tuning" investment. Not only was the solution easier on the system, using the online form was actually more convenient for the users than trying to visually pluck details out of an inch-thick report.

My *hotsos.com* company cofounder, Gary Goodman, tells stories of application implementation projects he led while he was at Oracle Corporation. One technique that he practiced during an implementation was to simply turn off every application report on the system. When users would come asking for a report they were missing, his project team would reactivate the requested report. In Gary's experience, not once did he ever reinstate more than 80% of the system's original reporting workload. Can you figure out which 20% of *your* reports your users never use?

At the business requirement layer in your technology stack, the right question for you to answer is:

> Which apparent business requirements are actually *legitimate* business requirements?

For user actions that provide no legitimate business value, simply turn them off. For user actions that really are necessary, try to eliminate any unnecessary work within them (Chapter 11 describes several ways). Your performance diagnostic data will drive your analysis from the bottom up, but it's usually cheaper to implement solutions from the top down. For example, find out whether a report should be deactivated before you tune it. Don't limit your optimization work to studying only the technical details of how something works. As I described in Chapter 1, the optimal performance analyst must also invest himself into understanding the relationship between technical workload and the business requirements that the workload is ostensibly required to support.

Finally, don't forget that from a business's perspective, the users don't just *use* a system, they are *part* of the system. A story told by my colleague Rick Minutella illustrates. A company had called him to optimize the performance of a recently upgraded order entry application. Table 10-1 shows the performance difference before and after the upgrade. In a classic Big Meeting with the company's CFO, users, IS department managers, and hardware vendor all in attendance, the company demanded that Oracle Corporation fix the performance of the order entry form because it was killing their business.

Table 10-1. Order Entry performance before and after an upgrade

Performance measurement	Value before upgrading	Value after upgrading
Order throughput	10 calls/hr	6 calls/hr
Entry form response time	5 sec/screen	60 sec/screen

Waiting 60 seconds for a response from an online order entry form is almost certainly much too long. However, the argument that "performance of the *order entry form* is killing our business" is simply not true. Here's why. If the business processes an average of six calls per hour, then the average duration per phone call is ten minutes. Example 10-4 shows the resource profile for such a call using a 60-second form.

Example 10-4. Resource profile for the order entry process when the form is behaving objectionably

```
Before optimizing the online order entry form
Response Time Component              Duration        # Calls    Dur/Call
---------------------------      ----------------  --------------  ------------

other                              540s  90.0%           1         540s
wait for the order entry form       60s  10.0%           1          60s
---------------------------      ----------------  --------------  ------------

Total                              600s 100.0%
```

What is the maximum impact to the business that can be obtained by optimizing the form? Example 10-5 shows the answer. If the form's response time can be *completely eliminated*, total order processing time will drop only to nine minutes.

Example 10-5. Resource profile for the order entry process if the form's response time could be entirely eliminated

```
Response Time Component              Duration        # Calls    Dur/Call
---------------------------      ----------------  --------------  ------------

other                              540s 100.0%           1         540s
wait for the order entry form        0s   0.0%           1           0s
---------------------------      ----------------  --------------  ------------

Total                              540s 100.0%
```

The problem is that this isn't good enough. If an order clerk could process an order in an average of nine minutes, then a single clerk could process an average of only 6.67 orders per hour. This of course is still well short of the ten calls-per-hour requirement. Fixing the performance of this business's online order entry form, by itself, will never improve throughput to the required ten calls per hour. It's not the form that's "killing the business," it's what the order takers are doing for the other nine minutes.

Solving this performance problem will require thinking outside the box of conventional "system tuning." What is it that consumes this "other" time? A few possibilities include:

- If most of the "other" duration results in customer inconvenience (for example, long waits for product ID lookups), then you should find ways to reduce the "other" duration.

- If most of the "other" duration is spent improving the company's relationship with the customer, then perhaps it's a better idea to hire more clerks so that an average per-clerk order throughput of about six calls per hour yields sufficient total order throughput for the business.

Another interesting problem to figure out is whether the "clustering" in time of incoming calls occurs in such a manner that customers spend a lot of time on hold during busy parts of the day. The queueing theory lessons presented in Chapter 9 can help you understand how to deal with peak incoming call times more effectively by either using more clerks or reducing per-call durations. There's a lot to think about. The point is not to constrict your view of your "system" to just a few bits of hardware and software. Your business needs you to think of the "order entry system" more broadly as *all* the participants in the order entry process that influence net profit, return on investment, and cash flow.

Eliminate Inter-Process Competition

What happens when you have eliminated all the unnecessary calls that you can in the user action under diagnosis, but its response time is still unacceptable? Your next step is to assess whether its individual per-call latencies are acceptable. Understanding whether a given latency is acceptable requires some knowledge of what numbers you should expect. There are surprisingly few numbers that constitute such knowledge. The ones that Jeff and I have found to be the most important are listed in Table 10-2. These constants will evolve as hardware speeds improve, but the numbers are reasonable upper bounds for many systems at the time of this writing in 2003. In particular, LIO numbers vary as CPU speeds vary, and of course CPU speeds are a rapidly moving target these days. The footnote to Table 10-2 explains.

Table 10-2. Useful constants for the performance analyst [Millsap and Holt (2002)]

Event	Maximum tolerated latency per event	Events-per-second rate at this latency
Logical read (LIO)[a]	20 μs or 0.000 020 s	50,000
Single-block disk read (PIO)	10 ms or 0.010 000 s	100
SQL*Net transmission via WAN	200 ms or 0.200 000 s	5

Event	Maximum tolerated latency per event	Events-per-second rate at this latency
SQL*Net transmission via LAN	15 ms or 0.015 000 s	67
SQL*Net transmission via IPC	1 ms or 0.001 000 s	1,000

[a] Experiments published by Jonathan Lewis indicate strongly that you can expect a CPU to perform roughly 10,000 LIO/sec per 100 MHz of CPU capacity [Lewis (2003)]. Hence, on a 1 GHz CPU, you should expect performance of roughly 100,000 LIO/sec, or 10 μs per LIO. If you are using a 500 MHz system, you should average approximately the 20-μs numbers listed here.

Latencies that violate the expectations listed in Table 10-2 sometimes indicate malfunctioning devices, but more often they indicate resource queueing delays. What causes long queueing delays? The most likely answer by far is—can you guess?—excessive demand for the resource. What could be causing that excessive demand? The answer to this question is, of course, one or more other programs that are competing for resources your targeted user action needs while it is running.

How to attack a latency problem

Example 10-6 depicts a situation in which the overall response time of a targeted user action is excessive because of excessive individual I/O call latencies. By the time this resource profile was generated, the analyst had eliminated unnecessary disk read calls, leaving only eighteen necessary calls. However, the average disk read latency of more than 2.023 seconds per call is far out of bounds compared to the expectation of 0.010 seconds from Table 10-2. From this resource profile alone, it is impossible to determine whether, for example, each of the 18 disk reads consumed 2.023 seconds apiece, or just one of the disk reads consumed so much time that it dominated the average. (Remember, it is impossible to extrapolate detail from an aggregate...even in resource profiles.)

Example 10-6. A resource profile for a user action whose response time is dominated by unacceptable disk I/O latencies

```
Response Time Component          Duration       # Calls    Dur/Call
-------------------------    -----------------  -------------  -----------
db file sequential read      36.4s   98.9%           18    2.023048s
CPU service                   0.4s    1.1%            4    0.091805s
SQL*Net message from client   0.0s    0.0%            3    0.004295s
SQL*Net message to client     0.0s    0.0%            3    0.000298s
-------------------------    -----------------  -------------  -----------
Total                        36.8s  100.0%
```

However, one thing is clear: something is desperately wrong with the latency for at least one disk read call for this user action. The following steps will help you get to the bottom of the problem:

1. Which block or blocks are the ones participating in the high-latency I/O calls? Your extended SQL trace file contains the answers. Chapters 5 and 6 provide the information you need to find them.

2. Once you know which blocks are taking so long to read, you can work with your disk subsystem manager to figure out on which devices the blocks reside.

3. Once you've figured out exactly which devices are at the root of the problem, determine whether programs that compete with your targeted action for the "hot" devices themselves use those devices wastefully. If they do, then eliminating the waste will reduce queueing delays for the hot device.

4. Assess whether the configuration of the slow device is itself generating wasted workload. For example:

   - I've seen systems with two or more mirrors set up so that reads and writes to separate devices bottleneck on a single controller.

   - RAID level 5 disk systems commonly have inadequate I/O call capacities. Using RAID level 5 is not necessarily a mistake. However, people commonly fail to realize that to provide adequate I/O performance with a RAID level 5 configuration typically requires the purchase of two to four times more disk drives than they initially might have believed [Millsap (2000a)].

   - It is sometimes possible to move workload from a hot device to one that's less busy during the problem time interval. System administrators refer to this operation as *I/O load balancing*. In the early 1990s, I visited a lot of Oracle sites that had I/O latency problems caused by extremely poor file layouts (such as putting *all* of an Oracle database's files on one disk). I don't think this kind of thing happens very often anymore. However, if you happen to suffer from such a dreadful configuration problem, then of course it's highly likely that you'll be plagued by excessive I/O latencies, regardless of whether your application issues a wastefully large number of disk I/O calls or not.

   - Faulty hardware can of course cause performance problems as well. A bad disk controller that causes unnecessary retry or timeout operations can contribute significantly to response time. For inexplicably slow I/O devices, check your system logs to ensure that your operating system isn't having a hard time getting your hardware to cooperate.

Steps 3 and 4 are the ones in which experience and creativity can produce excellent payoffs.

How to find competing workload

The job of learning which programs are out there competing against your user action resembles conventional performance tuning, at least insofar as which tools you'll use.

 There are lots of tools available for analyzing a specific resource in detail. The Oracle fixed views described in Chapter 8 are excellent places to look first.

Though the job of digging through details about some high-latency device may remind you of the old trial-and-error tuning approach (Method C from Chapter 1), there is an important distinction. That distinction is the hallmark of Method R—the ever-present companion of deterministic *targeting*. You won't be sifting through innumerable performance metrics wondering which ones might have a meaningful performance impact and which ones don't. Instead, you'll know exactly which resource it is that you're trying to improve. You'll know, because your resource profile has told you.

The most difficult part of finding a user action's competitors is a problem with collecting properly scoped diagnostic data. This is when it would really pay off to have a detailed X$TRACE-like history of everything that happened on a system during your performance problem time interval. Without such a history of detailed diagnostic data, it can be difficult to find out which programs were competing against your targeted user action, even if the action you're trying to improve just finished running a few minutes ago. There are several ways to make progress anyway, including:

Batch queue manager logs
> Practically by definition, the most intensely competitive workload on a system is that motivated by batch programs. Most good batch management software maintains a log of which jobs ran at what times. Beginning with this information, it is often easy to guess which programs motivated significant competition for a given resource. You can graduate from guesses to complete information by collecting properly scoped diagnostic data for these programs the next time they're scheduled to run.

Oracle connect-level auditing
> It is easy to configure an Oracle instance to perform lightweight logging of session-level resource consumption statistics. These statistics can help you determine which sessions were responsible for the greatest workloads on the system over a specified duration. Once you have that information, then usually a brief end-user interview is all it takes to construct a good guess about which programs might have motivated the competition for a given device. Again, you can graduate from guesses to complete information by collecting properly scoped diagnostic data for the suspects at some time in the future. To get started, search your Oracle documentation for information about the DBA_AUDIT_SESSION view.

Operating system process accounting
> Some operating systems provide the capability to collect and record relevant performance statistics for individual programs. This capability can be important, because not all competition for a specified resource is necessarily motivated from another Oracle process.

Custom timing instrumentation
> There's nothing better for the performance analyst than application code that can tell you where it spends all of its time. If you have the ability to instrument

the code that is performing poorly (for example, because it is code that *you* wrote), then *instrument it*. Chapter 7 explains how, in detail.

When you find the programs that are competing with your targeted user action for a "hot" resource, use the techniques described earlier in "Eliminate Unnecessary Calls" Your job becomes the familiar one of determining whether the requirement to overburden the resource is really a legitimate requirement.

Upgrade Capacity

Capacity upgrades are the last place you should look for performance improvement opportunities. The reasons for last-place status are straightforward:

- It is seldom possible to make as much progress with an expensive capacity upgrade as you can make with an inexpensive round of wasted workload elimination.

- Capacity upgrades, if executed without sufficient forethought, can actually *degrade* the performance of the user action you're trying to improve.

Any capacity upgrade is a gamble. The first observation says that an investment into faster hardware has a potentially lower payoff than you'd like. Many managers think of capacity upgrades as guaranteed investment successes, because "How can you ever have too much CPU [or memory, or disk, or whatever]?" The popular belief is that even if the performance problem at hand doesn't benefit directly from the upgrade, how can it hurt? You'll use the spare capacity eventually anyway, right? Well, not exactly. The gamble has a downside that a lot of decision-makers don't realize. I've already described one downside situation in "Why targeting is vital." The case in "Case 1: Misled by System-Wide Data" in Chapter 12 is another example of the same problem:

> A capacity upgrade is going to help *some* part of a system's workload, but the key issue is whether a capacity upgrade will help a system in alignment with the *business priorities* of its owner.

The first formal explanation that I ever read about such a counterintuitive possibility was in Neil Gunther's *Practical Performance Analyst* [Gunther (1998) 117–122]. When I presented Gunther's example to Oracle conference audiences worldwide, participants without fail would approach the podium to share the news that by seeing Gunther's example they could *finally* explain the bizarre result that had plagued some past project. I was pleased but actually a little surprised by how many different people had seen hardware *up*grades *de*grade system performance. After gaining some intimacy with Amdahl's Law, it became clear to me that *any* capacity upgrade can degrade the performance of *some* user action by unleashing extra competition for a resource that was not upgraded. The real key is whether or not the harmed user actions are ever *noticed*.

When capacity upgrades fail to improve performance, the results are some of the worst project disasters imaginable. Here's what happens. A company lives with a performance problem long enough that the collective pain rises above some threshold that triggers the expenditure of cash for an upgrade. Expectations form in direct proportion to the size of the expenditure. So, on the Friday before the Big Upgrade, a whole company is nervously awaiting Monday, when "We're spending so much money to fix this problem that performance is bound to be *spectacular*." Then when Monday rolls around, not only is performance unspectacular, it's actually *worse*. By Tuesday, the business is assessing whether the person who suggested the upgrade should bother to come to work on Wednesday.

Capacity upgrades motivate interesting ironies:

- Decision-makers often regard capacity upgrades as inexpensive alternatives to expensive analysis, yet the upside potential of capacity upgrades is severely limited in comparison to the upside potential of workload reduction.

- Decision-makers often perceive capacity upgrades as completely safe, yet they bear significant downside risk. Their downside potential actually demands serious, careful, and possibly even expensive analytical forethought.

Even when capacity upgrades work, they usually don't work as well as the people doing the upgrade had hoped. When capacity upgrades *don't* work, they jeopardize careers. The failures are often so visible and so spectacular that the project sponsors never regain their credibility.

Are hardware upgrades ever necessary? Certainly, there are many cases in which they are. But I implore you not to consider hardware upgrades as a first-line defense against performance problems. Is your system really under-sized? Odds are that its workload is just bigger than it needs to be. So, please, eliminate wasteful calls to a resource before you upgrade it. And when you do upgrade a resource, then make sure you think it through first:

> Don't upgrade capacity until you know that the resource you're upgrading is going to (a) help important user actions, and (b) harm only unimportant ones.

And, of course, don't lose sight of the fact that a user action that's unimportant today might become important tomorrow if you slow it down.

How to Forecast Improvement

One of the nicest things about the resource profile format is the ease with which you can predict the impact of a proposed improvement activity. Figure 10-2 shows a simple Microsoft Excel workbook that you can use to accomplish this task.

In the workbook shown here, I have specified in my *Baseline* case that a component called "thing to be improved" presently consumes 300 seconds of duration and is called 200 times. Another response time component called "all other" accounts for 100 seconds of total duration and is called only once.

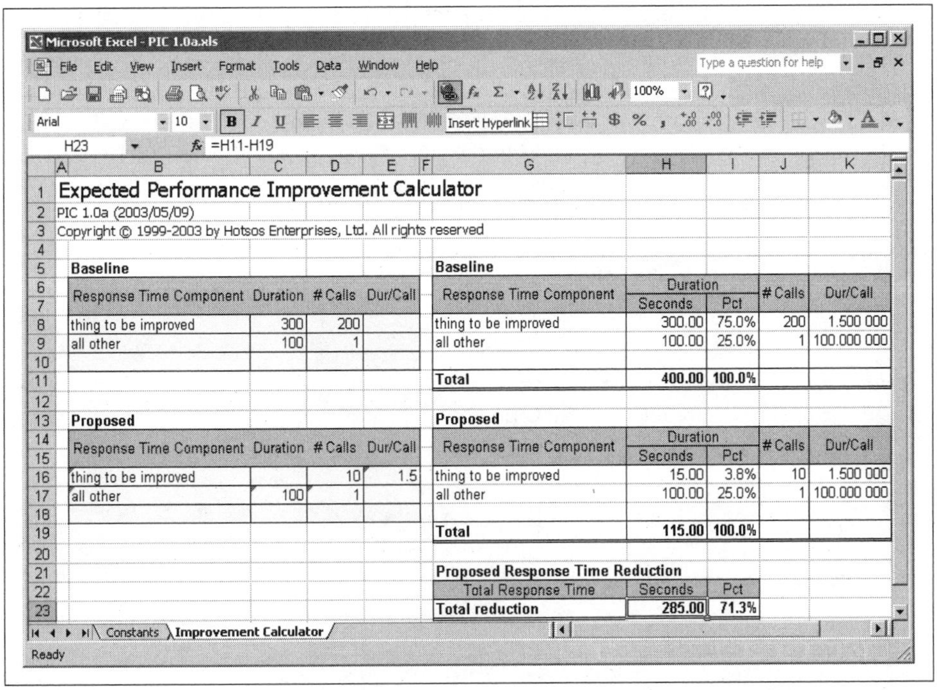

Microsoft Excel - PIC 1.0a.xls

Type a question for help

Arial   10   B I U   Insert Hyperlink $ % , .00 .00

H23   =H11-H19

Expected Performance Improvement Calculator

PIC 1.0a (2003/05/09)

Baseline

Response Time Component	Duration	# Calls	Dur/Call
thing to be improved	300	200	
all other	100	1	

Baseline

| Response Time Component | Duration | | # Calls | Dur/Call |
	Seconds	Pct		
thing to be improved	300.00	75.0%	200	1.500 000
all other	100.00	25.0%	1	100.000 000
Total	**400.00**	**100.0%**		

Proposed

Response Time Component	Duration	# Calls	Dur/Call
thing to be improved		10	1.5
all other	100	1	

Proposed

| Response Time Component | Duration | | # Calls | Dur/Call |
	Seconds	Pct		
thing to be improved	15.00	3.8%	10	1.500 000
all other	100.00	25.0%	1	100.000 000
Total	**115.00**	**100.0%**		

Proposed Response Time Reduction

Total Response Time	Seconds	Pct
Total reduction	**285.00**	**71.3%**

Constants \ Improvement Calculator

Ready

Figure 10-2. A simple performance improvement calculator that shows the expected response time benefit of reducing the number of calls of some "thing to be improved" from 200 calls to 10 calls

The call count that I enter for "all other" is irrelevant because I'm not going to be calculating the impact of any proposed change to its behavior.

In columns G through K, the workbook formats my input data into a full resource profile format.

In my *Proposed* case, I have specified that I think I can eliminate all but 10 of the calls to "thing to be improved." In cell E16, I have used the formula =K8 to denote that I believe my per-call latency will remain the same. In columns G through K, the workbook formats my *Proposed* case input data and produces a response time reduction summary. If I really can reduce the number of calls to "thing to be improved" from 200 to 10, then I should expect to see a response time improvement of about 285 seconds for this user action, or an elimination of about 71% of its response time.

Excel is a good tool for analyses like this one, because it allows you to see quickly "what if" you were to try a given performance improvement activity. For example, which is better, to reduce the call count for "thing to be improved" from 200 to 10? Or to reduce the per-call latency from 1.5 seconds to 0.5 seconds? Figure 10-3 shows that the better answer in this case is to reduce the call count. Of course, you could also use the tool to determine the impact of implementing both performance improvement activities.

 This simple model doesn't account for the secondary benefits that call count reduction is bound to have by reducing the queueing component of per-call latencies.

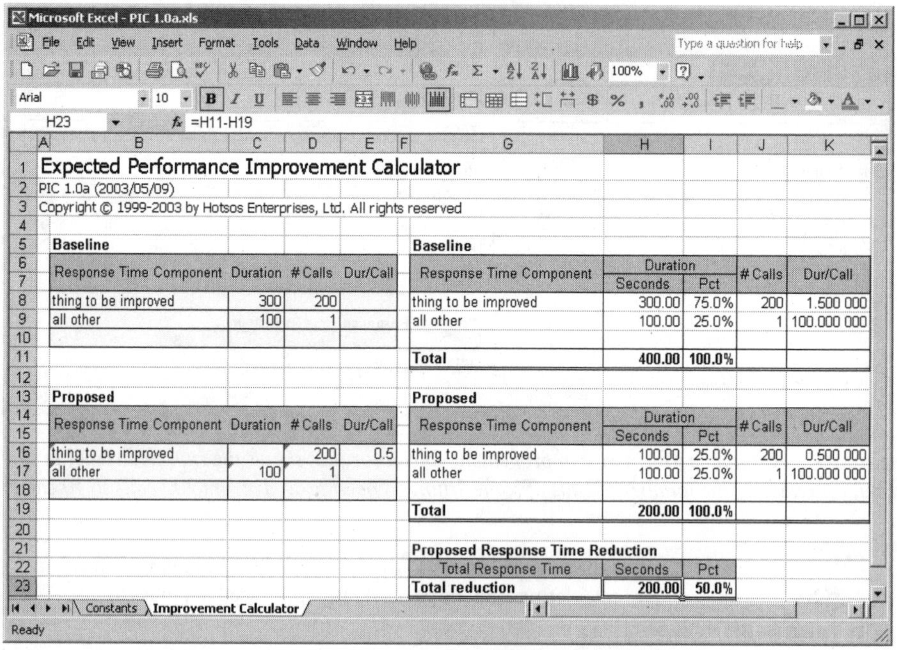

Figure 10-3. The performance improvement calculator shows plainly that reducing the duration per call from 1.5 sec/call to 0.5 sec/call for some "thing to be improved" can be expected to deliver less response time benefit than the benefit shown in Figure 10-2

How to Tell When Your Work Is Done

Of the profound problems that plague conventional Oracle tuning methods, one of the most serious is the absence of a termination condition. As a result, conventional performance improvement projects are notorious for lingering until either the patience or the money runs out (hence the *compulsive tuning disorder* (CTD) phenomenon I mentioned in Chapter 3). By contrast, Method R specifies a termination condition:

> If even the best net-payoff activity produces insufficient net payoff, then suspend your performance improvement activities until something changes.

How can you determine when the best net-payoff activity produces insufficient net payoff? If you can accurately forecast a performance improvement project's net payoff, then it's a straightforward financial analysis problem. Your company should allocate each unit of its cash to the activity that does the best job of net profit, return on investment, and cash flow simultaneously. If your project's expected financial performance is better than all the other ways your company could spend its next bit of capital, then your project should be next in line for implementation.

In reality, it is entirely appropriate for most performance improvement projects to be executed with no formal financial analysis. Many companies have full-time staff who are responsible for executing performance improvement activities whenever they're deemed necessary. In many circumstances, full-time analysts tinker with performance theories for a few hours each week. The incremental expense incurred by an analyst's affliction with even third-degree, adult-onset CTD is small enough to go unnoticed in most companies.

Even in situations where performance analysts have some extra time on their hands, it's still inconvenient not to be able to figure out whether a given user action has been truly *optimized*—that is, made as fast as it can possibly go. When you measure performance with the system-wide statistics that conventional tuning methods prescribe, it is virtually impossible to know. However, the response-time focus of Method R provides the means to know whether a user action contains any more room for performance improvement. It's actually pretty easy to determine from a resource profile and its underlying extended SQL trace data whether it's going to be possible to squeeze any more response time improvement out of a user action.

Example 10-7 illustrates what a resource profile looks like when a targeted user action has been *optimized*. Notice the following attributes of the pattern:

1. Total response time is small. This attribute is essential. If your total response time is not sufficiently small, then you're not done yet—it doesn't matter what other patterns exist within your resource profile. Your business defines the value of "sufficiently small," as I describe in Chapter 4.

2. Total response time is dominated by CPU consumption (usually more than 80% of total response time), but the application uses no unnecessary CPU capacity.

3. Database file reading or writing consumes more time than any response time component other than CPU service. The number of read or write calls is small.

4. Aside from CPU service and database file reads or writes, there's very little other time being consumed.

If a resource profile looks like Example 10-7, then you're finished if the total response time (❶) is small enough. If total response time is not small enough and the remaining attributes hold (❷, ❸, and ❹), then the only thing you can do to improve performance appreciably is to upgrade your CPU speed.

Example 10-7. The goal state resource profile

Response Time Component	Duration	# Calls	Dur/Call
CPU service	❷[*small*]s ≥80.0%		
[*database reads or writes*]	❸[*small*]s <20.0%	[*few*]	
[*everything else*]	❹[*small*]s <10.0%	[*few*]	
Total	❶[*small*]s 100.0%		

Why does an optimal resource profile have CPU service and physical I/O at the top? It's natural, really. *Something* has to be at the top, of course, as long as the total response time is non-zero. What would you like it to be? A database has a very simple job to do, really: to manage data held in long-term storage. A database reads, processes, and writes data. CPU service shows up ahead of physical I/O in an optimal resource profile because I/O performance problems are usually cheaper and easier to fix (usually by optimizing application SQL). When a problem is cheap to fix, you're likely to fix it, which reduces the duration motivated by that problem until another event surfaces to the top of the profile. Thus, CPU service bubbles to the top of the profile on a system as its performance is improved. Even when the CPU service number is small, it usually becomes the top-line item because most applications force Oracle to spend a lot more time processing data than reading or writing it.

All other activities that a database does are generally "necessary but unwanted." For example, the latch free event denotes the use of a resource that is necessary to prevent the corruption of several Oracle internal data structures under conditions of high concurrency use [Millsap (2001c)]. We all need for the "sleep if a latch is unavailable" feature to be there, but our applications will run faster if we can make them wait for latch free events as infrequently as possible. This "need the feature but want to avoid using it" category accounts for the vast majority of Oracle's few hundred so-called wait events.

If a query is well-tuned, then it will probably consume more CPU than any other resource. However, this is *not* equivalent to saying, "If a query consumes more CPU than anything else, then it is well tuned." It is quite possible that a query can consume less CPU capacity than it does and still return the correct answer. The most likely way to accomplish this is... (drum roll, please) ...eliminate unnecessary LIO calls.

You're finished when the cost of call reduction and latency reduction exceeds the cost of the performance you're getting today.

## CHAPTER 11

Responding to the Diagnosis

To improve Oracle performance, you must of course understand the technology of each response time component that contributes significantly to your targeted user action's response time. The place you should begin your research is the Oracle *Database Concepts* guide at *http://technet.oracle.com*. The response time components that show up in your resource profiles associate directly to instrumented Oracle kernel actions described in the *Concepts* guide. For example, it describes how the Oracle LGWR process copies content from the redo log buffer to an online redo log file. An Oracle kernel process accounts for the time it spends waiting on LGWR to perform this particular action with the wait event called log file sync.

There are lots of other such events. The number of wait events inside the Oracle kernel has grown with each new release, as shown in Table 11-1. Thankfully, it is not important for you to know a lot of details about every Oracle wait event. You usually don't need the gory details in your brain for any more than a couple of wait events at a time—the ones that are dominating your targeted user action at the moment. This is excellent news, because some of the events require some study time to understand. Rather than learn and try to retain a lot of details about dozens of events, I think it is more important to focus on the following:

- Know how to *target* the events that are important to you right now. I describe how to do this in Part I.
- Retain a general knowledge about the meanings of just a few response time components that will occur frequently on your system, including:
  - CPU service
  - unaccounted-for
  - SQL*Net message from client
  - The various read events
  - The one or two other events that occur frequently on your system

You can acquire this knowledge by studying this book, the Oracle *Database Concepts* guide, and the response time behavior of targeted user actions on your own system.

- Know where to find the details about a response time component when you need them. My favorite tools for finding wait event information are:

  — Oracle database product documentation at *http://technet.oracle.com*

  — Oracle *MetaLink* support bulletins and bug reports at *http://metalink.oracle.com*

  — Anjo Kolk and Shari Yamaguchi's *YAPP* paper [Kolk and Yamaguchi (1999)]

  — Steve Adams's bumblebee book [Adams (1999)], and his web site at *http://www.ixora.com.au*

  — The Google search engine at *http://www.google.com*, which helps me find wait event documentation throughout the Internet

Table 11-1. The number of Oracle wait events grows with each Oracle release (source: select count(*) from v$event_name)

Oracle release	Number of wait events
7.3.4	106
8.1.7	215
9.0.1	287
9.2.0	361
10.0.1	500 (est.)

Beyond the Resource Profile

The resource profile is an excellent first step that allows you to target the right piece of a user action's response time for detailed analysis. But once you understand which response time component dominates your user action's response time, what do you do next? The answer is simple:

> Find the source text (the SQL or PL/SQL) of the cursor that contributes the most to the duration of the component.

Doing this with extended SQL trace data is straightforward, as I explain in "Forward Attribution" in Chapter 5. Once you have found the SQL text of the first cursor action that contributes the most to your top response time component duration, you're well on the way to constructing a remedy. Your next step is to learn why the source code you've found motivates so much time spent at this component. The next section describes how to find out.

Response Time Components

When I began work on this chapter, I had in mind that I would write details about the twenty or so Oracle wait events that you would encounter most commonly in your work. However, Oracle Corporation has done such a good job improving its wait event documentation in the past few years that I think rehashing that information would be a waste of your time. The Oracle9i release 2 performance documentation [Oracle (2002)] is actually quite good. Rather than rehash what you can obtain freely from other sources, I focus my effort in this book upon three topics that are missing from the standard Oracle documentation:

- Treatment of the two pseudoevents ("events" that are not really events) whose durations you can obtain from extended SQL trace data: CPU service and unaccounted-for time.

- More comprehensive description of a few so-called *idle wait events* that other authors dismiss as unimportant. These events become very important in light of the improved diagnostic capabilities that you gain if you collect performance diagnostic data with proper time and action scope.

- More emphasis on how to *eliminate wasteful workload* in reaction to the appearance of various wait events.

In this section, I cover the pseudoevents and so-called idle wait events. Later in the chapter, I cover the topic of workload elimination.

Oracle Pseudoevents

You may by now have noticed that I use the term "response time component" in places where you might have expected the term *Oracle* "wait event." The reason I do this is simple. What I'm calling response time components consists of two different things: actual Oracle wait events described in V$EVENT_NAME, and two other important components of response time that do not show up in V$EVENT_NAME:

```
CPU service
unaccounted-for
```

Though neither of these components is officially an "Oracle wait event," each is a *measurable* (and often significant) component of response time for every user action imaginable. I include them on par with the Oracle wait events because every microsecond an Oracle kernel process spends "working" contributes just as much to user action response time as a microsecond spent "waiting." Recent versions of *Statspack* include CPU time in its list of top five "wait events" as well.

CPU service

CPU service will be a response time component of virtually every Oracle resource profile you'll ever see. It is often the dominant contributor to response time, both for efficient user actions and for extremely inefficient ones. The key is to understand whether the apparent requirement to consume as much CPU capacity as you're seeing is actually a legitimate requirement (Chapter 5).

Your first step in diagnosing excessive CPU service durations is to learn which database calls are predominantly responsible. Forward attribution is not necessary for determining the root cause of excessive consumption of CPU capacity, because the c statistics that define CPU service durations sit right on the trace file lines for the database calls themselves. Once you've identified the calls that are most responsible for the CPU service consumption, it's easy to search backward in the trace file for the appropriate PARSING IN CURSOR sections that identify the source text (SQL or PL/SQL) motivating those calls.

The database calls you should attend to first are the ones with the greatest progeny-*exclusive* c values. If a database call's high c value is the result of consumptions rolled up from its expensive recursive children, then determine the call's progeny-exclusive CPU capacity consumption by using the technique described in "Recursive SQL Double-Counting" in Chapter 5. Remember, a database call's CPU and LIO statistics (c, cr, and cu) are among those that roll up from child to parent.

Once you've found the database calls that contribute the most to your targeted user action's CPU service duration, the following items describe what action to take, depending upon the type of database call that has consumed the most CPU service:

Large c value for a FETCH, EXEC, UNMAP, or SORT UNMAP database call
> If you have many small c values distributed across a large number of FETCH or EXEC calls, then eliminate as many unnecessary database calls as possible, and consolidate the calls that remain into the smallest number of database calls that you can (for example, process arrays of rows instead of processing one row at a time).

> If you have a large c value for an individual FETCH or EXEC database call, then first determine whether the large CPU duration was due to logical I/O (LIO) processing:

High LIO count (more than about 10 LIO calls per non-aggregate row returned per table in the FROM clause)
> If the LIO count for the call is high, then optimize the SQL as I outline in "Logical I/O Optimization" later in this chapter.

Low LIO count
> If the call's LIO count is low, then the Oracle kernel process may have consumed an excessive amount of CPU capacity performing sort or hash operations. Events 10032 and 10033 provide detailed information about Oracle sorting operations, and event 10104 provides detailed information about hash joins.

Another possibility is that the time consumption was the result of type coercion operations. For example, a table scan that does a date comparison for every row could use a lot of CPU.

Finally, perhaps the time consumption was the result of excessive PL/SQL language processing. For example, PL/SQL instructions of course consume CPU capacity, even when they don't make any database calls. High c durations in EXEC trace file lines for PL/SQL blocks that have low progeny-exclusive LIO counts often indicate that branching, assignments, and other language processing elements are consuming excessive CPU capacity. You can use Oracle's DBMS_PROFILER package to diagnose PL/SQL language processing performance in detail [Kyte (2001)].

Large c value for a PARSE call

If you have many small c values distributes across a large number of PARSE calls, then eliminate as many parse calls as you can, using methods outlined in "Parse Optimization" later in this chapter.

If you have a large c value for a PARSE call, then investigate whether the SQL statement can be simplified. Also consider reducing the value of OPTIMIZER_MAX_PERMUTATIONS (see *http://www.ixora.com.au/q+a/0010/19140702.htm* for more information).

unaccounted-for

As I describe in Chapter 7, there are five sources of unaccounted-for time in a trace file, which create non-zero Δ values in the equation $e = c + \sum ela + \Delta$:

- Measurement intrusion effect
- Double-counting of CPU service between c and ela statistics
- Quantization error
- Time spent not executing
- Un-instrumented time

Having so many unknowns in a single equation might suggest that it is impossible to isolate the effect of any one contribution to Δ. However, in reality dealing with unaccounted-for time is simple. Three of the five sources of unaccounted-for time are constrained so that their overall impact upon response time tends to be negligible. If unaccounted-for is the largest component of a user action's resource profile for *properly scoped diagnostic data*, then the indication is almost always either *un-instrumented time* or *time spent not executing*. If un-instrumented Oracle kernel code is the source of your unaccounted-for time, then you're probably an Oracle patch application away from reducing the number of material unaccounted-for time sources to just one.

Most real-life instances of large unaccounted-for time durations are caused by errors in data collection such as the ones described in Chapters 3 and 6. If you are very careful to target *exactly* the data you need when you collect your performance diagnostic data, then you can exploit the full benefit of the knowledge contained within your unaccounted-for component durations.

Chapter 7 explains the details of the five different contributors to unaccounted-for response time components. Here is a recap:

Measurement intrusion effect
> The effect of measurement intrusion is small (on the order of a few microseconds per gettimeofday or getrusage call), so overall it is generally safe for you to ignore it. If you are concerned about measurement intrusion, you can measure its exact effect using techniques outlined in Chapter 7. Measurement intrusion effect influences Δ slightly in the positive direction.

Double-counting of CPU service between c and ela statistics
> The double-counting effect is small for most events. The largest impact I've seen from this effect occurs with db file scattered read events involving large data transfers (on the order of 100 KB or more). In such cases, I have seen apparent CPU double-counting of roughly one centisecond per read event. CPU double-counting influences Δ slightly in the negative direction.

Quantization error
> The overall effect of quantization error is also small. Because positive and negative quantization errors occur with equal probability, the errors tend to counteract each other, resulting in a nearly net-zero effect upon Δ.

Time spent not executing
> If the magnitude of total unaccounted-for duration of a resource profile is significant, then you have almost certainly discovered either time spent not executing or un-instrumented time. A good rule of thumb is given in Table 11-2. Time spent not executing always influences Δ in the positive direction.

Un-instrumented time
> If your application executes a significant amount of un-instrumented Oracle kernel code path, then the effect in the resource profile is indistinguishable from the effect of time spent not executing. Chapter 7 describes how you can detect the existence of un-instrumented code path. If unaccounted-for time dominates total response time on even a system that's not excessively context switching, paging, or swapping, then patch your Oracle kernel so that the your user action's code path is correctly instrumented. Un-instrumented Oracle code segments always influence Δ in the positive direction.

Table 11-2. Rule of thumb for dealing with unaccounted-for duration Δ, where R is the total response time for the user action under analysis

Condition	Indication
Δ is negative and has magnitude of more than 10% of total response time That is, $\Delta < -0.1R$	This is an extremely rare (but hypothetically possible) case in which error from CPU double-counting dominates your statistics for an entire trace file. (You can usually detect this phenomenon by analyzing extended SQL trace data for only a single database call.)
Δ is between –10% and 10% of total response time That is, $-0.1R \leq \Delta \leq +0.1R$	Ignore the unaccounted-for duration. It is a small enough contributor to total response time that it is not necessary to understand the exact cause.
Δ is positive and more than 10% of total response time That is, $+0.1R \leq \Delta$	If unaccounted-for duration is not a dominant contributor to total response time, then ignore. Otherwise, if your user action spent little time in the ready to run OS state (Chapter 7), then check Oracle *MetaLink* for information pertaining to un-instrumented Oracle kernel code. If your user action spent a lot of time in the ready to run OS state, then the unaccounted-for duration was most likely caused by inadequate CPU or memory capacity for the given workload.

No Event Is Inherently "Unimportant"

In most publications that are in print while I'm writing this chapter, authors still distinguish carefully between events that are *idle* and events that are *non-idle*. Those authors generally describe the non-idle events as the important ones, and the idle ones as unimportant. However, I encourage you to make only one classification of Oracle wait events: the *between/within* distinction that I introduce in Chapter 5. You need to understand this distinction to use the fundamental relation among trace file statistics, $e \approx c + \sum ela$, without introducing omissions or double-counting errors. The reason I encourage you to make no other classification of Oracle wait events is that *any* event can be an important contributor to response time.

There is only one legitimate criterion for determining whether a response time component is important:

> If a component contributes significantly to the response time of a properly targeted user action, then it is important; otherwise, it is not.

Therefore, I disagree with generalized claims that some events are "important" and that others are not. *Any* event can be important. It doesn't matter what event it is or how many authors say it's not important. If an event contributes significantly to the response time of a properly targeted user action, then the event is important to you.

How can "idle" events ever be important? When the time spent executing them contributes significantly to response time. Two events that you will encounter in almost every resource profile you will ever see are the events SQL*Net message to client and SQL*Net message from client. The *from client* event is irrefutably a so-called idle event. The Oracle kernel uses these *to client* and *from client* events to measure the

"Idle" Is a Four-Letter Word

Any good book about the Oracle wait interface must discuss the so-called *idle wait events*. Authors tag "idle" events as special because they represent code path in the Oracle kernel in which a kernel process awaits an instruction to do something. System monitoring tools specifically omit statistics about idle wait events. For example, Oracle's *Statspack* utility contains a table called STATS$IDLE_EVENT that holds the names of events database administrators commonly omit from the *Statspack* reports upon V$SYSTEM_EVENT. Those events are:

```
dispatcher timer
lock manager wait for remote message
pipe get
pmon timer
PX Idle Wait
PX Deq Credit: need buffer
PX Deq Credit: send blkd
rdbms ipc message
smon timer
SQL*Net message from client
virtual circuit status
```

As you've already seen in Chapter 8 ("The "idle events" problem"), authors drop various wait events into the "idle" bucket to solve a problem that is caused by improperly scoped diagnostic data. Improperly scoped diagnostic data forces the analyst to ignore "idle" events, even when those events contain vital information. However, if you collect properly scoped diagnostic data, then whether an event is "idle" becomes an unproductive distraction. Rather than classify events as "idle" or "non-idle," in Chapter 5, I introduce the classification of events that execute *within* the context of a database call versus events that execute *between* database calls.

While it is tempting to equate what other authors refer to as *idle* events with what I refer to as *between*-call events, even this is not a reliable mapping. *Between-call events* and the *idle wait events* are not synonyms. For example, the PX Deq Credit: need buffer event is a *within*-call event. Other events that are often considered idle, like SQL*Net more data from client and SQL*Net more data from dblink, also occur within the context of a database call, not between calls.

---

performance of interprocess communications that take place through SQL*Net. Example 11-1 depicts how the events work inside the Oracle kernel.

Example 11-1. Typical code path that the Oracle kernel executes upon the completion of a database call

```
# database call completes here

# write the result of the db call to the client through SQL*Net
ela0 = gettimeofday;
```

Example 11-1. Typical code path that the Oracle kernel executes upon the completion of a database call (continued)

```
write(SQLNET, ...);
ela1 = gettimeofday;
nam = 'SQL*Net message to client';
ela = ela1 - ela0;
printf(TRCFILE, "WAIT #%d: nam='%s' ela= %d' ...", cursor, nam, ela, ...);
printf(TRCFILE, "\n");

# listen to SQL*Net for further instructions from the client
ela0 = gettimeofday;
read(SQLNET, ...);
ela1 = gettimeofday;
nam = 'SQL*Net message from client';
ela = ela1 - ela0;
printf(TRCFILE, "WAIT #%d: nam='%s' ela= %d' ...", cursor, nam, ela, ...);
printf(TRCFILE, "\n");

# next database call gets processed here
```

SQL*Net message to client events typically consume only a couple of microseconds. But SQL*Net message from client events can take much longer. For example:

User think time
> If you connect to Oracle at 08.00 and then not issue a single database call until 10.00, Oracle will tally 7,200 seconds of SQL*Net message from client to V$SYSTEM_EVENT.TIME_WAITED at 10.00.

Client program execution time
> An Oracle Applications *Financial Statement Generator* report (a batch program that executes as an Oracle client process) will typically make some database calls and then spend a comparatively long time executing C code in the client program upon the retrieved data. From the Oracle kernel process's perspective, this time consumed by the client is simply time consumed blocked upon the read call depicted in Example 11-1, so the time is logged as SQL*Net message from client.

Inter-call latency
> Even when an application issues two database calls in rapid succession, it is common for the SQL*Net message from client event that occurs between the calls to have a latency of hundreds of microseconds.

Notice a couple of things from these examples. First, from looking at diagnostic data alone, it is impossible to determine which "database idle" time is actually part of someone's response time, and which "database idle" time is simply time that a user spends not paying attention to her screen. Knowing the difference requires knowledge of the user experience. Second, although the latency between rapid-fire database calls is only a few hundred microseconds, the total time adds up. For example, even if your average SQL*Net message from client latency is a microscopic 500 µs, then 1,000,000 database calls will generate a full 500 seconds (8.3 minutes) of response time.

Responding to large SQL*Net response time contributions

These observations lead us to an understanding of how to respond to a resource profile that is dominated by between-call event durations. If a between-call event dominates your resource profile, here is what to do:

1. Confirm that the between-call event duration is actually a component of someone's response time. If not, then correct the data collection error and construct a new resource profile.

2. If a between-call event's response time contribution is high because of a few large latencies, then investigate why the application spends so much time between database calls.

3. Otherwise, if the between-call event's response time contribution is high because the number of calls to the event is so large, then investigate why the application makes so many distinct database calls.

4. If you cannot reduce the number of distinct database calls, then investigate whether you can improve the individual wait event's average latency. For example, eliminate other processes' unnecessary database calls that might be causing queueing delays for network resources.

 Notice that this sequence of steps is completely consistent with the procedure laid out in Chapter 5. First, eliminate unnecessary calls. Next, eliminate unnecessary interprocess competition.

The SQL*Net events whose latencies are most likely to dominate a resource profile are:

*SQL*Net message from client*
> The remedy for this event is to eliminate as many unnecessary database calls as possible. For example, eliminate redundant parse calls (see "Parse Optimization" for details). Use Oracle's array processing features to manipulate many rows per database call instead of just one.*

*SQL*Net more data from client*
> If you are passing enormous SQL text strings in your application's parse calls, then stop it. Instead, issue stored procedure calls from the application. However, if you are sending large arrays of values to be bound into placeholders ("bind variables") in your SQL text, then you may not be able to reduce the time spent waiting for this event without creating some other, worse problem.

---

* The same advice applies to the job of eliminating single-task message events. The single-task message event is not a SQL*Net event, but its use is the single-task analog of the SQL*Net message from client event on two-task process configurations.

SQL*Net message from dblink

Consider replicating data locally instead of joining across a database link. Replication can be operationally efficient, especially for tables that change very rarely, or for which using slightly stale data produces negligible functional harm. It may be possible to eliminate executions of this event by reworking a SQL statement's execution plan so that less data are transmitted between instances.

 You can derive a good approximation of the number of network round-trips an application generates by counting the number of event executions whose nam values have the string SQL*Net in them. Studying the ela values for these event executions of course results in powerful evidence about whether your network latencies are a contributor to a response time problem.

Responding to large response time contributions from other events

Occasionally, you'll find an unsatisfactorily large response time contribution from an event you've never heard of. There are many Oracle wait events that I don't cover in much detail within this book. However, the pattern of your response shouldn't vary, even when your number one performance problem is something you don't know how to fix. The sequence of steps should sound familiar to you by now:

1. Identify the event that's consuming most of your user action's response time.

2. Determine what action causes the event to be executed so many times.

3. Make the application do that action less often.

Of course, step 1 is pretty thoroughly documented throughout this book. Steps 2 and 3 are not much more difficult. The names of most events give you a big clue about their meanings. For example, the PX events are emitted by code path within Oracle's parallel execution capability. Once you learn how parallel execution works, the meanings of the PX events become clear: a master session assigns work to slave sessions and waits for the results. The slaves do most of the work. Another example: a global cache cr request event is what a RAC-enabled Oracle kernel process emits when it needs to access a database buffer held by another RAC instance. How do you get rid of global cache cr request executions? Require fewer buffers from the other instance, or perhaps fewer buffer visits in general (see "Logical I/O Optimization," below).

Even if the event is something you've never heard of, and you find its name completely incomprehensible, Method R takes you to the threshold of a solution. As I mention at the beginning of this chapter, there are several references available to you, free of charge on the Internet. Even the worst case imaginable isn't very bad. If you find absolutely no help on the Internet, your call to Oracle Corporation product support should be much easier than you might expect:

Support call without Method R: My system is slow. We're desperate, but we have no clue what to do. What can we do to fix it?

Depending upon which support analyst you get, be prepared for just about anything. However, with Method R, your support call should be considerably more tightly scoped.

> *Support call with Method R:* The response time for the most important user action on my system is 75.32 seconds. Of that time, more than 73 seconds are spent executing an event called resmgr:waiting in check2. Can you please tell me (1) what action in my application is causing this Oracle kernel code path to be executed? And (2) what can I do to execute it less often?

It's a rhythm you get into: find out why an event was executed; find out how to avoid it next time. It's a rhythm that works.

Eliminating Wasteful Work

Oracle Corporation's wait event documentation has come a long way since the old days when the *Oracle7 Server Tuning* guide provided its comically bad advice to users of the new V$SESSION_WAIT view (Chapter 8). There's one area to which I wish Oracle would devote more focus, however: *workload reduction*. I think one reason Oracle doesn't focus on workload reduction in its wait events reference is that the wait events reference appears in the chapter entitled "Instance Tuning." I think that in a chapter with such a name, an author feels constrained to limit his discussions to "tuning" activities that don't require application modifications.

You and I, however, live under no such restrictions. Even if you're using a third-party application that you cannot change without vendor participation, you still need to keep your mind open to the performance enhancement opportunities made possible by workload reduction. Of course, eliminating wasteful workload can sometimes call for application modification. Don't despair, however. It is often not as difficult as you might think to convince an application software vendor to improve the performance of a packaged application.

 Your best chance of convincing an application software vendor to improve the performance of your purchased application is to provide irrefutable quantitative evidence that your performance improvement suggestions will help their product make you—and your vendor's other customers—happier.

A great benefit of using Method R is that no matter what the cause of a user action's performance problem, you'll find it. Will it be bad news to learn that your application vendor made a terrible design mistake that will prohibit your happiness until it is fixed? It may be. But if the truth is that the only path to good performance is through your application vendor, you need to learn that fact as quickly as possible, so that you'll stop wasting resources on activities that are destined to fail.

Each of the following sections augments the wait event references you'll find at Oracle Corporation web sites and elsewhere on the Internet. Each section describes a few ways to eliminate wasteful workload and how the waste at issue can show up as components of user action response time.

Logical I/O Optimization

Much of the data manipulation performed upon an Oracle database takes place in the *database buffer cache* region of the Oracle kernel's collection of shared memory segments called the *system global area*. Therefore, all performance analysts pay attention to what goes on in the database buffer cache. The Oracle kernel reportedly uses hundreds of different code paths to access buffers in the database buffer cache [Lewis (2003)]. The most expensive of those buffer visits are called *Oracle logical I/O* (LIO) operations. A database call's LIO count is the sum of its cr and cu statistic values from SQL trace data.

At virtually every Oracle site I've ever visited, more than 50% of the total CPU capacity consumed by Oracle applications has been wasted on unnecessary LIO calls. In many cases, well over 90% of a system's total capacity usage can be eliminated with no loss of useful function whatsoever to the business.

Excessive buffer visits are the morbid obesity of the database. Just like carrying around an extra twenty pounds of body fat hurts virtually every subsystem in a human body (circulatory, renal, musculoskeletal, ocular...), extra LIO calls can degrade the performance of virtually every subsystem in an Oracle application.

Visiting too many buffers consumes unnecessary CPU service and causes time spent not executing that can show up in large unaccounted-for durations. Unnecessary LIO operations cause latch free waits for cache buffers chains latches, and it motivates unnecessary OS read calls that show up as db file sequential read or db file scattered read.

Many Oracle wait events are capable of revealing harmful performance side effects of unnecessary buffer visits. For example, *everybody's* performance degrades as CPU run queues grow longer. Oracle's log file sync wait event is one of the first events to show increased latencies due to the time a process spends waiting in a CPU run queue. Negative effects of excessive buffer visits show up in places you might never have expected. For example, when unnecessary buffer visits motivate unnecessarily intense competition for disk I/O, DBWR writes can queue behind read requests. When DBWR fails to keep pace with the buffer change rate, applications become susceptible to waits for free buffer waits, write complete waits, and even log file switch (checkpoint incomplete) events. The origin of buffer busy waits problems can often be traced back to an excessive number of LIO operations. Mistakes that lead to unnecessary LIO operations can even cause unnecessary SQL*Net message from client event executions.

Why LIO problems are so common

There are several reasons that so many systems suffer from excessive LIO processing. One reason is that we're all taught early and often that memory accesses are a lot faster than disk accesses, with the implication that lots of memory accesses are nothing really to worry about [Millsap (2001c)]. A deeper reason that so many Oracle applications suffer from excessive LIO processing is that there are so many ways that people can cause the problem. Here is a small sample:

Application users
> There are several ways that application users can cause an application to make unnecessary buffer visits. They can run unconstrained queries instead of filtered queries; for example, they can search for the vendor named "Xerox" by performing a blind query instead of specifying X% as a constraint on the name. They can run reports without appropriate arguments; for example, they can run the accidental "whole company's sales since inception" report instead of the intended "this month's sales for my department" report. Especially when systems slow down because of other LIO excesses, users can resubmit the same job several times, resulting in an execution of the same LIOs several times.

Application administrators
> Application administrators can make mistakes that result in unnecessary buffer visits, too. In configurable applications, like the Oracle e-Business Suite, charts of accounts configuration and setup decisions can make a tremendous difference in the LIO counts generated by common business functions. Some applications, like the Oracle General Ledger product, have their own query optimization features built in. Using features like these without careful consideration of their performance impact can cause lots of unnecessary LIO calls. Application administrators that do a poor job of data archiving and purging can inflict millions of unnecessary LIO calls upon an application.

Instance administrators
> Instance administrator mistakes that can cause unnecessary LIO processing include making poor choices for the dozens of instance parameters like HASH_AREA_SIZE and DB_FILE_MULTIBLOCK_READ_COUNT that influence the operation of the Oracle cost-based query optimizer.

Data administrators
> Data administrators can cause unnecessary LIO processing in an immense number of ways. Perhaps the most common is to provide poor quality information about tables and indexes to the Oracle cost-based query optimizer (CBO) by botching the statistics gathering process. Tables afflicted with severe row migration or row chaining problems consume more LIO processing than necessary.

Tables with poorly planned PCTFREE and PCTUSED values can drive unnecessary LIOs. Failing to use index-organized tables, clusters, and partitions in the right situations can result in unnecessary LIOs. Failing to declare constraints (like which columns are primary or foreign key columns, and which columns are NULL-able and which are not) can prevent the Oracle query optimizer from using reduced-LIO execution plans. Of course, having too few indexes—or simply the *wrong* indexes—can cause unnecessary LIO operations for queries, and having too many indexes can cause unnecessary LIOs for INSERT, UPDATE, and DELETE statements.

Application developers

Applications development decisions of course have immense impact upon LIO counts. Several types of SQL design mistakes make it impossible for the Oracle kernel to use efficient query execution plans. For example, using a WHERE clause predicate like TRUNC(START_DATE) = TO_DATE(:b1,'mm/dd/rr') might prevent an Oracle kernel process from using an index upon START_DATE that might have provided excellent LIO count reduction. Application code can use perfect SQL and still execute too many LIO calls. For example, an application coded to fetch one row at a time from an Oracle cursor can execute a hundred times more LIO calls than the same application designed to use the Oracle *array fetch* mechanism to fetch 100 rows in a single LIO call. Neglecting to use Oracle's array features puts extra load not just on the database, but also on the network; the extra database calls required to process larger numbers of smaller row sets produce more SQL*Net message from client event executions, which contribute quickly to user action response times.

Application data designers

Application designers can also make it impossible to build an efficient, low-LIO application. One inventory tracking application that Jeff worked on a few years ago made it impossible to determine the location of an inventory item without constructing the entire history of where the item had been. Instead of a quick indexed "where is it?" lookup, the application required a complicated and long-running CONNECT BY query.

With so many people in the mix who have to do their jobs well to prevent LIO problems, it's no wonder that most sites generate excessive LIO calls.

How to optimize SQL

Optimizing inefficient SQL is easily the most important performance repair tactic that you'll need as an Oracle performance analyst. If a database call motivates more than about ten LIO calls per row returned per table listed in the FROM clause of the SQL text motivating the call, then the SQL statement's efficiency can probably be improved. For example, a three-table join operation that returns two rows should probably require fewer than about 60 LIO calls.

Any ratio is unreliable in certain circumstances. One such circumstance for this ratio occurs when a query's result set is the result of an aggregation. For example, a query returning a sum (one row) from a million-row table will legitimately require more than ten LIO calls.

Applications executing SQL resulting in large numbers of LIO calls create massive scalability barriers for systems with large user counts. Not only do unnecessary LIO calls motivate excessive CPU capacity consumption, they often drive large numbers of latch free waits for cache buffers chains latches [Millsap (2001c)]. Attempted latch acquisitions in and of themselves can cause excessive CPU capacity consumption, especially in environments where analysts have increased the value of _SPIN_ COUNT beyond its default value (as a general rule, *don't*).

There are several good resources available today that explain how to optimize SQL: [Ensor and Stevenson (1997a, 1997b); Harrison (2000); Lewis (2001b, 2002); Kyte (2001); Adams (2003); Lawson (2003); Holt et al. (2003)].* Contributors to various mailing lists like Oracle-L (*http://www.cybcon.com/~jkstill*) do an excellent job of helping list users write efficient SQL. Each of these sources includes good advice about how to write efficient SQL using methods including (but by no means restricted to) the following:

- Diagnosing the behavior of SQL statement executions with tools like *tkprof*, EXPLAIN PLAN, and debugging events like 10032, 10033, 10046, 10079, 10104, and 10241.

- Diagnosing the behavior of the Oracle query optimizer using debugging events like 10053.

- Manipulating SQL text to permit the use of more efficient execution plans.

- Defining an efficient index strategy to aid in better data reduction for queries without producing excessive overhead for INSERT, UPDATE, MERGE, and DELETE operations.

- Using the stored outlines feature to force the Oracle query optimizer to use the plan of your choosing.

- Creating appropriate table, index, and database statistics to better inform the Oracle query optimizer about your data.

- Designing physical data models that facilitate the storage and retrieval operations your application requires.

- Designing logical data models that facilitate the storage and retrieval operations your application requires.

---

* I'm also eager to see the new SQL optimization book that Dan Tow (*http://www.singingsql.com*) is reportedly writing as I finish this book.

Parse Optimization

Excessive parsing is a sure-fire way to ensure that an application will never scale to large user counts [Holt and Millsap (2000)]. The general sentiment that students seem to bring to our classrooms is that hard parses are huge scalability inhibitors for transaction processing systems, but "soft parses" are okay. More to the point, perhaps people believe that hard parses are avoidable, but "soft parses" are not. Both sentences are only half true. Hard parses *are* as awful as people expect, and you can avoid them by using bind variables instead of literal values in your application SQL. However, so-called soft parses are awful in their own right, and you can avoid more of them than you might have thought.

Many authors use the term "soft parse" as a synonym for "parse call." I prefer the term "parse call," because it focuses your attention upon the application, where you can actually implement a remedy action. Using the term "soft parse" seems to draw people's focus to the database, which is *not* the stack layer where you can fix the problem. Here's why. Any time an Oracle kernel process receives a parse call from an application, that kernel process must consume CPU capacity on the database server. If the kernel finds an appropriately sharable cursor for the query either in the session cursor cache or the Oracle library cache, then the parse call never motivates a *hard parse*, and the parse call ends up being cheaper than it might have been. However, even cheaper than a soft parse is *no parse*. Applications scale best to large user counts when they parse as infrequently as possible. You should strive to eliminate unnecessary parse calls whenever you can.

In fact, applications scale best when they make the smallest number of *database calls* that they can. The evolution of the Oracle Call Interface (OCI) reflects this goal. For example, the release 8 OCI reduces client-server round trips in a number of clever ways (*http://otn.oracle.com/ tech/oci/htdocs/Developing_apps.html*). The release 9.2 OCI goes even further to prevent many database calls in the application from ever even reaching the database (*http://otn.oracle.com/tech/oci/htdocs/ oci9ir2_new_features*).

On high concurrency systems with unnecessarily high parse call counts, large CPU service numbers often correlate with large numbers of latch free waits for library cache, shared pool, and other latches. Attempted latch acquisitions in and of themselves can cause excessive CPU capacity consumption, especially in environments where analysts have increased the value of _SPIN_COUNT (again, as a general rule, *don't*). Furthermore, excessive parse calls cause unnecessary SQL*Net message from client latencies, which can add up to several seconds of response time waste for every second of actual work done inside the database. Finally, parse calls that use long SQL texts create unnecessary SQL*Net more data from client latencies, which can also add up to big response time numbers.

If your performance problem is caused by large numbers of parse calls, then consider the following workload reduction strategies:

- Don't use string literals in SQL WHERE clauses. Use bind variables (placeholders) instead, especially when the literal string has high cardinality (that is, when the literal string has many possible values). Using string literals instead of bind variables consumes CPU service and, on high concurrency systems, it causes unnecessary latch free waits for shared pool, library cache, and row cache object latches.

- Extract parse calls from within loops so that an application can reuse the cursor prepared by a single parse call many times. The pseudocode of Example 11-2 shows how.

Example 11-2. Parsing inside of a loop creates a dreadful scalability inhibitor

```
# BAD, unscalable application code
for each v in (897248, 897249, ...) {
  c = parse("select ... where orderid = ".v);
  execute(c);
  data = fetch(c);
  close_cursor(c);
}

# GOOD, scalable application code
c = parse("select ... where orderid = :v1");
for each v in (897248, 897249, ...) {
  execute(c, v);
  data = fetch(c);
}
close_cursor(c);
```

- Deactivate application-to-database driver features that motivate more *parse* database calls than are apparent in the application source code. For example, the Perl DBI provides a prepare-level attribute called ora_check_sql whose default value of 1 motivates two parse calls per Perl prepare function call. The first parse call is performed to help the application SQL developer more quickly debug his application source code by providing more detailed diagnostic information in response to failed parse calls. However, on production systems, this feature should be deactivated because it motivates unnecessary parse calls.

- Use a multi-tier application architecture in which each application service parses all of its SQL statements exactly one time and then reuses cursors for the duration of its uptime.

- Don't send long SQL text stings in parse calls. Use stored procedure calls instead. Sending long SQL text strings in parse calls consumes unnecessary CPU service consumption on the server—even when they use bind variables. Even when the SQL text is completely shareable, the Oracle kernel must validate object permissions each time it receives a SQL text string from a new user ID (when the kernel receives a stored procedure call, the procedure executes in its owner's context, so the permissions on objects inside the package need to be checked only once—if the application developer doesn't specify the use of the invoker's rights) [Adams (2003) 371-372]. Passing long SQL text strings also causes unnecessary network load, which manifests as SQL*Net more data from client latency for the Oracle kernel process making the parse call, and as longer SQL*Net message from client latencies for everyone else.

- Reduce the application's use of public synonyms if you have an extraordinarily large number of object references [Adams (2003) 373-375]. Search *google.com* with site:www.ixora.com.au "public synonym" for additional information.

Write Optimization

The design of the Oracle kernel centralizes its writing tasks nicely into a small set of specialized background processes. The processes that do most of Oracle's write operations are DBWR, LGWR, and ARCH. Most databases do far more reading than they do writing. However, many systems have important service level agreements on business functions that require high-performance writing, and even on systems where writing takes a back seat to reading, slow writes can mess up performance for reads in indirect ways. For example, the poor performance behavior of a slow DBWR process can show up as free buffer waits events in query response times. Excessive write operations can queue at storage devices ahead of legitimate read requests, resulting in degraded db file sequential read, db file scattered read, or direct path read performance.

There are several ways that workload optimization can improve DBWR, LGWR, and ARCH write performance. The most commonly required optimization is actually to eliminate unnecessary LIO operations (see "Logical I/O Optimization"). Unnecessary LIO operations can motivate unnecessary OS read calls, which can queue ahead of DBWR writes, which can inspire longer-than-expected write latencies on db file single write and db file parallel write operations executed by a DBWR process.

Next, you should ensure that all the writes your application does are truly necessary. There are lots of sneaky ways that an application can generate more writes than it really needs to. For example:

- The Oracle kernel generates redo and undo for every index block that is changed by an INSERT, UPDATE, or DELETE statement, so the presence of unnecessary indexes can generate lots of unnecessary undo in transaction processing systems. For example, an insert into a table with three indexes generates roughly ten times more workload than an insert into an unindexed table [Ensor and Stevenson (1997a), 147].

- Some applications generate unnecessary undo by updating columns to the same value they already had. For example, in a SQL statement that sets a status flag from N to Y based on some set of conditions, make sure that your WHERE clause includes a predicate that specifies AND STATUS='N'. Automatic application generators often update columns to values they already had. They do it when they generate an UPDATE statement that updates every column that has a value shown on the current screen. Instead of updating *all* the columns with on-screen values, they should update only the columns that the user has *changed*.

- Application users and database administrators can execute table and index operations that use the LOGGING designation by default, but that could have been performed just as well with the NOLOGGING designation. (The keywords LOGGING and NOLOGGING replace the deprecated keywords RECOVERABLE and UNRECOVERABLE.)

> Using NOLOGGING is not a good idea if you actually want an operation to be recoverable. For example, you don't want to use NOLOGGING operations on a database that participates in a hot standby architecture. Oracle9*i* provides a FORCE LOGGING mode to stop developers from successfully using the NOLOGGING option.

Your system configuration decisions influence the amount of workload your system must endure, too. For example, RAID level 5 disk configurations are particularly vulnerable to write-induced waiting. Every write performed by an Oracle DBWR process is a single-block write, which RAID level 5 handles very inefficiently unless it has been configured with a sufficient amount of cache. When sustained write rates overwhelm the storage capacity of the cache, the performance of a RAID level 5 disk group degrades to roughly four times worse than the array's expected operational throughput. Your best solution is to eliminate enough wasted workload that your sustained I/O rate to the device drops to a suitable level. Failing that, you can choose one of the following courses of action:

- Increase the size of the cache (which will only defer the problem, but perhaps you can defer it long enough to suit your application for the duration of its peak I/O load).

- Increase the number of RAID level 5 disk groups dedicated to servicing your database application's read and write requests.

- Reconfigure your disks into a different RAID organization that allows you to achieve higher I/O throughput rates without the need to buy additional memory or disks. For example, use striping and mirroring.

Attributes of a Scalable Application

Building scalable applications is hard work. It's a lot harder than anything that fits in just one or two pages can solve. But by now, I'm sure you have noticed a couple of ideas about Oracle performance that I consider axiomatic:

---

1. Most systems have plenty of hardware dedicated to them; they are slow because of *waste*.

2. *Eliminating* that waste is much more economically efficient than trying to cover up the problem by adding more capacity to the system.

I therefore submit that building fast, scalable applications requires adherence to a kind of Golden Rule of Application Design:

> Don't design your application to do *anything* that isn't absolutely necessary.

It sounds horribly lazy, in direct violation of the sound work ethics that our good fathers and mothers have taught us. But doing things an application doesn't *need* to do is exactly what makes it slow, unscalable (which is different from *slow* [Millsap (2001a)]), and—in the end—economically inefficient. The following few bits of advice bring some concreteness to this Golden Rule:

1. Don't run reports that nobody reads.

2. Don't generate more output than you need.

3. Don't execute a business process any more often than the business needs.

4. Don't write SQL that visits more blocks in the database buffer cache than necessary.

5. Don't update a column's value to the same value it already has.

6. Push data when it's ready instead of forcing applications to poll to see if there's any work to do.

7. Don't generate redo and undo when you don't need the recoverability benefits provided by generating it.

8. Don't parse any SQL statement that you could have pre-parsed and shared.

9. Don't process DML one row at a time; use array fetches, bulk inserts, etc.

10. Don't lock data any more often or for any longer than is absolutely necessary.

While I won't pretend that the list is complete, I do believe that it should help you get into the spirit of understanding what an appropriately lean application should look like.

CHAPTER 12

Case Studies

If you've read the whole book to this point, then, conceptually, you're ready to do performance improvement projects in a whole new way. However, being "conceptually ready" to do something and actually committing yourself to the experience of doing it are two completely different things. Because the new Method R contradicts convention, it can be especially difficult to commit to using it. Virtually every book, paper, newsletter, web page, software tool, consultant, colleague, and friend who has ever occupied your attention before this book has given you advice about "tuning" that radically contradicts what I'm telling you to do here. In an attempt to convince you to try Method R, this chapter contains some examples to show you how it works in practice. My hope is that by showing you how my colleagues and I respond to some patterns that we commonly see in our optimization work, you'll imagine more vividly how Method R can work for you.

Think of learning Method R in the same way that you learned to speak your native language. You began by observing other people performing the act you were trying to learn. Specifically, you did *not* learn how to speak as a child by studying syntax diagrams and declension tables. If you studied those things at all, you did so *after* you had gained significant familiarity with the language. Your teachers probably forced you to study them in school. Your educational system's motive for exposing you to the underlying rules of the language was to enable you to subject your use of language to a more formal analysis that would help you communicate more effectively later in life.

I want to help you learn Method R in a similar way. In the following sections, I present a few examples of common Oracle performance improvement projects that you can follow from beginning to end. My plan is that by studying these examples, you'll quickly notice the emergence of key behavior patterns that you'll be able to copy in situations that differ from my examples. If you evolve more deeply into Oracle performance improvement as a specialty, then you'll need the syntax rules and declension tables that I provide in Part II.

The case studies in this chapter derive from a variety of sources, including:

- Hotsos Profiler customers who have submitted trace files to *hotsos.com* for analysis
- Hotsos Clinic students who have brought a trace file to class for live, in-class analysis
- Client visits performed by Hotsos performance specialists
- Questions and answers appearing on public news groups

All the examples are real. I do not reveal the source of each case, nor do I identify the people involved, but every case described in this chapter came to us as a legitimate pain that had, until submission to Method R, evaded solution. As you will see as you gain experience with the method, correct use of Method R leads inevitably to one of two conclusions:

- You find the root cause of a performance problem, and you're able to determine how much performance improvement you should expect.
- Or, you become able to prove that improving performance for the user action under analysis is not economically justifiable.

Case 1: Misled by System-Wide Data

After several months of trying to arrange a sales call into a local account in Dallas, our *hotsos.com* sales staff finally got a phone call on a Monday. The people with whom we'd been trying to arrange a visit had finally reached their wits' end with a performance problem, and they were going to give us a shot at fixing it. So on Wednesday, we got our chance.

The scenario was similar to ones we had seen before. The company had been fighting a performance problem with a particular program's response time for several months. All of the in-house experts had given the problem their shot over those months. None of their attempts had resulted in any appreciable performance gains. They had finally reached the level of frustration with the problem that management had decided to invest a large chunk of cash into fixing the problem. So on the weekend prior to our phone call, the company upgraded their system's CPUs. The upgrade process went successfully, and of course everyone was excited—perhaps a bit nervous—to see the improvement on Monday.

To their horror, the performance of the slow program was *actually worse* after the very expensive upgrade. Not just "seemed worse," *was* worse; measurably worse. So, on Monday we got a phone call. Our invitation said, "Come in and show us what you can do." Two days later, we got in our car and drove across town. This is what we found:

- The company used the Oracle Payroll product. It was configured in a conventional way, with batch jobs running on the database server, and dozens of browser-based users scattered throughout the building on a local area network (LAN).

- PYUGEN program performance had been hurting the business for several months. When we arrived, the PYUGEN program—a batch job—was able to process about 27 assignments per minute. Targeted performance was twice this throughput.

- The customer used an internationally renowned, full-featured performance monitoring tool that queried data from fixed views like V$SYSTEM_EVENT and V$LATCH. This tool showed that the system's bottleneck was waits for the Oracle latch free wait event. The vast majority of latch free waits were waits for cache buffers chains latches.

- The customer understood correctly that contention for cache buffers chains latches was a likely indication of inefficient (that is, high-LIO) SQL. However, the customer's application developers had analyzed the PYUGEN program and found no way to reduce the SQL's LIO count.

- A recent upgrade of all twelve of the system's CPUs from 700 MHz to 1 GHz had made PYUGEN performance measurably *worse*. Failure of the CPU upgrade to improve performance was the "final straw" motivating the customer to invite *hotsos.com* staff to come onsite.

Targeting

By the time we arrived onsite, the customer had already completed the user action targeting step by identifying PYUGEN as the system's more important performance problem. Thus, our first step with the customer was to begin the collection of properly scoped diagnostic data. At this customer, collecting Oracle extended SQL trace data was straightforward because user action response time consisted exclusively of PYUGEN program execution. We used our free tool called Sparky (*http://www.hotsos.com*) to manage the extended SQL trace activation and deactivation.

The execution that we traced consumed slightly more than half an hour, producing roughly 70 MB of extended trace data. After the program completed, we executed the Hotsos Profiler upon the data, producing the resource profile shown in Example 12-1.

Example 12-1. Resource profile for an Oracle Payroll program

Response Time Component	Duration		# Calls	Dur/Call
SQL*Net message from client	984.0s	49.6%	95,161	0.010340s
SQL*Net more data from client	418.8s	21.1%	3,345	0.125208s

Example 12-1. Resource profile for an Oracle Payroll program (continued)

db file sequential read	279.3s	14.1%	45,084	0.006196s
CPU service	248.7s	12.5%	222,760	0.001116s
unaccounted-for	27.9s	1.4%		
latch free	23.7s	1.2%	34,695	0.000683s
log file sync	1.1s	0.1%	506	0.002154s
SQL*Net more data to client	0.8s	0.0%	15,982	0.000052s
log file switch completion	0.3s	0.0%	3	0.093333s
enqueue	0.3s	0.0%	106	0.002358s
buffer busy waits	0.2s	0.0%	67	0.003284s
SQL*Net message to client	0.2s	0.0%	95,161	0.000003s
db file scattered read	0.0s	0.0%	2	0.005000s
SQL*Net break/reset to client	0.0s	0.0%	2	0.000000s
Total	1,985.3s	100.0%		

The data in the resource profile came as a surprise to everyone who had worked on the project for the past few months. From the resource profile alone, we could already determine beyond the shadow of a doubt that waits for latch free were virtually irrelevant in their influence over total PYUGEN response time. If the company had been completely successful in eliminating latch free waits from their system, it would have made only about a 1% difference in the runtime of this program.

 This kind of thing happens frequently in our field work: you can *not* detect many types of user action performance problems by examining system-wide data. The data from V$SYSTEM_EVENT was true; it was just irrelevant to the problem at hand. You cannot extrapolate detail for a specific session from aggregated system-wide data.

Actually, the V$SYSTEM_EVENT view had indicated clearly that the top wait event was SQL*Net message from client, but of course every good Oracle performance analyst knows that you have to discard all the SQL*Net events because they are "idle" events.

Roughly 50% of the total PYUGEN response time was consumed by executions of read system calls to the SQL*Net mechanism. The occurrence of SQL*Net message from client events at the top of the resource profile motivated a quick re-check of the collected data to ensure that the prominence of this between-calls event was not the result of data collection error. It wasn't. The SQL*Net message from client events and their durations were distributed uniformly throughout the trace file. These wait events were the results of thousands of database calls. When you add in the effect of the other SQL*Net event, SQL*Net more data from client, we had discovered the cause for over 70% of PYUGEN's total response time.

Diagnosis and Response

You of course cannot ignore 70% of a program's response time, even if people do call the motivating events "idle." Idle or not, this time was part of someone's response time, so we needed to deal with it. If we hadn't collected our statistics so carefully (with proper time scope and proper program scope), then we would have seen probably much more SQL*Net message from client time in our data. If you make that particular collection error, then you *must* disregard the so-called idle wait time.

The top line of the resource profile was naturally the symptom we investigated first. Because this was a prepackaged application, we expected that the number of database calls would be difficult for us to manipulate, so we let our attention wander to the duration-per-call column. Here, we found a number that looked suspiciously LAN-like (on the order of 0.010 seconds, as described in Chapter 10), not IPC-like (on the order of 0.001 seconds or less). So we reconfirmed that the PYUGEN batch program had indeed run on the database server host (with the PYUGEN process's corresponding Oracle kernel process) by checking the V$SESSION data collected automatically by Sparky upon collection activation (Example 12-2).

Example 12-2. The data that Sparky obtained from V$SESSION verified that the PYUGEN process was in fact running on the same host as its Oracle kernel process

```
   Oracle instance = prod (8.1.6.3.0)
              host = dalunix150.xyz.com (OSF1 V5.1)
           program = PYUGEN@dalunix150.xyz.com (TNS V1-V2) (session 611)
        trace file = /prod/u001/app/oracle/admin/prod/udump/ora_922341.trc
        line count = 1,760,351 (0 ignored, 0 oracle error)
                t0 = Wed Sep 12 2001 14:10:27 (388941433)
                t1 = Wed Sep 12 2001 14:43:32 (389139973)
 interval duration = 1,985.40s
      transactions = 672 (672 commits, 0 rollbacks)
```

Sure enough, the hostname reported to the right of the @ character in V$SESSION exactly matched the Node name reported in the preamble of the SQL trace file. PYUGEN had definitely run on the same host as the database server. So why would the PYUGEN program suffer from such large SQL*Net message from client latencies? We examined the system's *tnsnames.ora* file to find out. It turns out that to conserve system administration effort, the system's managers had decided to use a single TNS alias system-wide. The batch jobs were using the same TCP/IP protocol adapter as the system's browser clients were using.

It was easy to devise a strategy that was perfectly acceptable in terms of system administrative overhead. We could add a second alias to the existing *tnsnames.ora* file. The second alias would be identical to the existing alias except that it would have a different name, and it would use the syntax (PROTOCOL=BEQ) instead of (PROTOCOL=TCP). The customer would shut down the Oracle Applications Concurrent

---

Manager and restart it, specifying the new alias that used the *bequeath* protocol adapter. The new *tnsnames.ora* file could be pushed out to everyone on the system without side effect. Everyone except for the person who started the Concurrent Manager would use the same TNS alias as before.

Before implementing this change, the customer ran a simple test. He executed and timed a SELECT statement that would require a few thousand database calls from a SQL*Plus session executed on the database server itself. He ran it once through a session established with the old alias that used the TCP/IP protocol adapter. He then ran the statement again through a session established with the new alias that used the *bequeath* protocol adapter. The test showed that using the *bequeath* protocol adapter reduced SQL*Net message from client latencies to less than 0.001 seconds. We could expect to eliminate at least 40% of the program's total response time by executing this one change alone, as shown in Figure 12-1.

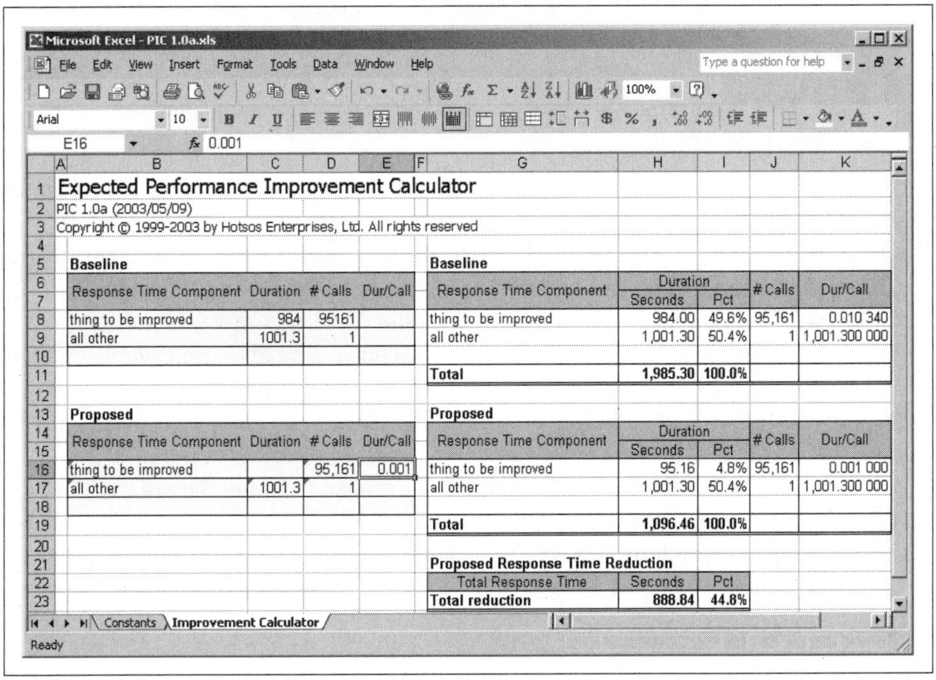

*Figure 12-1. We could expect that reducing the per-call latency of SQL*Net message from client events from 0.010 seconds to 0.001 seconds would eliminate more than 40% of PYUGEN's response time*

We actually had reason to expect better than a 40% improvement. The second most important contributor to PYUGEN response time was another SQL*Net event called SQL*Net more data from client. The cause of this event was a sequence of parse calls that passed excessively long SQL text strings through SQL*Net from the client to the server (instead of using stored procedure calls to accomplish the same thing). The long SQL text strings wouldn't fit into a single SQL*Net packet, so the Oracle kernel spent a considerable amount of time awaiting second and subsequent SQL*Net packets during parse calls. Of course, because Oracle Payroll was a prepackaged application, our short-term hopes for reducing the number of executions of this event were dim. However, we had reason to believe that because some of the `SQL*Net more data from client` latency was network transport, the protocol adapter change would improve the performance of this event's executions as well.

Results

The bottom-line results were excellent. Payroll processing performance improved from executing 27 assignments per minute to 61 assignments per minute. The proposed *tnsnames.ora* change took 15 minutes to test and about a week to navigate through change control. Our whole engagement at the client lasted less than four hours. Of this time, two hours were consumed installing Sparky (which required a Perl upgrade on the database server host), and a little more than half an hour was consumed by letting the `PYUGEN` program run with a level-8 extended SQL trace turned on. The remaining hour and a half contained the whole meeting, greeting, analysis, testing, and recap activities.

Oh yes... Why did the Payroll program get *slower* after the CPU upgrade? Not much Payroll program time was spent consuming CPU service, so the upgrade had very little direct positive effect upon `PYUGEN`. Most of the program's time was spent queueing for the network. Other programs ran at the same time as this Payroll job. The CPU upgrade made *them* faster, which intensified *their* number of network calls (which remained unchanged after the upgrade) into a smaller time window. The result was increased competition for the network during the Payroll run. Therefore, every network I/O call the Payroll program made was a little slower than before the CPU upgrade. The degradation in network response time overwhelmed the small direct improvement of the CPU time reduction, resulting in a net degradation of Payroll performance...not a good thing, because this Payroll program had a higher business priority than everything else on the system.

Lessons Learned

This case is a classic illustration of the following important points:

- Don't let your V$ data tell you what your system's problem is. Your business should decide that. The real performance problem in your system is whatever it is that is causing response time problems for your business's most important user action.

- You can't extrapolate detail from an aggregate. You cannot necessarily determine what's wrong with an individual program by examining only the system-wide statistics for an instance.

- Capacity upgrades are a riskier performance improvement activity than many people think. Not only can they waste a lot of money by being ineffective, they can actually degrade performance for the very programs you're trying to improve.

- It's nearly impossible to find and repair your performance problems by executing the old trial-and-error approach. There are just too many things that *might* be your performance problem. Instead of checking everything that *might* be causing your performance problem, it's easy enough to simply ask your targeted user actions what *is* causing your performance problem.

Case 2: Large CPU Service Duration

One of our first *hotsos.com* customers was an Oracle Financial and Manufacturing Applications site. The customer was experiencing poor response times in several different programs—some stock, some custom. This customer engaged us not to fix performance problems, but to teach their staff how to do it. Job one was to teach the customer's new performance analyst how to collect and use good diagnostic data. Job two was to hack our own pre-beta Sparky and Hotsos Profiler software into usable shape so the customer could use it after we had gone home. It was a nice experience for us. The new performance analyst was an applications administrator and had never actually done much performance improvement work before this project.

Over the course of a couple of months, our contact with the new performance analyst dwindled from daily phone calls to weekly emails. One day we received a call just to say hello and to brag a little bit about one of his day's accomplishments. This is the story of that accomplishment.

Targeting

Over the previous few weeks, our friend had done an excellent job of working down his company's list of targeted slow user actions. He described that he had actually gotten to the point where the conspicuous absence of performance complaints had left him with more free time at work than he was accustomed to having. So, with some of his free time, he had decided to investigate why a particular batch job had always taken so long. (Remember, the new performance analyst had worked closely with the applications before this performance improvement project, so he knew first-hand how long this thing took.) So he traced the program. Example 12-3 shows the resource profile for the trace file.

Example 12-3. Resource profile for Oracle Purchasing program

Response Time Component	Duration		# Calls	Dur/Call
CPU service	1,527.5s	60.8%	158,257	0.009652s
db file sequential read	432.0s	17.2%	62,495	0.006913s
unaccounted-for	209.6s	8.3%		
global cache lock s to x	99.9s	4.0%	3,434	0.029083s
global cache lock open s	85.9s	3.4%	3,507	0.024502s
global cache lock open x	57.9s	2.3%	1,930	0.029990s
latch free	26.8s	1.1%	1,010	0.026505s
SQL*Net message from client	19.1s	0.8%	6,714	0.002846s
write complete waits	11.1s	0.4%	155	0.071806s
enqueue	11.1s	0.4%	330	0.033606s
row cache lock	11.1s	0.4%	485	0.022887s
log file switch completion	7.3s	0.3%	15	0.487333s
log file sync	3.3s	0.1%	39	0.084872s
wait for DLM latch	3.0s	0.1%	91	0.032418s
global cache lock busy	1.5s	0.1%	11	0.139091s
DFS lock handle	1.4s	0.1%	43	0.032558s
global cache lock null to x	0.9s	0.0%	8	0.112500s
rdbms ipc reply	0.6s	0.0%	7	0.081429s
global cache lock null to s	0.4s	0.0%	7	0.060000s
library cache pin	0.1s	0.0%	7	0.015714s
SQL*Net message to client	0.0s	0.0%	6,714	0.000003s
file open	0.0s	0.0%	13	0.000000s
SQL*Net more data from client	0.0s	0.0%	2	0.000000s
Total	2,510.5s	100.0%		

As you can see, CPU service and database file reading dominate the profile with almost 80% of the total response time. Roughly 10% more of the response time is consumed by global cache lock operations required by Oracle Parallel Server, and the final 10% was distributed over a few percentage points of unaccounted-for time and lots of inconsequential events.

There's no way by looking only at the resource profile to determine whether the CPU service consumption shown here is excessive, but to make a material impact upon the almost 42-minute response time will certainly require a reduction of the duration of the CPU service component. The first question you answer in a case like this is, "Which SQL is responsible for this CPU service consumption?" The Hotsos Profiler makes this task particularly easy, by providing a section in its output that lists the top five SQL statements that contribute to each response time component, as shown in Example 12-4.

Example 12-4. The Hotsos Profiler identifies the contribution to CPU service duration by SQL statement

SQL Statement Id	Duration	
704365403	1,066.4s	69.8%
3277176312	371.9s	24.3%

Example 12-4. The Hotsos Profiler identifies the contribution to CPU service duration by SQL statement (continued)

```
1107640601              8.5s    0.6%
3705838826              6.5s    0.4%
529440951               6.0s    0.4%
111 others             68.7s    4.5%
-----------------   ------------------
Total                1,527.5s  100.0%
```

Two SQL statements completely dominate the session's consumption of CPU capacity. In the Hotsos Profiler output, each statement ID is a hyperlink that takes you to the data shown in Example 12-5. With Oracle's *tkprof* utility, you can accomplish the task by specifying the sort order sort=prscpu,execpu,fchcpu. With this sort order, the SQL statement that you're searching for will then show up at the top of the output.

Example 12-5. SQL text and performance statistics for statement 704365403, the top contributor to the session's CPU service consumption

```
Statement Text
update po_requisitions_interface set requisition_header_id=:b0
where (req_number_segment1=:b1 and request_id=:b2)
```

```
Statement Cumulative Database Call Statistics
Cursor  Action         ------ Response Time -------        LIO        PIO
Action  Count  Rows    Elapsed      CPU    Other        Blocks     Blocks
------- ------ ------  ---------  --------- --------   ----------  ----------
Parse      0      0       0.0        0.0      0.0             0           0
Execute 1,166     0   1,455.0    1,066.4    388.6     8,216,887       3,547
Fetch      0      0       0.0        0.0      0.0             0           0
------- ------ ------  ---------  --------- --------   ----------  ----------
Total   1,166     0   1,455.0    1,066.4    388.6     8,216,887       3,547

Per Exe    1      0       1.3        0.9      0.3         7,047           3
Per Row 1,166     1   1,455.0    1,066.4    388.6     8,216,887       3,547
```

The information in Example 12-5 is quite revealing. Here are some interesting observations:

- The statement that contributes the most CPU time to the session's response time is a very simple UPDATE that is executed 1,166 times.

- However, 1,166 executions of this UPDATE statement never processed a single row.

- Each execution required an average of 7,047 LIO operations (that's 8,216,887 LIOs divided by 1,166 executions) to determine that no rows matched the statement's simple WHERE clause predicate.

- The database buffer cache hit ratio for this statement is very "good." It is:

$$CHR = \frac{LIO - PIO}{LIO}$$
$$= \frac{8,216,887 - 3,547}{8,216,887}$$
$$= 0.999568$$

Ironically, one of the reasons that this statement never percolated to the top priority for the system's performance analysts may have been that its cache hit ratio was so good, the system's performance monitoring tools regarded the statement as exemplary.

Diagnosis and Response

In Chapter 11, I describe a simple rule of thumb about LIO call counts: if a SQL statement requires more than about ten LIO operations per row returned per table in the FROM clause, then the statement is probably doing too many LIOs. Well, this UPDATE statement isn't a query with a FROM clause, but nevertheless, it does execute much of the same Oracle kernel code path as would the following query:

```
select requisition_header_id=:b0
from po_requisitions_interface
where (req_number_segment1=:b1 and request_id=:b2)
```

How many LIOs should be required to determine that this query returns no rows? My estimation is fewer than ten. Here's why: if a composite index existed upon the two columns REQ_NUMBER_SEGMENT1 and REQUEST_ID, then the Oracle kernel should be able to determine that the query returns no rows by simply plunging the index from root to leaf. The number of LIO operations required to execute this plunge is the height of the index. The height of an index is its BLEVEL value (for example, from DBA_INDEXES, for index segments you have analyzed) plus one. The most enormous indexes I've ever heard of have heights of seven or less. Therefore, you should expect with a composite index upon REQ_NUMBER_SEGMENT1 and REQUEST_ID, the number of LIO operations per executions will be seven or less.

Remember, a database call's CPU consumption is usually proportional to the number of LIO operations it performs. Therefore, if you can reduce a call's number of LIO operations from 7,047 to just 7, then you can expect to reduce the database call's total CPU consumption by a similar factor of 1,000. You can thus expect for the LIO reduction to cause a total CPU consumption reduction for executions of this UPDATE statement from 1,066.4 seconds to roughly 1 second. This expected improvement of roughly 1,000 seconds is a big enough chunk of response time reduction that it's worth testing the result at this point. The recommended performance improvement activity is to create a composite index upon the two columns REQ_NUMBER_SEGMENT1 and REQUEST_ID.

Results

The total program response time actually dropped by far more than the 1,000-second savings that I forecast. The overachievement came from collateral benefits, including:

- The second largest SQL contributor to the session's CPU service consumption, statement 3277176312, used the exact same WHERE clause as statement 704365403 used. The index creation thus had a tremendous performance improving effect upon both of the top contributors to the session's total response time.

- LIO reduction reduces total session workload, not just in the CPU service category, but in other categories as well. Notably, if you can eliminate many of a session's database buffer visits, then you will usually eliminate many of the session's motives for performing disk read operations as well. Eliminating LIO operations almost always produces the collateral benefit of reduced PIO call counts as well. Reducing LIO call count can reduce waits for global cache lock... events, latch free events, and others as well.

Creating a new index also creates the risk of collateral *damage*, however. In this case, the risk of query damage was minimized because the base table was an interface table that was referenced by only a few SQL statements in the application. To be completely thorough when you create a new index (or drop an old one), you should re-check all of your application's execution plans to ensure that any plan changes introduced by the schema change are not harmful. (The Project Laredo tool described at *http://www.hotsos.com* is one way to accomplish this.)

Lessons Learned

This case highlights several important ideas:

- SQL optimization is often simpler than you might expect. The key is in knowing *which* SQL you need to optimize.
- The collateral benefit of LIO call reduction is extremely powerful.
- Creating or dropping an index provides opportunity for both collateral benefit and collateral damage. Mitigating your risk requires analysis of *all* the potential execution plan changes that the index manipulation might inspire.
- A SQL statement's database buffer cache hit ratio is not a valid measure of its efficiency.

Case 3: Large SQL*Net Event Duration

This case came to us in the final segment of a Hotsos Clinic. The game is that another instructor and I lecture for two and a half days, and then at the end of the course, we offer to open up people's trace files and try to diagnose them in a public forum. The theory is that we're brave enough to try to diagnose the trace file of anyone who is brave enough to show off their slow applications in public. It's great fun. The students get to see whether the techniques we've been talking about actually work in reality, and they get to practice their new ideas by shouting them out in the classroom. The submitter usually gets a serious problem fixed. And we get to see lots of very interesting application performance problems.

In this class, a very nice young lady who had sat at the back of the class handed us a CD on the final day of the course. The trace file on this disk, she explained, was the trace file from a purchased application built with PowerBuilder that had been slow for as long as she could remember. In fact, the company across the street used the same application and was having severe performance problems with it as well. At every local user group meeting, her story continued, she and the other users would routinely ask each other whether anyone had yet figured out how make this thing run faster. Nobody had figured out why it was so slow.

No pressure.

Targeting

It seemed like an excellent opportunity to demonstrate the power of Method R—how great of a setup is a performance problem that people have looked at for years without solving it. It was an opportunity straight out of the first few paragraphs of Chapter 1!

My heart sank when we looked at the resource profile for the file. What we saw is in Example 12-6: lots of SQL*Net message from client, and not really much else. The first sentence out of my mouth expressed my disappointment that we might not be able to help as much as we would like to, because this resource profile apparently included a lot of user think time, or time spent in a probably un-instrumented application server tier, or something like that.

Example 12-6. Resource profiler for an application written in PowerBuilder

Response Time Component	Duration		# Calls	Dur/Call
SQL*Net message from client	166.6s	91.8%	6,094	0.027338s
CPU service	9.7s	5.3%	18,750	0.000515s
unaccounted-for	1.9s	1.1%		
db file sequential read	1.6s	0.9%	1,740	0.000914s
log file sync	1.1s	0.6%	681	0.001645s
SQL*Net more data from client	0.3s	0.1%	71	0.003521s
SQL*Net more data to client	0.1s	0.1%	108	0.001019s
free buffer waits	0.1s	0.0%	4	0.022500s
db file scattered read	0.0s	0.0%	34	0.001176s
SQL*Net message to client	0.0s	0.0%	6,094	0.000007s
log file switch completion	0.0s	0.0%	1	0.030000s
latch free	0.0s	0.0%	1	0.010000s

```
log buffer space              0.0s   0.0%            2    0.005000s
direct path read              0.0s   0.0%            5    0.000000s
direct path write             0.0s   0.0%            2    0.000000s
--------------------------    ---------------   --------------   -----------
Total                       181.5s  100.0%
```

No, she asserted, she had in fact been awake for the duration of the course. She sincerely and patiently explained that she knew what collection error and think time were, and this trace file didn't have any. She had begun the extended SQL trace data collection immediately before a user clicked an OK button to initiate an online action, and she had stopped the data collection immediately after she had noticed that the system had returned the result, by having the user disconnect from the application. The user had actually waited about three minutes from button click to disconnect. This was a two-tier application, with no application middle tier and consequently no un-instrumented application server code. And furthermore, she had used our Sparky tool to collect the data.

Oh.

I had missed a clue, actually. In addition to the average duration per call information, our actual Hotsos Profiler output shows the minimum and maximum single wait time for each event. (It's too much information for me to show in the limited page width allowed for Example 12-6.) The longest wait for a SQL*Net message from client event had been on the order of a few seconds. And of course, the call count (# Calls in Example 12-6), had I paid more attention to it, was actually a big clue that this wasn't a collection error or a think time problem.

At the time, I really wasn't certain of how to attack the problem, so, with Jeff's lead, we starting looking through our Hotsos Profiler output. Using the principle of *forward attribution* as our guide (Chapter 11), we looked for database calls that followed the SQL*Net message from client events. Hotsos have since modified the code so that this type of problem is very easy to solve within just a couple of minutes. I'll describe the diagnostic process in terms of an analysis that would take place today with the improved Hotsos Profiler.

Diagnosis and Response

To tie up any possible loose ends, we examined the SQL*Net message from client time a little more closely. Example 12-6 doesn't show it, because the pages of this book aren't wide enough, but the Hotsos Profiler output showed that the maximum SQL*Net message from client execution duration was 17.43 seconds. A quick search in the raw trace file for the string ela= 1743 (notice the blank space that the Oracle kernel emits between the = and the 1), revealed that there *was* actually a bit of collection error at the tail of the file. Sitting between two XCTEND lines was a SQL*Net message from client execution with an ela value of 17.43 seconds. The first commit had been the end of the user action. The second commit occurred when the user disconnected from the application. It had taken the ladies a few seconds to notice that the action had completed. After correcting for this little bit of collection error, the resource profile for the user action is the one shown in Example 12-7.

Example 12-7. The resource profile from Example 12-6, after correcting for a 17.43-second collection error

Response Time Component	Duration		# Calls	Dur/Call
SQL*Net message from client	149.2s	91.0%	6,093	0.024482s
CPU service	9.7s	5.9%	18,750	0.000515s
unaccounted-for	1.9s	1.2%		
db file sequential read	1.6s	1.0%	1,740	0.000914s
log file sync	1.1s	0.7%	681	0.001645s
SQL*Net more data from client	0.3s	0.2%	71	0.003521s
SQL*Net more data to client	0.1s	0.1%	108	0.001019s
free buffer waits	0.1s	0.1%	4	0.022500s
db file scattered read	0.0s	0.0%	34	0.001176s
SQL*Net message to client	0.0s	0.0%	6,094	0.000007s
log file switch completion	0.0s	0.0%	1	0.030000s
latch free	0.0s	0.0%	1	0.010000s
log buffer space	0.0s	0.0%	2	0.005000s
direct path read	0.0s	0.0%	5	0.000000s
direct path write	0.0s	0.0%	2	0.000000s
Total	164.0s	100.0%		

The next question to answer in this situation is, "Which SQL is responsible for the remaining SQL*Net message from client duration?" The Hotsos Profiler output provides the answer automatically, as shown in Example 12-8.[*]

*Example 12-8. The Hotsos Profiler identifies the contribution to SQL*Net message from client duration by SQL statement*

SQL Statement Id	Duration	
1525010069	23.1s	15.5%
2038166283	18.7s	12.5%
1966856986	17.6s	11.8%
1547563725	13.9s	9.3%
3230460720	10.8s	7.2%
77 others	65.1s	43.6%
Total	149.2s	100.0%

From the percentages shown in the Example 12-8 list of SQL statements, you can see that no single SQL statement accounts for a disproportionately large part of the

---

[*] Unfortunately *tkprof* and Trace File Analyzer provide no help on this type of problem. However, using the principal of forward attribution, you can find the top contributing statements by searching the raw trace data.

SQL*Net message from client contribution. Therefore, to make a big impact upon the reduction of message from client time, it will actually be necessary in this case to look at more than just one SQL statement. However, we began by looking at the first one, whose statement text and statement statistics are shown in Example 12-9.

*Example 12-9. SQL text and performance statistics for statement 1525010069, the top contributor to the session's SQL*Net message from client duration*

```
Statement Text
INSERT INTO STAGING_AREA (
  DOC_OBJ_ID, TRADE_NAME_ID, LANGUAGE_CODE, OBJECT_RESULT, GRAPHIC_FLAG,
  USER_LAST_UPDT, TMSP_LAST_UPDT
) VALUES (
  1000346, 54213, 'ENGLISH', '<BLANK>', 'N', 'sa',
  TO_DATE('11/05/2001 16:40:54', 'MM/DD/YYYY HH24:MI:SS')
)
```

```
Statement Cumulative Database Call Statistics
Cursor  Action         ------ Response Time -------     LIO        PIO
Action  Count  Rows    Elapsed    CPU     Other       Blocks     Blocks
------- ------ ------  --------- -------- --------    ---------- ----------
Parse    696     0       0.9      0.8      0.1            0          0
Execute  348    348      1.7      1.6      0.0         5,251       351
Fetch      0      0       0.0      0.0      0.0            0          0
------- ------ ------  --------- -------- --------    ---------- ----------
Total   1,044   348      2.6      2.4      0.1         5,251       351

Per Exe    1      1       0.0      0.0      0.0           15          1
Per Row    1      1       0.0      0.0      0.0           15          1
```

Though I've not shown it in the output here, the Hotsos Profiler revealed that there were 347 "similar" statements in the trace file. The Profiler defines two SQL statements as *similar* if and only if the statements are identical (as regarded by the Oracle kernel) except for literal string values in the statements. Oracle's *tkprof* would not have aggregated the unshared SQL statements this way; instead, it would have listed all 348 distinct SQL texts as each consuming a very small amount of capacity. This, of course, makes analysis a bit more difficult, but all the information you need to determine that the statements should have been sharable is present in the SQL trace file.

The data in Example 12-9 make it clear why there were so many distinct SQL texts. The statement uses several string literals instead of placeholder ("bind") variables:

```
1000346
54213
'ENGLISH'
'<BLANK>'
'N'
'sa'
'11/05/2001 16:40:54'
```

The value that sticks out immediately as completely unsharable is the date value in the final variable position. This value corresponds to a column called TMSP_LAST_ UPDT—the timestamp of the last update. How many times would you expect for an application to ever reuse the exact SQL text that contains a hard-coded timestamp value with one-second resolution?

Right, you would expect the answer to be zero, but actually there's a little twist to the answer. This particular application reused the statement exactly once (that is, the application used this statement twice in total). Notice the action count for parses and executions of this statement (and its similar statements): the 348 statements accounted for a total of 696 parse calls and 348 executions. That's right, it accounted for exactly twice as many parses as executions! In "Parse Optimization" in Chapter 11, I admonish you to extract parse calls from within loops so that an application can reuse the cursor prepared by a single parse call many times. The Hotsos Profiler output shows (it's not shown in Example 12-9) that for the 696 parse calls, there are 348 misses on the library cache (from the mis statistic of the raw trace data). What's happening here is that, incredibly, this application actually parses each of these SQL statements *twice* for each execute call, as shown in Example 12-10.

Example 12-10. An application that parses twice for every execution...a really bad idea

```
# REALLY BAD, unscalable application code
for each v in (897248, 897249, ...) {
  c = parse("select ... where orderid = ".v);  # just ignore the result
  c = parse("select ... where orderid = ".v);  # do the same parse again
  execute(c);
  data = fetch(c);
  close_cursor(c);
}
```

The first parse call for each statement results in a library cache miss (a "hard" parse), and the second parse call for each statement results in a library cache hit (a "soft" parse).

At this point, it's important to remember our overall goal. Executions of the SQL*Net message from client wait event dominate user action response time. Example 12-7 shows that this user action executes a total of 6,093 such events, for a total response time contribution of 149.2 seconds, each consuming an average of 0.024482 seconds per call. SQL*Net message from client is a wait event that the Oracle kernel executes between database calls. Therefore, eliminating database calls will eliminate some response time attributable to SQL*Net message from client events. Happily, we had just found an opportunity to eliminate 348 parse calls. Simply find a way to stop parsing twice for every execute call. The expected savings: about 8.5 seconds for the session (about 5% of the session's total response time).

Not a huge start, but we're not done yet. As I mention in Chapter 11, by extracting a parse call from within a loop, the student should be able to eliminate *all but one* parse call. Using bind variables and making the code look like the scalable application code shown in Example 10-3 will result in the elimination of 695 unnecessary parse calls. Expected total impact to our student's user action: about 17 seconds, or about 10% of total session response time.

We wondered how many other SQL statements might be suffering from the same problems as the first one we examined? By visiting the detailed statistics for all the SQL statements in the Hotsos Profiler output, we found that over 3,000 total database calls should be candidates for elimination. Expected total impact to the user action: over 73 seconds, or about 45% of the session's total response time.

But even that's not all. Remember, the user clicked OK once and then waited over 180 seconds for a result, with no opportunity for further input provided to the application. But look again at Example 12-9. It is a single-row INSERT statement, executed 348 times, manipulating a grand total of 348 rows. Why would the application need to make 348 database calls to insert 348 rows? Oracle provides an array insert function that might reduce the number of insert statements from 348 to perhaps 4 (if the application could use an array size of 100 rows). If this database call reduction could be implemented, it would reduce the session's total database call count further by more than 650 calls. Expected additional impact to the user action: about 16 seconds, for 10% more of the session's total response time.

If all the proposed database call eliminations could be implemented, the total savings would amount to the elimination of more than 3,650 calls, for a grand total of roughly 89 seconds saved, or a 54% reduction in response time. If the database calls could be eliminated, the user could expect a response time improvement from 164 seconds to about 75 seconds. It is possible that if a lot of users run applications like this one simultaneously, then a lot of the network subsystem's capacity is eaten up by wasted database calls. If this is the case, then eliminating those wasteful calls might reduce network queueing delays so that the 0.024-second latency of SQL*Net message from client events might actually drop to about 0.015 seconds. If this were to happen, then the approximately 2,400 SQL*Net message from client events that remain after optimization might consume only about 37 seconds, which would represent a grand total of about 110 seconds' worth of response time reduction.

Results

When we assess trace files in class, we don't always get to see the end result of our recommendations. This case is one such example. Because the user action in question was part of a packaged application, the three manipulations that we suggested require vendor participation. The student did pass our suggestions to the vendor:

- Don't execute each parse call twice, to cut the number of parse calls for many cursors in half.
- Use bind variables and extract parse calls from loops to reduce the number of parse calls further to one per cursor.

- Reduce overall database calls counts by using array processing instead of processing only one row at a time.

While I write this chapter, the student and I are still waiting to see what might happen. Her company is planning to upgrade to the vendor's next release shortly after this book goes to print. We'll keep you posted on the Web.

Lessons Learned

This case highlights the following important ideas:

- You can't just ignore SQL*Net message from client wait events. When they contribute significantly to the response time of a properly targeted user action, you have to pay attention to them.

- Too many database calls can ruin your performance, even when your SQL is just fine. In this case, the SQL might have in fact been wasteful. But fixing it before fixing the problem with too many database calls would have produced unnoticeably small results.

Case 4: Large Read Event Duration

Regularly, we get nice letters from people who are interested in letting us know that our method and tools are helping. This case is the result of one such letter from a friend in Iceland who reduced the response time of a query from 6.5 hours to 10.9 seconds—and fixed a previously undiscovered functional bug—by adding four bytes to its SQL text. This is the story of how Method R helped him identify the SQL statement that was causing the problem. In the end, he improved the response time of an important batch job from nearly eight hours to just one hour.

Targeting

Application targeting in this case was typical. The system owner was a bank. One of the application's batch jobs was taking so long to run that it was unable to finish in its assigned batch window. The job started at 11:00 p.m. each night, and it would sometimes run until noon the next day. The bank was limiting the number of accounts to update so that the batch job would finish before opening hours. So our friend targeted this batch job for the collection of extended SQL trace data. Example 12-11 shows the resource profile for a run that consumed nearly eight hours of run time.

Example 12-11. Resource profile for a batch job that consumed almost eight hours

Response Time Component	Duration		# Calls	Dur/Call
db file scattered read	19,051.1s	68.4%	1,828,249	0.010420s
CPU service	6,889.3s	24.7%	959,148	0.007183s

db file sequential read	1,892.7s	6.8%	406,417	0.004657s
latch free	29.0s	0.1%	1,071	0.027106s
log file switch completion	1.6s	0.0%	14	0.112143s
SQL*Net message from client	0.3s	0.0%	10	0.034000s
log buffer space	0.1s	0.0%	1	0.100000s
log file sync	0.1s	0.0%	4	0.022500s
file open	0.1s	0.0%	54	0.001296s
buffer busy waits	0.0s	0.0%	14	0.002143s
undo segment extension	0.0s	0.0%	2,111	0.000014s
SQL*Net message to client	0.0s	0.0%	10	0.000000s
Total	27,864.4s	100.0%		

The top lines of Example 12-11 bear the distinct signature of inefficient SQL: lots of file reading and CPU capacity consumption. The next task is to determine which SQL statements are consuming so many resources. In this case, executing *tkprof* with the option sort=prsdsk,exedsk,fchdsk will produce a report with the SQL having the largest number of PIO blocks at the top.

Notice, however, that basing your *tkprof* sort order upon the PIO block *count* is not the same thing as sorting by total PIO call *duration*. What you really want is statements sorted by total I/O call duration, but *tkprof* does not provide this information unless you're using the 9i version. Therefore, when you use *tkprof*, you have to examine your output visually to make sure you have identified the SQL statement that you really want to analyze.

The analyst in this story knew which SQL statement contributed the most to the db file scattered read problem, because he used the Hotsos Profiler contribution table shown in Example 12-12.

Example 12-12. The Hotsos Profiler identifies the contribution to db file scattered read duration by SQL statement

SQL Statement Id	Duration	
1163242303	19,028.9s	99.9%
1626975503	6.7s	0.0%
808413641	5.2s	0.0%
3187134541	3.7s	0.0%
1594054818	2.4s	0.0%
8 others	4.3s	0.0%
Total	19,051.1s	100.0%

Diagnosis and Repair

The hunt thus progressed quickly to the performance analysis of the SQL statement 1163242303 (this is the statement's hv value in the PARSING IN CURSOR section of the raw trace data). Example 12-13 shows the text and performance statistics for this statement.

 Note that hv is only *almost* unique (that is, hv is *not* unique). Two different SQL statements *can* share the same hv value. You won't see it very often, but it can happen.

Example 12-13. SQL text and performance statistics for statement 1163242303, the top contributor to the session's db file scattered read duration

```
Statement Text
SELECT EIGANDI,INNLENT_ERLENT,VERDTRYGGING,SKULDFLOKKUN,VBRTEGUND,FLOKKUR
FROM V_SKULDABREF_AVOXTUN
WHERE EIGANDI = :b1
AND INNLENT_ERLENT = :b2
AND ((RAFVAETT = :b3 )
OR ((RAFVAETT = :b4 )
AND (INNLAUSN IS NULL
OR INNLAUSN > :b5 )
AND (VIDMIDDAGS <= :b6 )))
GROUP BY EIGANDI,INNLENT_ERLENT,VERDTRYGGING,SKULDFLOKKUN,VBRTEGUND,FLOKKUR
ORDER BY EIGANDI,INNLENT_ERLENT,VERDTRYGGING,SKULDFLOKKUN,VBRTEGUND,FLOKKUR
```

```
Statement Cumulative Database Call Statistics
Cursor  Action        ------ Response Time -------      LIO         PIO
Action  Count  Rows    Elapsed     CPU    Other      Blocks      Blocks
-------  ------ ------  ---------  --------- --------  ----------  ----------
Parse   3,739    0        1.9      0.7      1.2          147          17
Execute 3,739    0        1.7      1.6      0.2            0           0
Fetch   4,212   473   23,466.4  4,135.6 19,330.8  36,566,201  36,550,345
-------  ------ ------  ---------  --------- --------  ----------  ----------
Total   11,690  473   23,470.0  4,137.9 19,332.1  36,566,348  36,550,452

Per Exe     1     0        6.3      1.1      5.2        9,780       9,092
Per Row     8     1       49.6      8.8     40.9       77,307      71,868
```

The SQL text for this statement is not too difficult to understand. In spite of the Icelandic object names, the statement is simply a query from a single object. There's apparently not even a join. However, the statement's execution plan obtained from the trace file's STAT lines and shown in Example 12-14 reveal a different story.

Something a little more complicated than a simple one-table query is going on here. In fact, V_SKULDABREF_AVOXTUN is a view. The raw trace file confirms it. The parse call for the SELECT shown in Example 12-13 required a recursive parse, execute, and fetch calls against VIEW$, in the same manner as the query from DBA_OBJECTS that I describe in Chapter 5. The definition of the view V_SKULDABREF_AVOXTUN becomes the next target of our attention. One thing that an Oracle extended SQL trace file does not contain is the definition of each view accessed by SQL identified within the trace file. However, because the trace file makes it clear that V_SKULDABREF_AVOXTUN *is* a view, it's a simple enough matter to query DBA_VIEWS to determine the definition. Example 12-15 shows that definition.

Example 12-14. The execution plan for the time-consuming SELECT statement before optimization

```
         Rows Row Source Operation (Object Id)
--------------- ----------------------------------------------------------------
          473 SORT ORDER BY
          473  SORT GROUP BY
          974   VIEW V_SKULDABREF_AVOXTUN
          974    SORT UNIQUE
          974     UNION-ALL
          686      HASH JOIN
          886       TABLE ACCESS FULL SKULDABREF_AVOXTUN(21435)
      103,247       TABLE ACCESS FULL VBR_FLOKKAR(19409)
          288      FILTER
          288       HASH JOIN
          940        TABLE ACCESS BY INDEX ROWID BREF(19460)
        2,649         INDEX RANGE SCAN(20593)
       10,744        TABLE ACCESS FULL VBR_FLOKKAR(19409)
```

Example 12-15. The definition of the view behind the performance problem

```
CREATE OR REPLACE VIEW v_skuldabref_avoxtun (
   eigandi,
   innlent_erlent,
   verdtrygging,
   skuldflokkun,
   vbrtegund,
   flokkur,
   rafvaett,
   ostadladur,
   brefnumer,
   vidmiddags,
   innlausn,
   nafnverd,
   kaupkrafa,
   ees,
   vextir )
AS
select
   s.eigandi,
   s.innlent_erlent,
   s.verdtrygging,
   s.skuldflokkun,
   s.vbrtegund,
   s.flokkur,
   'N' rafvaett,
   nvl(f.ostadlad,'N') ostadladur,
   s.brefnumer,
```

```
    s.vidmiddags,
    s.innlausn,
    s.nafnverd,
    s.kaupkrafa,
    s.ees,
    null vextir
from fjastofn.vbr_flokkar f,
     fja_pfm.skuldabref_avoxtun s
where f.audkenni=s.flokkur and
      f.rafvaett is null
union
select
    s.eig eigandi,
    'I',
    Fja_pfm.Ymis_Foll.TegundTryggingar(f.visitala) verdtrygging,
    f.skuldaranumer skuldflokkun,
    f.vbrtegund vbrtegund,
    s.aud flokkur,
    'J' rafvaett,
    'N' ostadladur,
    'x' brefnumer,
    to_date(null) vidmiddags,
    to_date(null) innlausn,
    s.nav nafnverd,
    0 kaupkrafa,
    '+' ees,
    null vextir
from fjastofn.vbr_flokkar f,
     fja_pfm.bref s
where f.audkenni=s.aud and
      f.rafvaett is not null
/
```

The analyst discussed the view definition with a developer who understood its business purpose. From that discussion, the analyst and developer were able to prove that the view definition was flawed. Using a UNION of the two SELECT statements in the view definition instead of a UNION ALL was causing *two* problems:

- It caused a very costly but unneeded SORT UNIQUE row source operation. (The new data that the Oracle release 9.2 kernel emits in the STAT lines would better highlight the enormous cost.)

- It caused a bug as well, because the UNION erroneously eliminated rows that the application users needed.

Example 12-16 shows the execution plan of the statement shown in Example 12-13 after the view definition was corrected by inserting the bytes ALL into the view definition.

Example 12-16. The execution plan for the time-consuming SELECT statement after optimizing the view definition

```
       Rows Row Source Operation (Object Id)
--------------- ------------------------------------------------------------
        473 SORT ORDER BY
        473  SORT GROUP BY
        974   VIEW V_SKULDABREF_AVOXTUN
        974    UNION-ALL
        686     HASH JOIN
        886      INDEX RANGE SCAN(21436)
    103,314      TABLE ACCESS FULL VBR_FLOKKAR(19409)
        288     FILTER
        288      HASH JOIN
        940       INDEX RANGE SCAN(29887)
     10,744       TABLE ACCESS FULL VBR_FLOKKAR(19409)
```

Example 12-17 shows the more exciting news. The query that had previously consumed 23,470.0 seconds of response time now consumes only 10.9 seconds. It produces the same (actually better) application output; it just consumes about 6.5 fewer hours to do it.

Example 12-17. SQL text and performance statistics for statement 1163242303, after the view definition change. Note that this is the same SQL text as shown in Example 12-13; only the underlying view definition has changed. Total time reduction for the statement: from over 23,000 seconds to just over 10 seconds

```
Statement Text
SELECT EIGANDI,INNLENT_ERLENT,VERDTRYGGING,SKULDFLOKKUN,VBRTEGUND,FLOKKUR
FROM V_SKULDABREF_AVOXTUN
WHERE EIGANDI = :b1
AND INNLENT_ERLENT = :b2
AND ((RAFVAETT = :b3 )
OR ((RAFVAETT = :b4 )
AND (INNLAUSN IS NULL
OR INNLAUSN > :b5 )
AND (VIDMIDDAGS <= :b6 )))
GROUP BY EIGANDI,INNLENT_ERLENT,VERDTRYGGING,SKULDFLOKKUN,VBRTEGUND,FLOKKUR
ORDER BY EIGANDI,INNLENT_ERLENT,VERDTRYGGING,SKULDFLOKKUN,VBRTEGUND,FLOKKUR
```

Statement Cumulative Database Call Statistics

Cursor Action	Action Count	Rows	------ Response Time ------- Elapsed	CPU	Other	LIO Blocks	PIO Blocks
Parse	3,722	0	2.0	0.6	1.4	44	1
Execute	3,722	0	1.3	1.4	-0.1	14	0
Fetch	4,195	473	7.6	2.8	4.8	44,764	792
Total	11,639	473	10.9	4.8	6.2	44,822	793
Per Exe	1	0	0.0	0.0	0.0	12	0
Per Row	8	1	0.0	0.0	0.0	95	2

Results

The results were stunning. Example 12-18 shows the resource profile for the job after optimization. Total response time for the eight-hour batch job dropped to slightly more than one hour.

Example 12-18. Resource profile for the same batch job that consumed almost eight hours (compare Example 12-11). After optimization, the job consumed only slightly more than one hour

Response Time Component	Duration		# Calls	Dur/Call
CPU service	2,684.7s	73.9%	953,452	0.002816s
db file sequential read	847.6s	23.3%	77,944	0.010874s
unaccounted-for	93.2s	2.6%		
db file scattered read	5.8s	0.2%	295	0.019627s
log file switch completion	1.6s	0.0%	7	0.234286s
latch free	1.0s	0.0%	362	0.002873s
file open	0.1s	0.0%	49	0.002041s
log file sync	0.1s	0.0%	7	0.011429s
buffer busy waits	0.0s	0.0%	1	0.010000s
SQL*Net message from client	0.0s	0.0%	10	0.001000s
SQL*Net message to client	0.0s	0.0%	10	0.000000s
Total	3,634.1s	100.0%		

Before correcting the view definition for V_SKULDABREF_AVOXTUN, the bank had restricted the number of accounts upon which they would allow the job to run. Otherwise, the job's execution would violate the morning's online window by several hours. After making the correction, they can feed virtually any parameters they want to the query and it will not take considerably longer to run. Since optimization, the batch job has never even gotten close to the eight-hour runtime that the "before" job required.

Lessons Learned

This case illustrates the following points:

- The resource profile pattern of large db file... and CPU service durations usually indicates the use of inefficient SQL somewhere within the user action. To fix the problem, you have to find that SQL.

- The extended SQL trace file contained exactly the information that the analyst needed to optimize the targeting process for finding the root cause of his batch job's performance problem. Even though the view definition was not present in the trace data, the trace file contained information that focused our attention upon the view definition as the source of the performance problem.

- Sometimes, the scrutiny of performance analysis exposes functional bugs. In this case, the performance analyst was able to determine that not only was a specific query doing more work than it should have, it was actually returning an incomplete result set in some circumstances.

Conclusion

When I departed Oracle Corporation in 1999 to create this business called *hotsos. com*, I wasn't actually very good at Oracle performance optimization. I had the idea that at one point in history I *had* been, but it turns out that even that wasn't really true. But in the four years that have elapsed since beginning this company, I think I've gotten better. I've had the luxury of learning through what I believe to be the two most powerful learning tools available within the human experience:

Immersion
> I've been able to commit to *immersing* myself in the domain of Oracle performance optimization. For four years, learning, doing, and teaching Oracle performance optimization have been the focus of my professional life.

Copying good examples
> I've had the opportunity to learn from Jeff Holt and the many ladies and gentlemen that I've listed in the Preface of this book.

The immersion decision is of course your own. But I sincerely hope that you'll find this new book a helpful source of good ideas and good examples that you can copy in your day-to-day professional lives to remove performance pain faster and more completely than you've ever experienced.

Thank you for reading this book. I hope it will help you.

## PART IV

Appendixes

Glossary

Amdahl's law

A vital insight recognized by Gene Amdahl [Amdahl (1967)], which allows a performance analyst to compute the relevance of various proposed performance improvements:

> The performance enhancement possible with a given improvement is limited by the fraction of the execution time that the improved feature is used.

Arrival rate (λ)

The rate of arrivals into a queueing system per unit of time during a specified time interval.

Chi-square goodness-of-fit test

A statistical test that is useful in determining whether a data sample is sufficiently likely to belong to a specified distribution.

Clock interrupt

An *interrupt* that notifies the operating system kernel that one more time interval has elapsed [Bovet and Cesati (2001) 140].

Closed form solution

A mathematical result that can be expressed exactly in symbolic form. Contrast a mathematical result that can be expressed only approximately in numeric form.

Code path

The computer instructions that are executed to produce a given result. *Code path reduction* is the process of improving performance by eliminating code path without diminishing the functional result.

Collateral benefit

An unintended positive side effect of an action. A benefit yielded serendipitously by attending to something else.

Collateral damage

An unintended negative side effect of an action.

Completion rate (X)

The *throughput* of a queueing system.

Compulsive tuning disorder (CTD)

A term created by Gaja Vaidyanatha and Kirti Deshpande to describe an effect of using a performance improvement method that has no terminating condition:

> Many DBAs have gotten into the habit of tuning until they can't tune anymore. This not only drives them (and their customers) crazy with late hours and system downtime, but also it doesn't tend to result in much improvement in performance. We are absolutely convinced that there is a growing number of DBAs out there who suffer from the malady of Compulsive Tuning Disorder (CTD). [Vaidyanatha and Deshpande (2001) 8]

Concurrency

A measure of parallelism, usually used when describing the number of users and batch jobs that demand services simultaneously.

Connection

See *Oracle connection*.

Connection pooling

A technique whereby a large number of user sessions share a smaller number of Oracle sessions. The technique is designed to reduce the number of *connect* and *disconnect* database operations, resulting in better performance for systems with very large user counts.

Coordinated Universal Time (UTC)

The international time standard. *UTC* is the current term for what was commonly referred to as Greenwich Meridian Time (GMT). Zero hours UTC is midnight in Greenwich, England, which lies on the zero longitudinal meridian. Universal time is based on a 24-hour clock, therefore, afternoon hours such as 4:00 p.m. UTC are expressed as 16:00 UTC ("sixteen hours, zero minutes"). (Source: *http://www.ghcc.msfc.nasa.gov/utc.html*.)

Cost-based optimizer (CBO), Oracle cost-based query optimizer

A component of the Oracle kernel that computes the execution plan for a query by selecting the candidate execution plan with the smallest expected cost. Input factors that influence the CBO include session- and instance-level Oracle parameters, database table and index statistics, Oracle instance CPU and I/O statistics, database schema definitions, stored outlines, SQL text, and the Oracle query cost model embedded within the Oracle kernel code.

Cumulative distribution function (CDF)

The probability that a random variable X takes on a value that is less than or equal to a specified value x, denoted $P(X \leq x)$. The CDF of response time is especially valuable in service level agreement construction because it permits the formulation of p and r in statements of the form, "Response time of user action f will equal r seconds or less in at least p percent of executions of f."

Database buffer cache hit ratio

The ratio $(L - P)/L$, where L is a count of Oracle *logical I/O* calls (LIO), and P is a count of Oracle *physical I/O* calls (PIO). See *ratio fallacy*.

Database call

A subroutine in the Oracle kernel.

Data definition language (DDL) statement

A SQL statement that creates, alters, maintains, or drops a schema object, or that manipulates user privileges.

Data manipulation language (DML) statement

A SQL statement that queries, inserts, updates, deletes, or locks data.

Dynamic performance view

See *fixed view*.

Erlang, Agner Krarup (1878–1929)

A Danish mathematician who was the first person to study the problem of telephone networks. Erlang is known as the father of queueing theory.

Event-based measurement

A measurement technique by which a process measures a phenomenon by recording a timestamp each time a system's state changes. Contrast *polling*.

Expected value (*E*[*X*])

The mean (i.e., average) of a random variable.

Exponential distribution

A distribution with a probability density function of the form:

$$f(x) = \frac{1}{\theta} e^{-x/\theta}, \quad 0 \leq x < \infty,$$

where θ is the mean of the distribution. The exponential distribution is important to queueing theorists because interarrival times and service times in nature are often exponentially distributed. (It is equivalent to say that arrival processes and service processes are often Poisson distributed.)

First-come, first-served (FCFS)

A queue discipline that provides the next unit of service to the earliest request in the queue, regardless of its class of service. Also called *first-in, first-out* (FIFO).

Fixed view

An Oracle pseudo-table whose name begins with a prefix like V\$ or GV\$, which provides SQL access to instance information stored in shared memory. Also called *dynamic performance view*.

Forward attribution

The method by which the duration of a WAIT #n trace file line is attributed to the first database call for cursor #n that *follows* the WAIT line in the trace file. Attributing Oracle wait event durations this way helps you accurately identify which application source code is responsible for motivating the "wait" time.

Frequency (clock frequency)

The number of ticks generated by a discrete clock in a given unit of time. Clock frequency is the reciprocal of clock resolution.

Glossary

A textbook appendix in which an author works largely beyond the scrutiny of his editor to define terms in whatever manner he believes might marginally improve reader satisfaction.

Idle event

An Oracle wait event that occurs between database calls. The word "idle" denotes that during the execution of such an event, the Oracle kernel has completed a database call and is awaiting the next database call request. Many analysts teach that you should ignore the appearance of idle events in your diagnostic data. However, in properly time-scoped and action-scoped diagnostic data, idle events have as much diagnostic value as any other event.

Instrumentation

Lines of code that are inserted into a program's source code in order to measure that program's performance.

Interarrival time (τ)

The duration between adjacent arrivals into a queueing system. Interarrival time is the reciprocal of arrival rate.

Interrupt

A signal transmitted from hardware to the operating system kernel. From [Bach (1986) 16, 22]:

> The Unix system allows devices such as I/O peripherals or the system clock to

interrupt the CPU asynchronously. On receipt of the interrupt, the [OS] kernel saves its current *context* (a frozen image of what the process was doing), determines the cause of the interrupt, and services the interrupt. After the kernel services the interrupt, it restores its interrupted context and proceeds as if nothing had happened.... On Unix systems, interrupts are serviced by special functions in the operating system kernel, which are called in the context of the currently running process.

Interval bisection

A numerical method for approximating the solution to a mathematical equation. When it is not possible to compute a symbolic result, you must resort to numerical methods of solution, of which interval bisection is one. The method is demonstrated in the following pseudocode:

```
function solve(function f, real s, real
delta, real a, real b) {
    # We wish to find the value of x
where f(x) == s.
    # Return value is an interval
containing x, with interval size <
delta.
    # Solution is known to exist in
interval [a,b] (i.e., a ≤ x ≤ b).
    # Function f must be continuous and
monotonic for all x in [a,b].
    # Method terminates when x is within
delta of true solution.
    f = f - s;
# f == s when f - s == 0
    if (not (f(a) < f(b))) f = -f;
# ensure that f is ascending
    while (not (b - a < delta))
        if (f((a+b)/2) < 0)  a = (a+b)/2;
# solution is right of (a+b)/2
        else               b = (a+b)/2;
# solution is at or left of (a+b)/2
    return [a,b];
}
```

Interval timer

A digital time-keeping device that ticks in regular intervals.

Knee (ρ*)

The utilization value at which the response time divided by utilization (R/ρ) achieves its minimum value. The knee is often considered the optimal utilization for a queueing system because it simultaneously minimizes user response time while maximizing the amount of system capacity being consumed.

Latch

A data structure used to ensure that two processes cannot execute a specified segment of Oracle kernel code at the same time. Oracle kernel developers adhere to a simple latch acquisition protocol that prevents the code they write from corrupting objects stored in shared memory. Oracle's latching protocol looks roughly like this [Millsap (2001c)]:

```
while the latch for a desired operation
is unavailable {
  wait
}
obtain the latch
perform the required operation
release the latch
```

Latency

A synonym for *response time*.

Logical I/O (LIO), Oracle logical I/O, Oracle logical read

An operation in which the Oracle kernel obtains and processes the content of an Oracle block from the Oracle database buffer cache. The code path for an Oracle LIO includes instructions to determine whether the desired block exists in the buffer cache, to update internal data structures such as a buffer cache hash chain and an LRU chain, to pin the block, and to decompose and filter the content of the retrieved block. Oracle LIO operations occur in two modes: *consistent* and *current*. In consistent mode, a block may be copied (or *cloned*) and the clone modified to represent the block at a given point in history. In current mode, a block is simply obtained from the cache "as-is."

M/M/*m* (or M/M/*c*) queueing model

A set of mathematical formulas that can predict the performance of queueing systems that meet five very specific criteria:

- The request interarrival time is an exponentially distributed random variable.

- The service time is an exponentially distributed random variable.

- There are *m* parallel service channels, all of which have identical functional and performance characteristics, and all of which are identically capable of providing service to any arriving service request.

- There is no restriction on queue length. No request that enters the queue exits the queue until that request receives service.

- The queue discipline is first come, first served (FCFS). The system honors requests for service in the order in which they are received.

Mathematica

An application software package that performs fast and accurate symbolic, numerical, and graphical mathematical computations.

Maximum effective throughput (λ_{max})

The maximum throughput that can be attained in a queueing system without causing the average response time to exceed a specified user tolerance.

Measurement intrusion effect

A type of systematic error that occurs because the execution duration of a measured subroutine is different from the execution duration of the subroutine when it is not being measured.

Method

A deterministic sequence of steps. The quality of a method can be judged by its impact, efficiency, measurability, predictive capacity, reliability, determinism, finiteness, and practicality.

Methodology

The theoretical analysis of methods. "In recent years, however, the word "methodology" has used as a pretentious substitute for "method" in scientific and technical contexts.... The misuse of "methodology" obscures an important conceptual distinction between the tools of scientific investigation (properly "methods") and the principles that determine how such tools are deployed and interpreted—a distinction that the scientific and scholarly communities, if not the wider public, should be expected to maintain." (Source: *American Heritage Dictionary of the English Language*)

Microstate accounting

A name used by Sun Microsystems to describe the feature through which an operating system measures CPU capacity consumption with event-based instrumentation instead of polling. The result is much reduced *quantization error*.

Net payoff

The present value (PV) of a project's benefits minus the present value of the project's costs.

Optimize

To maximize the economic value of some target. Compare *tune*.

Oracle connection

From the *Oracle Database Concepts Guide*:

> A *connection* is a communication pathway between a user process and an Oracle instance. A communication pathway is established using available interprocess communication mechanisms (on a computer that runs both the user process and Oracle) or network software (when different computers run the database application and Oracle, and communicate through a network).

Oracle session

From the *Oracle Database Concepts Guide*:

> A *session* is a specific connection of a user to an Oracle instance through a user process.

Oracle does make a distinction between a *connection* (a communication pathway) and a session. You can be connected to Oracle and not have any sessions. On the other hand, you can be connected and have many simultaneous sessions on that single connection.

Over-constrained

An attribute of a requirement that specifies conflicting constraints. For example, the following requirement is over-constrained: "The value of x must be smaller than 0.001.... The value of x must be greater than 0.009." More commonly, such conflicting constraints are concealed within more complicated requirements, where the conflicts cannot be observed without significantly more analysis and, usually, expense.

Overflow error

An error that occurs when the result of an addition or multiplication operation exceeds the capacity of the result's storage mechanism. For example, an n-bit unsigned integer variable j can represent values between 0 and 2^{n-1}. Incrementing j when $j = 2^{n-1}$ would result in assignment of $j = 0$.

Paging

The process of writing pages from memory to disk in response to memory demands that exceed memory supply.

Parallel service channel

See *service channel*.

Physical I/O (PIO), Oracle physical I/O, Oracle physical write

An operation in which the Oracle kernel obtains one or more Oracle blocks via an operating system read call. In most cases, a PIO call is motivated by an LIO call, but not all PIO calls are managed in the Oracle buffer cache. Note that a PIO is not necessarily truly "physical" either, because PIO calls may be fulfilled from cache in the operating system, the disk array, or even the disk itself.

Poisson distribution

A distribution with a probability density function of the form:

$$f(x) = \frac{\lambda^x e^{-\lambda}}{x!}, \quad x = 0, 1, 2, \ldots,$$

where λ is the mean of the distribution. In 1909, Agner Erlang showed that the arrival rate of phone calls in a telephone system has a Poisson distribution. Many arrival processes and service processes in computer systems also obey the Poisson distribution.

Polling

A measurement technique by which a process measures a phenomenon by checking the state of a system at predefined, usually constant, time intervals. Also called *sampling*.

Present value (PV)

The present value (PV) of a cash flow is given by the following formula:

$$PV = \frac{C_1}{1+r}$$

where C_1 is the future cash flow, and r is the reward that investors demand for accepting delayed payment [Brealey and Myers (1988), 12–13]. The PV formula allows you to compare the values of cash flows that will take place at different times in the future. For example, if your expected annual rate of return is $r = 0.07$, then the PV of a $10,000 project payoff expected one year from now is only $9,345.79. If you could invest $9,345.79 today at 7% interest, then one year from now the investment would be worth $10,000.

Probability density function (pdf)

The probability that a random variable X will take on a specific value x, denoted $f(x) = P(X = x)$. For example, the pdf of a random variable simulating the result of the toss of a fair coin is:

$$f(x) = \begin{cases} 0.5, & \text{if } x \text{ is heads;} \\ 0.5, & \text{if } x \text{ is tails.} \end{cases}$$

Program

A sequence of computer instructions that carries out some business function.

Quantization error

The difference between an event's actual duration and the duration of that event as measured on a discrete clock.

Queue discipline

The rules that define how service will be allocated among competing demanders. Examples of queue disciplines are *first-come, first served* (FCFS); highest priority first; and sharpest elbows first.

Queueing delay (W)

The time consumed in a queueing system by an arriving request that is waiting to receive service from a resource that is busy serving another request. Queueing delay is *not* the same thing as the ela figures that the Oracle kernel emits in its WAIT trace data lines.

Queueing theory

A branch of mathematics that allows for the prediction of various attributes of performance, such as response time and queueing delay.

Random variable

A function whose value is a random number. A random variable is characterized by its mean, its distribution, and possibly other parameters such as standard deviation.

Ratio fallacy, ratio games

A deficiency inherent in *any* ratio that permits the performance of a system being measured to become worse while the apparent goodness of the ratio value improves. Ratio fallacies exist because any ratio's value can be manipulated by modifying *either* its numerator or its denominator. Improving a ratio's value by degrading the value of the system being measured is called *gaming* the system.

For example, a consultant whose bonus is proportional to his billable utilization can game his compensation plan by negotiating a reduction in his billable capacity. A sales representative can game his sales win ratio by making fewer sales calls on prospects that are less likely to buy. A database administrator can game the database buffer cache hit ratio by increasing the number of LIO calls to memory-resident blocks. *Any* ratio can be gamed.

Recursive SQL

Any SQL statement that appears in Oracle SQL trace data as having a cursor with a dep value that is greater than zero.

Reliable

The capacity of a method to produce the same degree of correctness *every time* it is executed. For example, a method that produces an incorrect answer every time it is executed is reliable. A method that produces a correct answer every time it is executed is also reliable. A method is unreliable if it sometimes produces a correct answer and sometimes produces an incorrect answer.

Resolution (clock resolution)

The elapsed duration between adjacent ticks of a discrete clock. Clock resolution is the reciprocal of clock frequency.

Resource profile

A table revealing a useful decomposition of response time. Typically, a resource profile reveals at least the attributes of (1) response time component, (2) total duration consumed by actions in that category, and (3) the number of calls to actions in that category. A resource profile is often presented in descending order of elapsed time consumption.

Response time (R), latency

The time that a system or functional unit takes to react to a given input. In a queueing system, response time equals service time plus queueing delay.

Risk

Uncertainty about future benefits or costs. We quantify that uncertainty using probability distributions [Bodie, et al. (1989) 112].

Round robin (RR)

A queue discipline in which processes are selected one after another so that all members of the set have an opportunity to execute before any member has a second opportunity [Comer (1984) 56].

Rule-based optimizer (RBO), Oracle rule-based query optimizer

A component of the Oracle kernel that computes the execution plan for a query using a static precedence list of row source operations. Input factors that influence the RBO include only the database schema configuration, the SQL text, and the operator precedence list embedded within the Oracle kernel source code.

Sampling

See *polling*.

Scalability

The rate of change of response time with respect to some specified parameter. For example, one may speak of the scalability of a query with respect to the number of rows returned, the scalability of a system with respect to the number of CPUs installed, and so on.

Scheduler

An operating system subroutine that is responsible for allocating CPU cycles among competing operating system processes.

Sequence diagram

A graphical depiction of response time in which a sequence of parallel timelines represent the resources in the technology stack. Consumption of a given resource is represented as a region on that resource's timeline. Supply and demand relationships among resources are represented by directed lines connecting the timelines.

Service channel, parallel service channel (m, c, or s)

A resource in a queueing system that provides service to requests arriving into the system. The number of parallel service channels in a queueing system is denoted with the variable m in this text (as in M/M/m). It is called c or s in some queueing theory texts (as in M/M/c).

Service level agreement (SLA)

An agreement between an information supplier and an information demander that defines expected application performance and availability levels.

Service rate (μ)

The number of arrivals that can be processed by a single channel in a queueing system within a specified unit of time. Service rate is the reciprocal of service time.

Service time (S)

The amount of resource capacity consumed by an arriving request in a queueing system. Service time is the reciprocal of service rate.

Session

See *Oracle session*.

Specification

A formal written statement of a project's intended result.

SQL optimization

The process of eliminating code path in operations executed by the Oracle kernel in response to instructions written in SQL.

Stable queueing system

A queueing system whose per-server utilization is in the range $0 \leq \rho < 1$. In a stable queueing system, the long-term number of completions equals the long-term number of arrivals.

System

To an information provider, a *system* is typically regarded as a collection of processes, files, and shared memory segments that comprise an application. To an information consumer, a *system* is an entity that provides service in response to user actions. The mismatch between these two perceptions often results in "optimizations" executed by information providers that affect the performance of important user actions either negligibly or even negatively.

System call, sys call

A subroutine in the operating system kernel [Stevens (1992) 20].

Systematic error

The result of some experimental "mistake" that introduces a consistent bias into its measurements. Systematic errors tend to be constant across all measurements, or slowly varying with time [Lilja (2000)].

Technology stack

A model that considers system components such as the hardware, the operating system, the database kernel, the application software, the business rules, and the business users as layers in a stratified architecture.

Think time

Time consumed in an architectural tier that rests in a level higher in the technology stack than the one you're analyzing.

Thrashing

The act of consuming an excessive amount of capacity just to administer a system's own overhead. For example, an operating system's CPU scheduler typically consumes less than $x\%$ of a system's total CPU capacity (on many systems today, $x = 10$). When the system's workload is increased so much that the CPU scheduler consumes more than $x\%$ of capacity just to allocate CPU, the CPU scheduler is said to be thrashing.

Throughput (X)

The rate of completions of a queueing system per unit of time during a specified time interval.

Traffic intensity (ρ)

The mean utilization per parallel service channel in a queueing system.

Tune

To improve the performance of some target. Compare *optimize*.

User action

A unit of work whose output and performance have meaning to the business, such as the entry of a field or form, or the execution of one or more whole programs.

UTC

See *Coordinated Universal Time*.

Utilization

Resource usage divided by resource capacity for a specified time interval.

Waste

Anything that can be eliminated with no loss of anything useful. In the context of computer system workload, *waste* is any workload that can be eliminated with no loss of functional value to the business.

Greek Alphabet

The following table gives the letters of the Greek alphabet and their English equivalents. Where the English pronunciation of a Greek letter is not obvious, the table gives an example. Thus, the Greek letter alpha is pronounced as the "a" in *father*, the Greek letter êta as the "e" in *hey*, and so forth.

Greek letter		Greek name	English equivalent	English pronunciation
A	α	alpha	a	"father"
B	β	beta	b	
Γ	γ	gamma	g	
Δ	δ	delta	d	
E	ε	epsilon	e	"end"
Z	ζ	zêta	z	
H	η	êta	ê	"hey"
Θ	θ	thêta	th	"thick"
I	ι	iota	i	"it"
K	κ	kappa	k	
Λ	λ	lambda	l	
M	μ	mu	m	
N	ν	nu	n	
Ξ	ξ	xi	ks	"box"
O	o	omikron	o	"off"
Π	π	pi	p	
P	ρ	rho	r	
Σ	σ, ς	sigma	s	"say"
T	τ	tau	t	
Y	υ	upsilon	u	"put"
Φ	φ	phi	f	

Greek letter		Greek name	English equivalent	English pronunciation
X	χ	chi	ch	"Bach"
Ψ	ψ	psi	ps	
Ω	ω	omega	ô	"grow"

Source: *http://www.ibiblio.org/koine/greek/lessons/alphabet.html*

Optimizing Your Database Buffer Cache Hit Ratio

Shortly after I joined Oracle Corporation in 1989, several of my technical mentors taught me that just about the only thing you could tell from looking at a database's buffer cache hit ratio is that when it's really high, it's usually a sign of trouble [Millsap (2001b)]. In the several years that have passed since my first exposure to that lesson, the battle has raged between advocates of using the buffer cache hit ratio as a primary indicator of performance quality and those who believe that hit ratio metrics is too unreliable for such use. It's not been much of a battle, actually. The evidence that hit ratios are unreliable is overwhelming, and similar ratio fallacies occurring in other industries are well documented (see, for example, [Jain (1991)] and [Goldratt (1992)]).

One of the most compelling (and funniest) proofs that hit ratios are unreliable is a PL/SQL procedure called choose_a_hit_ratio written by Connor McDonald. Connor's procedure lets you increase your database buffer cache hit ratio to any value that you like between its current value and 99.999 999 9%. How does it work? By adding wasteful workload to your system. That's right. You specify what you want your database buffer cache hit ratio to be, and choose_a_hit_ratio adds just enough wasteful workload to raise your hit ratio to that value. What you get in return is proof positive that having a high database buffer cache hit ratio is no indication that you have an efficient system. In his original text at *http://www.oracledba.co.uk*, Connor thanks Jonathan Lewis for some of the strategy that he used. And I thank Connor for his letting me use his work in this book.

You can find Connor's original PL/SQL at *http://www.oracledba.co.uk*. Example C-1 expresses the same idea in Perl, which enables me to do a little bit more, like prompting and printing timing statistics on the LIO generation. You can download the code as part of the examples for this book, from the O'Reilly catalog page: *http://www. oreilly.com/catalog/optoraclep/*.

Example C-1. A Perl program that will enable you to increase your database buffer cache hit ratio to virtually any value you want

```perl
#!/usr/bin/perl

# $Header: /home/cvs/cvm-book1/set_hit_ratio/set-bchr.pl,v 1.3 2003/05/08 06:37:50 cvm Exp
$
# Cary Millsap (cary.millsap@hotsos.com)
# based upon the innovative work of Connor McDonald and Jonathan Lewis
# Copyright (c) 2003 by Hotsos Enterprises, Ltd. All rights reserved.

use strict;
use warnings;
use Getopt::Long;
use Time::HiRes qw(gettimeofday);
use DBI;

# fetch command-line options
my %opt = (
    service     => "",
    username    => "/",
    password    => "",
    debug       => 0,
);
GetOptions(
    "service=s"  => \$opt{service},
    "username=s" => \$opt{username},
    "password=s" => \$opt{password},
    "debug"      => \$opt{debug},
);

sub fnum($;$$) {
    # return string representation of numeric value in
    # %.${precision}f format with specified separators
    my ($text, $precision, $separator) = @_;
    $precision = 0   unless defined $precision;
    $separator = "," unless defined $separator;
    $text = reverse sprintf "%.${precision}f", $text;
    $text =~ s/(\d\d\d)(?=\d)(?!\d*\.)/$1$separator/g;
    return scalar reverse $text;
}

sub stats($) {
    # fetch LIO and PIO stats from the given db handle
    my ($dbh) = @_;
    my $sth = $dbh->prepare(<<'END OF SQL', {ora_check_sql => 0});
select name, value from v$sysstat
where name in ('physical reads', 'db block gets', 'consistent gets')
END OF SQL
    $sth->execute();
    my $r = $sth->fetchall_hashref("NAME");
    my $pio = $r->{'physical reads' }->{VALUE};
    my $lio = $r->{'consistent gets'}->{VALUE} + $r->{'db block gets'}->{VALUE};
    if ($opt{debug}) {
```

```perl
            print "key='$_', val=$r->{$_}->{VALUE}\n" for (keys %$r);
            print "pio=$pio, lio=$lio\n";
    }
    return ($lio, $pio);
}

sub status($$$) {
    # print a status paragraph
    my ($description, $lio, $pio) = @_;
    print "$description\n";
    printf "%15s LIO calls\n", fnum($lio);
    printf "%15s PIO calls\n", fnum($pio);
    printf "%15.9f buffer cache hit ratio\n", ($lio - $pio) / $lio;
    print "\n";
}

# fetch target hit ratio from command line
my $usage = "Usage: $0 [options] target\n\t";
my $target = shift or die $usage;
my $max_target = 0.999_999_999;
unless ($target =~ /\d*\.\d+/ and 0 <= $target and $target <= $max_target) {
    die "target must be a number between 0 and $max_target\n";
}

# connect to Oracle
my %attr = (RaiseError => 0, PrintError => 0, AutoCommit => 0);
my $dbh = DBI->connect(
    "dbi:Oracle:$opt{service}", $opt{username}, $opt{password}, \%attr
);
END {
    # executed upon program exit
    $dbh->disconnect if defined $dbh;
}

# compute and display the baseline statistics
my ($lio0, $pio0) = stats $dbh;
status("Current state", $lio0, $pio0);

# compute and display the amount of waste required to
# "improve" the cache hit ratio by the requested amount
my $waste;
if ($target < ($lio0 - $pio0)/$lio0) {
    die "Your database buffer cache hit ratio already exceeds $target.\n";
} elsif ($target > $max_target) {
    die "Setting your hit ratio to $target will take too long.\n";
} else {
    # following formula is courtesy of Connor McDonald
    $waste = sprintf "%.0f", $pio0/(1 - $target) - $lio0;
}
my ($lio1, $pio1) = ($lio0 + $waste, $pio0);
status("Increasing LIO count by ".fnum($waste)." will yield", $lio1, $pio1);
```

Example C-1. A Perl program that will enable you to increase your database buffer cache hit ratio to virtually any value you want (continued)

```
# inquire whether to actually change the ratio
print <<"EOF";
*******************************************************************
                              WARNING
Responding affirmatively to the following prompt will create the
following effects:
1) It will degrade the performance of your database while it runs.
2) It might run a very long time.
3) It will "improve" your system's buffer cache hit ratio.
4) It will prove that a high database buffer cache hit ratio is
   an unreliable indicator of Oracle system performance.
*******************************************************************

EOF
print qq(Enter 'y' to "improve" your hit ratio to $target: );
my $response = <>;
exit unless $response =~ /^[Yy]/;
print "\n";

# create a table called DUMMY
my $sth;
$sth = $dbh->prepare(<<'END OF SQL', {ora_check_sql => 0});
drop table dummy
END OF SQL
$sth->execute if $sth;   # ignore errors
$sth = $dbh->prepare(<<'END OF SQL', {ora_check_sql => 0});
create table dummy (n primary key) organization index as
select rownum n from all_objects where rownum <= 200
END OF SQL
$sth->execute;

# disable 9i connect-by features to ensure lots of LIO
# idea is courtesy of Connor McDonald
$sth = $dbh->prepare(<<'END OF SQL', {ora_check_sql => 0});
alter session set _old_connect_by_enabled = true;
END OF SQL
$sth->execute if $sth;   # ignore errors

# perform the requisite number of LIO calls
# following query is courtesy of Jonathan Lewis
$sth = $dbh->prepare(<<'END OF SQL', {ora_check_sql => 0});
select count(*)
from (select n from dummy connect by n > prior n start with n = 1)
where rownum < ?
END OF SQL
my $e0 = gettimeofday;
$sth->execute($waste);
my $e1 = gettimeofday;
my $e = $e1 - $e0;
$sth->finish;
printf "Performed %s LIO calls in %.6f seconds (%s LIO/sec)\n\n",
```

Example C-1. A Perl program that will enable you to increase your database buffer cache hit ratio to virtually any value you want (continued)

```
    fnum($waste), $e, fnum($waste/$e);

# compute and display the final statistics
my ($lio2, $pio2) = stats($dbh);
status("Final state", $lio2, $pio2);

exit;

__END__

=head1 NAME

set-bchr - set your database buffer cache hit ratio to a higher value

=head1 SYNOPSIS

set-bchr
  [--service=I<h>]
  [--username=I<u>]
  [--password=I<p>]
  [--debug=I<d>]
  I<target>

=head1 DESCRIPTION

B<set-bchr> computes your present buffer cache hit ratio (using the
traditionally accepted formula), computes how much wasted workload must be
added to increase your hit ratio to I<target>, and then provides the
option to actually perform the wasted work that will raise the hit ratio
to the desired I<target> value. I<target> must be a decimal number between
0 and .999999999.

Using B<set-bchr> can increase the value of your system's database buffer
cache hit ratio, but IT WILL DEGRADE THE PERFORMANCE OF YOUR SYSTEM WHILE
IT RUNS. The intent of B<set-bchr> is to demonstrate humorously but
unequivocally that the database buffer cache hit ratio is an unreliable
indicator of system performance quality. If you intend to use this program
to trick customers or managers into believing that you are doing a better
job than you really are, then, well, good luck with that.

=head2 Options

=over 4

=item B<--service=>I<h>

The name of the Oracle service to which B<vprof> will connect. The default
value is "" (the empty string), which will cause B<vprof> to connect
using, for example, the default Oracle TNS alias.

=item B<--username=>I<u>
```

Example C-1. A Perl program that will enable you to increase your database buffer cache hit ratio to virtually any value you want (continued)

The name of the Oracle schema to which B<vprof> will connect. The default value is "/".

=item B<--password=>I<p>

The Oracle password that B<vprof> will use to connect. The default value is "" (the empty string).

=item B<--debug=>I<d>

When set to 1, B<vprof> dumps its internal data structures in addition to its normal output. The default value is 0.

=back

=head1 EXAMPLES

Use of B<set-bchr> will resemble something like the following, in which I used the tool to "improve" my database buffer cache hit ratio to approximately 0.92:

```
$ set-bchr --username=system --password=manager .92
Current state
      37,257,059 LIO calls
       3,001,414 PIO calls
      0.919440394 buffer cache hit ratio

Increasing LIO count by 260,616 will yield
      37,517,675 LIO calls
       3,001,414 PIO calls
      0.920000000 buffer cache hit ratio


********************************************************************
                            WARNING
Responding affirmatively to the following prompt will create the
following effects:
1) It will degrade the performance of your database while it runs.
2) It might run a very long time.
3) It will "improve" your system's buffer cache hit ratio.
4) It will prove that a high database buffer cache hit ratio is
   an unreliable indicator of Oracle system performance.
********************************************************************

Enter 'y' to "improve" your hit ratio to .92: y

Performed 260,616 LIO calls in 46.592340 seconds (5,594 LIO/sec)

Final state
      37,259,288 LIO calls
       3,001,414 PIO calls
      0.919445213 buffer cache hit ratio
```

Example C-1. A Perl program that will enable you to increase your database buffer cache hit ratio to virtually any value you want (continued)

```
=head1 AUTHOR

Cary Millsap (cary.millsap@hotsos.com), heavily derived from original work
performed by Connor McDonald.

=head1 BUGS

B<set-bchr> doesn't necessarily improve the database buffer cache hit
ratio to exactly the value of I<target>, but it gets very close.

B<set-bchr> computes the Oracle database buffer cache hit ratio using the
traditional formula R = (LIO - PIO) / LIO, where LIO is the sum of the
values of the Oracle 'consistent gets' and 'db block gets' statistics, and
PIO is the value of the Oracle 'physical reads' statistic. The computation
of LIO in this way is itself deeply flawed. See [Lewis (2003)] for
details.

=head1 COPYRIGHT

Copyright (c) 2003 by Hotsos Enterprises, Ltd. All rights reserved.
```

APPENDIX D

M/M/m Queueing Theory Formulas

Table D-1 provides a convenient summary of the M/M/m queueing theory formulas described in Chapter 9.

Table D-1. M/M/m queueing theory formulas

Definition	Formula
Average number of arrivals	A
Average number of completed requests	C
Measurement period	T
Average busy time	B
Number of parallel service channels	m
Average arrival rate	$\lambda = \dfrac{A}{T}$
Average interarrival rate	$\tau = \dfrac{1}{\lambda}$
Average system throughput	$X = \dfrac{C}{T}$
Average service time	$S = \dfrac{B}{C}$
Average service rate	$\mu = \dfrac{1}{S}$
Average total utilization	$U = \dfrac{B}{T}$
Average server utilization or load (m servers)	$\rho = \dfrac{U}{m}$

Table D-1. M/M/m queueing theory formulas (continued)

Definition	Formula
Probability that arriving request will be enqueued (*ErlangC*)	$C(m,\rho) = P(\geq m \text{ jobs}) = \dfrac{\dfrac{(m\rho)^m}{m!}}{(1-\rho)\displaystyle\sum_{k=0}^{m-1}\dfrac{(m\rho)^k}{k!} + \dfrac{(m\rho)^m}{m!}}$
Average queueing delay	$W = \dfrac{C(m,\rho)}{m\mu(1-\rho)}$
Average response time	$R = S + W$
Cumulative distribution function of response time	$P(R \leq r) = F(r) = \dfrac{m(1-\rho)-W_q(0)}{m(1-\rho)-1}\left(1-e^{-\mu r}\right) - \dfrac{1-W_q(0)}{m(1-\rho)-1}\left(1-e^{-(m\mu-\lambda)r}\right)$ where $W_q(0) = 1 - \dfrac{(m\rho)^m p_0}{m!(1-\rho)}$, and $p_0 = \left(\displaystyle\sum_{n=0}^{m-1}\dfrac{(m\rho)^n}{n!} + \dfrac{(m\rho)^m}{m!(1-\rho)}\right)^{-1}, \quad \rho < 1$

APPENDIX E

References

[Adams (1999)]
> Adams, S. 1999. *Oracle8i Internal Services for Waits, Latches, Locks, and Memory*. Sebastopol CA: O'Reilly & Associates.

[Adams (2003)]
> Adams, S. 2003. *Oracle Internals and Advanced Performance Tuning*. Copenhagen: Course presented at Miracle Master Class 2003, 13–15 Jan. 2003.

[Allen (1994)]
> Allen, A. O. 1994. *Computer Performance Analysis with Mathematica*. Cambridge MA: AP Professional.

[Amdahl (1967)]
> Amdahl, A. 1967. "Validity of the single processor approach to achieving large scale computing capabilities" in *AFIPS Conf. Proc.*, vol. 30.

[Ault and Brinson (2000)]
> Ault, M. R.; Brinson, J. M. 2000. *Oracle8 DBA: Performance Tuning Exam Cram*. Scottsdale AZ: Coriolis.

[Bach (1986)]
> Bach, M. J. 1986. *The Design of the UNIX Operating System*. Englewood Cliffs NJ: Prentice Hall.

[Bentley (1988)]
> Bentley, J. 1988. *More Programming Pearls: Confessions of a Coder*. Reading MA: Addison-Wesley.

[Bodie, et al. (1989)]
> Bodie, Z.; Kane, A.; Marcus, A. J. 1989 *Investments*. Homewood IL: Irwin.

[Bovet and Cesati (2001)]
> Bovet, D. P.; Cesati, M. 2001. *Understanding the Linux Kernel*. Sebastopol CA: O'Reilly.

[Brealey and Myers (1988)]
 Brealey, R. A.; Myers, S. C. 1988. *Principles of Corporate Finance* (3ed). New York: McGraw-Hill.

[Breitling (2002)]
 Breitling, W. 2002. "A look under the hood of CBO: the 10053 event." *http://www.hotsos.com*: Hotsos.

[Chiesa (1996)]
 Chiesa, D. P. 1996. *Unix Performance Measurement. http://www.transarc.ibm.com/Library/whitepapers/tg/node14.html.*

[Cockroft (1998)]
 Cockroft, A. 1998. "Prying into processes and workloads," in *Unix Insider*, 1 Apr. 98. *http://www.sun.com/sun-on-net/itworld/UIR980401perf.html*: Sun.

[Comer (1984)]
 Comer, D. 1984. *Operating System Design, the XINU Approach.* Englewood Cliffs NJ: Prentice-Hall.

[CRC (1991)]
 Standard Mathematical Tables and Formulae (29ed). Boca Raton FL: CRC Press.

[Dowd (1993)]
 Dowd, K. 1993. *High Performance Computing.* Sebastopol CA: O'Reilly.

[Engsig (2001)]
 Engsig, B. 2001. "Efficient use of bind variables, cursor_sharing and related cursor parameters." *http://otn.oracle.com/deploy/performance*: Oracle Corp.

[Ensor and Stevenson (1997a)]
 Ensor, D.; Stevenson, I. 1997. *Oracle Design.* Sebastopol CA: O'Reilly.

[Ensor and Stevenson (1997b)]
 Ensor, D.; Stevenson, I. 1997. *Oracle8 Design Tips.* Sebastopol CA: O'Reilly.

[Erlang (1909)]
 Erlang, A. K. 1909. "The Theory of Probabilities and Telephone Conversations," *Nyt Tidsskrift for Matematik B*, vol 20, 1909.

[Erlang (1917)]
 Erlang, A. K. 1917. "On the rational determination of the number of circuits," in *The Life and Works of A. K. Erlang*, 1948. Brockmeyer, E.; Halstrom, H.; Jensen, A. (eds.). *Trans. Danish Academy of Tech. Sci.* See also *http://plus.maths.org/issue2/erlang/#allref* for information about the life of Agner Erlang.

[Feuerstein (1998)]
 Feuerstein, S.; Beresniewicz, J.; Dawes, C. 1998. *Oracle PL/SQL Built-ins Pocket Reference.* Sebastopol CA: O'Reilly.

[Feynman (1999)]
 Feynman, R. P. 1999. *The Pleasure of Finding Things Out.* Cambridge MA: Perseus.

[Frisch (2002)]
> Frisch, Æ. 2002. *Essential System Administration* (3ed). Sebastopol CA: O'Reilly.

[Frisch (1998)]
> Frisch, Æ. 1998. *Essential Windows NT System Administration*. Sebastopol CA: O'Reilly.

[Goldratt (1992)]
> Goldratt, E. M. *The Goal: a Process of Ongoing Improvement* (2ed). Great Barrington MA: North River Press.

[Gray and Neuhoff (1998)]
> Gray, R. M.; Neuhoff, D. L. 1998. "Quantization" in *IEEE Transactions on Information Theory*, Vol. 44, No. 6, October 1998.

[Gross and Harris (1998)]
> Gross, D.; Harris, C. M. 1998. *Fundamentals of Queueing Theory* (3ed). New York: Wiley.

[Gunther (1998)]
> Gunther, N. J. 1998. *The Practical Performance Analyst: Performance-by-Design Techniques for Distributed Systems*. New York: McGraw-Hill.

[Gurry and Corrigan (1996)]
> Gurry, M.; Corrigan, P. 1996. *Oracle Performance Tuning* (2ed). Sebastopol CA: O'Reilly.

[Hailey (2002)]
> Hailey, K. 2002. "Direct Oracle SGA Memory Access." *http://oraperf.sourceforge.net*: SourceForge.

[Harrison (2000)]
> Harrison, G. 2000. *Oracle SQL High-Performance Tuning* (2ed). Upper Saddle River NJ: Prentice Hall PTR.

[Hawking (1988)]
> Hawking, S. W. 1988. *A Brief History of Time*. New York: Bantam.

[Hogg and Tanis (1977)]
> Hogg, R. V.; Tanis, E. A. 1983. *Probability and Statistical Inference*. New York: Macmillan.

[Holt (2000a)]
> Holt, J. 2000. "Predicting multi-block read call sizes." *http://www.hotsos.com*: Hotsos.

[Holt (2000b)]
> Holt, J. 2000. "Why are Oracle's read events 'named backwards'?" *http://www.hotsos.com*: Hotsos.

[Holt and Millsap (2000)]
> Holt, J.; Millsap, C. 2000. "Scaling applications to massive concurrent user counts." *http://www.hotsos.com*: Hotsos.

[Holt et al. (2003)]

Holt, J.; Millsap, C.; Minutella, R.; Goodman, G. 2003. *Hotsos Clinic OP101: Optimizing Oracle SQL. http://www.hotsos.com*: Hotsos.

[Jagerman (1974)]

Jagerman, D. L. 1974. "Some Properties of the Erlang Loss Function" in *Bell Sys. Tech. J.* **55**: 525.

[Jain (1991)]

Jain, R. 1991. *The Art of Computer Systems Performance Analysis*. New York: Wiley.

[Kachigan (1986)]

Kachigan, S. K. 1986. *Statistical Analysis: an Interdisciplinary Introduction to Univariate and Multivariate Methods*. New York: Radius Press.

[Kennedy and Everest (1994)]

Kennedy, J.; Everest, A. 1994. *Effective Interviewing! An Advanced Seminar for Achieving Superior Results*. San Rafael CA: Management Team Consultants, Inc.

[Kleinrock (1975)]

Kleinrock, L. 1975. *Queueing Systems, Vol. 1: Theory*. New York: Wiley.

[Knuth (1971)]

Knuth, D. E. 1971. "Empirical Study of FORTRAN Programs" in *Software—Practice and Experience*, April/June 1971, Vol. 1, No. 2, pp. 105–133.

[Knuth (1981)]

Knuth, D. E. 1981. *The Art of Computer Programming (2ed), Vol. 2 Seminumerical Algorithms*. Reading MA: Addison-Wesley.

[Kolk (1996)]

Kolk, A. 1996. *Description of Oracle7 Wait Events and Enqueues*. Redwood Shores CA: Oracle Corp. internal document.

[Kolk and Yamaguchi (1999)]

Kolk, A.; Yamaguchi, S. 1999. *Yet Another Performance Profiling Method (or YAPP-Method). http://www.oraperf.com*: OraPerf.

[Kolk (2001)]

Kolk. A. 2001. *New Oracle9i Timing Features. http://www.oraperf.com*: Precise Software Solutions.

[Kyte (2001)]

Kyte, T. 2001. *Expert One-on-One Oracle*. Birmingham UK: Wrox.

[Kyte (2002)]

Kyte, T. 2002. "Reducing LIOs" in *AskTom. http://asktom.oracle.com/pls/ask/f?p=4950:8:1683948::NO::F4950_P8_DISPLAYID,F4950_P8_CRITERIA: 6749454952894*: Oracle.

[Laplace (1812)]

de Laplace, P. S. 1812. *Théorie Analytique des Probabilités*.

[Lawson (2003)]

Lawson, C. 2003. *The Art and Science of Oracle Performance Tuning.* Birmingham UK: Curlingstone.

[Lewis & Papadimitriou (1981)]

Lewis, H. R.; Papadimitriou, C. H. 1981. *Elements of the Theory of Computation.* Englewood Cliffs NJ: Prentice Hall.

[Lewis (2001a)]

Lewis, J. 2001. "Folk Lore and Fairy Tales," *http://www.jlcomp.demon.co.uk/myths.html*: JL Computer Consultancy

[Lewis (2001b)]

Lewis, J. 2001. *Practical Oracle8i: Building Efficient Databases.* Upper Saddle River NJ: Addison-Wesley.

[Lewis (2002)]

Lewis, J. 2002. *Optimising Oracle.* Course presented at Miracle Master Class 2003, 23–25 Jan. 2002.

[Lewis (2003)]

Lewis, J. 2003. "The database gets better but the metrics look worse," in *IOUG Live 2003 Proceedings. http://www.ioug.org.*

[Lilja (2000)]

Lilja, D. J. 2000 *Measuring Computer Performance: a Practitioner's Guide.* Cambridge UK: Cambridge Press.

[Maloney et al. (1992)]

Malony, A. D.; Reed, D. A.; Wijshoff, H. A. G. 1992. "Performance Measurement Intrusion and Perturbation Analysis" in *IEEE Transactions on Parallel and Distributed Systems,* July 1992, Vol. 3, No. 4, pp. 433–450.

[McDonald (2000)]

McDonald, C. 2000. Various hints, tips, and observations, *http://www.oracledba.co.uk.*

[Millsap (1999)]

Millsap, C. V. 1999. "Performance Management: Myths & Facts," *http://www.hotsos.com*: Oracle.

[Millsap (2000a)]

Millsap, C. V. 2000. "Is RAID 5 Really a Bargain?" *http://www.hotsos.com*: Hotsos.

[Millsap (2000b)]

Millsap, C. V. 2000. "Batch Queue Management and the Magic of '2'," *http://www.hotsos.com*: Hotsos.

[Millsap (2001a)]

Millsap, C. V. 2001. "Scalability is a Rate of Change," *http://www.hotsos.com*: Hotsos.

[Millsap (2001b)]
> Millsap, C. V. 2001. "Why a 99%+ Database Buffer Cache Hit Ratio is *Not* Ok," *http://www.hotsos.com*: Hotsos.

[Millsap (2001c)]
> Millsap, C. V. 2002. "Why You Should Focus on LIOs Instead of PIOs," *http://www.hotsos.com*: Hotsos.

[Millsap (2002)]
> Millsap, C. V. 2002. "When to Use an Index," *http://www.hotsos.com*: Hotsos.

[Millsap and Holt (2002)]
> Millsap, C. V.; Holt, J. L. 2002. "Useful Constants for the Oracle Performance Analyst," *http://www.hotsos.com*: Hotsos.

[Morle (1999)]
> Morle, J. 1999. *Scaling Oracle8i: Building Highly Scalable OLTP System Architectures*. Upper Saddle River NJ: Addison-Wesley.

[Musumeci and Loukides (2002)]
> Musumeci, G. D.; Loukides, M. 2002. *System Performance Tuning* (2ed). Sebastopol CA: O'Reilly.

[Nemeth et al. (2000)]
> Nemeth, E.; Snyder, G.; Seebass, S.; Hein, T. R. 2000. *Unix System Administration Handbook* (3ed). Englewood Cliffs NJ: Prentice-Hall PTR.

[Olkin et al. (1994)]
> Olkin, I.; Gleser, L. J.; Derman, C. 1994. *Probability Models and Applications* (2ed). New York: Macmillan.

[Oracle (1996)]
> Oracle Corp. 1996. *Oracle7 Server Tuning. Redwood* Shores CA: Oracle Corp.

[Oracle OCI (1999)]
> Oracle Corp. 1999. *Oracle Call Interface Programmer's Guide*. Redwood Shores CA: Oracle Corp.

[Oracle (2002)]
> Oracle Corp. 2002. *Oracle9i Database Performance Tuning Guide and Reference Release 2 (9.2)*. Redwood Shores CA: Oracle Corp.

[Pelz (2000)]
> Pelz, D. 2000. *Dave Pelz's Putting Bible: the Complete Guide to Mastering the Green*. New York: Doubleday.

[Rivenes (2003)]
> Rivenes, A. 2003. *Oracle 9.2 Event 10046 Segment-Level Statistics. http://www.appsdba.com*: AppsDBA Consulting.

[Schrag (2002)]
> Schrag. R. 2002. *Interpreting Wait Events to Boost System Performance. http://www.dbspecialists.com/presentations/wait_events.html*: Database Specialists.

[Stanford (2001)]

Stanford University. 2001. *Human Subjects Manual: a comprehensive reference guide for Stanford researchers, administrators, students, and staff involved in human subjects research, http://humansubjects.stanford.edu/manual*: Stanford University.

[Stevens (1992)]

Stevens, W. R. 1992. *Advanced Programming in the Unix Environment*. Reading MA: Addison-Wesley.

[Vaidyanatha et al. (2001)]

Vaidyanatha, G. K.; Deshpande, K.; Kostelac, J. A. Jr. 2001. *Oracle Performance Tuning 101*. New York: Osborne/McGraw-Hill.

[Vernon (2001)]

Vernon, M. K. 2001. *CS 547: Computer System Modeling Fundamentals. http://www.cs.wisc.edu/~vernon/cs547/01/assignments/s5.pdf*: University of Wisconsin Madison.

[Wall et al. (2000)]

Wall, L.; Christiansen, T.; Orwant, J. 2000. *Programming Perl*. Sebastopol CA: O'Reilly & Associates.

[Wolfram (1999)]

Wolfram, S. 1999. *Mathematica*. Champaign IL: Wolfram.

[Wood (2003)]

Private conversation with Graham Wood of Oracle Corporation's Server Technologies group.

Index

About the Authors

Cary Millsap is a designer, developer, and instructor of the Hotsos educational curriculum, on which this book is based (*http://www.hotsos.com*). Prior to co-founding Hotsos in 1999, he served for ten years at Oracle Corporation as one of the company's leading system performance experts, where he founded, and served as vice president of, the System Performance Group. He has educated thousands of Oracle consultants, support analysts, developers, and customers in the optimal use of Oracle technology through his commitment to writing, teaching, and speaking at public events. Cary is also a founding member of the Oak Table Network (*http://www.oaktable.net*), an informal association of Oracle scientists well-known throughout the Oracle community.

Jeff Holt is a software developer, support analyst, curriculum designer, classroom instructor, and field consultant at Hotsos (*http://www.hotsos.com*). He is a former support analyst and consultant at Oracle Corporation, where he served as a tech-nology leader in the System Performance Group. He has improved system performance for hundreds of Oracle customers around the world since 1987. Since 1999, he has dedicated much of his time to constructing the Hotsos Profiler and Laredo software tools, which automate important tasks required during Oracle performance improvement projects. Jeff is also a member of the Oak Table Network (*http://www.oaktable.net*).

Colophon

Our look is the result of reader comments, our own experimentation, and feedback from distribution channels. Distinctive covers complement our distinctive approach to technical topics, breathing personality and life into potentially dry subjects.

The animals on the cover of *Optimizing Oracle Performance* are yellowjackets. Though frequently mistaken for bees, yellowjackets are a type of wasp. They can be distinguished from bees by their lack of hair. They also often have brighter black and yellow coloring on their tails. Yellowjackets are around half an inch long, and the queen is about three-quarters of an inch long. They can be found throughout North America. Wasps build nests by chewing bits of wood and leaves into a paper-like pulp. The nest is built in a dry, protected place such as a tree, log, shrub, or hole in the ground, or attached to a building.

Yellowjackets live in large colonies comprising a queen, female workers, and males. In the spring, the queen, who is the only yellowjacket that breeds, builds a small nest and lays eggs. When they hatch, the female workers expand the nest, look for food, and take care of the queen and the colony. The males fertilize the queen, who continues to lay eggs and expand the colony. In the winter, all yellowjackets except the queen die.

Yellowjackets are scavengers. They eat other insects, rotting fruit, and garbage. They are often considered to be pests because they are attracted to the food at picnics. Yellowjackets can sting repeatedly. Humans should avoid yellowjackets, which are attracted to bright clothing and sweet smells. If you encounter a yellowjacket, stay calm and walk away slowly. Swatting at it may anger it and cause it to sting. Furthermore, if hit, a yellowjacket may release venom into the air, which is an alarm signal that will summon other yellowjackets. Yellowjackets are beneficial because they eat large numbers of agricultural pests.

Jane Ellin was the production editor and proofreader for *Optimizing Oracle Performance*. Emily Quill provided quality control. James Quill and Jamie Peppard provided production support. Nancy Crumpton wrote the index.

Ellie Volckhausen designed the cover of this book, based on a series design by Edie Freedman. The cover image is a 19th-century engraving from the Dover Pictorial Archive. Emma Colby produced the cover layout with QuarkXPress 4.1 using Adobe's ITC Garamond font.

David Futato designed the interior layout. This book was converted by Joe Wizda to FrameMaker 5.5.6 with a format conversion tool created by Erik Ray, Jason McIntosh, Neil Walls, and Mike Sierra that uses Perl and XML technologies. The text font is Linotype Birka; the heading font is Adobe Myriad Condensed; and the code font is LucasFont's TheSans Mono Condensed. The illustrations that appear in the book were produced by Robert Romano and Jessamyn Read using Macromedia FreeHand 9 and Adobe Photoshop 6. The tip and warning icons were drawn by Christopher Bing. This colophon was written by Jane Ellin.